COLLECTED PAPERS

VOLUME ONE

COLLECTED PAPERS

PAPERS

VOLUME ONE

KENNETH E. BOULDING

FRED R. GLAHE, EDITOR

COLORADO ASSOCIATED UNIVERSITY PRESS

BOULDER, COLORADO

COLORADO ASSOCIATED UNIVERSITY PRESS
BOULDER, COLORADO

Copyright © 1971

Colorado Associated University Press
1424 Fifteenth Street
Boulder, Colorado 80302

Library of Congress Card Number 77-135288

ISBN 87081-011-1

CONTENTS

INTRODUCTION TO THE COLLECTED PAPERS OF KENNETH E. BOULDING

VOLUME I

I suppose the main justification for gathering stalks into a sheaf is that they are then easier to handle, and the same principle no doubt applies to collected papers. The reader, who would certainly not find it worth the trouble of searching the scattered journals in which these papers occur, will find them collected here into a sheaf and may perhaps have some pleasure, or even profit, in following the unfolding of ideas in a single mind. It is not for me to say anything about the quality of that mind, though I might have some discreet views about it. Any single mind, however, is a glass through which we can view the world, and even though through some corners of the glass we may see the world rather darkly, the experience of seeing the world through the mind of another has a peculiar, and sometimes an agreeable quality of its own.

This indeed is the only conceivable justification for a volume of collected papers which are inevitably of very uneven quality, as over against the anthology of the best works from a variety of minds. An anthology is like the eye of a fly, which sees the world through many prisms, and so perhaps comes close to the truth, but at the cost of fragmentation. A volume of collected papers sees the world through the single eye of the author, which means that the view is biased by the very position of the eye itself, and at the same time has a unity which an anthology rarely achieves.

All this abstract argument may be merely a coverup for the slight embarrassment I feel that anybody should think my papers worth collecting, an embarrassment which is probably only a disguised form of vanity, and it is my own vanity (of course my collected papers are worth publishing!) at which I am embarrassed. One reason why perhaps they are worth publishing is that they are in a sense a record of failure, and as it is only by failure that we ever learn anything, this might be the best justification. In many ways I see myself as a voice crying in the wilderness, to which nobody has paid much attention. In spite of the fact that I see myself as not much of a radical, being close to the "main line" of economic thought that goes from Adam Smith to Ricardo, Mill, Marshall, and Keynes, in terms of the reception of my ideas I feel much closer to the heretics, especially to the American institutionalists — to Veblen, Wesley Mitchell, and especially to John R. Commons, who has achieved the remarkable distinction of being perhaps the most influential and most neglected American thinker of the twentieth century.

The papers have been placed in chronological order, not only because this is the salient solution to the problem of arrangement, but also because as collected papers are the record of a single mind, what comes later must in a sense develop out of what comes earlier. The first paper of March 1932 I wrote when I was an undergraduate at Oxford. I sent it to Keynes, who was the editor of *The Economic Journal*, and I shall never forget the look of absolute astonishment on the face of my tutor when I told him it had been accepted. When I went to the University of Chicago as a Commonwealth Fellow in the fall of 1932, I presented this intellectual offspring with great pride to Professor Frank Knight and received from him a little note which simply said, "Professor Knight thanks Mr. Boulding for his paper, which he thinks is as wrong and as confused as possible." He was probably right, and after this auspicious beginning I went on to learn more from Frank Knight I think than from any other teacher I ever had, except perhaps Schumpeter, with whom I studied briefly at Harvard in the fall of 1933.

This perhaps is as good a place as any to tell how I came to be an economist. I went up to New College, Oxford, with a scholarship in chemistry in 1928 and after "reading" chemistry for the year, as the Oxford language puts it, I decided very firmly that chemistry was not for me and I was not for chemistry. The College generously allowed me to keep my scholarship in chemistry and study in the honor school of politics, philosophy, and economics. So in June 1929 I went to see Lionel Robbins, who was just about to leave New College to go to his professorship at the London School of Economics. Lionel Robbins very probably has no recollection of this incident, but I have a very clear recollection of him sitting in the window seat in his room in the garden quad, illuminated by the watery Oxford sun, and this shy, gauche, undergraduate from Liverpool asking him what he should read in the summer in economics. I had never even heard of economics before and had not the slightest idea what it was all about. I got out a pencil and paper and Robbins drawled cheerfully, "Well, you might read Marshall, *Principles of Economics*, Pigou, *The Economics of Welfare*, Cassell, *Theory of Social Economy*, and Hawtrey, *The Economic Problem*." I wrote these books down, never having heard of them, went to the library and got them out. They seemed rather large, but I had a whole summer to read them in, so I went back to Liverpool and read them. I came back to Oxford the next October to find Henry Phelps-Brown installed as the economics tutor. He promptly proceeded to give me a little examination, which in those days was called a collection, in which I scored an alpha, the Oxford for an A. Obviously economics was something that I could do, and I have continued to do it on and off ever since. This incident illustrates the deplorable principle, which research in the teaching of economics seems to substantiate, that the best way to teach people economics is to send them away with some books and tell them not to come back for several months, rather than to pester them with classes and lectures and other trivia of academic life.

To get back now to the papers, perhaps I should call the attention of the reader to certain themes which run through them, so that if he wishes to read them in topical rather than chronological order he may do so. The first and earliest theme is that of the theory of population and its application to the dynamics of populations of artifacts or poputions of capital. Papers Nos. 2, 4, 5, 27, and 28 in Volume I fall into this category. I suspect my later interest in general systems goes back to this very early perception in these papers of the mid-1930's, when I was a very young man, that the world consisted of populations of all kinds and that therefore the general theory of population was a very important general theory indeed. In my later years this has led to an interest in ecology as the theory of the interaction of populations, as developed in my first chapter of *The Reconstruction of Economics* (1949) and a paper on "Economics and Ecology" in 1966.

The second theme, which in a sense arises out of my interest in population analysis and capital theory, is that of the relation of stocks and flows. In this volume Nos. 3, 11, 18, 20, 22, and 25 are on this theme, also extensively developed in *The Reconstruction of Economics*. The basic theme of these papers is perhaps my principle heresy: that the welfare of a person is much more closely related to his condition, which is a stock variable related to his total assets, than it is to his income or consumption, that is, the input and output which are necessary in order to maintain or expand his total stock or condition. It seems to me so obvious that welfare is related to use rather than to consumption that it is a real puzzle to me that economists have been so persistently blind to this obvious truth.

Now when we come to realize that a high consumption economy is going to deplete and pollute the earth, these obvious truths may become more popular, but it is clear to me that formal economic training produces, in the words of Veblen, a "trained incapacity" in this regard. It is not, of course, that the input and output variables are unimportant;

in certain cases, as is the need for variety and activity in itself, they are very closely related to welfare — it is hard, for instance, to conceive of unconsumable food. Even here, though, I suspect that the value attached to consumption is derived in part, at least, by association with the stock variable, being well fed. This emphasis on stocks rather than on flows comes in part also from my view of the theory of the firm, or of social organization generally, as consisting essentially of a succession of states or position statements.

The third theme is that of the theory of the firm, or more generally the theory of a single social organization. In this collection Nos. 7, 10, and 23 follow this theme, which expanded in later years into work in the general theory of organization and the theory of such organizations as the university, the foundation, and of course the state.

The fourth group of papers revolves around price theory in a more technical sense. It includes in this collection paper No. 9, which I think perhaps I would nominate as my most important contribution to economics (although, again, one to which nobody has paid much attention), and papers Nos. 13 and 14. Perhaps No. 24 falls into this category, since welfare economics, which I must confess I regard as more beautiful than useful, is in effect a kind of coda to classical price theory.

The fifth group consists of papers concerned primarily with the rather slow development of a theory of economic and social dynamics, with which I am now mainly concerned. Papers Nos. 6, 12, 16 — and, oddly enough, 29, for my defense of statics is simply that disgracefully enough it is all we have — all fall a little uneasily into this category.

Finally, there is a group of papers oriented towards policy questions— Nos. 8, 15, 19, 21, and perhaps 26 fall into this group. In this volume there is only a single representative of what has developed into an important interest in later years, which might be called the scope, method, and justification of economics. Paper No. 17 in this volume represents my first effort in this direction; I recall it was commissioned for the Hundredth Anniversary of the American Association for the Advancement of Science, so perhaps began what has later become a strong interest, that of explaining economics to non-economists.

I find it hard to leave these productions of my earlier years without a word about the places and the circumstances of their origins. Following No. 1, my first Oxford undergraduate paper, Nos. 2, 3, and 4 were written as a graduate student when I was a Commonwealth Fellow at the University of Chicago. No. 5, too, came out of that period, though I think it was written when I was a humble assistant at the University of Edinburgh from 1934 to 1937. In 1937 I came to the United States, and papers Nos. 6 and 7 came out of my four years at Colgate University. The basic ideas of paper No. 9 developed while working as an economist for the League of Nations in Princeton, New Jersey, 1941-42; I think the paper was actually written when I went down to Fisk University the following year. Papers Nos. 8 and 10-19 came essentially out of the years at Iowa State College at Ames, although paper No. 19 is almost the only evidence that I went to Ames at the invitation of Theodore F. Schultz to become a labor economist. I did not really succeed in becoming a labor economist, but the effort ruined me as a pure economist. I became convinced that in any applied field one had to use all the social sciences and indeed developed a general social science, as all the social sciences were essentially studying the same thing, which was the social system. This led eventually to General Systems, but that is another story. The papers from No. 20 on came out of the years at the University of Michigan and reflect my gradual transformation from a pure economist into a very impure one.

I am particularly grateful to Professor Fred Glahe for the hard work he has put into this volume.

Boulder, Colorado 1971

Kenneth E. Boulding

THE PLACE OF THE "DISPLACEMENT COST" CONCEPT IN ECONOMIC THEORY

Economic Journal, 42, 165 (Mar. 1932): 137-141

THE PLACE OF THE "DISPLACEMENT COST" CONCEPT IN
ECONOMIC THEORY

THE notion of the displacement of resources from one employment to another, and the study of the principles which govern this displacement, has been of profound importance to economic thought from very early days.   With the development of mathematical economics, and the discovery of the indifference curve analysis, this idea of displacement, expressed quantitatively in the concept of a displacement cost, has become almost supreme in the exposition of economic theory : the easy appearance of exactitude which the displacement cost analysis exhibits has tended to draw economists away from the thornier path of analysis in terms of the elusive concepts of real cost and real income.   It may be useful, therefore, to define as accurately as we can our concept of displacement costs, and to investigate the conditions which limit its application.

The displacement cost concept is derived from that of an " economy " or a " displacement system " : a displacement system being the result of a division of a given quantity of something—which we may call " resources "—among a number of different uses or " employments."   Thus the landowner has to determine the distribution of a given quantity of land—his " resources "—among a number of different " employments," park land, house land, farm land, etc. : every individual has to distribute his money income among various possible lines of expenditure, and has to distribute his time income among the various uses to which his time can be put.   The economist himself is concerned principally with the "social economy," the division of the "resources"—of a society among their various possible uses. A displacement system is not, of course, the process by which resources are distributed, but the result of a distribution. For each mass of resources there are an infinite number of possible displacement systems.

The fundamental characteristic of a displacement system is that the total quantity of resources is fixed. Then, and only then, it follows that a change in the quantity of resources which we employ on any one employment involves a change in the opposite sense in the quantity of resources employed on all the remaining possible employments taken together. This may be called the "slices of cake" view of economic life; the bigger the slice which Johnny gets the less there is for Susie and Jimmie and all the rest of them taken together. This does not mean, of course, that the "cost" of Johnny's extra cake falls equally upon all the remaining participants, but their total loss must equal Johnny's gain.

This we may call the "sacrifices" view of cost: the cost of a thing is what we have to give up in order to get it: it is this view that is at the back of the concept of displacement cost. As a loose concept employed in the general description of economic life this view of cost has considerable value. But when we try to interpret it in a quantitative fashion grave difficulties arise.

We must first note a difficulty arising from the fact that in general the resources which we are considering are not merely divided but employed: they are transmuted into something else. For instance, we are concerned not with the mere division of our money income or our time income among various uses; we are interested in the result of so much money or time spent, in the products which the expenditure of a given quantity of money or time produces. It is not enough to know that we spend so much of our money or time income on procuring boots or so much on procuring hats: we want to know the number of boots and hats obtained per unit of money or per unit of time. We are interested, that is to say, in price: for price as an economic dimension as distinct from mere exchange ratios is "the efficiency of the employment of resources"—the ratio between the quantity of resources applied and the corresponding quantity of resultant product. We usually think of displacement cost in these terms; the displacement cost of three hats is one pair of boots, because in order to obtain those three hats we must give up one pair of boots. Where these hats and boots are on the margin of their own particular line of expenditure the displacement cost gives the exchange value, but of course the displacement cost concept holds for other than small changes. This argument is mere child's play to the economist. Nevertheless, the significant implications are often missed. The statement that the displacement cost of three hats is one pair of boots is only valid if three conditions are fulfilled. (1) Definite quantities of hats and boots must be produced by definite quantities of resources—*i.e.* they must each have an unequivocal price in terms of resources. (2) The resources by whose employment they are produced must be homogeneous—*i.e.* must be capable of measurement by a common unit—and must, of course, be fixed in total quantity. (3) There must be only two things producible by these resources.

(1) must be satisfied because it is the resources themselves which are really " displaced." The displacement cost of three hats is one pair of boots, because if we spend x units of resources more on hats we must spend x units of resources less on boots (assuming condition (3) to be fulfilled); and hence if we cannot measure units of product in terms of units of resources unequivocally we cannot compare the two products.

The second condition follows from the first : for if the resources cannot be measured by a common unit the displacement has no quantitative meaning. The third condition holds because we cannot, if there are more than two employments, express the displacement cost of the product of one employment in terms of the products of all the others without an extension of our knowledge into the region of the structure of demand. Thus, suppose I am dividing 20s. among various lines of expenditure; say, bread, milk, coal and hats. Let p_b, p_m, p_c, p_h, be their respective money prices. Then the displacement cost of x shillings more spent on bread, *i.e.* of $\dfrac{x}{p_b}$ units of bread, is equal to the product of x shillings less spent on all the rest put together; *i.e.* to $\dfrac{a}{p_m} + \dfrac{b}{p_c} + \dfrac{c}{p_h}$, where the only condition is that $a + b + c$ together $= x/\text{-}$. An infinite number of combinations is clearly possible. If we are to give a quantitative meaning to displacement costs in this case we must know the movements of a, b and c with respect to movements of x : that is to say, we must have a fairly intimate knowledge of the structure of demand. Granting this, however, we may extend the concept of displacement costs to the case where there are any number of employments.

Let us now consider where we shall find a displacement system in economic life ; for there only shall we find pure displacement costs.

The " economy of money income " is perhaps the most obvious and the most important example of a displacement system. If we abstract from the actual discontinuities in the flow of money in and out of one's pocket, and think of one's income as if it were a continual steady stream which one divides into a number of smaller streams representing different lines of expenditure, then in the division of this flow of income at a point of time into a number of smaller flows of " outgo " representing different lines of expenditure we have a perfect displacement system : the resources are homogeneous, for there is not the slightest difference between one unit of money and another : the quantity of resources is fixed, for we are considering a point of time only ; and provided we know the structure of demand for the different lines of expenditure we can apply the concept of displacement costs quantitatively and unequivocally. This is true also of the economy of time income, abstracted from reality in a similar way.

The concept of displacement costs, however, seems to apply perfectly only to these two abstract cases ; as soon as we move further into the region of real economic life it ceases, first to have quantitative meaning, and finally it ceases to have any validity at all. It can be applied vaguely to such displacement systems as the stock of land or of man-made goods existing at a point of time : the condition of homogeneity of resources is lacking here, but as long as the quantity of resources is fixed we can apply the concept of displacement costs in a loose, non-quantitative way.

When we turn to what are loosely called " productive resources " or " resources in general," however, and when we remove the abstraction that the division takes place at a point of time, the concept breaks down completely. The phrase " productive resources " like the word " scarcity," is the philosopher's stone of muddled economists : its magic deludes them into the belief that they are thinking clearly. In the first place, " resources in general," which usually mean nothing more than a hotch-potch of the old " factors of production," are certainly not homogeneous. We cannot add a unit of labour, a unit of capital (whatever that may be), and a unit of land, with perhaps a little entrepreneurial ability thrown in as seasoning, and expect a fine pudding composed of homogeneous " units of productive resources." A yet more significant objection is that as soon as we turn from the consideration of these abstract displacement systems at a point of time to consider economic processes through time; as soon as we exchange the magic-lantern for the cinematograph, the concept of a displacement system breaks down because our resources are not fixed in quantity. Thus it is not necessarily true that if I employ a certain quantity of productive resources on a certain object I necessarily withdraw them from something else; for in the first place, productive resources are not homogeneous but have a specific character to different employments : hence there is unemployment; and in the second place, considered over any period of time, however short, productive resources are not constant in quantity : hence an increase in the demand for productive resources in one employment may not lead to a decrease in the amount of productive resources in other employments, but may merely lead to an increase in the total quantity of productive resources.

We are now in a position to appreciate more fully the value of the concept of displacement costs for the interpretation of economic life. When we come to this interpretation we find two kinds of facts with which we must deal. The most obvious of these is the observed spectacle of economic process through time; this manifests itself quantitatively through " time series " —the movements of various economic magnitudes with the progress of time. The economist cannot stop with these, however : if he is to analyse time series themselves successfully, he must trace them back to certain psychical and physical facts (such, for instance, as the ordinary supply and demand curve represent), which must be expressed not in terms of movements through time, but as a series of conditional sentences which hold good at a moment of time, irrespective of whether they are realised in the future or not. It is here that we shall find the real place of the concept of the displacement system; in these abstract, ultimate conditions of economic process, not in the study of the processes themselves. Indeed, it is only through the concept of a displacement system that we can understand the nature of these vitally important underlying " General conditions of supply and demand." On the demand side, our resources are our money income : on the supply side, our resources are our income of labour time, qualified by some factor representing the efficiency of labour in the production of real income. The system of displacement costs of the two displacement systems gives us the " general conditions of supply and demand " at a point of time. These systems both determine, and are in part determined by, the economic processes through time : but the pure concept of displacement costs must not be extended into the analysis of process as such if it is to retain its usefulness.

THE APPLICATION OF THE PURE THEORY OF POPULATION CHANGE TO THE THEORY OF CAPITAL

Quarterly Journal of Economics, 48 (Aug. 1934):
645-666.

THE APPLICATION OF THE PURE THEORY OF POPULATION CHANGE TO THE THEORY OF CAPITAL

One of the earliest, and one of the most persistent views of the nature of capital is that which regards it as a sustaining fund which supports factors of production during a period of production. This view goes back at least to Adam Smith; it dominated the English classical school, and it is an essential part of the theories of Böhm-Bawerk and his modern followers. Underlying all such views of capital is the concept of a period of production; and it is hoped that this paper will make some contribution towards the clarification of this concept and the view of economic life on which it rests.

We may conveniently start from the exposition of Böhm-Bawerk. He conceived the economic process as if it started from the application of "primary" factors of production, labor and land, the products of which were then worked up into the final product through successive applications of more labor and land throughout the process of production. He did not himself choose to express his theories in mathematical

form, but we can easily write his basic assumption in the
form of an equation. If S represents the subsistence fund,
i.e., total capital; W the rate of wages; N the number of
laborers and T the total period of production; then if wages
represent the only outgoings to factors of production, and
if the augmentation of the value of products proceeds at a
steady rate through the period of production, we may write:

$$S = \tfrac{1}{2}TWN \tag{1}$$

We can modify this equation a little to make it more representative of economic realities. Böhm-Bawerk himself
meant by "wages" all payments to factors of production,
and by $\tfrac{1}{2}T$ the average period of production. So that we
can replace the WN of (1) by B, the total income of factors
of production, and the $\tfrac{1}{2}T$ of (1) by V, the "average period
of production," and write our formula:

$$S = VB \tag{2}$$

Consider for a moment the dimensions of this equation.
S is the total value of existing capital, expressed, let us
say, as a number of dollars. B is total money income, expressed, say, as a number of dollars per year. The ratio, $\dfrac{S}{B}$,
is clearly a period of time — a number of years. Leaving
aside all theoretical implications, then, we can take equation
(2) to be a mere definition of V, expressing the formal
dimensional relation, that the ratio between capital and
income has the dimension of time. V is then defined as the
period over which total money income must be summed in
order to equal the value of total capital. Then there are
two theoretical problems which arise in the interpretation of
equation (2). The first is whether V corresponds to any
economically significant time quantity such as an average
period of production; for a quantity may have the formal
dimensions of length of time and yet not represent any time
interval. The period of purchase, for instance (the reciprocal
of the rate of interest), corresponds to no time interval which
is significant in economic relations. If, however, we can
establish a definition for V independent of the definition

which could be provided by equation (2), the second problem arises: which of the variables of this equation are dependent and which are independent. Böhm-Bawerk, and indeed most of the classical economists, would have answered the first question in the affirmative, identifying V with the average period of production. Böhm-Bawerk would also have regarded S as the independent variable — the "subsistence fund," which is a given factor at any moment in economic life; S being given, V and B are mutually determined by the principle of the maximization of profit under free competition.[1] This is the logical development of the confused wage-fund theory of the English school.

There are really two interpretations of the formula in Böhm-Bawerk. One is the subsistence fund interpretation; the other we may call the "lake and stream" interpretation, which is latent to a very large extent in Böhm-Bawerk's general view of the economic process, altho it is in many respects contradictory to the subsistence fund theory which he uses in his theory of the determination of wages and profit. According to this interpretation, capital consists of the totality of goods in existence at a moment of time; this is the "lake." Income is a stream of services of factors of production, which flow into the lake by becoming embodied as goods, and flow out of the lake as consumption-services. In monetary terms, B is the total money income of factors of production, while S is the total money value of all existing goods, whether the so called "capital goods" or "consumption goods." V, then, may be thought of as the time it would take for the income stream to fill up the capital lake, were income independent of the amount of capital; or otherwise, as the average time taken for the "water" — the services of productive factors — to pass through the lake from the incoming to the outgoing stream.

The difficult question is how to define our factors of production. For Böhm-Bawerk the incoming stream consists only of the services of labor and land, which he thought were the only true factors of production, for we can always analyze

1. Böhm-Bawerk, Positive Theorie des Kapitals, 4th ed., bk. iv, ch. 3.

back the services of capital goods into the labor and land
which produced these capital goods. Objection has been
made to this that it makes the period of production infinite,
or at least indefinite — for we can trace our productive
process back to the primordial amoeba if we are energetic
enough. This in itself would not be enough to vitiate the
argument; for the average period of production may be finite
even if certain portions of the process can be traced back
indefinitely, provided these portions are infinitely small.
The analogy of the lake will help us here; there may be some
portion of the water that flows into a lake that never gets out,
or that only gets out after a very long period of time; but that
does not prevent the average time taken for water to pass
through the lake from being finite, for the portion that never
gets out is infinitesimally small.

The "lake and stream" analogy, however, will not carry
us very much further. The dilemma is this: are we to regard
the inflowing stream of productive services as a stream of the
services of some "primary" factors of production — labor,
or labor and land — which grows in size the longer it stays
in the lake, so that the output is always greater than the
input; or are we to regard the incoming stream as a stream
of the services of all the usual factors of production, including
the services of capital, in which case we must regard the
size of the inflowing stream as a function of the size of the
lake? Both these alternatives stretch the physical analogy
to the point of absurdity, but that need not worry us were
there not graver issues involved. Ricardo, Marx, Böhm-
Bawerk, Hayek, look at economic life from the point of view
of the first of these alternatives. For them the formation of
capital consists in the cumulative embodiment of some
"primary" factor or factors of production in the form of
goods. As a picture of a physical historic process this view is
tenable; but what we want principally for economic theory
is a picture of a "reproducing economy" — a network of
flows and counterflows whose cross-section, apart from
seasonal and other regular variations, is invariant; for such a
system the period of production from "primary" factors has

no meaning. What is relevant to the economic situation at any one time is not past acts but present resources, and a period of production which looks back to "primary" factors may be mathematically definable in physical terms,[2] but has no relevance to economics.

There is no need, however, to go back to "primary" factors to discover a process of production. The basic idea of a "process" of production is that goods are embodied services; services which are "bottled" and in the course of being carried from a factor of production, where they originated, to an ultimate consumer, where they are given up. Thus from all factors of production at a point of time there proceeds a flow of services which we may call "real outgo," or current *input*. Part of this input, the direct personal services of men or of things, is realized immediately as "real income," or *output*. Part of this input is not realized immediately, but is embodied in the form of goods, and realized as output after varying periods of time. Thus the aggregate of goods in existence at a point of time represents an integral, or sum, of past input which it is hoped will be realized as an integral of future output. If we think of input and output as value flows (dollars per "year"), the cost of the total stock of goods (measured, say, in dollars) is equal to the sum of all the items of input that have been embodied in it, each weighted by the period of time over which it was applied: the value of the total stock of goods is equal to the anticipated sum of all the items of output which will be "disembodied" out of it, each weighted by the period of time over which it will be applied. We define equilibrium conditions in this connection by the equation, value of the total stock of goods is equal to its cost.

In such a scheme input is not a flow of labor or labor and land services, but the flow of the services of all factors of production; it includes the services for which profits and interest are paid, as well as services for which wages are paid. It is measured by the total net money incomes of all factors

2. Compare C. H. P. Gifford, "The concept of the length of the period of production," Economic Journal, December, 1933.

of production. Output is the flow of services into consumption; it is measured by the total net money expenditures of the owners of all factors of production. In between input, considered as a value inflow, and output considered as a value outflow stands the "stock of value" — the sum of the value of all existing goods.

One point of causal connection must be made clear. Goods have a value not because they represent embodied services but because they have the power to render up services. The fallacy of the "cost of production" theories of value is that they reverse this causal connection, and make it appear that the value of products is derived from the value of the services embodied in them. In a state of equilibrium this fact would not matter, for there would be no losses; every anticipation would be justified, and for practical purposes we could assume that every item of input that went into embodiment would be released sooner or later as an exactly equivalent item of output. In actual economic life, of course, we cannot make this assumption. It is true that input is embodied in the expectation that it will later be released as an equivalent item of output; but this expectation is not necessarily fulfilled. From this arises the many phenomena connected with uncertainty. From the point of view of equilibrium theory, however, we can neglect the uncertainty factor and concentrate on the simple process of embodiment and release of the flow of services.

For a system such as we envisage here the analogy with the movement through time of an abstract population will be more helpful than the "lake and stream" picture. A population may be defined as an aggregation of disparate items, or "individuals," each one of which conforms to a given definition, retains its identity with the passage of time, and exists only during a finite interval. An individual enters a population, or is "born," when it first conforms to the definition which identifies the population; it leaves the population, or "dies," when it ceases to conform to this definition. The commonest example of a population is of course human population; but any aggregate conforming to the above criterion can be treated according to the principles evolved in the pure theory of population.

Now it is clear that the aggregate of goods is something which is subject to "birth" and "death," and hence might be treated as a population.[3] We cannot treat it thus, however, without making further assumptions, for we have no simple unit of goods, no individual according to which we could number the population. The difficulty is easily seen in a simple example: suppose we add a grand piano to our population, and subtract a flock of sheep; has our population increased or diminished? We cannot say; and until we have some criterion of the size of our population and the size of the inflows and outflows which pertain to it, we cannot apply population theory.

We do in practice, however, reduce our heterogeneous aggregate of goods to homogeneity by means of the device of valuation in some "numéraire"; we reduce it, that is, to a sum of "dollars." This being done, there is an undoubted opportunity for the application of pure population theory; the value of all goods becomes our "stock" or "population" of value; input corresponds to the flow of births into this population; output corresponds to the flow of deaths out of this population, and the average period of production corresponds to the average length of life. Other analogies will present themselves when we have discussed further the principal properties of an abstract population system. The analogy must not be applied too rashly, of course; we must not imagine that each newborn value goes through life with a tag round its neck; there are considerable difficulties of imputation, due to the chaotic complexities of the capital structure. But the analogy is worth pursuing, and we shall find that subject to certain conventions and limitations, it holds.

3. Compare Irving Fisher, Economic Journal, vi, 534, in his article, What is Capital? "Just as population is correlative to the various rates of births, deaths, marriages, 'coming of age,' emigration, immigration, etc., so capital is correlative to income, expenditure, production, consumption, 'ripening' of goods in process of production, exports, imports, monetary circulation, etc."

The theory of capital is thus resolved partly into an actuarial problem. In its more refined branches it would require fairly advanced mathematics for its development; but we can demonstrate the propositions in which we are interested by the use of a very simple device for illustrating the movement of a population through time.

Thus suppose we take a population, in the year S, of size P_s. Now suppose we classify the individuals of this population according to age, taking a "year" to represent any convenient unit of time. Then if $_rA_s$ represents the number of individuals between the ages of $r-1$ and r years, in the year S, we have

$$\sum_{r=1}^{r=n} {}_rA_s = P_s \tag{3}$$

and we may call the series

$$_1A_s, \; _2A_s, \; _3A_s, \; \cdots \; _nA_s,$$

the *age grouping* for the year S, where $_nA_s$, the nth age group, contains the oldest individuals.

The *age distribution*, represented by the series

$$_1a_s, \; _2a_s, \; _3a_s, \; \cdots \; _na_s,$$

is obtained by dividing each item of the age grouping by the total population, so that

$$_rA_s = P_s \cdot {}_ra_s. \tag{4}$$

The *death grouping*, represented by the series

$$_1D_s, \; _2D_s, \; _3D_s, \; \cdots \; _nD_s,$$

shows the number of deaths in the year S in each age group. Thus $_rD_s$ is the number of deaths in the year S in age group $_rA_s$.

The *death distribution*, represented by the series

$$_1d_s, \; _2d_s, \; _3d_s, \; \cdots \; _nd_s,$$

shows the proportion of deaths in the year S in each age group.

Thus, $_rD_s = {}_rA_s \cdot {}_rd_s = P_s \cdot {}_ra_s \cdot {}_rd_s. \tag{5}$

The *net births* B_s of year S, is the total number of births taking place in that year which survive into the year $S+1$. Now given the age grouping, the death grouping, and the net births of year S we can deduce the age grouping, and hence the total population, of year $S+1$. For the rth age group of year S becomes the $(r+1)$th age group of year $S+1$; hence the size of the $(r+1)$th age group of year $S+1$ is equal to the size of the rth age group of year S, less the number of deaths which have occurred in that age group in the year. That is:

$$_{r+1}A_{s+1} = {_r}A_s - {_r}D_s. \tag{6}$$

Substituting from equations (4) and (5), we have:

$$_{r+1}a_{s+1} = {_r}a_s(1 - {_r}d_s). \tag{7}$$

Then as the first age group of the year $S+1$ is equal to the number of net births in the year S, we have also:

$$_1A_{s+1} = B_s.$$

We can therefore derive all the age groups of the year $S+1$ from those of year S. The process will perhaps be made clearer in the following table:

TABLE 1

								Totals
1	Year S, age grouping		12	15	10	8	5	50
2	Year S, death grouping		1	2	2	4	5	14
3	Year $S+1$, age grouping	10	11	13	8	4	—	46

Line 1 represents the age grouping into five age groups of a population of 50 individuals in the year S; the age groups being 0–1 years; 1–2 years; 2–3 years; 3–4 years and 4–5 years. Line 2 represents the death grouping of the population for that year. Line 3 results by subtraction of line 2 from line 1, and the addition of the number of net births, assumed to be 10, occurring in year S. As long as we know the net births and the death grouping for each year we can follow out this process for an indefinite number of years.

By means of this device we can develop the mechanism of population change under all kinds of different conditions. Thus, if we assume a constant death distribution and a constant number of net births per year, we can show that starting from any arbitrary age distribution and population we finally arrive at an equilibrium population and age distribution, which is then maintained indefinitely. This equilibrium is attained after a number of years equal to the number of terms in the death distribution — the last term of which must be equal to unity; for after this period of time the youngest members of the original population have all died out, and the influence of the original population is thereby removed entirely. The age distribution and the total population in the equilibrium condition can be derived from the number of net births per year and the death distribution. The fundamental condition for an equilibrium population is that the number in the rth age group of the year S should be equal to the number in the rth age group of the year $S+1$. That is:

$$_rA_s = {_r}A_{s+1} \tag{9}$$

But we know already from equation (6) that

$$_rA_{s+1} = {_{r-1}}A_s - {_{r-1}}D_s; \tag{10}$$

hence in the equilibrium population, in the year S,

$$_rA_s = {_{r-1}}A_s - {_{r-1}}D_s; \tag{11}$$

a condition which we may also write, substituting from equations (4) and (5),

$$_ra_s = {_{r-1}}a_s(1 - {_{r-1}}d_s). \tag{12}$$

Then we also have

$$_1a_s \cdot P_s = {_1}A_s = B_{s-1} = B, \tag{13}$$

where B is the constant number of net births per year. From these equations (12) and (13) we can derive the whole age distribution and the population. Thus:

$$_1a_s = \frac{B}{P_s}$$

$$_2a_s = \frac{B}{P_s}(1-_1d_s)$$

$$_3a_s = \frac{B}{P_s}(1-_1d_s)(1-_2d_s)$$

$$\cdot \quad \cdot \quad \cdot \quad \cdot \quad \cdot \quad \cdot \quad \cdot \quad \cdot$$

$$_ra_s = \frac{B}{P_s}(1-_1d_s)(1-_2d_s) \cdots (1-_{r-1}d_s) \tag{14}$$

Summing these equations to the nth and last equation we have:

$$1 = \frac{B}{P_s}[1+(1-_1d_s)+(1-_1d_s)(1-_2d_s)+ \cdots$$
$$+\{(1-_1d_s)(1-_2d_s) \cdots (1-_{n-1}d_s)\}] \tag{15}$$

As we have supposed the death distribution constant we can write:

$$V=1+(1-_1d_s)+(1-_1d_s)(1-_2d_s)+\cdots$$
$$+\{(1-_1d_s)(1-_2d_s) \cdots (1-_{n-1}d_s)\} \tag{16}$$

where V is a constant. Equation (15) then becomes:

$$P_s = VB \tag{17}$$

The similarity of formula (17) to formula (2) is apparent immediately. It now remains to be shown that in an equilibrium population V is equal to the average length of life.

Table 2 illustrates the progress of a stationary equilibrium population through time.

TABLE 2

							a	b	c	d	e

Year S							a	b	c	d	e
Year $S+1$						a	b	c	d	e
Year $S+2$					a	b	c	d	e
Year $S+3$				a	b	c	d	e
Year $S+4$			a	b	c	d	e
Year $S+5$		a	b	c	d	e
Year $S+6$	a	b	c	d	e

*

The rows of such a table represent the age grouping for each year; the columns represent what we may call the *survival grouping* of the batch of births of the year previous to the year of the head of the column. Thus in the column marked *
a is the number of births of the year S which survive into the year $S+1$; b is the number surviving into the year $S+2$, and so on. Now let us assume that all births of the year S survive into the year $S+1$, and that thereafter deaths occur at a uniform rate during each year. The number of deaths of those born in year S occurring in the year $S+1$ is therefore $(a-b)$, at an average age of 1 year: the number occurring in year $S+2$ is $(b-c)$, at an average age of 2 years, and so on. The average length of life is therefore

$$L = \frac{(a-b)+2(b-c)+3(c-d)+\text{etc.}}{a} \tag{18}$$

$$= \frac{a+b+c+\text{etc.}}{a}$$

If our "year" is taken to be small enough any errors which arise from the initial assumptions become negligible, and we can affirm in general that the average length of life is equal to the sum of the figures of the survival grouping divided by the number of births. If we divide each figure of a survival grouping by the corresponding number of births we get a series which we may call the *survival distribution*, whose sum is equal to the average length of life.

Now we see from table 2 that in an equilibrium population the age grouping and the survival grouping are identical and constant through time. Hence $a+b+c+\text{etc.}=P$, the constant population, and we have

$$L = \frac{P}{B} = V \tag{19}$$

We thus see that Böhm-Bawerk's fundamental assumption, which we expressed in equation (2), is justified in a system of stationary equilibrium; for the ratio between total capital (P) and total income (B) is constant and is equal to the average period of production.

The question now arises, whether any other system is possible besides that of stationary equilibrium in which the period of production, or more generally equation (2), has any definite significance.

Let us first assume stability of age and death distributions with a changing total population. The condition for stability of age distribution from year to year is:

$$_r a_s = {_r a_{s+1}} \tag{20}$$

We have, therefore, by equation (4),

$$\frac{_r A_s}{P_s} = \frac{_r A_{s+1}}{P_{s+1}} \tag{21}$$

Whence:

$$\frac{P_s}{P_{s+1}} = \frac{_r A_s}{_r A_{s+1}} = \frac{_r A_s}{_{r-1} A_s (1 - {_{r-1} d_s})} = \frac{_r a_s}{_{r-1} a_s (1 - {_{r-1} d_s})} \tag{22}$$

Then as we have assumed both the age distribution and the death distribution constant we may write (22)

$$\frac{P_s}{P_{s+1}} = k, \tag{23}$$

where k is a constant. In order to have a constant age and death distribution, therefore, the population must increase geometrically, with k as the yearly rate of increase. In the limiting case where our "year" becomes indefinitely small the population increases exponentially. This condition we may call the *exponential moving equilibrium* of population. Stationary equilibrium is a special case of this, where $k = 1$. In an exponential moving equilibrium where $k \neq 1$ we can show that the number of births per year still bears a constant ratio, V, to the population; but that V is not equal to the average length of life, L, tho this itself is also constant.

An illustration again will easily demonstrate this proposition. Suppose we have a population, say, of five age groups, a, b, c, d, e, in the year S, and suppose the yearly rate of increase is k. Then the progress of this population over a period of years will be as in table 3:

TABLE 3

												. . . . Total
Year $S-1$						a/k	b/k	c/k	d/k	e/k		P/k
Year S							a	b	c	d	e	P
Year $S+1$					ka	kb	kc	kd	ke			k^2P
Year $S+2$				k^2a	k^2b	k^2c	k^2d	k^2e				k^2P
Year $S+3$			k^3a	k^3b	k^3c	k^3d	k^3e					k^3P
Year $S+4$		k^4a	k^4b	k^4c	k^4d	k^4e						k^4P
Year $S+5$	k^5a	k^5b	k^5c	k^5d	k^5e							k^5P

. . . .

Now suppose we take any year, say the year $S+1$. Then as in equation 18 we see that the average length of life of those born in the previous year is

$$L = \frac{ka + k^2b + k^3c + k^4d + k^5e}{ka}$$
$$= \frac{a + kb + k^2c + k^3d + k^4e}{a} \tag{24}$$

Dividing numerator and denominator of this fraction by P_s we get:

$$L = \frac{{}_1a_s + k \cdot {}_2a_s + k^2 \cdot {}_3a_s + k^3 \cdot {}_4a_s + \text{etc.}}{\dfrac{a}{P_s}} \tag{25}$$

where ${}_1a_s, {}_2a_s, \cdots$ etc. represents the constant age distribution. But for any year, $S+u$, we have

$$\frac{\text{Population}}{\text{Births}} = \frac{k^u \cdot P_s}{k^{u+1} \cdot a} = \frac{P_s}{ka} = V \tag{26}$$

where V is constant.

We can therefore write (25):

$$L = (k \cdot {}_1a_s + k^2 \cdot {}_2a_s + k^3 \cdot {}_3a_s + \text{etc.}) \cdot V \tag{27}$$

L is therefore constant, and bears a constant ratio to V. V is clearly smaller than L if the population is increasing ($k > 1$) and is larger than L if the population is decreasing ($k < 1$).

Having now established some few principles governing population movements through time, we can proceed to elaborate the analogy with movements of a system of capital and income through time.

We have already seen that the real outgo from all factors of production — which is the same thing as the input into the productive process — corresponds to the births of our population system, and that the real income of consumers, or the final output from the productive system corresponds to the deaths in our population system. We have to be careful, however, in defining our age distribution, if we are to avoid the fallacy of tracing all capital back to some "primary" factors of production. The concept is established most easily by considering the movement of a system forward from a given date. Thus suppose in a certain year S current input into the system was B_s dollars per year; i.e., $\$B_s$ was received as money income by factors of production during that year. A certain proportion of the value created by this input, $_0d_s$, "dies at birth" — or during the year S; i.e., becomes immediately available as output. Such items of input are personal services, such as the services of houses, household furniture, house servants, barbers, shoeblacks, etc. At the beginning of the year $S+1$, therefore, we have a proportion $(1-{_0d_s})$ of the current input of year S which is still embodied in the form of goods, which in a perfectly adjusted system would have a value of $\$B_s \cdot (1-{_0d_s})$. In conformity with our population notation we may write this amount $\$_1A_{s+1}$. Then during the year $S+1$ a certain proportion, $_1d_s$, of this value will be realized as output, leaving $\$_1A_{s+1}(1-{_1d_{s+1}})=\$_2A_{s+2}$ to pass on into the year $S+2$. The series $_1A_{s+1}$, $_2A_{s+2}$, etc. is clearly the survival grouping of the current input of the year S; it represents the gradual realization as output of this input. We can construct similar survival groupings for the current input of the years $S+1$, $S+2$, etc., and so build up a complete population table; the horizontal rows of this table represent genuine age groupings of the total population of value existing in any one year: age groupings with reference not to the dates of input of any "primary" factors of production but with reference to some year's current input.

It must be clearly understood that the input for a given year consists only of the services for which money income is paid during that year. Thus the goods existing in a previous year do not in themselves constitute input. A stock of wheat, for instance, which was grown in the year $S-1$ and is turned into flour in the year S is not input for the year S; the interest due during the year S to the owner of this stock of wheat, however, or rather the services, whatever they are, for which this interest is paid, does constitute input for the year S. It follows from this that in calculating the amount of the input of one year which survives into another year we must not add interest; for the interest on capital existing in any given year is input for that year, and must not be considered as an addition to the embodied input of previous years. In this way our births into the value population will eventually give rise to an exactly equal number of deaths.

What is perhaps even more important, the reinvestment of current income, such as that which occurs in a process of amortization and replacement of capital, must be regarded as a new birth, and not as a continuance of an old "life." An example will perhaps make these points clearer. Suppose in the year S I build a house with current resources at a cost of $10,000. By the rent of this house I obtain a subsequent income of $1,000 a year, and furthermore suppose that it costs me $500 a year to replace the wear and tear of the house. Whether I can replace the wearing out as it goes along, or whether I have to set aside a depreciation fund with which to rebuild the house completely after so many years does not matter for the present argument; for simplicity we can assume that the expenditure of $500 each year leaves the house at the end of the year in exactly the same condition in which it was found at the beginning. The question is, when is the $10,000 input of the year S realized as output? Now in order to replace the house after a year's wear I have to spend $500 of current input; hence it is clear that $500 of output comes out of the house every year. But according to our system there cannot be more output than input from a given item of input; hence as the original input was $10,000, the output must be $500 a year for twenty years, and in this case the average period of production from the input involved in building a house is ten years. But there remains to me, after I have replaced all wear and tear, an income of $500 from the house. This is interest; and it must be considered each year as an item of current input resulting from the house as source. In this particular case this input results simultaneously in output; for the service rendered by a house is personal service resulting in goods of zero durability. In the case of a factory, however, or some item of industrial equipment this current input itself is embodied and has its own period of production, which must not be confused with the period of production of its source. This confusion between the period of production of a source itself, and the period of production of the income from it is probably the origin of nearly all the confusion which today surrounds this concept.

The simple age distribution of a value population, it must be noticed, does not correspond to any particular classification of the goods whose value constitutes the value population. We must not think of the items of value which were embodied, say, three years ago as corresponding to a certain class of half finished goods. All goods contain items of value of different ages, and all items of value of the same age are distributed over a great variety of goods. Thus the value of a new automobile, for instance, will represent some items of current input of a few days age (retailing services); some of a month or so (transport services, etc.); some of several months (manufacturing services), and so on. The cumulative age distribution of the population of value, however, corresponds fairly closely to certain classifications of goods. Thus suppose we consider a single manufacturer whose process is completely integrated, i.e., who buys no products of other firms for eventual resale. Then his unfinished product in any stage of completion will embody in it all the value of age less than the age of the oldest value embodied in it. The classification of his total stock of goods into more or less finished products thus corresponds to the cumulative age grouping of the value which these goods represent. The division of this integrated process among two or more entrepreneurs clearly does not invalidate this conclusion, as long as there

is a single finished product at the end of the process. When
we consider the whole productive process, however, this
simple relation breaks down; for in the cumulative age
group which includes, say, all items of the population of
value which are under one year old, we shall have some finished products — those which take a year to finish — and
some unfinished products — those which take more than a
year to finish. Hence the general classification of the stock
of goods according to the criterion of degree of completion
does not correspond exactly to the classification of the population of value into cumulative age groups. Nevertheless,
given a constant system of production, a relative increase of
less finished over more finished goods would be reflected in a
shift of the cumulative age distribution (and hence of the
simple age distribution) of the population of value into the
younger age groups; so that the age distribution, while not
actually descriptive of the classification of goods into more
or less finished goods, serves as an index of changes in this
classification.

Similarly the survival groupings — the vertical columns of
our population table — do not correspond to any direct
classification of the productive process into later or earlier
stages, but any change in the productive process which favors
earlier or later stages is reflected in the survival groupings
of input.

The death grouping, it must be noticed, expresses the
value of the finished goods in each cumulative age group;
thus in our former notation $_rD_s$ would' signify the value of
those goods existing in the year S, in which the oldest item
of current output embodied is r years old, and which are
finished in the sense that they will be consumed before the
next year.

Having now established the concept of a productive process in general, it remains to inquire what type of productive
process, corresponding to what type of population change, is
likely to be met with in modern society. The system of stationary equilibrium clearly has no reference to any system
of real economics with which we are likely to come into con-

tact. The modern economy is generally a progressive economy; hence we should expect to find a closer approximation
to modern economic systems in the theory of an increasing
population of value. The exponentially increasing economy
is likely to be a very special case, for we have no reason to
expect constancy of any of the factors of population growth.
What we are faced with in reality is an irregularly increasing
economy with several very peculiar features.

Perhaps the most significant feature of the actual system
of production is that the disposal of current input determines
to a considerable extent the survival grouping of that input.
This occurs because of the lack of mobility of most sources
and most intermediate goods between different forms of
employment; the form of existing sources determines to a
large extent what forms current input will take; and not
merely the forms of the sources but the forms of existing
intermediate goods determine the way in which current input can be applied. These propositions are amply demon-
strated in the familiar observations that one cannot make
shoes with a shipyard; that a bricklayer cannot make walls
unless he has bricks; and that bricks cannot be made into
walls unless there are bricklayers. These rigidities in the
productive process are not absolute; and the longer the period
considered the less important they become. But from the
point of view of the disposal of current input they dominate
the situation. In terms of our population process this means
that the magnitude and form of the births into the population of value are determined to some extent by the age distribution in any given year; and that once given the form of
the births the survival distribution of those births is very
largely determined at the outset.

Now, a progressive productive process requires the making
of *investment*. Investment may be defined as the process of
the application of current input to the production of new
sources of current input. Input, then, is divided at the outset into two parts: investment, that part which goes to the
production of new sources; and that part which we may call
reproductive input which goes simply to keeping the old system going, which in a stationary equilibrium would consti-

tute the whole of input. The division of a given year's input between investment and reproductive input is important in determining what will be the survival grouping of that year's input. But investment has another property; by determining the sources of future input, and hence the form of that input, investment affects the survival grouping of future input. Hence we should expect the survival grouping, and with it the average period of production, to change in a progressive society. Whether it will increase or decrease depends upon technical considerations; there is no necessary economic reason why the movement should be one way rather than the other; investment will generally tend to shorten the average period of production of some items of input and lengthen that of others; investment that is embodied in very durable goods may lengthen it; but even investment in durable goods may have a great influence in shortening the period of production of current input in other forms. The improvement of transport is a case in point: the period of production of those items of current input which go into the means of transportation may be lengthened; but the period of production of almost all other input will be shortened, and there is no necessity that one will outbalance the other.

The average period of production itself is difficult or virtually impossible to measure. We can easily measure V, however, the ratio between the value of capital and total income, and hence if we can get some idea of the relation between L, the average period of production, and V, we can obtain some idea of the magnitude of L. In an exponentially advancing society, as we have already seen, L is greater than V. This is generally true of any advancing population unless the period of production is decreasing very rapidly. Table 4, which represents the survival grouping and the age grouping corresponding to a given year, will illustrate this:

TABLE 4

Year S	a	b	c	d	e
Year $S+1$	b'				
Year $S+2$	c'				
Year $S+3$	d'				
Year $S+4$	e'				

a, b, c, d, e, is the age grouping for the year S; a, b', c', d', e' is the survival grouping for births B_{s-1} of the year $S-1$; B_s is the number of births of the year S.

Then

$$L = \frac{a+b'+c'+d'+e'}{B_{s-1}} \tag{28}$$

$$V = \frac{a+b+c+d+e}{B_s} \tag{29}$$

Now in an advancing society we should expect b' to be greater than b; for it descends from a larger number of births. Similarly we should have $c'>c$, $d'>d$, $e'>e$. We also have $B_s>B_{s-1}$; L is therefore clearly greater than V.

Where the period of production is increasing we should expect b', c', etc. to be still greater than they would be in an advancing society of constant period of production; in this case the disparity between L and V will be increased. Where the period of production is diminishing, however, b', c', etc. will be less than they would be otherwise, and the disparity between L and V is diminished. If the period of production is decreasing very rapidly we might conceivably have L less than V, but this is very unlikely to occur.

This argument does not give us an exact measure of the average period of production, but it enables us to form some idea of its order of magnitude. As V, the ratio $\dfrac{\text{Total Capital}}{\text{Total Income}}$ is somewhat less than the reciprocal of the rate of interest, which is the ratio $\dfrac{\text{Total Capital}}{\text{Income from Capital}}$; and as L in a progressive society is somewhat more than V, we may expect L to be of the order of the reciprocal of the rate of interest. L must therefore be something between 10 and 20 years.

This analogy of the productive process to a population process must be used cautiously; it applies strictly only to an economy in which there are no losses, in which all anticipations are realized; for only then is the value of capital equal to the value of all the input which has been embodied in it. Within these limitations it enables us to get an accurate picture of the progress of the productive process through time, and furthermore enables us to define a "period of production" which has some reference to economic life. When we remove these limitations: when we allow for changes in the price system, for frictions in the price system, for any other causes of loss of capital: our simple picture of a population of value breaks down, but the underlying concept of a physical process of production remains, even tho we can no longer reduce it to homogeneity. The rigidity of this physical process of production, in fact, is very largely responsible for the disruptions in the price system and the losses of capital which prevent our reducing it to simple value terms. For as we have seen, the output of a given year is very largely determined by the input of a number of previous years; the physical output is to that extent unalterable. Unless this physical output corresponds exactly to the general demand structure at existing prices and incomes there will be some disruption of the price structure. This correspondence will only be realized if entrepreneurs have been perfectly wise in their anticipations; as this is very unlikely we may reasonably expect some disturbance of the price system to be going on continually. The effects of such price disturbances lie outside the scope of this paper; the population analogy is not adaptable with any exactitude to a system of continuous price disequilibrium, and in such a system the concept of a process of production — and with it the concept of a period of production — becomes rather vague. This does not invalidate the concept, however, as a structural concept; for the anticipated process of production as it exists in the minds of the entrepreneurs at a point of time is one of the principal determinants of the actual disposal of current input. The period of production — or more accurately, the survival grouping of current input — thus takes its place with the demand and supply functions as a psycho-physical determinant of the course of economic life, whose importance is in no way diminished by the fact that it may never be realized in practice.

A NOTE ON THE CONSUMPTION FUNCTION

The Review of Economic Studies,
2, 2 (Feb. 1935): 99-103.

A Note on the Consumption Function

By the consumption function of an individual I mean that function which expresses the relation between the price structure with which he is confronted, the money income which he receives, and the way in which he divides that income among the various lines of expenditure which are open to him. Thus, if on one commodity, of price p_1, he spends $x_1/\text{-}$; on another commodity of price p_2 he spends $x_2/\text{-}$; on an " n^{th} " commodity of price p_n he spends $x_n/\text{-}$, and so on, there must be some relation between all these quantities and his money income, $r/\text{-}$, which we may write formally :

$$F(r, x_1, x_2, \ldots x_n, p_1, p_2, \ldots p_n) = 0.$$

From the point of view of an individual we may regard the money income and the various prices as independent variables, which serve to determine the distribution of expenditures ; for each income and price system there is a corresponding system of distribution of expenditures. Expressed mathematically, if we write the function

$$F(x, r, p_1, p_2, \ldots p_n) = 0,$$

then for each system of values of $r, p_1, p_2, \ldots p_n$ this equation will have n roots when solved for x which will be the n values $x_1, x_2, \ldots x_n$.

A formal function is, of course, of very little use to us until we can find some means of investigating its properties. This we can conveniently do by a system of graphical analysis, taking sections of the function in various dimensions. Figure 1 shows how the distribution of expenditures is likely

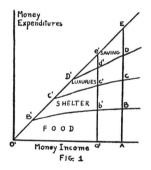

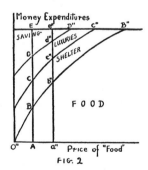

to vary with a change in money income, the price system being constant. Corresponding to any income, $O'A$, we have an equal total expenditure, AE. The line representing the relation between total income and total expenditure is clearly a straight line at an angle of 45° to the axis. As, however, all expenditures have the same dimension—that of money per unit of time— we can express the division of expenditures simply by dividing the line AE

into a number of segments, AB, BC, CD, etc., where each represents the expenditure on a particular commodity. For simplicity I have supposed four lines of expenditure, " Food ", " Shelter ", " Luxuries ", and " Savings ". The latter, it must be noticed, is just as much a line of " expenditure " as any other when we are considering the distribution of income at a point of time. The order in which we range these lines of expenditure segments along the total expenditure line is not strictly relevant to the consumption function as such, but there is a convenient order which enables us, as we shall see later, to extend the usefulness of the concept. Thus we can suppose that there is some income of very small dimensions at which only one commodity will be purchased ; we will suppose it to be food, this being an absolute necessity of existence. As money income increases, we shall find that there comes a point at which another commodity enters the scheme of expenditure—shelter. Above this point there will therefore be a division of the expenditure line into two parts, and it will be convenient to place the " shelter " part above the " food " part. Then as succeeding commodities enter into the expenditure system, with increase of money income, we place the segment of expenditure of each commodity above those which had preceded it. We thus obtain a kind of " order of importance " of commodities, a range showing the degree to which they are necessitous. The position of a commodity on this range corresponds more or less to the classical idea of its " value in use " ; the lower the commodity in the scale, the greater its " value in use ". Then the loci, BB', CC', etc., of the points B, C, etc., on AE, traced out as we change money income, give us our picture of this section of the consumption function. Generally we should expect each particular expenditure to increase as income increases, though as a rule at a smaller rate than the rate of increase of income, for as our income increases we do not devote all the increase to a single line of expenditure. With some commodities it is conceivable that with increase of income the expenditure in that particular line should decrease, or even drop out altogether. Margarine, for instance, is consumed more at low income levels than at high. The lines BB', CC', etc., will not generally be continuous, but will proceed by steps and stairs ; the size of the steps being determined roughly by the smallest convenient unit of the commodity in question.

These relations between expenditures and money income are of considerable importance, and have been somewhat neglected in economic theory to date. We can, if our taste lies in that direction, construct elasticity concepts which will fit these curves ; we could, for instance, construct curves showing the relation between total money income and the rate of consumption of each commodity, and derive from these a concept of " income elasticity "—the ratio of a proportionate change in income to a proportionate change in the consumption of the particular commodity. But the advantage of the formulation adopted above is that it shows clearly in a single diagram the necessary relations between expenditures on all commodities, this being possible because we have taken expenditures, and not rates of consumption, as our fundamental system of variables.

Two further important plane sections of the consumption function diagram are represented in Figures 2 and 3, showing the relationship between the

expenditure system and the price of one commodity. In Figure 2 we exhibit
the relation between the price of " food " and the expenditure system. If we
assume that food is an absolute necessity of existence—i.e., a commodity for
which there is no possible substitute—then the expenditure on food will rise
continuously from the origin O'', as shown by the line $O''B''$, to the point B''
where the whole income is spent on this commodity. If the income of the
individual concerned is independent of the price of the commodity considered
—that is, if the individual is not a producer of that commodity—then the
total expenditure line, EB'', will be parallel to the price axis. Where the
individual is a producer of the commodity the total expenditure line will in
general rise with rise in the price of the commodity, as his income rises. The
complexities which the introduction of this case brings into the problem,
however, are very considerable ; and for the purposes of this short note we
may assume that the income of our individual is not derived from the sale of
any commodity which he himself produces. Figure
3 exhibits a typical plane section showing the
relation between the expenditure system and the
price of a commodity that is not absolutely necessary—say, "luxuries". The expenditure on luxuries will rise from zero to some positive quantities
as the price of luxuries increases, but will eventually
decrease to zero again when the price is so high
that no luxuries are bought. In either of these
cases, if $O''A$, $O'''A$, represent the price of their
respective commodities which underlies the system
of Figure 1, AB, BC, CD, DE, represent respectively the amounts spent on food, shelter, luxuries,
and saving, and must be equal to the AB, BC,

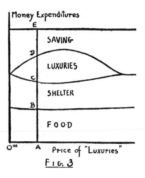

Fig. 3

CD, DE of Figure 1, in which $O'A$ represents the income which underlies
Figures 2 and 3.

We can clearly also construct a three-dimensional section of the consumption
function in which the price of (say) food, money income, and money expenditures are the co-ordinates. Figure 1 is a section of this figure parallel to the
money income, money expenditures plane ; Figure 2 is a section parallel to·
the price of food, money expenditures plane ; these two sections have a
common line AE, and are at right-angles to one another ; they will help us
to visualise the three-dimensional figure, which is something like a slice of an
onion with " skins " one inside the other.

If the commodities in our diagram are independent in consumption—
if our desire for any one commodity, that is to say, is independent of the
quantity of any other commodity which we may consume—then there is a
very simple relationship between two sections related as are Figures 1 and 2.
Given the curves of Figure 1, and the " food curve " of Figure 2, $O''B''$, we
can construct all the other curves of Figure 2. For let us take any point on
this food curve, say b'' in Figure 2 ; the perpendicular to the base line, $b''a''$
represents the expenditure on food ; the perpendicular to the total expenditure
line, $b''e''$ represents the total expenditure on other things than food. If now

we turn to Figure 1, there must be some intercept, $b'e'$, perpendicular to the income axis and cut off between the lines OE and $B'B$ which is equal to $b''e''$.[1] If this cuts the lines CC', DD' in c' and d' (Figure 1), then $b'c'$ represents the amount spent on shelter, $c'd'$ the amount spent on luxuries, $d'e'$ the amount saved, when we have the amount $b'e'$ to spend on shelter, luxuries, and savings put together. But we have also in Figure 2 an amount $b''e''$, to spend on shelter, luxuries, and saving, equal to $b'e'$. Hence if our consumption of food does not affect our consumption of any of the other objects of our expenditure, we shall divide the amount $b''e''$ in just the same way as we divided the amount $b'e'$; that is, we shall have $b'c' = b''c''$, $c'd' = c''d''$, and $d'e' = d''e''$. If the consumption of all other commodities is always independent of the amount of food that we consume, this relation will always be true whatever the position of b' and whatever two sections we take. This is true even if the other commodities are not independent in consumption among themselves, and this definition of independence therefore enables us to define it as a property of a single commodity.

Competitive and complementary relations between commodities are not so easy of definition by this method of approach, but a definition can be obtained. Thus, suppose $p'q'$ represents any division of $b'e'$, and $p''q''$ represents the corresponding division of $b''e''$. Then suppose in the first case that the relation between the price elasticity of demand and the income elasticity of demand for food is such that $a'b'$ represents a larger consumption of food than $a''b''$. Then if the commodity represented by the expenditures $p'q'$, $p''q''$ stands in a complementary relation to food, the greater consumption of food in the first case will divert expenditure toward this commodity and we should have $p'q' > p''q''$. If this commodity stands in a competitive relation to food we should similarly have $p'q' < p''q''$. These conditions will be reversed, however, if the relation between the price elasticity and the income elasticity is such that $a'b'$ represents a smaller consumption of food than $a''b''$. It must be noticed that according to this definition of complementary and competitive relations, if a commodity stands in a complementary relation to one other commodity it must stand in a competitive relation to all the others taken together. In general, in relation to any one commodity all others stand in varying degrees of complementarity or competitiveness. It may happen that in such a system there are some borderline cases in which $p'q' = p''q''$; but these do not signify any kind of true independence, for which all the corresponding expenditures must be equal.

This line of approach to the problem of the structure of demand is neither so deep nor so mathematically elegant as that recently set forth by Dr. Hicks and Mr. Allen.[2] Nevertheless, what it loses in elegance it may gain to some extent in directness, and the complexity of the problem is certainly sufficient to justify as many lines of attack as can be mustered. In essentials the conclusion from this approach is similar to that of Dr. Hicks and Mr. Allen ;

[1] If a' is the foot of the perpendicular from b' on to $O'A$, then Aa' represents a change in money income which is in some way equivalent to the change in price Aa''. Any definition of equivalence of price and money changes must be somewhat arbitrary, but this one is simple and reasonable and may well be adopted.

[2] *Economica*, February, 1934, p. 52, and May, 1934, p. 196.

that the problem of the structure of demand can be dealt with without any reference to a " utility function "—even without reference to a utility index. We must not imagine, however, that the troublesome ghost of utility is finally laid when we have constructed an equilibrium system without it. For whenever we come to enquire into the significance of physically-measured commodity quantities, whether directly or under the deceptive guise of " price ", we find ourselves immediately faced with what is essentially the utility concept, even though it may be hidden under the blessed phrase, " economic welfare ". The problems which this raises, however, are too deep for this short note.

THE THEORY OF A SINGLE INVESTMENT

Quarterly Journal of Economics, 49 (May 1935): 475-494.

THE THEORY OF A SINGLE INVESTMENT

We may conveniently start our exposition from the analysis of the single firm, as it has been developed in the last few years. This analysis runs as follows. A firm is an institution which is characterized principally by the possession of an income account, into which are paid revenues, derived from the sale of some product, and out of which are paid outlays, or costs, which are incurred in the production of this product. Over any period of time the residuum after costs have been subtracted from revenues we call "net revenues," and the elementary theory of the firm is worked out on the assumption that net revenues are maximized. These revenues, costs, and net revenues may be considered as money flows which are constant through time, or as integrals of money flow over any arbitrary period of time; their fundamental dimension, however, is that of money flow. On the assumption that costs and revenues are uniquely dependent on the output of product, it is easy to show that the output at which the net revenue is the greatest is the output at which the differential of revenue with respect to output (marginal revenue) is equal to the differential of outlay with respect to output (marginal cost). This analysis, however, is "timeless," in the sense that it neglects changes in capital values and also assumes that changes in costs result immediately in the changes in revenues to which they give rise. It is the purpose of this paper to extend this analysis by considering the element of time as an explicit variable of the problem.

We must first notice that even the "timeless" analysis applies not merely to a "firm," which is the largest unit of income accounting, but to all income accounts within the firm. The unit of organization with which we are concerned is not merely defined by unitary control, but by a unitary income account. Thus in the internal accounting of a firm, from the point of view of policy we can conceive each department, even each machine or operation, as if it were a separate enterprise, providing only that a separate income account is kept for it. Then, the complete history of an income account from the day of its inception to the day of its final liquidation is the history of a single investment; a single investment, that is to say, is defined by the complete history of an income account. Revenues, costs, and net revenues are still characteristics of such a history, but instead of regarding them as constant with respect to time we shall now consider their whole history. If we divide up the whole life of an investment into a number of equal periods of time, each of which is a "year," or an "accounting period," for each year we have a figure which represents the revenues actually accruing in that year, another figure which represents the outlays actually incurred in that year, and by subtraction another which represents the net revenue for that year. The complete series of these figures, for all the years in succession, we may call the "revenue series," the "outlay series" and the "net revenue series" respectively. It is with the properties of the net revenue series that we shall principally be concerned. But before we go on there is a difficulty in the very concept of a net revenue which must be noticed.

The concept of a gross revenue is a perfectly definite one which presents no difficulties. It is also clear that this gross revenue is divided between outlay and net revenue. The difficulty arises in deciding just where the dividing line shall come. All gross revenues are paid out to somebody, of course, but in order to have an unequivocal concept of net revenue we must have a clear distinction between those payments which are made in respect of costs and those which are not. The distinction rests ultimately on the division between the owners of the investment itself, that is, of the income account itself considered as an equity, and people who are not owners of the investment. Payments made into or out of the income account, by the owners of the investment, in respect of their capacity as owners of the investment, are net revenues; a negative net revenue indicates a payment into the income account on behalf of its owners; a positive net revenue a payment out of the income account towards its owners. Outlays are payments made for the purchase of "input" — that is, for anything which is bought from persons neither owning the investment nor acting in their capacity as owners of the investment. Outlays thus consist of payments for raw materials, labor or land services, immediate or capitalized, and even for the services of capital borrowed from outside at a contractual rate of interest.

A further point must be emphasized. In the elementary discussion of this paper we shall not consider the question of "futurity," or uncertainty, as it affects our net revenue series. What we shall be doing is more like the post-mortem of a bridge game than the theory of the game itself; we shall consider an investment as if it were all past history or, what is the same thing, as if all its future were perfectly foreknown, and consider what ought to have been, say, the capital value at any moment, the payments made to the investor, the rate of return on the investment. This is not, of course, an adequate theory of enterprise, but it is at least the foundation on which such a theory must be built.

Let us then return to the consideration of our net revenue series. Suppose we represent by x_r the net revenue of an investment in the rth year from its foundation. Then we can write our net revenue series:

$$x_1, x_2, x_3, \cdot \cdot x_r, \cdot \cdot x_n$$

x_1 is the net revenue of the year 1, x_n that of the year N, the last year in which the investment is in existence. In all that follows we shall assume for the sake of convenience that the net revenue of a given year all accrues on the last day of that year. It is clear that the early terms of the series will in general be negative; that is to say, in the "construction period" costs will be larger than revenues — indeed, revenues may be zero — and the investors will have to make payments into the account of the investment sufficient to bridge this gap. The later terms of the series will normally be positive; this is the period when the investors are receiving "returns" on their investment. Unless the enterprise is absolutely unprofitable, the sum of all the net revenues will be positive. It must be emphasized that both positive and negative net revenues are merely plus or minus values of essentially the same category.

We will now assume that there is some rate of return, i, which is characteristic of the investment as a whole. This is of course a rate of interest, or a rate of discount. But it must be emphasized that it is a rate of interest which the enterprise itself produces, and which, as we shall see later, is bound up with the very structure of the net revenues themselves. That is to say, it is an internal rate, and while it may be equal to external rates of interest it must not be confused with them. We shall assume in all that follows that all valuations within the investment are made at the internal rate; this either reduces to the assumption that the internal and external rates of interest are equal throughout the course of the investment, in which case there is no distinction between internal and external valuations, or that there are internal valuations, made, say, in calculating what dividends to declare, which are not identical with market valuations. This latter assumption is by no means unrealistic; accountants are constantly appealing to concepts of "book value" as opposed to "market value," and as we shall see this practice is quite justifiable.

We can now make two propositions: first, that the value of the enterprise at the end of the rth year from its inception, V_r, is equal to the sum of the present values at that date of all future net revenues, discounting at the internal rate of interest. That is:

$$V_r = \frac{x_{r+1}}{(1+i)} + \frac{x_{r+2}}{(1+i)^2} + \frac{x_{r+3}}{(1+i)^3} + \cdots + \frac{x_n}{(1+i)^{n-r}} \tag{1}$$

This proposition is derived from three subsidiary propositions: that the value of anything is the present value of the income stream pertaining to it, discounted at some rate of interest; that the net revenue series is the income stream which pertains to the investment as an entity; and that as this is an internal valuation the internal rate is the one concerned.

The second main proposition is that the amount of capital invested in the enterprise by the end of the rth year from its inception, I_r, is equal to the sum of the present values at that date of all past net revenues, discounted at the internal rate of interest, but with the sign changed. That is:

$$I_r = -x_1(1+i)^{r-1} - x_2(1+i)^{r-2} - x_3(1+i)^{r-3}$$
$$\cdots - x_{r-1}(1+i) - x_r \qquad (2)$$

This proposition is not obviously true at first sight, but its proof is by no means difficult. It again depends on three subsidiary propositions. The first of these is that the amount invested during a given year, R, or the rate of investment in that year, I_r', is equal to the total amount invested up to the end of that year, I_r, less the total amount invested up to the end of the previous year, I_{r-1}. That is:

$$I'_r = I_r - I_{r-1} \qquad (3)$$

This is, of course, a simple application of pure mathematical principles.

The second subsidiary proposition is that the amount invested in a given year R, I'_r, is equal to the amount paid in interest to the investors during that year, S_r, less the net revenue of that year, x_r. That is:

$$I'_r = S_r - x_r \qquad (4)$$

This follows from our definitions. We have already defined net revenue to mean the total of payments made out of the account of the investment in a given year to the owners of the investment. This is clearly made up of two parts: the payments whch are due to the investors on account of interest on previously invested capital, less the sum which the investors are adding to the amount invested in that year.

This gives us immediately equation (4); thus, when net revenue is negative, or if positive is less than the amount due in interest, there is a positive rate of investment. It follows from this, as we should expect, that when the rate of investment is zero — i.e. when the investment is neither being built up nor liquidated — the amount paid to the investors is equal to the net revenue, assumed of course to be positive.

The third subsidiary proposition is that the amount paid out to investors in a given year is equal to the total amount invested up to the beginning of that year (or what is the same thing, the total amount invested up to the end of the previous year), I_{r-1}, multiplied by the internal rate of return. For the internal rate is the rate which the investment "pays" as a whole; and at any date the amount of capital previously invested is the amount on which we should reckon the interest due to the proprietors. This proposition we may write:

$$I_{r-1} \cdot i = S_r \tag{5}$$

From equations (3), (4), and (5) we can derive equation (2) as follows. We have $I_0 = 0$; hence from (5), $S_1 = 0$.
Then we have:
from (3) and (4)

$$I_1 = I_1' = -x_1 \tag{6}$$

Then from (4), (5), and (6), we have:

$$I_2' = S_2 - x_2 = I_1 i - x_2 = -x_1 i - x_2 \tag{7}$$

Then from (3) and (7):

$$I_2 = I_2' + I_1 = -x_1(1+i) - x_2 \tag{8}$$

Similarly we have, from (4), (5), and (8)

$$I_3' = S_3 - x_3 = I_2 i - x_3 = -x_1(1+i)i - x_2 i - x_3 \tag{9}$$

and from (3), (8) and (9)

$$I_3 = I_3' + I_2 = -x_1(1+i)^2 - x_2(1+i) - x_3 \tag{10}$$

So we can go on cumulatively, finally building up equation (2).

Now we can go on to prove another important proposition. We have assumed as a first condition of our analysis that the net revenue series is known with absolute certainty.

It follows from this that there can be no capital losses or gains, for capital loss or gain can only arise where expectations are not fulfilled. Hence at any date the value of the enterprise will be equal to the amount of money invested in it. That is to say, we have:

$$I_r = V_r \qquad (11)$$

Substituting from equations (1) and (2) we have:

$$-x_1(1+i)^{r-1} - x_2(1+i)^{r-2} \cdots - x_{r-1}(1+i) - x_r$$

$$= \frac{x_{r+1}}{(1+i)} + \frac{x_{r+2}}{(1+i)^2} + \cdots + \frac{x_n}{(1+i)^n}$$

This equation we may more conveniently write, transposing and multiplying by $\dfrac{1}{(1+i)^r}$:

$$\frac{x_1}{(1+i)} + \frac{x_2}{(1+i)^2} + \cdots + \frac{x_r}{(1+i)^r} + \cdots + \frac{x_n}{(1+i)^n} = 0 \quad (12)$$

That is, we have:

$$V_0 = 0 \qquad (13)$$

The value of the enterprise, before it has begun, is zero; this is of course exactly what we should expect and confirms our previous assumptions. Similarly if we multiply equation (12) by $(1+i)^n$ we shall obtain the result

$$I_n = 0 \qquad (14)$$

That is, the total amount invested at the date of final liquidation is zero. We can similarly show that on our definitions the value of the investment and the amount invested at any date before the beginning or after the end of the investment is zero.

Equation (12), however, in whatever form we wish to take it, gives us a still more interesting result; it is an equation from which we can calculate the internal rate of return of the enterprise itself, treating the net revenue series as given and i as an unknown. The solution is not mathematically a simple one, but it is clear on general grounds that in most practical cases a single solution can be found. It is clear that V_0 will decrease as i increases; when i is zero

V_0 is the sum of the net revenues, which we assume to be positive if the investment is profitable at all. Hence as we increase i from zero, V_0 will decrease from some positive value, and for all ordinary net revenue series there will be some value of i for which V_0 is zero. This value is the internal rate of return in the investment, and if calculations are made, say in distributing profits to investors, at any other rate than this there will be no necessary equality between the amount of money invested and the value of the enterprise. Thus, bound up in the very structure of any net revenue series there is a rate of return which pertains to it, and which can be calculated if we know all the terms of the net revenue series and nothing else.

We must now enunciate the central proposition of this argument, which is that the magnitude which the perfectly rational and perfectly foreseeing investor wishes to maximize is this internal rate of return, if we are considering policy as it affects not merely a single year but the life of the investment as a whole. It is clear that the investor will not want to maximize the net revenue of a particular year at the expense of the net revenues of other years — indeed, the way to maximize the net revenue of a particular year is to liquidate the investment as quickly as possible! It is also clear on reflection that it is not the total excess of positive over negative net revenues that is to be maximized; this would assume that the investor is indifferent as to the date at which these surplus net revenues occurred. It is in fact the "rate of profit" in the classical terminology, the rate of return over the whole period of the enterprise, that is the real measure of its profitability, and it is this which we have to maximize.

I have deliberately used the terms "investment" and "investor," rather than "enterprise" and "entrepreneur" for two reasons: first because the "investment" aspects of enterprise need to be stressed and, secondly, because the above analysis applies quite generally to any kind of investment, i.e. to any equity with an income account — to the "investment" of an individual saver in securities which he sells after so many years as well as to the "real" investment of the entrepreneur in the purchase of factors of production and the building up of real capital.

We must now proceed to a more fundamental analysis, that of the enterprise and of the entrepreneur engaged in the production of commodities and the employment of factors of production.

We shall begin with a simple case: an entrepreneur-capitalist, using his own capital only, and producing a single product of price p_m. We will suppose that he buys several kinds of physical input with his outlays; for the sake of simplicity of exposition we will assume two kinds of input, A and B, of prices p_a, p_b, tho the argument applies equally well if we have any number of kinds of input. We will suppose furthermore that if a quantity q_a of input A and q_b of input B are applied to the enterprise, they result, by a directly traceable process of physical causation, in a quantity of product q_m after a period of time r. Then we shall assume that q_m depends on q_a, q_b, and r, in continuous variation; this function, $q_m = F(q_a, q_b, r)$, is the physical production function of the enterprise. In a great many cases r, which we may call loosely the "period of production," is fixed by technical considerations and need not be taken as a variable into the problem, but our case is more general. The simplest example in practice is that of a forest, and if we think of A as being input, say, of saplings, B the input of labor necessary to plant them, and grown trees the product, it is clear that the quantity of wood in the grown tree depends partly on the size and quality of the sapling, partly on the amount of care devoted to its planting, and partly on the length of time for which it is allowed to grow. The mere fact of physical growth in this case, while striking, is only incidental to the analysis, which is quite general.

Now let us suppose that the total outlay in one year expended by the entrepreneur in buying input A is $a(=p_a q_a)$, and in buying input B is $b(=p_b q_b)$, and suppose furthermore that after r years these input items give rise to a gross revenue $m(=p_m q_m)$ derived from the sale of the product.

Then starting from the beginning of the enterprise, for the first r years there will be a net revenue in each year of $(-a -b)$. In the year $R+1$ the revenue will come in from the sale of the first year's product — that is, from the product which results from the input of the first year. The net revenue in that year will be $(m -a -b)$, and will be positive if the enterprise is a profitable one. This will continue until the year $R+N$, in which year we will suppose that it is decided to liquidate the investment. The case where the investment is not liquidated, i.e. $N=$infinity, is of course only a special case of the present analysis. Then in the year $R+N+1$ there will be a revenue m derived from the outlays of r years back, but no outlays. This will continue for r years, until in the year $R+N+R$ the revenue

TABLE 1.

Year from Base Date	Net Revenue	Base Date Value of Net Revenue		
1	$-a -b$		$-a\dfrac{1}{(1+i)}$	$-b\dfrac{1}{(1+i)}$
2	$-a -b$		$-a\dfrac{1}{(1+i)^2}$	$-b\dfrac{1}{(1+i)^2}$
R	$-a -b$		$-a\dfrac{1}{(1+i)^r}$	$-b\dfrac{1}{(1+i)^r}$
$R+1$	$m -a -b$	$m\dfrac{1}{(1+i)^{r+1}}$	$-a\dfrac{1}{(1+i)^{r+1}}$	$-b\dfrac{1}{(1+i)^{r+1}}$
$R+2$	$m -a -b$	$m\dfrac{1}{(1+i)^{r+2}}$	$-a\dfrac{1}{(1+i)^{r+2}}$	$-b\dfrac{1}{(1+i)^{r+2}}$
$R+N$	$m -a -b$	$m\dfrac{1}{(1+i)^{r+n}}$	$-a\dfrac{1}{(1+i)^{r+n}}$	$-b\dfrac{1}{(1+i)^{r+n}}$
$R+N+1$	m	$m\dfrac{1}{(1+i)^{r+n+1}}$		
$R+N+2$	m	$m\dfrac{1}{(1+i)^{r+n+2}}$		
$R+N+R$	m	$m\dfrac{1}{(1+i)^{r+n+r}}$		

from the last input applied will be received. After that the enterprise will have been completely liquidated, and net revenues will be zero. In Table 1, then, we show the net revenue series of such an enterprise, together with the series of the base date values of these net revenues, discounted at the internal rate of return. Then, summing the base date values of the net revenues and putting the sum equal to zero, according to equation (12), we have:

$$\frac{m}{i(1+i)^r}\left(1-\frac{1}{(1+i)^{r+n}}\right) - \frac{a}{i}\left(1-\frac{1}{(1+i)^{r+n}}\right)$$
$$- \frac{b}{i}\left(1-\frac{1}{(1+i)^{r+n}}\right) = 0$$

As neither $i=0$ or $i=\infty$ are relevant solutions, this reduces to:

$$\frac{m}{(1+i)^r} = a+b \tag{15}$$

This beautifully simple result, it must be noticed, does not contain n; thus the rate of return on such an enterprise is independent of the number of years in which the enterprise is in full operation. Expressed in words, the rate of return in an enterprise is that rate which will make the present value of the product of input which is now going into the enterprise equal to the value of that input. The product of a given year's input will in general be greater in value than the input itself, but will appear at a later date; the rate of discounting necessary to bring the present value of this product down to the value of the input which produces it is the rate of return in the enterprise. We can think of input growing in value until it becomes output; the rate at which it has to grow in value in order to equal the value of output when it comes to fruition is the rate öf return. We have here assumed, it must be noticed, that all coöperating input is applied at the same time, and that the product arising from it all appears in one year. We shall relax this limiting assumption later, but meanwhile we may investigate the conditions, in our simple case, which make the rate of return a maximum.

We shall assume quite generally that p_m, p_a, and p_b are functions of q_m, q_a, and q_b respectively, and hence that m, a, and b are general functions of q_m, q_a, and q_b respectively. We shall not, that is to say, assume perfect competition in either the buying or selling markets of the enterprise — an enterprise being in a condition of perfect competition with respect to its selling market if the price of its product does not vary with the amount it sells, and in a condition of perfect competition with respect to its buying markets if for each item of input the price it pays is independent of the amount that it buys. We have already assumed that q_m is a function of q_a, q_b, and r; as m is a function of q_m it follows that m is a function of q_a, q_b, and r. Then, differentiating equation (15) partially with respect to r, q_a, and q_b, and putting in each case $\dfrac{\partial i}{\partial r} = 0$, $\dfrac{\partial i}{\partial q_a} = 0$, $\dfrac{\partial i}{\partial q_b} = 0$, respectively, we obtain three equations, which are the conditions for maximizing i. The simultaneous solution of these three together with equation (15) for r, q_a, q_b, and i gives us the maximum value of i and the optimum values of the other three quantities. The three conditions are:[1]

$$\frac{\partial m}{\partial x} \cdot \frac{1}{m} = \text{Log}_e\,(1+i) \tag{16}$$

$$\frac{\partial m}{\partial q_a} \cdot \frac{1}{(1+i)^r} = \frac{da}{dq_a} \tag{17}$$

$$\frac{\partial m}{\partial q_b} \cdot \frac{1}{(1+i)^r} = \frac{db}{dq_b} \tag{18}$$

If we are compounding interest continuously, as in strict

---

1. Taking logarithms of both sides of equation (15) we have:
$$\text{Log}_e m - r\text{Log}_e(1+i) = \text{Log}(a+b)$$
Differentiating, we have:
$$\frac{1}{m}\frac{\partial m}{\partial r} - \text{Log}_e(1+i) - \frac{r}{1+i}\frac{\partial i}{\partial r} = 0$$
Which, as $\dfrac{\partial i}{\partial r} = 0$ at the point of maximization of i, gives us equation (16).

The other two equations can easily be differentiated directly.

theory we should, these equations reduce to the following:[2]

$$\frac{\partial m}{\partial r} \cdot \frac{1}{m} = i \qquad (19)$$

$$\frac{\partial m}{\partial q_a} \cdot e^{-ir} = \frac{da}{dq_a} \qquad (20)$$

$$\frac{\partial m}{\partial q_b} \cdot e^{-ir} = \frac{db}{dq_b} \qquad (21)$$

All the quantities of these equations are important economic conceptions. The quantity $\dfrac{\partial m}{\partial r} \cdot \dfrac{1}{m}$ we may call the "rate of value growth"; it is the "per cent per annum" rate of growth of the value of a given input with lengthening of the period of production. To return for a moment to our original picture of a forest, the rate of value growth is the rate of

2. If we reckon interest continuously the discounted sum of our net revenues is:

$$m \int_{x=n+2r}^{x=r} e^{-ix} - (a+b) \int_{x=n+r}^{x=0} e^{-ix}$$

$$= \frac{m}{i} e^{-ir}(1 - e^{-i(r+n)}) - (a+b)(1 - e^{-i(r+n)}) = 0$$

which reduces to the equation

$$me^{-ir} = a+b$$

corresponding to equation (15).
Taking logarithms as before, we have:

$$\text{Log}_e m - ir = \text{Log}_e(a+b)$$

Differentiating partially with respect to r gives us equation (19); differentiating partially with respect to q_a and q_b in the original equation gives us equations (20) and (21). $\text{Log}_e(1+i)$ of equation (16) is of course the rate of discontinuous discounting which corresponds to a rate of continuous discounting, i. If we eliminate i from our four equations the remaining three are the same whether we discount continuously or not; viz.:

$$\frac{\partial m}{\partial r} \cdot \frac{1}{m} = \frac{1}{x} \text{Log}_e\left(\frac{m}{a+b}\right)$$

$$\frac{\partial m}{\partial q_a} \cdot \frac{a+b}{m} = \frac{da}{dq_a}$$

$$\frac{\partial m}{\partial q_b} \cdot \frac{a+b}{m} = \frac{db}{dq_b}$$

growth of the value, as present timber, of a single tree. Equation (19) then reduces to the familiar proposition that the age at which a tree is cut down is the age at which its rate of growth (strictly, its rate of value growth) is equal to the rate of interest on the investment. In more general terms we may say that when the period of production is of such a length that with given input items the rate of return on the investment is maximized, the rate of value growth of input is equal to this maximum rate of return, if interest is compounded continuously. It must be emphasized that the "value" which we conceive as "growing" in this concept is not the sales value of, say, intermediate products, but the sum which we would obtain for the product of our given input, if the period of production were such and such a length; it is a value derived from a conceptually actual product, not a conceptually anticipated product.

The magnitude $\dfrac{da}{dq_a}$ is the change in the total cost of input item A which is attendant upon a unit change in the quantity of A bought. That is to say, it is the marginal cost of input A. The "marginal cost of input" concept must not be confused with what is called marginal cost in the "timeless" analysis, which is rather the marginal cost of output. The separation which we have made between input and output, which is not made in the "timeless" analysis, necessitates this distinction. Similarly we may call the quantity $\dfrac{\partial m}{\partial q_a}$ the marginal revenue of input A; it is the change in revenue, other things being held constant, which results from a unit change in the quantity of input A. A more familiar term is available, for this quantity is what has been called the marginal value productivity, or more simply the marginal productivity, of input A. Then equations (17) or (20) reduce to the proposition that when the rate of return is maximized, the marginal cost of input A is equal to the present value, at the date of that input, of the marginal revenue of input A, that is, to the "discounted marginal productivity" of input A. Similar propositions are true for input B, and for any other inputs C, D, etc., for our analysis is not affected by the addition of new kinds of input, each new kind merely adding one unknown and a further equation of the type of (17) or (20) to the system.

We can derive an interesting corollary to this proposition. We have, as $a = p_a q_a$,

$$\frac{da}{dq_a} = \frac{d(p_a q_a)}{dq_a} = p_a + q_a \frac{dp_a}{dq_a} = p_a \left(1 + \frac{q_a}{p_a} \cdot \frac{dp_a}{dq_a}\right)$$
$$= p_a \left(1 + \frac{1}{\mu_a}\right) \tag{22}$$

where μ_a is the "individual elasticity of supply of input A" for the enterprise, expressed roughly, the percentage increase in the quantity supplied to the enterprise which is called forth by a one per cent increase in the price offered. Now, under conditions of perfect competition in the buying market, the price of input is fixed independently of the quantity which an enterprise will take or, more exactly, the slightest increase in the price offered will result in an infinite increase in the supply offered by the owners of the input item to that particular enterprise. That is, the individual elasticity of supply is infinite, and we have:

$$\frac{dm}{dq_a} \cdot \frac{1}{(1+i)^r} = \frac{da}{dq_a} = p_a \tag{23}$$

Similarly, of course, for all the other input items. This is the familiar "discounted marginal productivity" theory of distribution, expressed in symbolic form, and seen, as it were, from the side of the enterprise rather than that of the factor of production. We see that it is only true in conditions of perfect competition in the market for input; equation (22), however, gives us a formula which is true under imperfect competition; we might almost call the expression $1 + \frac{1}{\mu_a}$ the "coefficient of imperfection." In general as we proceed from perfect competition to complete monopoly in the market for input the "discounted marginal productivity" of input becomes greater than the price of that input.

In all our analysis so far we have assumed that all coöperating input is applied simultaneously and that its product is all sold within a given year. This is of course a very unrealistic assumption; it is approximately true only in a very few cases, such as the forest in which trees are not

Table 2.

Year From Base Date	Net Revenue	Base Date Value of Net Revenue		
1	$-a$		$-a\dfrac{1}{(1+i)}$	
2	$-a$		$-a\dfrac{1}{(1+i)^2}$	
S	$-a$		$-a\dfrac{1}{(1-i)^s}$	
$S+1$	$-a\ -b$		$-a\dfrac{1}{(1+i)^{s+1}}$	$-b\dfrac{1}{(1+i)^{s+1}}$
$S+2$	$-a\ -b$		$-a\dfrac{1}{(1+i)^{s+2}}$	$-b\dfrac{1}{(1+i)^{s+2}}$
R	$-a\ -b$		$-a\dfrac{1}{(1+i)^r}$	$-b\dfrac{1}{(1+i)^r}$
$R+1$	$m\ -a\ -b$	$m\dfrac{1}{(1+i)^{r+1}}$	$-a\dfrac{1}{(1+i)^{r+1}}$	$-b\dfrac{1}{(1+i)^{r+1}}$
$R+2$	$m\ -a\ -b$	$m\dfrac{1}{(1+i)^{r+2}}$	$-a\dfrac{1}{(1+i)^{r+2}}$	$-b\dfrac{1}{(1+i)^{r+2}}$
$R+N$	$m\ -a\ -b$	$m\dfrac{1}{(1+i)^{r+n}}$	$-a\dfrac{1}{(1+i)^{r+n}}$	$-b\dfrac{1}{(1+i)^{r+n}}$
$R+N+1$	$m\quad -b$	$m\dfrac{1}{(1+i)^{r+n+1}}$		$-b\dfrac{1}{(1+i)^{r+n+1}}$
$R+N+S$	$m\quad -b$	$m\dfrac{1}{(1+i)^{r+n+s}}$		$-b\dfrac{1}{(1+i)^{r+n+s}}$
$R+N+S+1$	m	$m\dfrac{1}{(1+i)^{r+n+s+1}}$		
$R+N+R$	m	$m\dfrac{1}{(1+i)^{r+n+r}}$		

specifically cared for between the date of their planting and of their cutting down. We have also assumed that the period of production is variable, and that the quantity of product is a continuous function of the period of production. This is also true only in a few special cases, of which the forest is one and the maturing of wines and spirits another. Normally there is some technically determined period connected with a specific enterprise such that any attempt to produce with a shorter period of production results in greatly diminished or even zero output, and production with a longer period (which can easily be obtained simply by holding stocks of the finished product or of some intermediate product) will not result in a greater value of output. This last condition is modified where the price of the product is rising continuously, but this case is too complex to be considered here. Normally, too, the input that gives rise to the product of a given date has been applied at various dates, and the product of input of given dates is sold at various dates. For the sake of simplicity of exposition we shall consider a case in which one item of input, A, is applied at the beginning of a process; a coöperating item, B, is applied to the input A after S years, and the product of these inputs emerges R years from the beginning. We can then construct our net revenue series as before; this series, and the corresponding series of base date values, is shown in Table 2.

As before, a, b, and m represent respectively the sums expended on input A and input B and received for the product; but input B only begins to be applied after S years have elapsed from the beginning; and in the liquidation B continues to be applied to previous applications of A for S years after the application of A has ceased. Summing the base date values as before and putting the sum equal to zero we get:

$$\frac{m}{(1+i)^r} = a + \frac{b}{(1+i)^s} \qquad (24)$$

an equation which we can also write in this form:

$$m = a(1+i)^r + b(1+i)^{r-s} \qquad (25)$$

That is, the rate of return on the investment is that which will make the value of the product equal at the date of emergence of the product to the present value of all the costs which have gone toward the production of the product. The analysis is clearly valid for any number of input items at whatever date they may be applied. It is also valid for any number of output items at whatever date they may emerge. For clearly, if we assume, to take the simplest example, that our costs a at the base date and b s years after produce a revenue m_1 r years after the base date and m_2 q years after the base date, the m_2 series in the net revenue table will be "stepped" relative to the m_1 series just as the b series is stepped relative to the a series in Table 2, and when we sum our base date values of the net revenues we shall get as our equation for i

$$m_2 + m_1(1+i)^{q-r} = b(1+i)^{q-s} + a(1+i)^q \tag{26}$$

It is clear that as we can multiply both sides of this equation by any power of $(1+i)$ without affecting its validity, we can formulate the general proposition thus: if in an enterprise we have a system of costs and revenues at different dates, which are connected through a physical substratum of causation, and which describe the element of the productive process which characterizes the enterprise, then the rate of return in the enterprise is that rate of interest which will make the present values at any date of the revenues equal to the present value of the costs at the same date.

Even from the most complicated systems of costs and revenues we can theoretically obtain the conditions for maximizing the rate of return, and so find the optimum rates of input, and optimum lengths of the various periods involved. The equations which give us the lengths of the various periods are very complex and intractable; however, as we have seen, it is by no means unrealistic to assume that these periods are fixed by technological considerations for any given productive process. In this case the only unknowns of the problem — the quantities which policy has to determine — are the rates of input, q_a, q_b, etc. In the case which is represented in equation (26) the conditions for maximizing i, obtained as before by differentiating partially with respect to q_a and q_b, and putting $\dfrac{di}{dq_a} = 0, \dfrac{di}{dq_b} = 0$ in the equations thus obtained are:

$$\frac{\partial m_2}{\partial q_a} + \frac{\partial m_1}{\partial q_a}(1+i)^{q-r} = \frac{da}{dq_a}(1+i)^q \tag{27}$$

$$\frac{\partial m_2}{\partial q_b} + \frac{\partial m_1}{\partial q_b}(1+i)^{q-r} = \frac{db}{dq_b}(1+i)^{q-s} \tag{28}$$

In words, for each input item, the present value at any date of the change in gross revenue which can be attributed to a unit change in the quantity of that input is equal to the present value at the same date of the change in the cost of that input which a unit change in the quantity entails. This is of course merely the generalized case of the simpler formula expressed in equations (17) and (18).

We may conveniently bring the present analysis to a close at this point. It must not be supposed that we have solved or even stated the problems with which an actual entrepreneur or investor is faced, for we have neglected both the uncertainty of those anticipations which are the data of the entrepreneur's judgment, and the effect of the existence of other enterprises or opportunities for investment upon the entrepreneur's policy. We have further avoided the problems connected with the shifts of demand and supply functions through time. In fact, our analysis, for all its introduction of time as a specific element, has not achieved much more than the "timeless" analysis in the task of interpreting economic history, or economic processes through time, which is one of the principal tasks of present-day economics. It tells us nothing, for instance, of the question when, and why, does the entrepreneur decide to liquidate; n, the length of time the entrepreneur carries on the enterprise, cancels out of our equations. Our conclusions are remarkably similar to those of the "timeless" analysis also; identify input with output and equations (17) and (18) become the familiar "marginal cost equals marginal revenue" formula. Nevertheless, it is to be hoped that the present analysis will at least provide a starting point from which the real problems of business policy may be attacked.

TIME AND INVESTMENT

Economica, NS 3, 10 (May 1936): 196-220.

Time and Investment

"An Investment" is the complete history of the payments made into and out of a day book account. It consists algebraically of a series of payments, i.e. of transferred sums of money, some of which are positive and some of which are negative, each being associated with a certain "date"; the "date" being the interval of time between the payment and a given base date. The base date can be any convenient point of time, and will generally be taken to be the point of time at which the first term of the payments series occurs. We will adopt the convention that time measured "forwards"—i.e. from past to future—is positive, while time measured "backwards" is negative. We can then write as a perfectly general formula, that if X_t is the "present value" of X_o at a date t years from X_o, and i is the rate of interest,

$$X_t = X_o(1+i)^t. \tag{1}$$

If X_t is "past" relative to X_o; then t is negative (say $-s$) and the equation becomes the ordinary "discounting" equation,

$$X_t = \frac{X_o}{(1+i)^s}.$$

We must also adopt a convention with regard to the algebraical sign of the payments; which convention we adopt is quite immaterial. The most obvious one is to look at the payments from the side of the investment itself and regard all payments made into the account (i.e. added to it) as positive, and all payments made out from the account (i.e. subtracted from it) as negative.

We can make no absolute definition of the limits of an individual account, nor can we construct any absolute criterion of relevance for a particular payment. We must simply accept the fact that payments are in practice classified into "accounts" by business men.

We shall consider first the simplest type of investment ; that in which all the payments of the payments series are made between the investor and his investment, and no payments are made to outsiders. Examples of this class are loans at interest, the purchase, holding, and sale of bonds or securities of any kind ; the simplest example is the loan repaid after a number of years with interest added. We have, say, a positive payment, m_0 (the loan) and a negative payment, n_1 (the repayment with interest) after t_1 years. Then the " yield " or the rate of return on this investment is defined by the equation

$$m_0(1 + i)^{t_1} - n_1 = 0 \qquad\qquad (2)$$

That is to say, the rate of return is the rate at which the positive payment must grow in order to be equal arithmetically to the negative payment after an interval of time equal to the interval between the two payments. If then there is to be a positive rate of return, two conditions must be fulfilled : first, the positive payment must be smaller than the negative payment—i.e. the payments out of the investment must exceed the payments in : " returns " must be greater than " outlay "—and secondly, the positive payment must be previous to the negative payment in time. In such a case it is obvious that the longer the interval between the two payments, the payments being constant, the smaller the rate of return ; the more time the payment has to grow, the smaller its rate of growth has to be. This case is illustrated graphically in Fig. 1. If we plot time

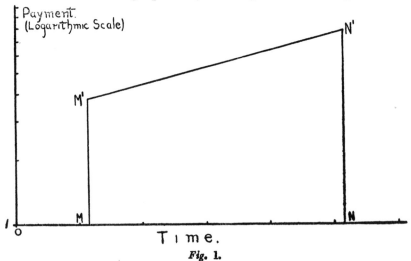

Fig. 1.

along the X axis, and plot the logarithm of the payments along the Y axis (i.e. if we plot our curves on semi-logarithmic paper), then growth, or compound interest curves, appear as straight lines—the slope of the line being the rate of growth—i.e. the rate of return.[1]   Then if MM', $N'N$ represent the values of the positive and negative payments respectively, at dates OM, ON, the line $M'N'$ represents the growth curve and its slope is the rate of return in the investment.   Clearly, if we keep MM', $N'N$ constant, increasing MN (the period of investment) lowers the slope of $M'N'$: increasing the ratio MM'/NN' raises the slope of $M'N'$. The algebraic sign of a payment in this figure is indicated by the direction in which the line representing it is measured: positive payments are measured as from M to M': negative payments as from N' to N.

In this case there is no question about the concept of the period of investment: it is simply the time distance between the two payments.   The question now arises, however, can we apply this analysis to the general case, where we have more than two payments?   In the general case we have positive payments, m_1, m_2, . . . m_h, at dates t_1, t_2, . . . t_h, and negative payments n_1, n_2, . . . n_k, at dates s_1, s_2, . . . s_k. The rate of return, i, is then defined by the equation:

$$m_1 (1 + i)^{-t_1} + m_2 (1 + i)^{-t_2} + . . . + m_h (1 + i)^{-t_h}$$
$$= n_1 (1 + i)^{-s_1} + n_2 (1 + i)^{-s_2} + . . . + n_k (1 + i)^{-s_k} \quad (3)$$

In words, the rate of return is a rate of growth which will make the positive payments grow into a sum, by a given date, equal arithmetically to the sum into which the negative

[1] In measuring the slope of growth curves on semi-logarithmic paper we must, of course, measure the vertical ordinates on a natural logarithmic scale.   If we compound interest continuously (as we are doing in Fig. 1), equation (2) becomes

$$m_0 e^{it} = n_1$$

This equation may also be written:

$$i = \frac{1}{t}(Log_e n_1 - Log_e m_0)$$

The right hand side of this equation is the slope of the compound interest line on the logarithmic diagram when the vertical ordinates are measured on a natural logarithmic scale.   In practice it is not easy to read off the slope of a growth line: perhaps the easiest method of finding what rate of return a given growth line represents is to find out from the figure how many years it takes a sum to double itself and then calculating, or finding from tables, the rate of return from that datum.

It must be noticed that on the logarithmic figures the points M and N do not represent zero payments but a payment of one unit: the lines MM', N'N therefore really represent a sum which is one unit less than the actual payment represented by the ordinates of M' and N'. This difficulty arises, of course, because the zero of the logarithmic scale is at minus infinity and cannot be represented on the diagram.   The difficulty, however, is only one of exposition: in the text I have treated the points M and N as if they truly represented zero payments. The same device has also been used in Fig. 2.

payments will grow by the same date. If the rate of return is positive the positive payments must be on the whole earlier than the negative payments and their sum must be smaller. There is no necessity, it must be observed, for *all* the positive payments to precede all the negative payments. We can think of the time-positions of positive and negative payments as "chords" on a time-scale; the chords may overlap, but the positive chord must be on the whole nearer the "past" end of the scale than the negative chord.

The question now arises, can we define an "average date" for the positive and negative payments respectively? Let us take first the positive payments, m_1, m_2 ... m_h at dates t_1, t_2 ... t_h. We shall define the "time centre" of these payments, for reasons which will appear shortly, not by any ordinary statistical average, but as follows. The *time centre* of a group of payments is that date at which the sum of the present values of the payments, discounting at the internal rate of return, is equal to the sum of the payments. Thus if T_m is the date of the time centre of the positive payments, T_m is given by the equation

$$m_1 (1+i)^{T_m - t_1} + m_2 (1+i)^{T_m - t_2} + \ldots + m_h (1+i)^{T_m - t_h}$$
$$= m_1 + m_2 + \ldots + m_h \quad (4)$$

It can be easily seen that T_m lies somewhere intermediate between t_1 and t_h, the first and last dates of the series. At the date t_1 the sum of the present values of the payments is less than the sum of the payments, for the present value of each payment is less than the payment itself. At the date t_1 the sum of the present values of the payments is greater than the sum of the payments; for the present value of each payment is greater than the payment itself. At some intermediate point the present value of some of the payments (the "past" payments) will be greater than the value of the payments themselves, while the present value of the other ("future") payments will be less; where these just balance is the "Time centre."

We can similarly define the centre T_n for the negative payments, n_1, n_2 ... n_k at times s_1, s_2 ... s_k by the equation

$$n_1 (1+i)^{T_n - s_1} + n_2 (1+i)^{T_n - s_2} + \ldots + n_k (1+i)^{T_n - s_k}$$
$$= n_1 + n_2 + \ldots + n_k \quad (5)$$

Now multiplying equation (4) by $(1+i)^{T_n - T_m}$ we have

$$(1+i)^{T_n}\left[m_1(1+i)^{-t_1}+m_2(1+i)^{-t_2}+\ldots+m_h(1+i)^{-t_h}\right]$$
$$= M(1+i)^{T_n - T_m} \quad (6)$$

where $M = m_1 + m_2 + \ldots + m_h$.

Equation (5) may also be written :

$$(1+i)^{T_n}\left[n_1(1+i)^{-s_1}+n_2(1+i)^{-s_2}+\ldots+n_k(1+i)^{-s_k}\right]$$
$$= N \quad (7)$$

where $N = n_1 + n_2 + \ldots + n_k$.

Now from equation (3), if i is the internal rate of return the quantities in the square brackets in equations (6) and (7) are equal. We have therefore :

$$M(1+i)^{T_n - T_m} = N. \quad (8)$$

The interval between the time centres of positive and negative payments, $T_n - T_m$ may properly be called the " Time spread " of the investment. It is the length of time for which a quantity equal to the sum of the positive payments would have to grow (at the rate of return) in order to equal the sum of the negative payments. This is the really *significant* period of investment.

It is interesting to trace the relation between this " Time spread " as defined above and the " average interval " between positive and negative payments. If the rate of return is small enough so that we can neglect its square and higher powers we can expand each term of equation (4) by the binomial theorem, taking the first two terms of the expansion only. We then have :

$$m_1(1+T_m i - t_1 i)+m_2(1+T_m i - t_2 i)+\ldots+m_h(1+T_m i - t_h i)$$
$$= m_1 + m_2 + \ldots + m_h$$

which reduces to :

$$T_m = \frac{m_1 t_1 + m_2 t_2 + \ldots + m_h t_h}{m_1 + m_2 + \ldots + m_h} = \bar{t} \quad (9)$$

Similarly we have :

$$T_n = \frac{n_1 s_1 + n_2 s_2 + \ldots + n_k s_k}{n_1 + n_2 + \ldots + n_k} = \bar{s} \quad (10)$$

That is, if i is small the time centre of each group of payments is the weighted arithmetical average of the dates of the payments, each date being weighted by the payment corresponding to it.

These equations are very useful in the arithmetical determination of the rate of return in any given investment. (See Appendix.)

The time interval $\bar{s} - \bar{t}$ is the most general formula for what is usually known as the "average period of investment." If we have only one positive payment at a point of time t_m, then

$$\bar{s} - \bar{t} = \frac{n_1 (s_1 - t_m) + n_2 (s_2 - t_m) + \ldots + n_k (s_k - t_m)}{n_1 + n_2 + \ldots + n_k}$$

The "average period" of investment in this case is the weighted average of the dates of the negative payments taken from the date of the positive payment as base date. Similarly if there are a number of positive payments and one negative payment the "average period" is the weighted average of the dates of the positive payments, reckoned from the date of the negative payment as the base date. These two cases correspond to the "average disinvestment period" and the "average construction period" respectively. The numerical divergence of the average period of investment from the time spread is not usually very large: but for theoretical purposes it is the "time spread" which is really important.

We shall now prove an important proposition: that if we take a certain payments series, with a time spread T, and repeat this payments series, beginning at any date but keeping the original intervals between the payments, both the time spread and the rate of return in the payments series formed by the original series and its repetition is the same as the time spread and the rate of return in the original series. This is true however many times we repeat the original series, and at whatever dates.

For the sake of obtaining simplicity in exposition without losing generality, suppose we take as our original payments series a series of four terms, two positive and two negative. The payments series may then be represented by Table I.

TABLE I.

Date	0	t_1	t_2	t_3
Payment	m_o	m_1	$-n_2$	$-n_3$

The base date is taken at the first payment for simplicity of exposition. Now suppose we repeat this series, beginning at a time t_4, which, it must be noticed, need not be later than the latest payment of the original series : there is nothing, that is to say, to prevent the repetition from beginning while the original series is still in process. Then the payments series of the investment formed by the original and the repeated series is :

TABLE 2

Date	o	t_1	t_2	t_3	t_4	t_4+t_1	t_4+t_2	t_4+t_3
Payment	m_o	m_1	$-n_2$	$-n_3$	m_o	m_1	$-n_2$	$-n_3$

Now, the rate of return, i, in the original investment is given by

$$m_o + m_1 (1 + i)^{-t_1} - n_2 (1 + i)^{-t_2} - n_3 (1 + i)^{-t_3} = 0$$

The rate of return, i', in the " duplicated " investment is given by

$$m_o + m_1 (1+i')^{-t_1} - n_2 (1+i')^{-t_2} - n_3 (1+i')^{-t_3} + m_o (1+i')^{-t_4}$$
$$+ m_1 (1+i')^{-t_4-t_1} - n_2 (1+i')^{-t_4-t_2} - n_3 (1+i')^{-t_4-t_3} = 0$$

i.e. by

$$(1 + (1 + i')^{-t_4}) \left[m_o + m_1 (1 + i')^{-t_1} - n_2 (1 + i')^{-t_2} \right.$$
$$\left. - n_3 (1 + i')^{-t_3} \right] = 0$$

whence it is clear that $i' = i$: i.e. the rate of return in the duplicated investment is the same as that in the original. Then the time spread, T, in the original investment is given by the equation :

$$(m_o + m_1) (1 + i)^T = n_2 + n_3 \qquad (11)$$

Similarly the time spread in the duplicated investment, T', is given by the equation :

$$2 (m_o + m_1) (1 + i')^{T'} = 2 (n_2 + n_3) \qquad (12)$$

Comparing equations (11) and (12), as $i' = i$, we have

$$T = T'.$$

The argument clearly holds for any number of repetitions. This result can also be proved directly by calculating the time centres of the two investments. It may seem surprising at first sight, but the logic of it is fairly clear. When we repeat the " element," we do of course move the time centres of each of the payment groups forward ; but each time centre is moved forward by exactly the same amount, and the interval between them is not changed. In any investment, therefore, which consists of repetitions, however ordered, of an elementary payments series, the time

spread of the element is characteristic of the investment
as a whole. This is true however many repetitions there
are, and however far they extend through time.

Now, there are three ways in which we may repeat an
element of investment : we may repeat it at random, we
may begin each new element immediately on the completion
of the old, or we may begin a new element each " year "—
a " year ", of course, being any appropriate unit of time.
The first mode of repetition need not detain us ; it is rare
in practice and has no theoretical significance. The other
two modes of repetition, however, are very frequent in
practice, and of very great theoretical significance ; for
by means of them we can turn an " element " of investment,
which is strictly bounded by " dates " in time, into a " continuous " investment which is not so bounded. In other
words, an " element " of investment : a single apple tree,
or a single house, or a single machine, must come to an
end sometime : but when repeated it forms an investment
which may stretch into the indefinite future. When, then,
we come to examine the relations between the time structure of an investment and its capital structure, we must
be very careful to distinguish these three forms of repetition.

In the first place let us consider the case of an element
of investment, i.e. a payments series which is not repeated
at all, and which cannot be analysed into repetitions of
any simpler series. Such an investment might be the
voyages of adventure of the mediæval merchants, each of
which represented a payments series not to be repeated,
or to be repeated only at random. Now, the total amount
invested in a given investment up to a certain date
is the net algebraical sum of all payments made to that
date, plus the accrued interest payments. Each time the
owner pays a sum into the account of the investment, the
capital increases by that amount ; each time the owner draws
a sum out of the investment the capital decreases by that
amount. And in the intervals of time between payments
the capital grows at the internal rate of return. Thus,
suppose I buy a security for £100 ; receive £5 after a year,
£5 after two years, and then sell the security for £100. The
rate of return on this investment, calculated by equation
(3), is .05 per annum. On the day I buy it, the capital
invested is £100. Throughout the first year the amount
invested grows, as interest accrues without being withdrawn.

At the end of the first year the capital is £105; I withdraw £5 and the capital sinks to £100 again. Similarly for the second, or any subsequent years, till I sell the security and the capital drops to zero. The simple general case of four payments is illustrated in Fig. 2. Along the X axis we plot time, on a linear scale; on the Y axis we plot the total capital invested, on a logarithmic scale, for the reasons mentioned earlier.

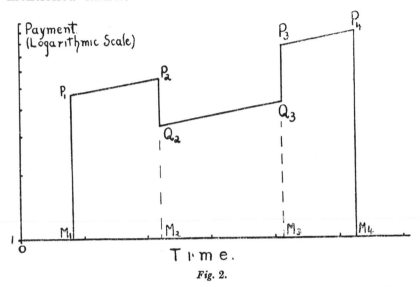

Fig. 2.

Thus, our net payments series is, we suppose, a positive payment M_1P_1 at a date OM_1, a negative payment P_2Q_2 at a date OM_2; a positive payment Q_3P_3 at a date OM_3, and a negative payment P_4M_4 at a date OM_4 which liquidates the investment. The line $M_1P_1P_2Q_2Q_3P_3P_4M_4$ exhibits the amount of capital invested at each date. The slope of the lines P_1P_2, Q_2Q_3, P_3P_4, which are parallel, show the internal rate of return. If the slope of these lines is not the internal rate of return—i.e. if we reckon accrued interest at any other rate than the internal rate—the investment will not be properly liquidated. Thus if we reckon interest accruals at above the internal rate, i.e. if the slope of the lines P_1P_2, etc., is too great, we shall arrive at a position at the time OM_4 in which the supposed amount of capital invested is greater than the last negative payment, and therefore cannot be liquidated by that payment. If we reckon interest accruals at a rate below the internal rate, the amount of capital believed to have been invested

by the date OM_1 will be less than the final payment, which
will "over-liquidate" the investment. This point cannot
be too strongly emphasised : that the very concept of the
amount of capital invested in an investment at a given
date involves knowledge of the "true"—i.e. the internal—
rate of return in the investment, and consequently pre-
supposes knowledge of the future course of payments. Of
course, in practice the future course of payments, and hence
the internal rate of return, can only be guessed at ; as time
proceeds these guesses are rectified by reckoning capital
losses or gains—i.e. by writing off or "writing on" capital.
If there were perfect knowledge, of course, there could be
no capital loss or gain. Now, the amount of capital necessary in an investment—i.e. the minimum amount of funds
which an investor must have control over if the investment
is to be carried through to its completion—is the maximum
amount of capital registered during the life of the investment. In an elementary investment, it must be noted,
there is no quantity that we can strictly call "the" capital :
the amount of capital in the investment is a function of
time. There is, however, some justification for calling the
maximum figure "the" capital of the investment. The
investor must have at least that quantity at the corresponding date if the investment is to be carried through ; failure
to have command over that quantity must mean the abandonment or sale of the investment before completion. Now,
as we have seen there will be, in general, several relative
maxima of the capital invested ; in fact, a relative maximum
will occur whenever a negative payment is made, as this
reduces the amount of capital invested. One of these
relative maxima will be the absolute maximum : but which
it is, we cannot say without an exact knowledge of the
payments series itself : there is no general rule. In the
figure taken as illustration it happens to be at the point
P_4 ; it might just as well have been at the point P_2 had
the sizes of the payments, or their times, been different.

Now, if we increase the "time spread" without changing
the magnitudes of the payments, we shall lower the rate of
return according to equation (8) ; but we cannot say even
in the case of one of the relative maxima whether the
amount of capital it represents will be raised or lowered
by the change unless we know all the dates, both new and
old, of all the payments : still less do we know whether

the absolute maximum has been raised or lowered, because the shift in the time positions of the various payments may dethrone the old absolute maximum and erect one of the previously inferior relative maxima in its place. Thus, if in both the old and the new positions the last relative maximum is the absolute maximum, the change in the time spread will not have changed the maximum capital at all: in both positions it is equal to the last negative payment. On the other hand, if some intermediate relative maximum is also the absolute maximum, under some conditions an increase in the time spread (without change in the payment quantities) will raise, under other conditions lower, the maximum capital employed.

This is also true of an investment of the second class of repetition, which we may call " end to end " repetition. This class of investment is quite common in everyday life. Indeed, it may be said that this case includes every investment involving the building up and ultimate expenditure of a depreciation fund. Investment in a car, a machine, a horse, where there is only one car, one machine, one horse, is of this type. The function showing the amount of capital invested at each point of time is a simple periodic repetition of the " elementary " function : the maximum capital of the elementary investment will also be the maximum of the repeated investment, and we cannot make any general proposition regarding the effect of a pure lengthening of the time spread upon the maximum capital employed.

The third class of repetition, however, which we may call *continuous* repetition, is much more tractable to analysis. Here a new element is begun every " year ", a " year " being any convenient accounting period. Then if the elementary payments series is $x_1, x_2 \ldots x_n$, for the years 1, 2, $\ldots N$, the payments series of the repeated investment will be as in Table 3. Some x's will of course be positive, some negative.

TABLE 3.

Year.	Payment.
1	x_1
2	$x_2 + x_1$
3	$x_3 + x_2 + x_1$
4	$x_4 + x_3 + x_2 + x_1$
N	$x_n + x_{n-1} + x_{n-2} + x_{n-3} + \ldots + x_2 + x_1$
$N+1$	$x_n + x_{n-1} + x_{n-2} + \ldots + x_3 + x_2 + x_1$

Clearly, after the year N the payment in each year will be constant and will be equal to the sum of all the payments of the elementary payment series. The amount of capital invested up to the year N, C_n, is the compounded sum of all preceding payments, i.e. :

$$C_n = x_1 \left[(1+i)^{n-1} + (1+i)^{n-2} + \ldots + (1+i) + 1 \right]$$
$$+ x_2 \left[(1+i)^{n-2} + (1+i)^{n-3} + \ldots + (1+i) + 1 \right]$$
$$+ \ldots + x_{n-1} \left[(1+i) + 1 \right] + x_n$$

$$= \frac{x_1}{i} \left[(1+i)^n - 1 \right] + \frac{x_2}{i} \left[(1+i)^{n-1} - 1 \right]$$
$$+ \ldots + \frac{x_{n-1}}{i} \left[(1\,i\,+)^2 - 1 \right] + \frac{x_n}{i} \left[(1+i) - 1 \right]$$

$$= \frac{1}{i} \left[x_1 (1+i)^n + x_2 (1+i)^{n-1} + \ldots \right.$$
$$\left. + x_{n-1} (1+i)^2 + x_n (1+i) \right]$$

$$- \frac{1}{i} \left[x_1 + x_2 + \ldots + x_n \right]$$

Whence, as by the definition of the rate of return,
$$x_1 (1+i)^n + x_2 (1+i)^{n-1} + \ldots + x_n (1+i) = 0, \text{ we have}$$

$$C_n = - \left(\frac{x_1 + x_2 + \ldots + x_n}{i} \right) \tag{13}$$

We can similarly show that $C_n = C_{n+1} = C_{n+2} =$ etc., and that $C_n > C_{n-1} > C_{n-2} >$ etc. Thus, when the continuously repeated investment is in full running order— i.e. when a new element is begun and an old element finishes each " year "—the total capital invested is constant, apart from changes within the " year " which we neglect, and is equal to the net annual negative payment divided by the rate of return. Moreover, this net annual negative payment or " net revenue " is itself equal to the algebraical sum of the terms in the payment series of the element of the investment. The time spread is constant, however long we continue the repetitions, and is equal to the time spread of the element. We can easily formulate the relationship between the time spread, the yearly net revenue, and the amount of capital employed. If M, N, are the arithmetical sums of the positive and negative payments of the element; the time spread, T, is given by:

$$(1 + i)^T = \frac{N}{M}$$

But by equation (13), $i = \dfrac{N - M}{C}$, where C is the total capital.

Hence we have:

$$T = \frac{Log_e \dfrac{N}{M}}{Log_e (1 + i)} = \frac{Log_e \dfrac{N}{M}}{Log_e \left(1 + \dfrac{N - M}{C}\right)} \tag{14}$$

If we assume continuous discounting instead of yearly discounting the formula becomes much simpler: equation (14) may then be written:

$$T = \frac{Log_e \dfrac{N}{M}}{i} = \frac{C}{N - M} \, Log_e \frac{N}{M} \tag{15}$$

If i is so small that its squares and higher powers can be neglected we can formulate an even simpler relation between the time spread and the capital invested. Writing equation (14) in the form

$$T = \frac{Log_e \left(1 + \dfrac{N - M}{M}\right)}{Log_e \left(1 + \dfrac{N - M}{C}\right)},$$

expanding, and neglecting terms involving squares or higher powers of $\dfrac{N - M}{M}$ and $\dfrac{N - M}{C}$, we have:

$$T = \frac{C}{M} \tag{16}$$

In equations (15) and (16), it will be noticed, if the terms of the payments series are constant—i.e. if N and M are constant—the capital is directly proportional to the time spread.

Thus, if our elementary investment is an apple tree, and our " continuous " investment is an orchard in which one tree is planted and one cut down each year, the composition of the orchard does not change from year to year, though its constituent apple trees are planted, grow, and die. The payments made each year in the whole orchard are identical in magnitude and object with the payments which constitute the investment in a single tree : the rate of return and the time spread are the same for the orchard and for a single tree, while if the time spread is altered merely by changing the dates and not the magnitudes of the payments series of the single tree, the capital invested in the orchard is directly proportional to the time spread.

This brings us to the next stage of the argument. We have so far been considering investment merely as investment—i.e. merely as a payments series between the investment and its owner. We must now carry the enquiry a stage further : for every investment ultimately rests upon, and is occasioned through, *production*. Beneath every elementary investment there lies a *process* of production, which consists of a series of *inputs*, each of which involves a *cost*, or *outlay*, and a series of *outputs*, each of which brings in a *revenue*. The cost-revenue series of a productive process underlies the positive and negative payments series of the investment which corresponds to the process. Thus suppose we take the elementary case of the production of a play. Abstracting from uncertainty, the play consists, from the economic point of view, of a number of costs at various dates—salaries, wages, royalties, rents, taxes, etc.— and a number of revenues of various dates—the receipts from the sale of tickets. In the simplest case, where there is no accumulation or decumulation of cash balances in the account of the investment, every time a cost is incurred— i.e. every time a payment is made from the account of the outside world—the investor must balance this by a positive payment equal in magnitude to the cost, paid into the account of the investment. Likewise every time a revenue comes in from the outside world, a negative payment must be made from the account of the investment in favour of the investor. Thus in this case there is a payments series, identical in magnitude but opposite in algebraical sign, which is necessitated by the cost-revenue series of the process. This payments series we shall call the " basic investment." Now, of course, once we relax the condition that the investment shall not hold a cash balance the actual payments series does not have to correspond to the basic payments series. Thus our investor may, and generally does, pay in a sum to the credit of the investment in advance of actual expenditures, while he will generally receive his returns more or less continuously, and not as revenues happen to come in. But we can formulate two propositions with certainty: that the total excess of negative over positive payments to the investor must be equal to the total excess of revenues over costs (because there can be no change in the cash balance over the whole life of the investment): and that the rate of return on the actual investment cannot exceed the rate of return in the basic investment. For if the actual and the basic payments series diverge, it is only because positive payments precede the costs which necessitate them and negative payments follow the revenues which provide them; hence the time spread must be greater in the actual than in the basic investment, and as the sum of the positive and negative payments is the same, the rate of return must be lower in the actual payments series. This would not be the case where the idle balances of the actual payments series could be invested in external investments at a rate of interest equal or greater than the rate of return; but this is unlikely, as in that event the original investment will not be made at all.

These complications, however, belong to monetary theory rather than to the theory of investment, and for the moment we can assume that the actual and the basic payments series are identical. Then the time spread of the basic payments series is the best meaning we can ascribe to the concept of the period of production in the *process*. Now, it must be emphasised that the period of production in the process is a half-physical, half economic entity which determines the time spread of the investment : the *nature* of the process in which investment is embodied *determines* the time spread of that investment : while underneath all apparently " pure " investments—i.e. investments without costs or revenues, but with positive and negative payments only—there are processes of production and " basic " payments series which " produce " the interest which the pure investment apparently pays without effort. In other words, all borrowed money is borrowed for something : the something for which it is borrowed is some productive process—a series of costs and revenues—and the rate of return in this process determines the rate of interest which the " pure " investment can pay.

To round off the argument we may consider two special cases which have given a great deal of trouble in this connection. First let us consider the case in which a single positive payment is associated with an infinite series of constant annual negative payments—i.e. where a perpetual income is bought for a capital sum. Such a series would be represented by Table 4.

TABLE 4

Year	0	1	2	3 . . . to infinity.
Payment	M	$-n$	$-n$	$-n$ . . . to infinity.

Applying equation (3) we have the rate of return given by :

$$M - n(1+i)^{-1} - n(1+i)^{-2} \dots \text{ to infinity, } = 0$$

Summing this infinite geometrical series we have :

$$M - \frac{n}{i} = 0, \text{ or } i = \frac{n}{M}$$

That is, the rate of return is equal to the yearly income divided by the capital sum. The total negative payment, however, is infinite, and as the rate of return is finite the time spread must also be infinite ; it would clearly take an infinite time for a finite sum to grow into an infinite sum at a finite rate of growth. In this case the concept of a time spread is of no importance whatever. We must, however, be very careful to distinguish this case from the case of continuous repetition of an element of investment, which, as we have already seen, gives us an infinite series of constant *net* annual payments which may also be purchased for a constant capital sum at any date. To illustrate with the simplest example : suppose our element of investment were a positive payment m and a negative payment, $-n$ after one year ; if this is repeated annually, our payments series looks like Table 5.

TABLE 5.

Date	0	1	2	3 . . . to infinity.
Payment	m	$m-n$	$m-n$	$m-n$ . . . to infinity.

The rate of return in this series is given by

$$i = \frac{n-m}{m},$$

while the time spread is one year, no matter how far the series is carried. Now, if we look only to net payments, Table 5 looks very much like Table 4 ; but if we consider *all* payments made in the course of an investment, a definite and significant time spread emerges. Thus a basic payments series with a definite time spread may be financed by a pure investment with an infinite time spread : but this infinite time spread is only apparent and is not characteristic of the underlying productive process. It must be admitted that cases are conceivable in which the basic payments series has an infinite time spread : the production of an immortal capital good which required no maintenance would be a case in point. But such cases are unlikely to occur in practice : even land, generally taken as the type of an immortal capital good, required constant maintenance of its qualities.

This brings us to the second special case : that in which a capital good is produced which requires maintenance. Suppose, for instance, we buy a house for £M ; and suppose in each year we receive a gross rent of £n, and we have to spend £m each year in maintaining the house—i.e. in restoring it to its initial value. Then the payments series is as in Table 6.

TABLE 6.

Year	0	1	2	.	.	.	R
Payment	M	$-n + m$	$-n + m$				$-M - n + m$

R is the year in which we sell the house. The rate of return in this payment series is $i = \dfrac{n - m}{M}$. The time spread, T_r, is given by the equation :

$$(1 + i)^{T_r} = \frac{M + rn}{M + rm} \tag{17}$$

Now, as r approaches infinity, $\dfrac{M + rn}{M + rm}$ approaches $\dfrac{n}{m}$.

Hence, if the date of liquidation is in the indefinitely remote future, the time spread, T_∞, is given by :

$$(1 + i)^{T_\infty} = \frac{n}{m} \tag{18}$$

Equation (18) may be written in the form :

$$T_\infty = \frac{Log\left(1 + \dfrac{n-m}{m}\right)}{Log\left(1 + \dfrac{n-m}{M}\right)} \qquad (19)$$

Now, if i is small, so that square and higher powers of i may be neglected, $n - m$ will be small, and in expanding

$$Log\left(1 + \frac{n-m}{m}\right) \text{ and } Log\left(1 + \frac{n-m}{M}\right)$$

we can neglect all terms after the first and write equation (19)

$$T = \frac{M}{m}$$

That is, in the case of a capital good which requires maintenance, the time spread approaches the ratio of the cost of the good to its annual maintenance charge, as the date of liquidation recedes into the indefinitely distant future and the rate of return approaches zero. The time spread in this limiting case is the number of years for which the maintenance change will have to be made in order to make the total paid out equal the initial cost. It will be seen, therefore, that though the time spread increases as we push the date of liquidation further and further into the future, it approaches a finite limit when the date of liquidation is indefinitely remote. In any case, the time spread is a perfectly definite quantity.

To summarise our conclusions : (1) A definite, valid, and significant concept of a " period of investment " in any single investment can be found in the concept of a " time spread." (2) Where the investment is made up of a number of repetitions of an elementary investment, the time spread of the investment is equal to the time spread of the element. (3) A continuously repeated element therefore has a finite time spread, although the investment itself may proceed indefinitely into the future. (4) In a continuously repeated investment, the amount of capital invested is constant, and is directly proportional to the time spread, where change in the time spread is effected only by changing the dates and not by changing the magnitudes of the quantities of the payments series. (5) In an investment which does not consist of the continuous repetition of a finite element the capital is not constant and the maximum capital invested bears no simple and direct relation to the time spread. (6) An investment which consists of a continuously *maintained* capital good has a finite time spread, however far into the future the investment proceeds.

So far we have been dealing exclusively with the properties of a *single* investment. The question naturally arises whether we can apply these results and concepts to investment as a whole—which means to-day practically the whole of economic activity : can we, for instance, apply the concept of the time spread to the whole process of production ? The problem is one of great difficulty. If we try to establish a concept of a " payments series " for the productive process as a whole we are faced with the difficulty that in the system as a whole " costs " and " revenues " are not independent, but are to a very large extent the same quantities : thus a " cost " to one process is a " revenue " to another : the " expenditure " of one person is the " income " of another, and we cannot assume for the whole economy a system of independent incomings and outgoings as we can for the individual person or the single process. This does not mean, of course, that the concept of an " average period of production " in the physical productive process is invalid, though it probably does imply that any physical " average period of production " is not capable of measurement. In the application of our results to the general theory of capital we must also be very careful, for we cannot assume in fact, as the " Austrian " school has often tended to do, that the process of production as a whole repeats itself continuously : there are elements of irregularity and discontinuity in the productive process which militate against any simple relationships between capital quantity and the time structure of the productive process. In spite of these unsolved problems, however, we cannot doubt that the connection between capital quantities and the time structure of production is very intimate. The very concept of investment involves the concept of a time interval of some kind between outlays and receipts, as we have seen, and the difficulties outlined above do not affect the fundamental conceptual relations.

THE PRACTICAL DETERMINATION OF THE RATE OF RETURN IN THE GENERAL CASE.

AN APPENDIX TO "TIME AND INVESTMENT."

The problem of the determination of the rate of interest in any given investment has never presented itself very acutely to economists. This is mainly because they have usually thought of the rate of interest in terms of two special types of investment. The first is that in which a constant yearly income is bought for a capital sum : the yearly income proceeding either to infinity or to liquidation for a capital sum equal to the original purchase price, in which case the general equation (3) reduces to the simple form

$$i = \frac{n}{M} \tag{A1}$$

i being the rate of return, n the yearly income, and M the capital sum. The second is that which consists of a single positive payment m and a single negative payment n, at one year's interval. Then equation (3) becomes :

$$1 + i = \frac{n}{m}, \text{ or } i = \frac{n}{m} - 1 \tag{A2}$$

Even where we have a single positive and a single negative payment with a number of years interval between them, T, the calculation of the rate of return is fairly easy. Thus we have

$$(1 + i)^T = \frac{n}{m}$$

$$\text{or } Log(1 + i) = \frac{1}{T} Log \frac{n}{m} \tag{A3}$$

from which $Log(1 + i)$, and therefore i, can easily be calculated with the aid of tables.

When, however, we come to the general case, where we have a number of positive payments, $m_1, m_2 \ldots m_h$, at dates $t_1, t_2, \ldots t_h$, and a number of negative payments $n_1, n_2, \ldots n_k$ at dates $s_1, s_2, \ldots s_k$, the rate of return is given by the equation :

$$m_1(1 + i)^{-t_1} + m_2(1 + i)^{-t_2} + \ldots + m_h(1 + i)^{-t_h}$$

$$= n_1(1+i)^{-s_1} + n_2(1+i)^{-s_2} + \ldots + n_k(1+i)^{-s_k} \tag{A4}$$

It is clear that with ordinary values for the various quantities there is a value of i which satisfies this equation: it is, however, a very awkward equation to solve. Indeed, a perfectly accurate general solution is not possible unless the payments series exhibits a regular form, and this is by no means always the case. The analysis of the preceding paper, however, will enable us to obtain very simply an approximate solution which is of a degree of accuracy sufficient for all practical purposes, a solution furthermore which is capable of giving as high a degree of accuracy as we wish.

It is clear that if we can find the time centres of the positive and negative payments, and thereby the time spread of the investment, we could easily find the rate of return. For if T is the time spread, and M and N the sum of the positive and negative payments respectively, we have:

$$(1 + i)^T = \frac{N}{M}, \text{ or } Log(1 + i) = \frac{1}{T}(LogN - LogM) \quad \text{(A5)}$$

which we can solve like equation (A3). Now, we cannot find the true values of the time centres without knowing the rate of return—the very thing we are trying to find: for equations (4) and (5) (page 199) which give the true value of the time centres contain i. But fortunately we have approximate formulæ for the time centres, $\bar{t}$ and $\bar{s}$, in equations (9) and 10 (page 200) which do not involve i, and which, moreover, are very easily evaluated. We can, then, find an approximate value for the time centres, and hence an approximate value for T, from equations (9) and (10). If T' is this approximate value, then

$$T' = \bar{s} - \bar{t} \quad \text{(A6)}$$

Then putting this value of T' in equation (A5) we get an approximate value for i, say i'. The value i' is sufficiently accurate in most practical cases. In any case, the value should always be checked by evaluating

$$m_1(1+i')^{-t_1} + m_2(1+i')^{-t_2} + \ldots + m_h(1+i')^{-t_h} = V'_m \text{ and}$$

$$n_1(1+i')^{-s_1} + n_2(1+i')^{-s_2} + \ldots + n_k(1+i')^{-s_k} = V'_n \quad \text{(A7)}$$

If $V'_m = V'_n$, then $i' = i$, the true value, and we need proceed no further. If, however, we desire to proceed to a further degree of approximation, we can do so as follows : From equations (4) and (5) (page 199) we have, if t'', s'' are the second approximations to the time centres,

$$(1 + i')^{t''} = \frac{M}{V'_m}, \quad (1 + i')^{s''} = \frac{N}{V'_n} \qquad \text{(A8)}$$

From equations (A8) we can evaluate t'' and s'', and therefore the second approximation for the time spread, $T'' = s'' - t''$. We then have, if i'' is the second approximation for the rate of return,

$$(1 + i'')^{T''} = \frac{N}{M}$$

from which we can evaluate i''. Then substituting i'' for i' in equations (A7) we obtain new values V''_m, V''_n; these should be more nearly equal to each other than V'_m and V'_n. If we desire further approximations we can go on to get i''' from V''_m and V''_n and so on *ad infinitum*, or rather until the strain on our tables of logarithms is too great. In practice, the first approximation is about as high as can be obtained with four- or even five-figure tables, and is about as much as most people would ever want, as may be seen in the following example[1].

Suppose a man buys some stock, one year from a base date, paying £100, and that a further £50 of the purchase money is called up three years after the base date. The nominal value and the nominal rate of interest are of course irrelevant ; we are here concerned with actual money payments and with real rates of return. Suppose further that he gets dividends of £2, £5, £10, £6 and £3, at dates 2, 3, 4, 5, and 6 years after the base date respectively. Suppose further that he sells the stock six years after the base date for £160. What rate of return has the investment paid ?

[1] The accuracy of this first approximation is at first sight quite surprising, for it depends upon the assumption that the squares and higher powers of i can be neglected in expansion. This is, of course, by no means the case, even where i is of the magnitude of .05. The secret of this method lies in the fact that the error introduced into the values of both the time centres by this assumption is in the same direction in each case, and is of the same order of magnitude in each case. The error in the *difference* between the time centres—i.e. the time spread—is therefore less than the error in the time centres themselves. This is not the case when there is only a single positive or a single negative payment, in which case the position of one of the time centres is exactly fixed by the position of the single payment, but the error becomes less when the number of positive payments approximates to the number of negative payments.

We first tabulate the history of the investment thus :—

TABLE A1.

Date (t_r)	Positive payments (m_r) £	$t_r m_r$	Negative payments (n_r) £	$t_r n_r$
1	100	100	–	–
2	–	–	2	4
3	50	150	5	15
4	–	–	10	40
5	–	–	6	30
6	–	–	3	18
6	–	–	160	960
Totals	150	250	186	1,067

As a first approximation, by equations (9) and (10) we have :

$$\bar{t} = \frac{\Sigma m_r}{M} = \frac{250}{150} = 1.66666(7)$$

$$\bar{s} = \frac{s_r n_r}{N} = \frac{1067}{186} = 5.73655(9)$$

Whence,

$$T' = \qquad \bar{s} - \bar{t} \qquad = 4.06989(2)$$

Then :

$$Log(1 + i') = \frac{Log186 - Log150}{4.06989(2)} = .022954$$

Whence,

$$i' = .0543 = \underline{5.43\%} \text{ p.a.}$$

We now proceed to evaluate V'_m and V'_n , the following tabular form being convenient :—

TABLE A2.

Calculation of V'_m.

t_r	m_r	$-t_r \, Log(1 + i')$	$(1 + i')^{-t_r}$	$m_r(1+i')^{-t_r}$
1	100	$-.022954 = \bar{1}.977046$	.94851(5)	94.851(5)
3	50	$-.068862 = \bar{1}.931138$	.85337(6)	42.668(8)

$$\text{Total} = V'_m = 137.52(03)$$

TABLE A3.
Calculation of V'_n.

s_r	n_r	$-s_r \, Log(1+i')$	$(1+i')^{-s_r}$	$n_r(1+i')^{-s_r}$
2	2	$-.045908 = \bar{1}.954092$	.89968(4)	1.799(4)
3	5	$-.068862 = \bar{1}.931138$	.85337(6)	4.266(9)
4	10	$-.091816 = \bar{1}.908194$	.80946(8)	8.094(7)
5	6	$-.114770 = \bar{1}.885230$	.76776(7)	4.606(6)
6	163	$-.137724 = \bar{1}.862276$	.72824(3)	118.703(6)

Total $= V'_n = 137.47\,(12)$

In the above example five-figure tables have been used, and it will be seen that the result is remarkably accurate : V'_m and V'_n are equal to four significant figures and differ only in the fifth figure, which is open to a measure of doubt in any case : the result is certainly as accurate as could possibly be obtained with four-figure tables. For most practical purposes there is no need to carry the approximation any further. If, however, we wish to proceed to the second approximation, we should proceed thus :—
We have from equations (A8) :

$$s'' = \frac{Log186 - Log137.47}{.022954} = 5.7200$$

$$t'' = \frac{Log150 - Log137.52}{.022954} = 1.6437$$

Whence,

$$T'' = s'' - t'' = 4.0763$$

Then,

$$Log(1+i'') = \frac{Log186 - Log150}{4.0763} = .022918(3)$$

This gives us

$$i'' = .0542 = 5.42\% \text{ p.a.}$$

We can see that this is a more correct result by calculating V''_m and V''_n, thus :

TABLE A4.
Calculation of V''_m.

t_r	m_r	$-t_r \, Log(1+i'')$	$(1+i'')^{-t_r}$	$m_r(1+i'')^{-t_r}$
1	100	$-.0229183 = \bar{1}.977082$	.948603	94.860(3)
3	50	$-.0687549 = \bar{1}.931245$	.853590	42.679(5)

Total $= V''_m = 137.53(98)$

TABLE A5.

Calculation of V''_n.

s_r	n_r	$-s_r \, Log(1+i'')$	$(1+i'')^{-s_r}$	$n_r(1+i'')^{-s_r}$
2	2	$-.0458366 = \bar{1}.954163$	.899813	1.799(63)
3	5	$-.0687549 = \bar{1}.931245$	.853590	4.267(95)
4	10	$-.0916732 = \bar{1}.908327$	.809712	8.097(12)
5	6	$-.1145915 = \bar{1}.885408$	.768080	4.608(48)
6	163	$-.1375098 = \bar{1}.862490$	.728600	118.761(80)

$$\text{Total} = V''_n = 137.53(49)$$

V''_m and V''_n are equal for as many significant figures as
we have in our tables, and therefore with five-figure tables
i'' is as accurate a value as we can obtain. With more
accurate tables of course a greater degree of accuracy could
be obtained by further approximations, but it is difficult
to see what practical purposes further approximations
would serve.

The practical usefulness of the above methods may be
considerable : a single example will serve to illustrate.
Mr. Walsh, in his interesting study of " The capital concept
applied to man " (*Q. J. E.*, February, 1935) made a comparison between the profitability of various lines of investment in human education. He did this by taking in each
case the costs, at various dates, of obtaining the particular
education in question, and the " revenues," at various dates,
or average excess income attributable to the education in
question. He then compared the present value of both
costs and revenues at a given date, using an arbitrary rate
of interest (4 per cent.) in finding the present values. There
is, of course, no objection to this method as a method of
comparison, but it would at least be more elegant to be
able to express the results in the form of the actual rates
of return yielded by the various forms of education—i.e.
the rate of compounding or discounting in each case which
would make the present value of the costs at a given date
exactly equal to the present value at that date of the
revenues. The method outlined above would provide a
simple means of finding these rates of return.

EQUILIBRIUM AND WEALTH: A WORD OF ENCOURAGEMENT TO ECONOMISTS

Canadian Journal of Economics and Political Science, 5 (1939): 1-18.

EQUILIBRIUM AND WEALTH : A WORD OF ENCOURAGE-
MENT TO ECONOMISTS

I. The Nature of Equilibrium

WHEN the founder of the science which has become Economics came
to write the title-page of his immortal work, he wrote boldly *An
Enquiry into the Nature and Causes of the Wealth of Nations.* From this
it might be thought that Economics was the science of wealth; that it
would tell us what are the conditions which make one society wealthy
and one poor, or which make for the growth and decline of wealth, in
general or in particular. In fact, however, the science has not developed
primarily along these lines, in spite of many interesting and important
observations on this subject on the part of the standard writers. Especially in these days we seem to be interested not in Plutology—the science
of wealth—but in Economy—the science of management, of budgeting,
of the distribution of *given* resources. In other words, our interest has
shifted from the study of the Nature and Causes of the Wealth of Nations
to the study of equilibrium and disequilibrium.

In many ways this shift of emphasis is regrettable, in spite of the
undoubted achievements of equilibrium theory. Part of the loss of prestige from which Economics has suffered is undoubtedly due to this very
point. To the general public, equilibrium seems to be a vague and irrelevant ideal. Most governments, and most individuals, would rather be
in chronic disequilibrium, and be rich, than be in glorious equilibrium,
and be poor. The assumption which frequently underlies economic homi-
letics—that equilibrium is synonymous with riches and disequilibrium
with poverty—is not one which can be long maintained.

Our first task, therefore, must be to make clear the nature of the
concept of equilibrium in economic life. When we say that any economic
organism, or any economic society, is in equilibrium we mean that *with
certain conditions given* the organism or society cannot improve its position by any action involving choice between alternatives. Thus a firm
is not in equilibrium so long as it can increase its profits by any course of

action; a consumer is not in equilibrium so long as he can increase his satisfactions by rearranging his mode of disposal of income; a society is not in equilibrium if any individual by any course of action—e.g., by working harder, or by changing his occupation, or by buying different things—can in his own estimation "better himself." A simple analogy will illustrate the point. A mountaineer is a person whose ambition it is, we will say, to get to the top of the mountain on which he stands. As long as it is possible for him to ascend, therefore, he will not be in mountaineering equilibrium, for he can improve his position (in this case, his altitude) by walking up the slope. In other words, so long as his "marginal altitude" (the amount by which his altitude changes as he proceeds a unit distance horizontally) is positive in any direction he will not be in equilibrium : he will continue to proceed in the direction in which marginal altitude is positive until, following the well-known law of eventually diminishing marginal altitude, he finds that he reaches a point where the marginal altitude is equal to zero in all directions—in less technical language, he will climb till he gets to the top of the mountain. There, and there only, will he be in equilibrium. But—and this is the important point—in all this discussion we have made no mention whatever of the altitude of the mountain top itself.

To carry the analogy back into economic life: the conditions of equilibrium tell us when we are as well off as we can be in the given circumstances. They tell us nothing about how well off we are when we have reached the position of equilibrium. Thus in the case of the equilibrium of the individual firm (assuming that the net revenue is the proper measure of profitability) the condition of equilibrium with respect to output is that the marginal cost should equal the marginal revenue. This condition, however, tells us nothing about *how profitable* the firm is at this point. In the case of the equilibrium of the individual consumer, who has a given income at his disposal, the condition of equilibrium is that the "weighted" marginal utility in all his lines of expenditure shall be equal. This condition does not tell us how well off the consumer is, however,—it merely tells us when he is as well off as he can be under the circumstances. Similarly in the case of the "static" equilibrium of society, the condition of equilibrium is that all employments, of labour, or land, or of capital, shall be equally advantageous, in the sense that no one who can shift his resources from one occupation to another wishes to do so. This condition also tells us nothing of how wealthy the society is—it merely tells us that with the resources available, the society is as wealthy as it can be.

II. Utility and Necessity

It is not difficult to explain why economics has concentrated its attention on the theory of equilibrium to the relative neglect of the theory of wealth. The explanation lies unquestionably in the fact that wealth, especially from a social point of view, is extremely difficult to measure in quantitative terms. A theory of wealth, however, implies inevitably that some form of measurement of wealth on an objective scale is possible, while a theory of equilibrium can be constructed without reference to any measurement of wealth beyond the fundamental principle that if any individual prefers one situation to another, the preferred situation is *ipso facto* a "wealthier" situation. The immeasurability of wealth arises because wealth—i.e., "well-being"—is in its essence not a physical concept but a psychological concept. That is, well-being is a state of mind, and not a state of physical nature. States of mind, however, are notoriously hard to reduce to quantitative terms. A courageous attempt to make such a quantification was implied in the concept of Utility. The concept of "Utility," "Satisfaction," "Economic Welfare"—whatever name we care to give it—is a recognition of the fact that the ultimate product of all economic activity is the creation and maintenance of certain desired states of mind. All physical goods (such as cheese) and all physical services (such as shoe-shines) are in reality intermediate products, even when they are purchased by final consumers, and the value of any physical goods or services depends on their ability to satisfy wants—i.e., to create "Utility." From the point of view of the theory of wealth, however, the concept of utility has been useless, although in a modified form the theory of utility has made important contributions to the theory of equilibrium. This is because the concept of utility has made no contribution to the problem of the *measurement* of wealth, and in so far as it is useful in the theory of equilibrium it must be divested of any traces of assumed measurability. It is clear that the conditions of equilibrium (i.e., of *maximum* utility) can be stated without the assumption of a measurable utility, for the conditions of maximization merely state that a small change in any one of the variables affecting utility will not change the total of utility: no conditions of maximization, as we have seen, involve any assumption as to how great is the maximized total. Consequently, through the device of indifference curves, the analysis of the equilibrium of the consumer has been formulated without any reference to a quantitatively measurable utility.

Where attempts have been made to apply the utility concept to a discussion of problems involving wealth, however, the result has been failure. Perhaps the most conspicuous attempt in this direction has been that body of theory which is based on the assumption that the marginal utility of money-income declines as money-income increases (with a given state of prices) in approximately the same degree for all individuals. On this assumption has been based the argument for progressive taxation, and sharp discussion has raged around it. Once it is realized, however, that this problem has nothing whatever to do with equilibrium theory, but is in effect a problem of the theory of wealth, much of the discussion on this topic is seen to be based on misunderstanding of the nature of the problem. The recent discussion between Professor Robbins and Mr. Harrod[1] has made it clear that Professor Robbins only objects to the presence of inter-personal comparisons of utility in equilibrium theory— in which theory they have no part anyhow. That is not to say, of course, that the principle of diminishing marginal—shall we say—"significance" of money-income, provided that it is not interpreted in a strictly quantitative sense, is unimportant. On the contrary, it is of the greatest importance in considering the problem of "ideal" distribution of income. It was not necessary, however, for the justification of progressive taxation to assume any rigidly measurable utility, and it is doubtful whether the introduction of the concept of utility into this problem did any more than create an erudite terminology and bestow a spurious appearance of mathematical accuracy to an argument which was only valid as long as it was vague.

The reason for the inutility of Utility in this connection seems to lie in the fact that the utility analysis neglects altogether the *differences* between commodities or lines of expenditure in respect of their significance for wealth. This neglect perhaps goes back to the Benthamite Utilitarianism from which, in spite of many disclaimers, the Utility analysis originates. For Bentham, all commodities or pursuits were comparable only as they gave pleasure; with rude logic he repudiated the doubts of the moralists and declared equally for pushpin or poetry, provided only that they gave the same amount of pleasure. Similarly from the point of view of utility theory all lines of expenditure rate equally, provided only that the marginal utility per dollar in all lines is the same; bread or diamonds, provided, of course, that they were infinitely divisible, stand on equal terms as far as the equilibrium of the consumer is concerned. In fact, however, as Adam Smith observed, bread and diamonds do not stand on equal terms as far as consumption is concerned— hence the paradox of "value in use" and "value in exchange," a paradox left largely unresolved by Smith himself. The Utility theory has gone a long way toward explaining the paradox as far as "value in exchange" is concerned, for that is primarily a problem of equilibrium; once the dis-

[1]*Economic Journal*, Sept., 1938, p. 383, and Dec., 1938, p. 635.

tinction between subjective and objective value is made clear the problems of exchange present little difficulty.   The concept of "value in use," however, seems to have remained largely unexploited since the days of Adam Smith.   It is clear that we cannot invoke the concept of total utility to account for it, as total utility, involving, as it does, the measurement of utility, is not a valid concept.   We must, therefore, turn aside

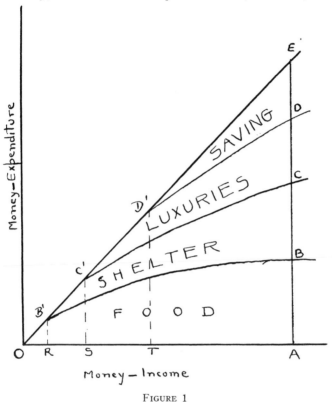

FIGURE 1

from the utility approach altogether, and seek an explanation in the concept of an *order* or *rank* of commodities.

An analysis of the consumption function along these lines may be found in my "Note on the Consumption Function."[2]   It is not necessary here to recapitulate the conclusions of that "Note," except in so far as they enable us to postulate an order of commodities arranged according to the order in which they begin to enter consumption as income rises. Thus figure 1 shows the way in which the distribution of outgoings be-

[2]*Review of Economic Studies*, Feb., 1935, p. 99.

tween various lines of disposal—reduced for the sake of simplicity to four, food, shelter, luxuries, and saving—will probably change in the case of a representative individual as income increases. It will be seen that for an income, OA, there will be an equal outgo, AE, divided up into various lines of disposal—AB for food, BC for shelter, CD for luxuries, and so on. Now, it is clear that for very small incomes food will be the only commodity purchased, this being more necessary even than shelter. As income rises to the level OR shelter begins to enter the budget: at a still higher income, OS, luxuries enter the budget, and at a still higher income, OT, saving enters the budget. In fact, of course, owing to the imperfect divisibility of most commodities, the lines $B'B$, $C'C$, $D'D$, etc., will not be smooth, but will exhibit discontinuous changes.

It is clear, therefore, that for any individual we can range the whole field of commodities which he will purchase at all incomes in this order, which we may call the "scale of necessity," with those commodities which he will begin to buy at low incomes at one end of the scale, such as potatoes, bread, cheese, coarse clothes, or small houses; those commodities in the middle of the scale which he will begin to buy at moderate incomes, such as villas, refrigerators, automobiles, or short trips, and those commodities at the other end of the scale which he will buy only if his income is very large, such as yachts, mansions, butlers, caviar, or world cruises. This "scale of necessity" is clearly what Adam Smith had in mind in his discussion of "Value in Use." Bread has a high "value in use" because it is high on the scale of necessity: diamonds have a low value in use because they are low on the scale of necessity: bread will be bought at very low incomes, but diamonds will be bought only at very high incomes.

We can now extend the concept of a scale of necessity to a whole society. Any extension of a concept involving relationship from an individual to society implies a certain degree of arbitrariness in the method of extension, but it is not difficult to formulate methods of constructing a scale of necessity, on a statistical basis, for society as a whole. It should be noticed that the difficulty which arises when we try to extend the utility concept from the individual to society—the difficulty that the satisfactions of different people are not commensurable—does not arise here, for in compiling a scale of necessity we make no reference to the level of satisfactions of enjoyments received. We are merely considering objective facts—that rich men will buy Rolls-Royces while poor men will not: we are not in any way comparing the satisfactions derived by the rich man from his Rolls Royce with the possibly much greater satisfactions derived by the poor man from his Ford. Consequently the dilemma of the Benthamite and the Brahmin need not worry us, as it seems to worry Professor Robbins,[3] for even though the Brahmin may be ten times more capable of enjoyment than the outcast, yet it remains true that if we reduced the Brahmin to the outcast's income he would consume much the same things as the outcast, while if we raised the outcast to the income of the Brahmin we may not unreasonably suppose that he would buy somewhat the same kind of commodities as the Brahmin does now.

It will be apparent from this example that in order to construct an absolutely rigorous and unequivocal social scale of necessity we should have to assume, not that the satisfactions or utilities received by all individuals were the same under similar conditions, but that their *tastes* were the same under similar conditions. The assumption of identity of tastes among all individuals is certainly less unreasonable than the assumption of identity of satisfactions, but it still cannot claim to be a very close approximation to the truth. Nevertheless as in the case of other economic problems—e.g., the construction of market demand curves—we may assume that the idiosyncrasies of individuals cancel out when we consider the character of a mass of individuals. Provided, therefore, that the diversity of tastes in a society is not so great as to render any statistical average meaningless—a very reasonable assumption—we may construct a statistical concept of the order of necessity of all the final consumption goods which a society produces.

One method of obtaining such a social order of necessity would be as follows. We could take any commodity—e.g., strawberries—, and from family budget studies we could find at what income group strawberries first entered the budget in appreciable quantities. The statistical definition of "appreciable," of course, would have to be a matter of taste—but any honest statistician would admit that most statistical techniques involve as much judgment as arithmetic. We could repeat this for all commodities, and then scale them according to the income groups in which their consumption first becomes appreciable. Thus we might find that the consumption of strawberries becomes appreciable in the income group $1,000-1,100, while the consumption of apples becomes appreciable in the $600-700 group. We should then be justified in ranging apples above strawberries in the scale of necessity.

Another possible way of obtaining a statistical concept of an order of necessity would be again to take a given commodity, say strawberries: find the consumption in each income group, and then find the "average" income at which strawberries are consumed. This average may be taken in any of the standard ways: the weighted arithmetical mean recommends itself as the simplest, and neither more nor less significant than any other

---

[3]Robbins, "Interpersonal Comparisons of Utility" (*Economic Journal*, Dec., 1938, p. 638).

average. This process can be repeated for all commodities, and the commodities can then be arranged as before in the order of the income groups which represent them. This method is less subject to the personal judgment of what is "significant" than the first; it may, however, give misleading results in the case of commodities which are consumed through a large section of society. Thus a commodity such as bread, consumed through all the income groups, might stand too near the middle of the scale on this criterion, along with, say, a commodity like Ford cars whose consumption is restricted to a group of incomes around the middle of the scale.

The actual statistical technique used in determining a social "order of necessity" is not, however, very important. For the purpose of this argument it is not necessary that we should be able to arrange all commodities in an order so that we will know whether any single commodity is higher or lower on the scale of necessity than any other. Lack of definition does not invalidate a distinction; the distinction between spring flowers and summer flowers is an important one even though we may sometimes catch a daffodil blooming with a rose. Likewise the distinction between "poor man's goods" and "rich man's goods" is an important one, even though we may be in some doubt as to the exact position of strawberries in the scale.

One further point in connection with the concept of a scale of necessity must be clarified before we proceed; the construction of any scale of necessity implies that the *prices* of all the commodities are given, and every scale of necessity must have reference to a given system of prices; a change in relative prices will in general shift the relative positions of commodities on the scale of necessity. Thus in the Orient rice is undoubtedly more of a necessity than wheat: a fall in the price of wheat relative to that of rice, however, might easily reverse that situation.

III. Some Propositions on Wealth

The first task of a theory of wealth[4] is, of course, to devise some method of measurement of wealth. Utility, as we have seen, cannot help us here. The concept of a scale of necessity, however, is more valuable, for although it cannot provide us with a simple numerical measure of wealth—a measure, indeed, which cannot even exist, since "wealth" is a concept too com-

[4] By "wealth" I mean, of course, wealth in the sense of income, not in the sense of a stock or aggregation of commodities, though these two concepts are likely to be related. With given techniques a society or country which has the larger stock of valuable things will also have the larger wealth-income. It is possible, however, for an improvement in the technique of income-production to go hand in hand with a reduction in the quantity or value of the things used in production.

plex to be represented in linear terms—it can give us certain insight into the nature of wealth, and what is perhaps even more important, can give us insight into its causes. A society, or an individual, is wealthy according to the degree to which it can afford to consume commodities which lie towards the "luxury" end of the scale of necessity. What these commodities will be will depend, of course, on the tastes of the times—they may be cathedrals in the twelfth century, palaces in the eighteenth, or yachts and skyscrapers in the twentieth. We make no judgment as to the moral virtue of "luxuries," but even so, in any given state of social taste we can always place them. We need no clearer definition of what we mean by wealth in order to reach important conclusions regarding the conditions which make a society wealthy or poor. Let us, to simplify the argument, suppose that we can classify commodities into two groups only on the scale of necessity—"necessities" and "luxuries." Then the proportion of the total expenditure of the society which goes to luxuries will be an excellent criterion of wealth—the wealthier a society, the greater the proportion of its expenditure which will go towards luxuries, and the smaller proportion which will go towards necessities.[5]

We are here investigating the deeper sources of social wealth. Consequently we must look beyond the expenditures and incomes of a society in terms of money, and must consider what are the forces which determine the division of the real resources of a society between necessities and luxuries. This question forces us back still further on to the question, "What are the real resources of society": what is it, in the last analysis, that is *divided* in the economic *mêlée* between various lines of employment: what is it, in other words, that a society has to spend? In a society without capital, or with immortal equipment, the answer would be easy: in the last analysis the thing which a society, like an individual, has to spend is the *time* of its members. Just as the most fundamental act of econo-

[5]It is interesting to note that this concept opens up the possibility of statistical comparisons of the wealth of widely different cultures and civilizations. "Luxuries" differ very greatly from culture to culture; consequently it is virtually impossible to construct any "price level" or "real income" concept which will cover both, shall we say, the Hottentot and the New Yorker. Necessities, on the other hand, differ much less from age to age and from civilization to civilization; the olives and wheat of the classical world are much the same commodities that they are today, while the chariots and nightingales' tongues cannot be compared with the Packards and *paté de fois gras* of today. If, therefore, between any two cultures we can prepare a list of basic necessities which are common to both, and find what *proportion* the expenditure on these necessities bore to the total expenditure of the society, in terms either of money or of man-time, we shall have an index of the relative wealth of the two cultures which is perhaps as good as we can hope to get, for we may assume that a society which spends a *small* proportion of its total resources on basic necessities is rich, no matter what strange forms its luxuries take.

mizing on the part of an individual is the division of the twenty-four
hours a day which he has to spend among the various uses to which those
hours can be put—earning, sleeping, spending, eating—so a society of,
shall we say, a hundred million people has twenty-four hundred million
man-hours to spend every day. This time has to be divided between all
the occupations of which man is capable. In a society with capital embodied in mortal goods—i.e., goods with a finite length of service life—
the situation is complicated by the fact that such a society can spend
currently beyond, or not up to, its "means" by the process of decumulating or accumulating valuable goods. It still remains true, however, even
in a society which has capital, that the *current* resources which are to be
used consist in the "time-income" at the disposal of its members, even
though these current resources may not bear fruit until some future dates,
and even though current wealth-income comes from resources which have
been employed in the past.

It may be objected that this view of "resources" as consisting of man-
hours sails dangerously near to the rocks of the labour theory of value:
surely, it will be said, we should count in our resources the services of land
and of existing equipment as contributing towards the total product. It
must be remembered, however, that we are considering here *not* the
determination of prices, nor the distribution of incomes, but the *sources*
of wealth. In this connection it seems to be perfectly legitimate to regard
man-time as an original, homogeneous resource, and to introduce the
factors which co-operate with man in the guise of "coefficients of transformation" of man-time into products (consumption goods). Thus the
assumption that man-time is the only original resource does not debar us
from considering the effects of an abundance or a scarcity of co-operating
land or of co-operating equipment. The presence or absence of these co-
operating factors can be reflected for our present purposes perfectly
adequately in the coefficients of transformation; when man is co-operating with large amounts of good land and equipment, or when his skill,
energy, and ability are high the coefficient of transformation of man-time
into product is high—i.e., one man-hour will produce a large quantity of
goods and services. When, on the other hand, man is co-operating with
relatively small or inferior quantities of land and equipment, or when his
skill, energy, and ability are low—then the coefficient of transformation
of man-time into product is low, and one man-hour will produce only a
small quantity of consumers' goods. The problem of transforming our
social time-income into consumers' goods (which, note, include in this
sense sleep, eating, and leisure) is thus seen to be analogous to the individual problem of transforming money into consumers' goods. Just as
we can assume in the problem of the expenditure of money-income that

we have a homogeneous "resource"—money—which is transformed into heterogeneous commodities by purchasing them at a money price, so we can assume in the problem of the expenditure of social resources that we have a homogeneous resource—man-time—with which society purchases commodities at a "man-time price." The "man-time price"—the number of man-hours necessary to produce a unit of commodity—is, of course, the reciprocal of the "coefficient of transformation"—the number of units of a commodity produced by a man-hour. In both these cases we throw all the heterogeneous factors in economic life into the concept of "price" in order to be able to establish a homogeneous concept of "resources."

We can now proceed to the formulation of three fundamental propositions of the theory of wealth. The first is that in general the wealth of any society depends upon the coefficients of transformation of man-time into commodities. We cannot, of course, *measure* wealth by any coefficient of transformation of man-time into commodities in general, for we cannot measure "commodities in general." What we can say, however, is that any change which results in an increase in the coefficient of transformation of man-time into any specific commodity, no matter where it stands on the scale of necessity, will result in an increased production of "luxuries" once equilibrium has been achieved again, and may therefore be regarded as increasing the wealth of the society concerned. The second theorem is that the effect of a change in the coefficient of transformation will be greater in the case of those commodities which are produced in large quantities than in the case of those produced in small quantities. Thus an improvement in the technique of wheat production will increase the wealth of society more than a corresponding improvement in, shall we say, salt production, even though these commodities stand on roughly the same level of the scale of necessity. The third theorem is in part an extension of the second. It is that in poor societies a given proportional increase in the coefficient of transformation of man-time into necessities will result in a greater increase in wealth than an equal proportional increase in the coefficient of transformation of man-time into luxuries. That is, the effect on wealth of a given proportional increase in the coefficient of transformation of man-time into any commodity will be greater the nearer the commodity is to the "necessity" end of the scale. In rich societies, on the other hand, the reverse is likely to be the case; i.e., a given proportional increase in the coefficient of transformation of a commodity will have a greater effect upon wealth if that commodity is at the "luxury" end of the scale.

We can illustrate these theorems with reference to a specially simplified case. Let us suppose that we have a society in which there are only two commodities, "Necessities" and "Luxuries." Let us suppose that the demand for necessities is completely inelastic—i.e., that the society must consume a given quantity of necessities, N, and no more and no less. Then let the total consumption of luxuries be X; let the total number of man-hours which the society has to "spend" in a given time be s; let the number of man-hours devoted to the production of necessities be s_n, and the number devoted to luxuries be s_x. Let the coefficients of transformation of man-time into necessities and luxuries be c_n and c_x respectively. Then we have :

$$s_n + s_x = s, \dots\dots\dots\dots\dots\dots\dots\dots\dots\dots\dots\dots (1)$$
$$N = s_n c_n, \dots\dots\dots\dots\dots\dots\dots\dots\dots\dots\dots (2a)$$
$$X = s_x c_x. \dots\dots\dots\dots\dots\dots\dots\dots\dots\dots\dots (2b)$$

Whence ;

$$X = c_x s - \frac{N c_x}{c_n}. \dots\dots\dots\dots\dots\dots\dots\dots\dots\dots (3)$$

Differentiating equation (2b) with respect to c_x and multiplying by c_x we have :

$$\lambda_x = \frac{dX}{dc_x} \cdot c_x = s_x c_x. \dots\dots\dots\dots\dots\dots\dots\dots (4a)$$

Similarly :

$$\lambda_n = \frac{dX}{dc_n} \cdot c_n = \frac{N c_x}{c_n^2} \cdot c_n = s_n c_x. \dots\dots\dots\dots\dots\dots (4b)$$

(We assume that c_x and c_n are independent of each other, and that N is constant.)

Now, λ_x may be defined as the change in the consumption of luxuries which results from a given relative change (say a one per cent change) in the coefficient of transformation of man-time into luxuries. Similarly, λ_n may be defined as the change in the consumption of luxuries which results from a given relative change (say one per cent) in the coefficient of transformation of necessities. We may note that, since we have assumed that the consumption of necessities is absolutely inelastic, any increase in the coefficient of transformation of man-time into necessities will result in a *transfer* of man-time from necessities to luxuries up to an amount which will enable the society to produce the same quantity of necessities as before. Now it is clear from equations (4) that λ_n will be greater than λ_x when s_n is greater than s_x. That is, when a society is devoting a large proportion of its man-time to the production of necessities (i.e., when it is poor), the effect of a given relative increase in the coefficient of transformation on the production of luxuries will be greater in the case of necessities than in the case of luxuries. But, as we have seen, the quantity of luxuries which a society can produce is the index of its wealth. Consequently in a poor society a given improvement in the technique of production of necessities will result in a greater increase in wealth—reflected in a greater increase in luxuries—than a corresponding improvement in the technique of production of luxuries.

Similarly, in a rich society, where a larger proportion of man-time is devoted to luxuries than to necessities $(s_x > s_n)$ we have $\lambda_x > \lambda_n$—i.e., the effect on wealth of a given relative improvement in the technique of production of luxuries is greater than the effect of a similar improvement in the technique of production of necessities. In this simple case, when the man-time of the society is equally divided between the production of necessities and luxuries $(s_x = s_n)$ we also have $\lambda_x = \lambda_n$—i.e., the effect on wealth of a given relative improvement of the technique of production of either necessities or luxuries will be the same.[6]

IV. Some Applications

The theorems outlined briefly above have several important—and somewhat neglected—applications. Perhaps the most important of these is their application to the interpretation of economic history and to the

[6]If we relax the assumption that the consumption of necessities is absolutely inelastic our results are slightly modified, but not substantially affected. Thus we now have:

$$\lambda_x = s_x c_x - \frac{c_x^2}{c_n} \cdot \frac{dN}{dc_x},$$

$$\lambda_n = s_n c_x - c_x \frac{dN}{dc_n}.$$

If now $\lambda_x = \lambda_n$, we have

$$s_x = s_n \left(1 + \frac{dN}{dc_x} \cdot \frac{c_x}{N} - \frac{dN}{dc_n} \cdot \frac{c_n}{N} \right)$$

$$= s_n(1 + \mu_x - \mu_n),$$

where μ_n is the elasticity of consumption of necessities with respect to the coefficient of transformation of man-time into necessities, and μ_x is the elasticity of consumption of necessities with respect to the coefficient of transformation of man-time into luxuries. We may reasonably expect that in general μ_n will be greater than μ_x; consequently when $\lambda_x = \lambda_n$, instead of having $s_x = s_n$ as we had before, we will have $s_x < s_n$. That is, the point where an improvement in the technique of production of necessities ceases to have a greater effect on wealth than a similar improvement in the technique of production of luxuries will take place at a rather "poorer" level of wealth than before. It should be noticed that it is only the very richest societies which, in fact, fall into the second category of theorem III. If we take agriculture as representative of the necessities industry, and manufactures as representative of the luxuries industry, very few societies indeed have achieved a state of wealth where the proportion of resources devoted to necessities has fallen to one-half of the total. In fact, it is probable that western capitalism is about the only society in history which has achieved even this moderate degree of wealth.

principles of economic development. This application depends on the assumption that roughly speaking, agriculture produces "necessities" while manufacturing industry produces "luxuries." There are, of course, notable exceptions on both sides—there are luxurious foods just as there are necessary clothes and utensils. Nevertheless it remains true that by and large food production is more of a "necessity" than the majority of industrial occupations. It follows immediately from the theorem (3) above that in poor societies economic development must come primarily from the improvements of technique in agriculture. This has been recognized by many economists, reaching at least as far back as the Physiocrats: Adam Smith himself and Davenport may be quoted in this connection.[7] This principle has not, perhaps, received the attention which it deserves from historians. Once it is grasped, the significant relationship between, for instance, the European "building boom" of the eleventh and twelfth centuries and the introduction of the three-field system, or again the relationship between the agricultural revolution of the eighteenth century and the industrial revolution which followed and went along with it, become apparent at once. If improvements in agriculture had not permitted a surplus of food for the cathedral builders to be drawn from the country, the cathedrals would never have been built. It was the introduction of the humble turnip and the consequent development of four-course rotation, winter feeding of cattle, and adequate manuring—with the immense breeding improvements which these changes made possible—which made the industrial revolution possible. Otherwise there would have been nothing with which to feed the workers in the factories. What is more, there might have been no workers to put into the factories. It is well known that the remarkable increase in population of the western world in the past two hundred years was due prim-

[7]Adam Smith, *Wealth of Nations*, book III, chap. I (vol. I, p. 356 of Cannan's edition): "As subsistence is, in the nature of things, prior to conveniency and luxury, so the industry which procures the former, must necessarily be prior to that which ministers to the latter. The cultivation and improvement of the country, therefore, which affords subsistence, must, necessarily, be prior to the increase of the town, which furnishes only the means of conveniency and luxury. It is the surplus produce of the country only, or what is over and above the maintenance of the cultivators, that constitutes the subsistence of the town, which can increase only with the increase of this surplus produce."

Davenport, *Economics of Enterprise*, p. 201 : "The growth of the city is not ultimately to be explained by the improvement of industrial processes. Only such men can work in manufacturing as the falling prices of food products relatively to manufacturing products dismiss from the processes of food production. So long as the food product from one man's labor sufficed for the food requirement of only one man, the entire population was compelled to occupy itself with agriculture: now, when one man's labor will feed three men, two thirds of the population may be urban."

arily to the fall in mortality, and particularly in infant mortality, which took place in the middle years of the eighteenth century. The connection between this fall in mortality and the improved nutrition which followed the agricultural improvements is clear, although, of course, it would be rash to assign any single cause to so momentous a movement. It is scarcely an exaggeration, therefore, to say that the turnip—the basis of the agricultural revolution, and therefore of the industrial revolution and of the expansion of the western world—is one of the prime sources of our civilization!

This brings us to another important part of the theory of wealth—one, moreover, which has received rather more attention at the hands of economists—the effect of population density on wealth. The classical economists perceived—although their statement was frequently obscure and misunderstood—that one of the results of the so-called "law of diminishing returns" was that the coefficient of transformation of man-time in agricultural production must eventually fall as the population of a given area of land increased, and that consequently, at least in a region of moderate density of population, an increase of population in the absence of technical improvement in agriculture itself must result in an increased proportion of resources in agriculture and a decline in the standard of life of the people. The fact that the output of food per acre is not indefinitely extensible means that as the population grows in a fixed area, in the absence of technical improvements it must get poorer. It was further argued that this process (increase of population and decline in wealth) would go on until a level of wealth was reached at which no further increase of population would occur. This was the "Subsistence level." In spite of many attacks—based mainly on the mistaken identification of the subsistence level with the minimum *physical* standard of subsistence and on the observation of the purely dynamic phenomenon of a rapid rise in the standard of life of the western world in the nineteenth century—this theory remains substantially true. The "subsistence level" may, of course, be at a very high standard of life; the indication seems to be that the subsistence level (i.e., the standard of life at which populations will just reproduce themselves) has been rising steadily, especially in the past fifty years, until now it is likely that it has reached a point that the actual standard of life can never reach. That is to say, whatever the standard of life possible under present techniques it will always be below the sub-sistence level—i.e., the population will never succeed in reproducing itself, and that consequently unless there is a change in the desire for children the population of the western world is doomed to extinction.

This modified Malthusian theory unquestionably explains in part the difference in the standard of life between the western world and the

Orient. The western world is rich not merely because it is virtuous and hard-working and enterprising, but because it has a great deal of land in proportion to its population. The Orient is poor because its population is crowded, and the niggardliness of the soil is an ever-present and pressing factor in its economic life. Moreover, the growth of the standard of life of the western world in the past century or so has been due in considerable measure to the fact that the improvements in transport have in effect increased the amount of land available for its population more quickly than the population itself has increased. This fact, coupled with the invention and use of labour-saving techniques in the newly opened lands have so increased the coefficient of transformation of man-time in agriculture that as Davenport suggests, one man can now produce enough food for three, so that two men out of every three are set free to produce buildings, clothes, automobiles, and the other "conveniences and luxuries of life." Perhaps, again, the coefficient of transformation of man-time into necessities is of significance not only in studying economic progress but also in studying economic decline. "Land" is not only area, but fertility, and fertility may be squandered, except in particularly favoured spots like the valleys of the Nile, the Ganges, and the Yellow River. May we not see in this fact an explanation of the persistence of the river civilizations, and of the impermanence of those founded on perishable soils? And may we not also look over our eroded plains with a little reminiscent shudder for Nineveh and Tyre?

The ramifications of the Theory of Wealth are great, and we cannot possibly follow them within the scope of a single article. We may, however, note briefly one further area of discussion which should be included in an adequate theory of wealth. This is the theory of the geographical distribution of wealth; the theory, if we like to think in national terms, of the "wealth of nations," or more scientifically, of the wealth of regions. To follow out the ramifications of these problems—the location of industries, the economics of cities, the judgment of governmental policies, the theory of taxation, of protection, of intervention: this would take not another article, but a treatise; we merely mention that these are essentially problems of the theory of wealth, and not, as they are so often regarded, of the theory of equilibrium. We may, however, notice in passing two points of interest on which the theory outlined above throws immediate light. The first is the position of *transport* in the theory of wealth. An improvement in the technique of transport has the effect of widening the *extent* of an economic society, and consequently of increasing the possibility of specialization. An improvement in the technique of transport, therefore, by making possible a more intricate "division of labour" than before, may increase the coefficients of transformation in all kinds of production. From the social point of view the Marshallian "external economies of large scale production" are precisely this phenomenon. Unless the improvement in transport affects the coefficients of transformation in agriculture more than in manufactures, however, it may not affect the fundamental distribution of population between town and country. It will, however, affect the *size* of the town. The giant city is entirely the product of swift, cheap transportation; without it, New York and London would be impossible.[8]

The second point concerns the position of agriculture in a progressive society. We have seen that as a society progresses in wealth a greater and greater proportion of resources will be devoted to the production of luxuries and a smaller and smaller proportion to the production of necessities. Agriculture, however, as we have seen, is largely concerned with the production of necessities. Consequently as a society progresses in wealth, the *relative* position of agriculture continually falls in relation to other industries. In a capitalist society this must be reflected in the relative unprofitability of agriculture, both for the capitalist, the worker, and the landowner, for relative unprofitability is the only means whereby a capitalist economy can cause a relative decline in an industry. This is borne out strongly in fact; for the past two hundred years men, enterprise, and land have been squeezed out of agriculture (relatively) because industry has been more attractive, wherever it has been a practicable alternative. This process has been disguised, especially in the New World, by the fact that it has been only relative—agriculture in the nineteenth century at least was expanding, but less rapidly than industry. Now, however, with the approach of stationary and declining populations, it has become evident that agriculture must actually contract as far as employment is concerned if progress is to continue. This relative unprofitability of agriculture in a progressive society is perhaps the real justification—if any can be found at all—for protectionism. Certainly in a state of equilibrium there is no reason to suppose that those engaged in agriculture—and therefore agricultural countries—will be less wealthy than those in manufactures; the classical free-trade doctrine in such a condition has no flaw. In a progressive society, however, those engaged in agriculture—and consequently those countries specializing in agriculture—will tend on the whole to be poorer than those people and coun-

[8]Davenport, *Economics of Enterprise*, p. 202: "Improving transportation, then, so far as it is not at the same time to be regarded as improving agriculture, has had its effect, not in emphasising the growth of urban as against rural population, but in fostering the growth of the small city as against the village, and of the great city as against the small city. Looked at from a more distinctly technological point of view, this truth would read that transportation has fostered the giant industry as over against many small competing industrial units."

tries specializing in manufactures. When one considers that for the past
two hundred years at least we have lived in a rapidly progressing economy
in the western world, the growth of protectionism on the part of those
countries not naturally fitted for specialization in manufactures is hardly
surprising.

The purpose of this paper has not been, of course, to present a complete, mathematically accurate, or even a particularly novel theory of
wealth. Nor is its purpose to decry the theories of equilibrium and disequilibrium which form the background of the study of the actual mechanisms of economic life. Theories of price determination, of distribution,
of the conduct of business or of consumption, of the trade cycle, of the
mechanism of exchange—these will no doubt always hold the centre of
the economic stage, and these too have considerable relevance to the
theory of wealth, for where disequilibrium results in lack of use, or misuse
of available resources these resources are just as if they had not been there
at all to contribute to the wealth of society. It will have served its
purpose if it calls to the attention of students who may be discouraged by
the difficulties and disagreements of equilibrium theory, by the apparent
emptiness of its acknowledged conclusions and the apparent dubiety of its
important conclusions, that there exists in the body of economic theory a
system of propositions and conclusions on the subject of wealth which can
claim without question to give us an insight into the processes of social
life possessed perhaps by no other of the social sciences. In this theory
we have a key which must be held by historians, by sociologists, by
anthropologists, by political scientists alike if they are to unlock their
own peculiar mysteries. It is an achievement of which economists may
be proud; and it is a line of enquiry, too much neglected by the present
generation, which may well be pressed anew.

THE THEORY OF THE FIRM
IN THE LAST TEN YEARS

American Economic Review 32, 4 (Dec. 1942):
791-802

THE THEORY OF THE FIRM IN THE LAST TEN YEARS

It is probable that when future historians of economic thought look back over this century, the thirties will appear as an era of rapid development in economic theory. Not only has there been unusual activity in monetary theory, but extensive transformations have also been made in the basic theory of value. The outstanding publications in this field are, of course, Joan Robinson's *Theory of Imperfect Competition* and Chamberlin's *Theory of Monopolistic Competition*, the first produced in Cambridge, England, and the second in Cambridge, Massachusetts. These volumes mark the explicit recognition of the theory of the firm as an integral division of economic analysis upon which rests the whole fabric of equilibrium theory. General equilibrium is nothing more than the problem of the interaction of individual economic organisms, under various conditions and assumptions; as a necessary preliminary to its solution, an adequate theory of the individual organism itself is necessary. This consists of two main parts: first, an account of the circumstance, or environment, facing an economic organism, described in individual demand curves, purchase curves, expectations, and so on, together with a "principle of maximization," a criterion by which to judge the various possible actions of the organism in order to select the "best." Second, from the principles discovered in the first part of the theory, a technique must be devised to describe the *reactions* of an organism to changes in its environment: how, for instance, a change in the demand for its product will affect its sales.

The "Cambridge Theory"—if so we may describe the essentially similar[1] doctrines of Mrs. Robinson and Professor Chamberlin—made one important step forward in the techniques of analysis, *i.e.*, the use of

---

[1] Probably neither Mrs. Robinson nor Professor Chamberlin would agree that their doctrines are essentially similar: indeed, in regard to the theory of the "industry" and of general equilibrium there are significant divergences between them. In respect to their theory of the firm *per se*, however, there is little difference between them. Compare Kaldor, "Market Imperfection and Excess Capacity," *Economica* (1935), p. 33: Joan Robinson, "What Is Perfect Competition?" *Quart. Jour. of Econ.* (1934-35), p. 104: E. H. Chamberlin, "Monopolistic or Imperfect Competition," *Quart. Jour. of Econ.* (1936-37), p. 557.

the marginal revenue curve, and one very important advance in generality in showing clearly that the theory of the firm under perfect competition was merely a special case of the theory of the firm under monopoly, worked out long before but without very fruitful techniques, by Cournot and Marshall. The Cambridge Theory has been of great importance in simplifying the exposition of economic theory, and it is in the field of elementary exposition that these doctrines have been of most value. Comparing the lucidity of Meyer's *Elements of Modern Economics,* for instance, with any text published in the pre-marginal revenue era will illustrate the point. The student of today, if he is inclined to crab at the geometry with which he is usually presented in his elementary course, should take a look at Marshall's fearsome "nests of rectangular hyperbola" or at Cournot's even more repulsive calculus, and thank his stars that he was not born ten years earlier.

Nevertheless, for all the importance of this contribution, neither Professor Chamberlin nor Mrs. Robinson added very much to the theory of the firm itself, as outlined by Cournot or by Marshall in his chapter on monopoly. Cournot's assumptions are unchanged: that the total cost and total revenue vary continuously with output, and that the "best" position of the firm is that in which the net revenue, the difference between total revenue and total cost, is a maximum. The "marginal cost equals marginal revenue" condition, on the one hand, and the analogous "marginal value productivity equals price of factor" condition, on the other, are both merely convenient expressions of the maximization of net revenue. The firm is conceived either as an organism receiving a constant flow of revenue, and disbursing a constant flow of costs, or as an instantaneous enterprise conceived and liquidated within so short a period of time as to make the cost and revenue items virtually simultaneous.

The weakness of this Cambridge Theory was that it completely neglected the time element in enterprise, and consequently worked with a concept of the firm so far from reality that it cannot be considered more than a rough—though useful—first approximation. It was therefore forced to abstract from an essential feature of enterprise—uncertainty; it made no contribution to capital theory, and it invariably broke down when any attempt was made to account for *profits.* Because of its lack of dynamic character, it also failed to give any satisfactory account of interfirm relationships, for instance, in duopoly, where anticipations form an essential part of the data and where the position of equilibrium is determined by the *path in time* which is taken in reaching it.

Most of the work of the past ten years has been directed toward building up a more accurate picture of the nature and reactions of a firm, particularly expressed in explicit time relationships. We now conceive the firm not as the recipient of a continuous flow of revenues and costs, but as an *account,* consisting of a large number of different input and output items, each with a specific date attached, and strung out in time like washing on a line. Under these circumstances we can no longer assume that the net revenue is to be maximized, for the entrepreneur might prefer a smaller net revenue that accrued earlier to a larger net revenue that accrued later.[2] The problem, "What does the entrepeneur maximize?" therefore, becomes an acute one.

Most of the writers[3] who have tackled this question assume that the entrepreneur wishes to maximize the *discounted* net revenue of his enterprise; *i.e.,* the difference between the present value of all future receipts and the present value of all future outlays. The discounting presumably is to be done for each period of time at that rate of interest which represents the alternative cost of employing capital in the occupation in question; that is, at the rate which the entrepreneur could obtain in other investments. This assumption is implicit, of course, in Taussig's *Wages and Capital,* as in any theory equating the price of a factor of production to its *discounted* marginal product. The conditions of maximization, corresponding to the "marginal cost equals marginal revenue" condition of the Cambridge Theory, are that for each variable the *discounted* marginal cost must be equal to the *discounted* marginal revenue. The "discounted marginal product" theory of wages is of course a special case of the above condition of maximization. It should be noticed that this refinement of the Cambridge Theory is not as revolutionary as might at first sight appear. Indeed, if we define marginal cost to mean the increase in total cost which results from a unit change in output, and define total cost (as we must) to include interest and "normal profit" charges, the marginal cost is seen to be the same as the "compounded marginal outlays"; *i.e.,* the sum of previous outlays, plus interest and profit accruals. If, then, the revenues are assumed to occur at a single date, the Cambridge criterion and the "discounted net receipts" criterion give the same result. This is generally true if the time relationships of the various inputs and outputs are not variable, as in many instances is the case. If the time relationship between input

[2] This fact would seem to vitiate Gerhard Tintner's otherwise interesting article on "Monopoly Over Time" in *Econometrica,* Vol. 5 (1937), pp. 160-70.

[3] H. Hotelling, "The Economics of Exhaustible Resources," *Jour. of Pol. Econ.* (April, 1931); Dr. J. R. Hicks, in "Wages and Interest, the Dynamic Problem," *Econ. Jour.* (Sept., 1935); also in *Value and Capital* (Oxford, 1939); A. G. Hart, "Anticipations, Business Planning, and the Cycle," *Quart. Jour. of Econ.* (Feb., 1937); P. A. Samuelson, "Some Aspects of the Pure Theory of Capital," *Quart. Jour. of Econ.* (Aug., 1937).

and output is a variable of the problem, as, for instance, in the classic example of the maturing of wines or of the growth of trees, the Cambridge Theory breaks down.

Another suggestion in regard to the maximization problem I made myself:[4] that the entrepreneur should maximize the internal rate of return on his investment, or the "rate of profit" which the investment actually earns. This gives the same criterion of maximization as the "discounted net receipts" formula, with the exception that the rate of interest used in discounting in the first case is the "internal" rate and in the second is the "alternative" rate, or rather scheme of rates, which is regarded as normal. If the economic rent of an enterprise is included as one of its outlays, then even this distinction disappears, for if we discount (or compound) any series of net receipts *including* economic rent at a rate equal to the "alternative rate," the result is the same as if we had discounted (or compounded) the same series—not including economic rent—at the internal rate. The criterion of maximizing the internal rate of return is thus seen to be a special case of the "discounted net receipts" criterion.

The "discounted net receipts" criterion in its turn has not proved altogether satisfactory; for, although it takes into account the time relations of inputs and outputs, it abstracts from the most essential feature of enterprise—its uncertainty. Every decision must be made in the expectation of certain future events, and the expectations, by the very fact that they refer to the future, are uncertain. The problem of relating this uncertainty to the conduct of enterprise is therefore a major one. Indeed, in general theory, "profit" is usually regarded as the reward of "risk-bearing"—or rather, to use Professor Knight's more exact term, "uncertainty-bearing," an uncertainty being an uninsurable risk, and a necessary and characteristic feature of all enterprise.

One method of surmounting this difficulty is to express an expected future magnitude—receipt or expense—not as a single figure but as a probability distribution, showing the probability of each of a series of possible magnitudes for the variable in question. Thus a manufacturer may think that there is a 50 per cent chance of his receipts next month being $10,000, a 20 per cent chance of their being either $9,000 or $11,000, a 4 per cent chance of their being $8,000, or $12,000, and so on. This method of expressing the probability of future magnitudes has been used by many authors: Irving Fisher used it as far back as 1906.[5] and it has entered into almost all discussions of the topic in the past ten years. As a first approximation, the "expected value" of the variable

[4] K. E. Boulding, "The Theory of a Single Investment," *Quart. Jour. of Econ.*, Vol. 49, pp. 475-94.

[5] Irving Fisher, *Capital and Interest*, Appendix to chap. XVI.

in question, *i.e.*, the average of all possible values, each weighted by its probability, may be substituted for the probability distribution, and then treated as if it had 100 per cent probability, thus eliminating uncertainty altogether. This procedure, however, is dangerous, for, in effect, it abstracts once more from the fact that differing degrees of uncertainty may involve various choices, and consequently may draw attention away from the most essential questions posed by the existence of uncertainty. Professors Marschak and Makower, in their remarkably interesting article on "Assets, Prices, and Monetary Theory,"[6] offer a suggestion that there are at least three aspects of the probability distribution of a net receipts item to take into account: *lucrativity*, expressed by the expected value of the item; *safety*, measured by the smallness of the dispersion of the probability distribution; and *asymmetry*, measured by the skewness of the distribution, important in the case of "long odds enthusiasts" who are more eager to take a small chance of a large gain rather than a mathematically equivalent large chance of a small gain. These authors suggest also that uncertainty equivalents may be expressed by a process analogous to discounting; that is to say, we should be able to set up a system of preferences of any individual, expressing the equivalence, in terms of "utility" or indifference, of various sums of various dates, degrees of safety, skewness, etc. The process of discounting in the ordinary sense is that of equating in "value" different sums because of their difference of time position. In other words, if the rate of interest is 5 per cent per annum, we say that $100 now is equivalent to $105 in one year's time, because if an individual can earn 5 per cent per annum on his money he does not care whether he has $100 now or $105 next year, provided that his demands do not alter and that the sums in question are absolutely certain. If, however, the sums are not certain, we can still say of a given individual that he does not care whether he has $100 now or, say, the probability of getting various sums next year, the probability distribution having a known expected value, dispersion, and skewness. The $100 this year is then the "discounted equivalent" of the whole probability distribution of next year.

An apparent difficulty of this line of analysis is that it takes away the *objectivity* of the discounting process. As long as we regard the external rate of interest as the controlling factor in the discounting process, it appears to be quite mechanical and objective. If we include the elements of time and uncertainty preference immediately there is a different rate of discounting for each individual, and the objective rate of interest disappears. This, however, is a marked step toward reality; for "the rate of interest" that figures so largely in economic

⁶ H. Makower and J. Marshak, *Economica* (1938), pp. 261-88.

discussion is an illusion created by the fact that some future events—
e.g., the payment of obligations under a government bond—are so probable that we regard them as absolutely certain. Consequently, the price
of these obligations in the market "determines" a rate of interest which
is as objective as the fulfilment of the obligations is certain. But in
strict theory we must recognize that all future events are uncertain—
i.e., have less than 100 per cent probability—and that consequently
what is determined in the capital market is not a rate of interest, but the
price, or present value, of more or less uncertain future payments. The
rate of interest to which each price corresponds is a purely subjective
matter, depending on the expectations and on the preferences of the
individual concerned. Indeed, these expectations involve preferences
so complex that we will probably have to abandon the simple concept
of interest as a "rate of time transference," and recognize it for the
multidimensional complex that it is.

Mr. Kalecki has developed an interesting special case of these general
principles in his "Principle of Increasing Risk."[7] He points out that one
of the limitations preventing the indefinite expansion of an enterprise,
even under conditions where there are no other limiting conditions,
such as imperfect markets or decreasing returns, is the decline in the
proportion of the total investment represented by the entrepreneur's
own capital, and the corresponding increase in the proportion of borrowed capital. The smaller the proportion of the total investment
represented by the entrepreneur's equity, the greater will be the proportionate loss of that equity for a given proportionate loss of the total
investment. Thus, if the total investment is $1,000,000, of which
$500,000 is the entrepreneur's equity and $500,000 is borrowed, a 10
per cent loss of the total investment represents a 20 per cent loss in the
entrepreneur's equity. If, however, the entrepreneur's equity in this case
were only $100,000, a 10 per cent loss on the total investment would
wipe out the entrepreneur's equity completely. Consequently, the more
an enterpreneur borrows in order to expand his business, the greater
the risk of loss of his own capital, or the greater the dispersion of the
probability distributions of the expected receipts from the entrepreneur's own capital. An entrepreneur will cease to expand at the
point where he reckons the gain in "lucrativity" to be just balanced by
the loss in "safety," to use the language of Marschak and Makower.

Another interesting approach in the direction of quantifying these
relationships is that of Mr. R. H. Coase,[8] who develops an idea of
Pareto in showing the most preferred point graphically by means of
indifference curves relating income and probability, the assumption

[7] M. Kalecki, *Essays in the Theory of Economic Fluctuations*, pp. 95-106.

[8] R. H. Coase, "Some Notes on Monopoly Price," *Rev. of Econ. Stud.*, Vol. 5, p. 17.

being that an entrepreneur will not care whether he has a large income of low probability or a small income of high probability. This approach by means of indifference curves is worthy of more attention; Mr. Coase does not solve all the problems he raises, and he seems to have the probability curves drawn rather inaccurately, but the idea is a most valuable one and may prove useful in future developments. It has the great merit that it assimilates the theory of the firm still more closely to the theory of the consumer, recognizing that the conduct of enterprise and the conduct of consumption are merely cases of one general principle of choice.

For all these fruitful suggestions, it cannot be said that this chapter in the development of economic thought is closed. Not only do we wait for a method of analysis, perhaps a graphical device like the marginal revenue curve, which will free the theory of uncertainty from its present formality and enable us to reach more conclusions than now seems possible; we also need much more work on the nature of uncertainty and of profit. It can be argued that all argument in terms of probability distributions is concerned only with *risk,* in Professor Knight's terminology, and not with uncertainty at all. If we know the probability of a future event we can insure against it, and hence eliminate the risk altogether. An event is not uncertain unless we know that it does not have 100 per cent probability of occurrence, and we do *not* know the actual probability of occurrence. Thus, there are three degrees of knowledge: certainty, which is 100 per cent probability: risk, which is a known probability; and uncertainty, which is an unknown probability. Enterprise concerns itself largely with the last of these three, and the theory of probability does not seem to have been extended to this case.

The uncertain position of the theory of uncertainty is reflected in the equally unsatisfactory nature of the theory of profits. This lies rather beyond the scope of the theory of the firm, but we may notice that the part played by profits in the various forms of competition is still much open to doubt. One of the most attractive conclusions of the theory of monopolistic competition (to be attributed principally to Chamberlin) is that the end result of monopolistic competition is not to permit profits above normal, but to make the number of firms in an industry larger than would be the case under perfect competition. The monopolistic element works itself out not in permitting higher profits to the marginal firm, but in permitting more firms to make at least normal profits. This conclusion has been attacked by Mr. Kaldor[9] and Mr. Triffin,[10] both of whom really wish to abolish the concept of an

[9] M. N. Kaldor, "Market Imperfection and Excess Capacity," *Economica* (1935), p. 33.
[10] Robert Triffin, *Monopolistic Competition and General Equilibrium Theory* (Harvard, 1940).

"industry" altogether on the grounds that it is impossible to fix boundaries between one industry and another. Hence, the concept of a "marginal firm" also seems to disappear, except in perfect competition, the profits of each firm being determined with reference to the possibility of producing substitutes for its product. But this means virtually the abandonment of the theory of imperfect competition. We seem almost to be back at Marshall again, with a fairly clear theory of monopoly, a fairly clear theory of perfect competition, and a twilit region in between where our theory gives us few clear conclusions, and where, unfortunately, most of the economic world resides. All this discussion reflects the generally unsatisfactory state of the theory of profits: even an authority like Professor Hicks finds it an easily exhaustible mine of useful results.[11]

In connection with the theory of uncertainty the study of Dr. Albert G. Hart[12] deserves particular mention, as constituting perhaps the most exhaustive study to date of these aspects of the theory of the film. Dr. Hart lays particular stress on the phenomenon of capital *rationing*—a limiting factor in the expansion of an enterprise of great importance in present circumstances. He also points out the importance of "flexibility" of plan, that is, the element in present decisions which permits of future adjustments. For "flexibility" of assets a firm may sacrifice lucrativity up to a certain point.

The theory of the reactions of a firm naturally lags behind the theory of the principles which govern a firm. Nevertheless, there have been some important contributions in recent years, mostly in the direction of a more realistic account of the *variables* with which a firm is likely to be concerned and of the functional relationships between these variables.

Progress has been made, for instance, in the description of the production function, which expresses the necessary relationships between quantities of input and output. The graphic representation of the production function as a three-dimensional surface, relating the quantities of two inputs and one output, has been valuable in clarifying the nature of input-output relationships. Especially valuable has been the use of contour-lines of this three-dimensional figure or "isoquants," showing on a plane graph whose axes represent quantities of two inputs those combinations of input-quantities which yield a given output. The "isoquants" are at the same time "revenue contours," for any two combinations of inputs which yield the same output will also yield the same

[11] J. S. Hicks, "The Theory of Uncertainty and Profit," *Economica* (May, 1931), p. 170-89.

[12] A. G. Hart, "Anticipations, Uncertainty, and Dynamic Planning," *Jour. of Bus., Univ. Chicago,* spec. suppl.

revenue. On the same figure "cost contours" or "isocosts" can be drawn, showing these combinations of inputs involving the same total expense. The point at which an isoquant is touched by a cost contour represents a "least cost combination" of inputs, or the cheapest way of producing the output given by the isoquant. The locus of all such points has been called the "expansion path" by Carlson, following Frisch.

The effect of a change in price of one input can easily be analyzed by the above tools. If the price of Input A rises, while that of Input B remains the same, the result is to steepen the isocost lines, making them more nearly parallel to the B axis, as a larger amount of B is now equal in total cost to a unit of A. The expansion path is therefore shifted toward the B axis, and the cheaper B is substituted for the more expensive A. This is known as the "substitution effect." There is also a "scale effect"—a contraction in scale necessitated because the rise in the price of input has raised the marginal cost at each output. At the old optimum output the marginal cost is now greater than the marginal revenue. When the price of Input A rises, the substitution effect operates to reduce the purchase of A and increases that of B. The scale effect operates to reduce purchases of both inputs. If the scale effect is great enough it may counterbalance the substitution effect in the case of B and cause a net decline in the purchase of B, even though relative to A its price has risen.

This type of analysis is exactly analogous to the analysis of the reactions of a consumer by means of indifference curves. Indeed, a consumer is merely a "firm" whose product is "utility." The indifference curves are analogous to the isoquants, or product contours, the only difference being that they cannot be assigned definite quantities of utility. The utility surface, whose contours form the system of indifference curves, is a "mountain" whose shape we theoretically know, but whose height at any point probably cannot be known; by contrast, we can assume that both shape and height of the production surface are known. The "substitution effect" and the "scale effect" are likewise known in consumption theory, where the scale effect is usually called the "income effect." Thus, a rise in the price of a single object of consumption will have a substitution effect tending to reduce the consumption of that object as cheaper alternatives are substituted for it. There will also be an "income effect" tending to reduce all consumption, as the higher price makes the consumer poorer. The effect of a given rise in price, therefore—i.e., the elasticity of demand—depends first on the substitutability of the commodity concerned, and, secondly, on its importance in the total expenditure. This is true either of a consumption good or of a factor of production.

This unified theory of production and consumption is itself the product of many hands. It was first developed in the theory of consumption: the concept of indifference curves goes back to Pareto,[13] the analysis in terms of substitution and income effects was made, though in a highly mathematical form, by Slutsky,[14] and interpreted by Hicks and Allen[15] in a celebrated article. The applications to the theory of production may be traced back as far as Wicksell, and to Wicksteed, who drew attention to the essential symmetry of the classical law of diminishing returns. The use of isoquants to describe the production function did not develop to any great extent until the thirties. Frisch[16] Schneider,[17] and Hicks[18] make use of them. Carlson[19] uses them extensively, and in my *Economic Analysis*[20] I have extended this type of analysis to cover even the theory of selling cost, relegating the once predominant theory of consumption to its place as a special case of the general theory of an economic organism.

It is not difficult to extend this type of analysis to cover the case of joint products (*cf.* Carlson[21]). What is more important, it can be extended to cover the case of an enterprise in time. The great defect of the Cambridge Theory was that it took no account of the position of inputs and outputs in *time*. With the aid of the "substitution effect" and "income effect" concepts this difficult problem can be tackled. It is merely necessary to assume that time position, as well as kind or quality, separates one factor from another. Thus, "this week's labor" is a different factor from "next week's labor." Once this is recognized, the effects of expectations can be analyzed. Thus, suppose that an entrepreneur expects that labor will be cheaper next year. This expectation will have two general effects: first, next year's labor will be substituted in some degree, not only for other factors of next year, but also for this year's labor: *i.e.*, the purchase of labor will be postponed. Secondly, there may be a scale effect—in this case a general increase in scale —which will further tend to expand the purchases of next year's labor. In regard to the purchases of this year's labor, however, the substitution and the scale effects would be in opposite directions, the substitution

[13] V. Pareto, *Manuale di Economia Politica*, cap. III, sect. 54.

[14] E. Slutsky, "Sulla teoria del bilancio del consumatore," *Giornale di Economisti* (July, 1915).

[15] J. R. Hicks and R. D. G. Allen, "A Reconsideration of the Theory of Value," *Economica* (1934).

[16] R. Frisch, "Tekniske og Økonomiske Producktivitetlover" (mimeograph lectures, Oslo University).

[17] E. Schneider, *Theorie der Produktion* (1934), p. 4.

[18] J. R. Hicks, *Value and Capital* (1939), p. 91.

[19] S. Carlson, *A Study in the Pure Theory of Production* (1939), p. 19.

[20] K. E. Boulding, *Economic Analysis* (1941), chaps. 23 and 26.

[21] Carlson, *op. cit.*, chap. 5.

effect tending to diminish, the scale effect tending to augment the pur-chases. The net effect will depend on their relative magnitudes: if next year's labor can easily be substituted for this year's labor, that is, if the purchase of labor can easily be postponed, the result of an anticipated fall in wages will probably be a decline in present employment. If, however, this year's and next year's labor are not easily substitutable, and if the scale effect is considerable, the expansion of scale may begin this year and the expectation of a fall in wages will cause a rise in this year's employment.[22]

Closely related to the theory of the individual firm is the theory of duopoly, or oligopoly—i.e., the theory of the interactions of two or more firms operating under the condition that each firm in drawing up its own policy considers in some way the reactions of other firms, and the con-sequent repercussions on itself of any policy it may pursue. The theory resolves itself into a comparative study of the results obtained when various assumptions are made regarding the expectations of the two firms and the nature of the repercussions. The theory in one form is as old as Cournot; Chamberlin[23] and Stackelberg[24] have given more gen-eral treatments. No very far-reaching developments seem to have been made in this part of theory in the last few years, though the work of Smithies and Savage[25] is worth mention as providing a dynamic ap-proach in terms of the path to equilibrium. The problem has so many degrees of freedom that it is not easily tackled with existing tools.

In sum, we see that considerable advance has been made in the past few years toward a more realistic and fruitful theory of the firm. Nevertheless, much remains to be done. The picture of the firm on which much of our analysis is built is crude in the extreme, and in spite of recent refinements there remains a vast gap between the elegant curves of the economist and the daily problems of a flesh-and-blood executive. Economics describes as a science what business practices as an art, and much of the theory of the firm is an attempt to describe ex-plicitly principles which a business man follows unconsciously. But economists have undoubtedly neglected the most difficult problem of business: how to make judgments when essential data are missing. The theoretical economist blithely assumes that anything that ought to be known can be known. Cost and revenue curves are data which must be known if profits are to be accurately maximized: ergo, says the economist, as profits are to be maximized we must assume cost and

[22] Carlson, op. cit., chap. 6; and Hicks, op. cit., chap. 15.

[23] E. H. Chamberlin, The Theory of Monopolistic Competition, chap. 3.

[24] H. von Stackelberg, Marktform und Gleichgewicht (Wien, 1934).

[25] A. Smithies and L. J. Savage, "A Dynamic Problem in Duopoly," Econometrica, Vol. 8 (1940), p. 130.

revenue curves to be known, although somewhat vaguely. Recently, however, the disturbing notion has been gaining ground that, as the business man cannot know the data on which to maximize profits, the very principle of maximizing profits is a false one. Hicks has suggested that a quiet life may be the most desired fruit of monopoly, and a good deal of evidence is accumulating to show that except in times of abnormal instability many, if not most business men, are content to follow rules of thumb in their price and sales policy, without bothering too much about whether a little adjustment here or there would not yield them a larger profit. Thus the studies of the Oxford economists[26] revealed the fact that many firms fix prices according to a more or less conventional "full cost" figure (average total cost, including profit) and are very loathe to change prices to meet changed conditions. In part, as R. L. Hall and C. J. Hitch[27] have shown, this behavior may not be inconsistent with a policy of maximizing profits, particularly in oliogopolistic conditions where there may be discontinuities in the firm's individual demand curve. It may also in part be due to a strong tendency for people untrained in functional thinking to regard the "cost of production" as something absolute and constant, a tendency which is sometimes expressed in legislative attempts to "fix prices according to cost of production."

It is probable that we are entering on a period when the main contributions to the theory of the firm will spring out of econometric investigations. The studies already made on statistical cost curves[28] have borne some fruit. Nevertheless, a great deal remains to be done in the investigation of actual decisions made by business men and their relation to the environment which surrounds these decisions. It is surprising that more has not been done on these lines in this country, where the art of asking pertinent and impertinent questions has perhaps developed most fully. The Oxford inquiry, for all the interest of its results, shows marks of the gentleman-amateur. One would like to see one of our high-powered fact-factories, armed with modern statistical equipment, a staff of inquisitive ex-social workers, and a grain or two of common sense, set off in pursuit of the elusive policy-maker and track down the minutest detail of his thoughts and actions. The results might be surprising, and might necessitate the recasting of a good deal of our analytical machinery.

[26] *Oxford Economic Papers:* Oct., 1938; May, 1939; and Feb., 1940.

[27] R. J. Hall and C. J. Hitch, "Price Theory and Business Behaviour," *Oxford Economic Papers,* May, 1939, p. 12.

[28] H. Staehle, "The Measurement of Statistical Cost Functions: An Appraisal of Some Recent Contributions," *Am. Econ. Rev.,* Vol. XXXII (June, 1942), pp. 321-33.

DESIRABLE CHANGES IN THE NATIONAL ECONOMY AFTER THE WAR

Journal of Farm Economics, 26, 1 (Feb. 1944): 95-100

DESIRABLE CHANGES IN THE NATIONAL ECONOMY AFTER THE WAR

B EFORE we can answer the question "What are the desirable changes in the economic system" we need to ask two other questions: first, what is the function of the economic system and what tasks is it called upon to perform, and second, in what directions is it failing to fulfil these functions and to perform these tasks. Not until we have a reasonably clear answer to these questions can we hope to judge what changes it is desirable to make.

There seem to be three main functions which an economic system is called up to perform. The first is to ensure a reasonably rapid rate of economic progress. The second is to provide for a reasonable amount of stability, so that extreme booms and depressions are avoided. The third is to provide for equity in the distribution of the product of economic activity. It should be clearly recognized that these three aims are not necessarily compatible—that is to say, they are to some extent alternative goods between which we must choose. Thus it may only be possible to achieve a rapid rate of economic progress at the cost of a certain degree of instability and inequity. Similarly measures taken to distribute the product more justly may result in a check to economic progress or may accentuate instability. As long as these alternatives are clearly recognized, however, they should not present any great difficulty to the policy-maker. Choice between recognized alternatives is the essential characteristic of economic activity, and the problem, for instance, how much progress to sacrifice for an increased degree of stability, is not essentially different from any other judgment of choice, even though it may be more difficult. Dangers are most likely to arise when the alternatives are not recognized as such, and when the policy-maker operates under the illusion that he can have his cake and eat it. Particularly dangerous is the piecemeal method of attempting to solve social and economic problems, for the man who has a single problem to solve frequently does so by creating worse problems that other people have to solve. It is perhaps the principal duty of the social scientist to reveal clearly just where the alternatives lie, for mistakes in social policy arise more from lack of appreciation of the true alternatives involved than from deliberate mischoice.

The economic system consists of three elements: laws, institutions, and individuals. Any discussion of changes in the system must therefore deal with each of these three elements. Change in laws is perhaps the easiest to achieve, though it must always be remembered that the effectiveness of laws depends on the willingness of people to obey and enforce them. Change in institutions comes more slowly—i.e. in the forms and ideals of corporations, trade unions, private businesses, banks, cooperatives, and all the other innumerable organizations that carry on economic activity. Change in the motives and patterns of behaviour of individuals comes most slowly of all, and yet is the most fundamental, for laws and institutions are but the creation and reflection of the character of individuals.

The first, and probably the most important task of the economic system is to permit a rapid rate of economic progress. This is particularly important for poor regions, and as the vast bulk of the world's population still is miserably poor, the problem of progress may not unreasonably be considered the world's number one economic problem. We are apt to be obsessed by the problem of instability in this country and to forget that the business cycle itself is a luxury of rich countries. The world's problem is how to extend the knowledge and practice of our best techniques to the 90 percent or more who do not know or practice them. And lest there are those who balk at world responsibility and feel concerned only for the inhabitants of the United States, it may be pointed out that one quarter to one third of our people live at a standard of life and techniques far below what the existing state of knowledge permits.

The principal conditions which permit rapid progress are (1) Laws which give security in the administration of productive property and in the enjoyment of a reasonable proportion of the fruits of individual change; (2) Institutions which permit of competition, in the narrow sense of the ability of better processes and products to displace the inferior; (3) Individuals with an adventurous disposition, a liking for change and a strong sense of the present value of prospective future benefits.

On the whole the American system has provided these conditions, and consequently has enjoyed over a period of two hundred years or more an astonishing rate of economic progress. Nevertheless there are certain improvements which might be made and certain dangers to be guarded against. There is little doubt, for instance, that our tenancy laws, particularly in the south, are seriously defective and need modifying in the direction of greater tenant right in security of tenure and in compensation for improvements. We have perhaps concentrated too much on the losing battle to prevent the spread of tenancy, and have not thought sufficiently about methods for rendering it innocuous, or even beneficial. On the negative side there has been an alarming spread in recent years of the doctrine that inferior processes and methods must be protected against the competition of the superior. The anti-chain store measures, for instance, which tax chain stores because they have lower costs than others; the so-called "scientific tariff," which taxes cheaper imports to prevent them from displacing the more expensive home product; even the "parity price" doctrine, which in the hands of some of its advocates would deprive the industrial population of the benefits of any technical progress in agriculture—all these are measures which may be inimical to economic progress, though there may be other justifications for them. More dangerous perhaps than any of these measures is the state of mind which they embody; an attitude that fears change, that seeks security at all costs, forgetting that danger is the price we pay for life and that absolute security exists only in the grave. This is not to say, of course, that we must be utterly ruthless and unconcerned with the human costs of progress. It is a just criticism of our system that the costs of progress are not adequately taken into our accounting. Nevertheless there is a world of difference with the attitude that insists on the "rights" of all established interests, and cares not whether progress be stifled in consequence, and the attitude which would increase the willingness to bear the costs of progress, vicariously if necessary, at the same time that it seeks to distribute the burden of these costs more equitably.

There is a real and a hard choice here between progress and equity, which is nowhere revealed more clearly than in agriculture. In a progressive society the relative importance of agriculture must continually decline, for agriculture produces, on the whole, basic necessities of relatively low income-elasticity. This decline can only be brought about, however, if agriculture is relatively less profitable that industry; capital and labor must be squeezed out of

agriculture and attracted into industry, and there is no way of
doing this other than by making agriculture less advantageous,
both to capital and labor, than industry. A relatively unprofitable
agriculture is a necessary accompaniment of a rapidly progressing
society; and the moment when agriculture ceases to be relatively
unprofitable will mark the beginning of our economic decline. The
only answer to this problem is to hasten by all possible means the
movement out of agriculture, for then a very slight inequity will be
sufficient to guarantee progress. There is danger, however, that
those whose whole energies are directed towards solving the problem of equity in distribution, or those whose personal interests are
adversely affected by progress, may try to "freeze" the existing
status of agriculture and by means of governmental subsidies make
it artificially profitable. If such were the object of the agricultural
interest and of its advocates it would indeed be true that no greater
menace to the welfare of society could be found than the pre-
dominance of the agricultural interest in the political scheme. The
history of some European countries—notably France—provides an
admirable but depressing illustration of the truth of this proposition.

Closely connected with the problem of progress is that of
stability. It is in this connection perhaps that the American economy is weakest; its violent fluctuations are too well known to need
description. It is probably true that a certain amount of instability
is a necessary cost of rapid progress. Progress means adventure;
and adventure inevitably leads to mistakes. Minor and local booms
and depressions therefore are inevitable in any progressive society;
we cannot prevent a boom in a new industry or a decline in a displaced one. But we can prevent *general* inflations and *general* depressions of the type that took place following 1929. The problem
here is that of preventing large fluctuations in the aggregate money
income of society. This is essentially a responsibility of government;
no other institution and no individual is powerful enough to accomplish this task. It can be accomplished through the instrument
of the tax system, if the tax system is designed consciously with
that end in view, and not regarded simply as a means for financing
government expenditures. The deficit-financing school is essentially
correct in supposing that budget deficits tend to increase money
incomes and budget surpluses to decrease them. When money incomes are declining, therefore, this decline can be offset by a suit-

able budget deficit, and when money incomes are increasing this can be offset by a budget surplus. The mistake of the New Deal was to treat government *expenditures* as the most variable item. It would be much better to set the level and kinds of government expenditure by rather long-run criteria, otherwise we fall into "boon-doggling" and waste. The required deficits or surpluses can then be achieved through appropriate fluctuations in tax rates and government receipts. It should not be impossible to devise a semi-automatic "adjustable tax plan" based on a widespread, deductible-at-source income tax not unlike the arrangement we now have, with the proviso that the rate of tax in each period (month or quarter) should be automatically determined by the *change* in aggregate money income in the preceding period. When money income fell, the tax rate would likewise fall—becoming zero or even negative if it were necessary to counteract a violently deflationary movement. If, on the contrary, money income rose beyond what was considered desirable, the tax rate should rise even more steeply until the inflationary movement was suppressed. Such a plan would not prevent all fluctuations; it would however confine them within relatively harmless limits. There is now no excuse for a repetition of the experience of 1929-32, provided that the people and the politicians can be persuaded to regard the budgetary and tax system as the steering wheel of the system and not as its sheet-anchor. The budget-balancers may then be seen as people who want to keep the steering wheel fixed at all costs, no matter what happens to the car! It may not be impossible to perform this educational task. It is so obvious at the moment that the purpose of taxation is not to "pay for the war" but to prevent inflation, that it should not prove too much of an intellectual step to regard taxes as likewise an instrument for preventing deflation.

There is not time in this short period to discuss at length the problem of equity in distribution. It must suffice to notice that in this connection government has many responsibilities. The distribution of income can be affected directly through the tax system and indirectly through the control of monopolies. The great unresolved problem in this connection is the *criterion* of justice. Most people nowadays would agree that extreme inequalities are undesirable, but there is room for much legitimate disagreement as to how far in the direction of equality we should move. One principle however is clear; that the state has a responsibility to see that none of its people fall below a certain minimum standard of life. How high this standard should be—whether it should be at the level of bare existence or at some level of "health and decency" is a difficult question, the answer to which must depend largely on the size of aggregate real income and on the amount of that income which is available for distribution. This latter quantity may be termed the "economic surplus"; it is the difference between the total product and the total supply price of all factors of production. Redistribution cannot cut below the level of this economic surplus without destroying production itself. It is highly desirable, therefore, to have a large economic surplus, otherwise the attempt to redistribute wealth may simply result in its destruction. This fact underlines more sharply than ever the importance of economic progress, for there is a real sense in which justice in distribution is a luxury which can only be afforded by rich societies. The economic surplus however depends not only on the total product, but on the willingness of the owners of scarce factors and abilities to put them to work at low prices. This in turn depends on the attitude of individuals towards riches. Justice in distribution perhaps depends more than many have realized on the attitudes of individuals, and there is a vast field for desirable change here. We need many more individuals with a developed "instinct of workmanship" and an atrophied sense of luxury and display. Indeed, a good slogan for the postwar world would be "it's ridiculous to be rich." A social climate in which productivity is honored and extravagance is despised is highly desirable; it is obviously desirable for a "war effort"; it should be equally recognized as desirable for the "peace effort"— the effort to maximize not our powers of destruction but the welfare of all people.

A LIQUIDITY PREFERENCE THEORY OF MARKET PRICES

Economica, NS 11, 42 (May 1944): 55-63.

A Liquidity Preference Theory of Market Prices

THE ultimate " causes of price "—to use a Classical term—lie deeply embedded in the psychology and techniques of mankind and his environment, and are as manifold as the sands of the sea. All economic analysis is an attempt to classify these manifold causes, to sort them out into categories of discourse that our limited minds can handle, and so to perceive the unity of structural relationship which both unites and separates the manifoldness. Our concepts of " demand " and " supply " are such broad categories. In whatever sense they are used, they are not ultimate determinants of anything, but they are convenient channels through which we can classify and describe the effects of the multitude of determinants of the system of economic magnitudes. These ultimate determinants are, on the one hand, the patterns of choice between alternatives of all individuals, and on the other, the pattern of technical limitation of resources such as labour time and raw materials and the transformation functions of these resources into commodities and services. It is possible to show, algebraically, how these billions of determinants operate to create and to change the structure of economic quantities (prices, volumes, etc.). Such algebraic demonstration, after the manner of the Lausanne school, though logically necessary, is not practically valuable in the solution of particular problems.[1] For this task we need to be able to divide the multitude of causes into a few broad workable categories, of which the Marshallian demand and supply analysis is an admirable example. It is not the purpose of this paper to overthrow the Marshallian methods, or to question their limited validity. Rather is it to suggest a new dichotomy of forces in the special case of market price in a competitive market, not into " demand " and " supply ", but into " price determining factors " and " quantity determining factors ". For many purposes it would seem that this new dichotomy is much more useful than the old, and leads to results which could not have been attained with the demand and supply apparatus.

It should be noted carefully that the situation discussed in this paper is that of the determination of market price in a perfectly competitive market on a single " day ", the " day ", of course, being as short as we wish to make it and being defined by the condition that the market is cleared and that all transactions which can be accomplished under existing conditions have been accomplished. This itself, of course, is a fiction, though a useful and necessary one: our mind finds it difficult to grasp the slippery and continuous processes of the actual world without first " fixing " each position in our mind before proceeding to the next. The simplest approach to dynamic economics is through a succession of static pictures, just as the representation of movement on the screen is obtained through a rapid succession of stationary projections. In the " market day " therefore we make the following assumptions: (i) the quantity of exchangeables (goods and money) possessed by all the people in the market does not change during the course of the " day ". All that happens is exchange, in the simplest and most literal sense of the world—i.e., a *rearrangement of ownership* of the goods and money in the market. At the end of the day some people have more money, some less; some have more commodity, some less, but the increases must be exactly balanced by the declines as the total quantities possessed by all marketers have not changed. (ii) We will assume that the price that clears the market is discovered immediately and prevails all through the " day ", and that all transactions made during the " day " are made at that price. This assumption does not quite correspond to reality: nevertheless if the " day " is sufficiently short no serious errors are likely to be introduced by it, and it enables us to sidestep a number of highly

---

[1] The brilliant work of Professor Leontief (*The Structure of American Economy, 1919—1929*) might seem at first sight to disprove this assertion. But even Professor Leontief has to simplify his system of simultaneous equations radically in order to obtain any results.

difficult problems of secondary importance concerning the effect of transactions on the market.[1]

The situation envisaged above must be distinguished sharply from the analysis of normal price by means of long-run demand and supply curves. In the normal price analysis we are considering an equilibrium of *flows* of commodity on and off the market. The demand curve in this case shows the average rate of consumption, and the supply curve the average rate of production, that would prevail at each price. It is dangerously easy to carry over habits of thought from the long-run analysis into the analysis of the market, yet the two are very distinct, and it must constantly be borne in mind in the following analysis that the quantities refer to *stocks*, both of commodity and money, that are shifted around in ownership, and do not refer to *flows* of production, consumption, or income.

We will begin the analysis by considering the situation of a single marketer in a one-commodity market, possessing a quantity of money m_1 and a quantity of commodity a_1. His willingness to buy or sell can be described by his individual market demand-supply curve or function, showing what quantities of the commodity he will buy or sell at each price. .This will normally be a continuous function: at high prices he will sell, at low prices he will buy, and at some intermediate price, which may be called the " null price " he will neither buy nor sell, being satisfied with the quantity in his possession. It is convenient to adopt the convention that purchases (because they add to the stocks of the purchaser) are positive in sign, and that sales are negative. We can then express the individual market demand-supply function by a single equation,

$$q_1 = f_1(p) \qquad (1)$$

A negative value of q_1 here represents an offer to sell, and a positive value an offer to buy.

In the market there will be a number of individuals, 1 to N, each having his own demand-supply function, $q_1 = f_1(p)$, $q_2 = f_2(p) \ldots q_n = f_n(p)$. Knowing these functions we can immediately derive the market demand and market supply schedules by adding, for each value of p, the positive q's to get the total quantity demanded, Q_d, and the negative q's to get the total quantity supplied, Q_s. Thus we obtain the demand function, $Q_d = F_d(p)$ and the supply function $Q_s = F_s(p)$, and the condition that the price must equate the quantity demanded and the quantity offered—i.e., $Q_d = Q_s$, gives us a third equation from which we can now derive the three unknowns, Q_d, Q_s, and p. This is the usual demand and supply market analysis.

There is, however, another way to approach the problem. If we add, algebraically, all the individual q's at each price we get a figure $Q_e = (Q_d - Q_s)$ which represents the excess demand or excess supply, according as it happens to be positive or negative. Thus by simple addition we derive from the individual demand-supply functions, an excess demand-supply function, $Q_e = F_e(p) = \Sigma f(p)$. Then at the equilibrium price we know that $Q_e = O$, i.e.,

$$\Sigma f(p) = O \qquad (2)$$

What has been done here is to separate out that element in the market situation which is responsible purely for the determination of price. Graphically, the price is given by the point at which the excess demand-supply curve (which I have elsewhere called the " total market curve "[2]) cuts the vertical (price) axis. The " height " of the excess demand-supply curve is in some sense an " average " of the heights of all the individual demand-supply curves from which it is derived. That is to say, the market price will be some kind of weighted average (the weight, of course, depending on the type of individual demand-supply function) of the " null prices " of the various marketers.[3]

---

[1] Marshall, we may note, avoided the same set of problems in his discussion of the " corn market " by assuming that the marginal utility of money remained constant.

[2] Boulding, *Economic Analysis*, p. 73. See also Hicks, *Value and Capital*, p. 63.

[3] It is easy to show that when the individual demand-supply functions are linear the market price is the weighted average of the null prices of all the marketers, weighted by the slopes of each individual demand-supply curve. Thus let the individual demand-supply functions be $p_1 = b_1 q_1 + c_1$, $p_2 = b_2 q_2 + c_2$ ..... $p_n = b_n q_n + c_n$. Then $c_1, c_2, \ldots c_n$ are the null prices of the various marketers. The equilibrium price p is given by equation (2), i.e.,

$$\frac{p}{b_1} - \frac{c_1}{b_1} + \frac{p}{b_2} - \frac{c_2}{b_2} + \ldots + \frac{p}{b_n} - \frac{c_n}{b_n} = 0$$

i.e., $p = \dfrac{\dfrac{c_1}{b_1} + \dfrac{c_2}{b_2} + \ldots + \dfrac{c_n}{b_n}}{\dfrac{1}{b_1} + \dfrac{1}{b_2} + \ldots + \dfrac{1}{b_n}}$

The " null price " of an individual's demand-supply curve is a measure of his willingness to buy, or what is the same thing, his unwillingness to sell. Any increase in his willingness to buy raises his whole demand-supply schedule, and with it raises his null price. A rise in the market price therefore can only result from a general net increase in the willingness to buy the commodity in question. It is this, and no other factor, that determines price.

It is possible also to separate out those elements in the total market situation which determine the quantity exchanged. If all the demand-supply curves of the individual marketers passed through the same point on the price axis—i.e., if all the marketers had the same null price—the demand and supply curves would intersect on the price axis and there would be no exchanges on the market at all. There might be a market price quoted, but as this would of necessity be equal to the null prices of all the marketers, nothing would be bought or sold at that price. It is only because the different marketers have different degrees of willingness to buy or sell that transactions can take place at all. This property of the market we may call its " divergence ", and it is this, and this alone, which determines the quantity exchanged. The greater the divergence of the individual demand-supply curves—i.e., the greater the spread of the null prices of the various marketers about the market price, the greater will be the quantity exchanged.[1]

We have now effected our new dichotomy of the forces in the market, dividing them not into " supply " and " demand ", but into " price determining " and " quantity determining " factors. The descriptive advantages of such a division are obvious, and it is interesting to compare the description of various changes under our analysis and under the old supply and demand analysis. Suppose, for instance, that we have a " pure " price-raising movement, through a uniform increase in the height of all the individual demand-supply curves. That is, there is a uniform increase in the willingness to buy, or what is the same thing, a uniform decrease in the willingness to sell. This is reflected merely in the price, the quantity exchanged remaining as before. In our analysis it is represented simply by a rise in the total market demand-supply curve, which now cuts the price axis at a higher price than before. In the demand and supply analysis this same movement would be represented by a rise in the market demand curve coupled with a fall in the market supply curve, the new point of intersection being at a higher price, but at the same quantity as before. These movements in the demand and supply curves, however, are not independent; they are both the result of a single force, the increase in the willingness to buy or unwillingness to sell expressed by the rise in the individual demand-supply curves. Indeed, a situation is hardly conceivable in which a change in market demand does not go hand in hand with a change in market supply. It is this interdependence of market demand and supply curves that makes them rather unsuitable for market analysis.

Similarly, when we have a " pure " change in market divergence, resulting in a change in the quantity bought without change in the price, the result is a change in both supply and demand curves, proceeding from the same cause. Suppose that the divergence of the various individual null prices becomes wider, without any change in the market price. The quantity exchanged will increase. The market demand and supply curves will both move to the right, intersecting at a point representing a larger quantity, but the same price as before. The movement of both demand and supply curves thus follows from exactly the same cause: viz., the increase in market

---

[1] Where the individual demand-supply functions are linear an algebraic formula for the quantity exchanged can be derived as follows, using the notation of footnote 3, p. 56. Let $c_1, c_2 \ldots c_k$ be the null prices of all those marketers whose null prices are greater than the market price, p. These are the buyers. The amount that buyer K will buy at the price p is $\dfrac{c-p}{b}$, and the total amount bought is

$$Q_d = \frac{c_1 - p}{b_1} + \frac{c_2 - p}{b_2} + \ldots + \frac{c_k - p}{b_k}$$

Similarly the marketers whose null prices are greater than p, $c_{k+1}, c_{+2} \ldots c_n$, are the sellers; and the quantity sold, Q_s, is given by :

$$Q_s = \frac{c_{k+1} - p}{b_{k+1}} + \frac{c_{k+2} - p}{b_{k+2}} + \ldots + \frac{c_n - p}{b_n}$$

Q_s, of course, is equal to Q_d. The quantity exchanged, therefore, is equal to the weighted sum of either the positive or the negative deviations of the null prices from the market price weighted according to the reciprocal of the slope of the individual demand-supply curve. The greater these deviations—i.e., the greater the " divergence " in the market, the greater the quantity exchanged. If all the null prices were the same, then we should have $c_1 = c_2 = \ldots = c_k = \ldots = c_n = p$, and both Q_d and Q_s would be zero.

divergence. It is evident that the division of the market situation into " demand " on the one hand, and " supply " on the other, does not correspond to any very significant distinction within the structure of the market. The reason for this is clear: in a competitive market " buyers " and " sellers " are not distinct groups of people, separate from each other. Any marketer may be a buyer at one price and a seller at a higher price: every rise in prices induces some who were previously in the buyer's camp to cross over into the seller's, and every fall in prices has the reverse effect. Hence the demand and supply curves cannot be independent: they represent only a momentary division of the market, and will invariably move together except in the unlikely case of exactly counterbalancing changes in eagerness to buy and in market divergence. This is not the case, it should be noticed, in the case of the long-run demand and supply analysis: the producers and consumers of a single commodity are usually different groups of people, with only a little overlapping. In this case it is reasonable to assume that demand and supply curves are independent of each other and of the price, and hence they have much more individual meaning and validity.

We can now take yet another step in the analysis, and actually define an equation for the individual demand-supply curve on a simple and plausible assumption. From this we shall go on to derive a simple yet revolutionary formula which gives us the market price itself. The assumption is that each marketer wishes to hold a certain proportion of his total capital resources in the form of money, which we will call the *preferred liquidity ratio*, r, or his " liquidity preference ", and that this proportion is independent of the absolute level of the price of the commodity. As we shall see, the preferred liquidity ratio is by no means independent of anticipated changes in prices, but there seems to be no reason to suppose that it would be affected by the actual level of absolute prices. This assumption alone is sufficient to give us an equation for the individual demand-supply curve and a simple formula for market price.

Let an individual marketer possess a quantity of money m_1, a quantity of commodity a_1, and suppose that his preferred liquidity ratio is r_1. Let q_1 be the quantity of commodity that he exchanges in the " day ": q_1 if positive will represent a purchase, if negative, a sale. Let the price be p_1. Then we will assume to begin with that he possesses only commodity A and money, and that no other commodities enter into the market, or, what is perhaps more realistic, that his other possessions and transactions do not affect his transactions in commodity A. Then after he has completed his transactions the total amount of commodity he possesses is $a_1 + q_1$, and the total amount of money is $m_1 - p_1q_1$. The total value of commodity possessed by him is $p_1a_1 + p_1q_1$. The total value of his holdings of money and commodity combined is therefore $(p_1a_1 + p_1q_1) + (m_1 - p_1q_1) = p_1a_1 + m_1$. It will be noticed that the total value of his holdings is not affected by the exchanges he makes, as what he receives is always equal in value to what he gives up. After his exchanges have been completed the ratio of the money he now possesses to the value of his total holdings should equal his preferred liquidity ratio, r_1, for presumably the *object* of his transactions was to rearrange the form of his possessions into the desired liquidity ratio. We have, therefore,

$$r_1 = \frac{m_1 - p_1q_1}{m_1 + p_1a_1} \tag{3a}$$

This equation can also be written:

$$p_1 = \frac{m_1(1 - r_1)}{r_1a_1 + q_1} \tag{3b}$$

or

$$q_1 = \frac{m_1(1 - r_1)}{p_1} - r_1a_1 \tag{3c}$$

This is the equation of the individual's demand-supply curve, for it shows what quantity of the commodity he will buy or sell at each price in order to achieve his preferred liquidity ratio. It is a rectangular hyperbola, asymptotic to the quantity axis at $q = \infty$, and to the line $q_1 = -r_1a_1$ at $p_1 = \infty$. This expresses the fact that an individual will never sell a greater proportion of the commodity that he possesses than his liquidity ratio, and will only sell all the commodity he possesses if he wants to have all his holdings in the form of money (i.e., if $r = 1$). The asymmetry between buying and selling is interesting: no matter how high the price rises the amount an individual is willing to sell cannot go beyond a certain point. There is no limit, however, to the increase in the amount that an individual is willing to buy as the price falls, for with each fall in price the purchasing power of his money increases.

It is now easy to obtain a formula for the market price, knowing the quantities of money and of commodity possessed by each marketer, and knowing the preferred liquidity ratio of each. Denoting the quantities associated with the various marketers by suffices $1, 2, \ldots n$, and applying equation 2 we have immediately the market price, p, given by equation (4):

$$p = \frac{m_1(1 - r_1) + m_2(1 - r_2) + \ldots + m_n(1 - r_n)}{r_1a_1 + r_2a_2 + \ldots + r_na_n} \tag{4}$$

This is a most instructive equation. It shows at once that an increase in the quantity of money, or a decrease in the quantity of commodity, possessed by any marketer, or a decrease in the preferred liquidity ratio of any marketer, will raise the price. It shows also that the effect on the price produced by a change in the quantity of money or of commodity possessed by any marketer depends on his preferred liquidity ratio. A change in the stock of commodity will have a larger effect on price if it is felt by those marketers with the higher liquidity preference. A change in the stock of money will have a larger effect on price if it is felt by those with a lower liquidity preference. Thus if new money gets into the hands of " hoarders " with high liquidity preference it will have less effect on price than if it gets into the hands of individuals with small liquidity preference (spenders). The equation also shows two interesting extreme cases: that if the preferred liquidity ratio is zero—i.e., if people do not wish to hold any money—the price will be infinite; if the preferred liquidity ratio is 1, so that people wish to hold all their resources in the form of money and none in the form of commodities, then the price will fall to zero. It also shows that when liquidity preference is high, a change in the stocks of commodity produces a greater effect on price than a change in the stocks of money. On the other hand, when liquidity preference is low, changes in the stocks of money produce more effect than changes in stocks of commodities.

If the preferred liquidity ratio of all individuals is the same and equal to r, equation (4) reduces to the very simple form

$$p = \frac{M(1 - r)}{Ar} \tag{5}$$

where M is the total stock of money in the market and A is the total stock of commodity. Even if the preferred liquidity ratios of the various individuals differ, equation (5) is still highly significant: r then means the " average " or " market " liquidity ratio. It is the proportion of the value of liquid property to the value of all property which the market as a whole feels is most desirable. The market liquidity ratio, r, is not a simple average of the individual ratios, however, but a complex weighted average.[1]

The important equation (5) can easily be derived directly, without reference back to individual preferences. The total value of goods and money owned by marketers is $pA + M$. If r is the preferred liquidity ratio for the market as a whole, therefore, we have

$$r = \frac{M}{pA + M,}$$

[1] We have, combining equations (4) and (5)

$$\frac{M(1 - r)}{Ar} = \frac{m_1(1 - r_1) + m_2(1 - r_2) + \ldots + m_n(1 - r_n)}{a_1r_1 + a_2r_2 + \ldots + a_nr_n}$$

whence $r = \dfrac{M\Sigma a_i r_i}{AM + M\Sigma a_i r_i - A\Sigma r_i m_i}$ (6)

If money and commodity were equally distributed among all the marketers this equation would reduce to the simple average of the individual r's—i.e., $r = \dfrac{\Sigma r_i}{n}$. Where there is not this equal division it should be noticed that the market liquidity ratio, r, could change somewhat even if the individual preferred ratios, r_1, r_2, etc., did not change, through a change in the a's and m's. It is not, therefore a wholly satisfactory measure of liquidity preference, but the same difficulty is encountered in any weighted average. Yet another simplification can be made : if it is assumed that the ratio of the amount of commodity to the amount of money possessed by each marketer is the same—i.e. $\dfrac{a_1}{m_1} = \dfrac{a_2}{m_2} = \ldots = \dfrac{a_n}{m_3} = K$, then equation 6 reduced to $r = \dfrac{\Sigma a_i r_i}{A}$, i.e., the market ratio is the weighted average of the individual ratio, weighted by the amount of commodity possessed by each marketer. In such a case a decline in the amount of commodity possessed by a marketer with a liquidity preference, above the average, would tend to lower the market ratio even if the individual ratios did not change. Such an interpretation of the market ratio, however, is not unreasonable, and the assumption on which it is based is not likely to be far from the truth.

which when transposed immediately gives equation (5). This equation should be compared with Fisher's equation of exchange, to which it bears some resemblance. The liquidity preference concept and the concept of velocity of circulation are at bottom different ways of expressing the same phenomenon. It would be quite possible to apply equation (5) to the general price level. In that case p would represent the price level, M the total quantity of money, A the total quantity of commodities and other valuta not including money, and r would be the general liquidity preference ratio. An increase in liquidity preference is the same thing as a decline in the velocity of circulation—i.e., it represents an increased desire for money and therefore a decreased willingness to spend it. The ratio $\dfrac{(1-r)}{r}$ may therefore be called the

" velocity ratio ", v: it rises and falls, along with the velocity of circulation of money, as r falls and rises. The differences between equation (5)—which may perhaps be called the " equation of price determination " and Fisher's equation of exchange are, however, highly significant. Equation (5) interprets prices in terms of *stocks* of commodities and of money, coupled with a preference factor. Fisher's equation describes simply an identity of *flows*: of money on the one hand and of the value of goods on the other. Although useful in many ways, it fails to give any causal explanations of the determination of price, for price and the quantity exchanged are always determined together; hence an equation which includes the volume of transactions is useless as an explanation of prices, for the volume of transactions is one of the unknowns which has to be determined along with price. Equation (5) has the advantage that all its components, except price, are historically determined or are given as data: the stock of money, the stock of goods, and the preferred liquidity ratios are objective facts at any moment of time, and may truly be described as the only short-run determinants of market price. There still remains the question " what determines the stocks and the preferences ": that, however, is a long-run problem of normal price.

From the stocks and preferences data we can also derive a formula which gives the quantity exchanged, or the volume of transactions in the " day ". The null price of marketer I, c_1, is found by putting $q_1 = O$ in equation 3b, whence

$$c_1 = \frac{m_1(1-r_1)}{r_1 a_1} \tag{7}$$

Substituting the value of $m_1(1-r_1)$ from equation 7 into equation (3c) we have:

$$q_1 = \frac{r_1 a_1}{p}(c_1 - p_1)$$

If the subscripts 1 to k represent the buyers in the market—i.e., those individuals whose null prices are greater than the market price, then the total volume of transactions, Q, is given by:

$$Q = \Sigma_1^k q_i = \Sigma_1^k \frac{r_i a_i}{p}(c_1 - p) \tag{8}$$

The volume of transactions is again seen to depend on the divergence of the null prices of the various marketers from the market price.

Substituting the value of p from equation 4 in equation 3c, summing $\Sigma_1^k q_1$ and simplifying, we arrive at the general formula for the quantity exchanged,

$$Q = \frac{M_d \Sigma_{k+i}^n r_i a_i - M_s \Sigma_i^k r_i a_i + (\Sigma_i^k r_i a_i)(\Sigma_{k+i}^n r_i m_i) - (\Sigma_{k+i}^n r_i a_i)(\Sigma_i^k r_i m_i)}{M - \Sigma_i^n m_i r_i} \tag{9}$$

If the liquidity preference of each marketer was equal to r, the formula simplifies to:

$$Q = \frac{r(A_s M_d - A_d M_s)}{M} \tag{10}$$

where A_d and A_s respectively signify the amounts of commodity possessed by buyers and by sellers, and M_d and M_s represent the quantity of money possessed by buyers and sellers. Although this formula is suggestive, it is not as useful as might at first sight appear, for as we have seen there is no clear distinction in the market between buyers and sellers. Nevertheless the formula suggests roughly that a rise in the quantity of commodity, or a fall in the quantity of money held by the " sellers " side of the market will tend to raise the volume of transactions, while a rise in the quantity of commodity or a fall in the quantity of money held by the " buyers " side of the market will have the opposite effect. It also suggests that a rise in liquidity preference, or a fall in the total quantity of money held in the market will have a general tendency to increase the volume of transactions, though this result is not necessary.

The analysis can now be extended without much difficulty to include any number of commodities. Suppose that there are Z commodities, $A, B, C, \ldots Z$. Let the total value of all these commodities, plus the money held by the marketers be v. By "commodity" we here mean anything that has monetary value: it therefore includes securities and other valuta. We can now express the "commodity preference" for each commodity as the preferred ratio of the value of the commodity to the total value of all things, including money, held in the market. Thus if p_a is the price of commodity A, and A is the amount held by the marketers, the "commodity preference ratio" for commodity A, r_a, is given by the equation:

$$r_a = \frac{A p_a}{v} \qquad (11)$$

If M is the total quantity of money held in the market, and r_m is the liquidity preference ratio, we have:

$$r_m = \frac{M}{v} \qquad (12)$$

Eliminating $\overset{\vee}{V}$ between these two equations we have:

$$p_a = \frac{M r_a}{A r_m} \qquad (13)$$

Similarly for the other commodities we have:

$$p_b = \frac{M r_b}{B r_m}, \quad p_c = \frac{M r_c}{C r_m} \ldots p_z = \frac{M r_z}{Z r_m} \qquad (13)$$

It follows that an increase in the quantity of money, or a decrease in liquidity preference, will raise *all* prices. An increase in the quantity of any one commodity will lower the price of that commodity; if the preferences of the market do not change, however, an increase in the quantity of one commodity will not change the prices of any other commodity.[1] This will only be true where the commodity is neither a substitute for nor a complement of any other commodity: i.e., where $\dfrac{\delta r_b}{\delta a} = \dfrac{\delta r_c}{\delta a,} = \ldots$ $= \dfrac{\delta r_z}{\delta a} = 0$. If the commodity A has a substitute, B, then an increased quantity of A in the hands of the marketers will cause a decrease in the preference for B: i.e., $\dfrac{\delta r_b}{\delta a}$ is negative. If the commodity A has a *complement*, C, then an increased quantity of A will cause an *increase* in the preference for C—i.e., $\dfrac{\delta r_c}{\delta a}$ is positive. In such a case an increase in the quantity of A will cause a decrease in the price of the substitute, B, and an increase in the price of the complement, C, according to equations (13). We see therefore that this method provides an easy solution for the problem of relatedness in demand.

It must be observed that there cannot be a change in one preference ratio without there being an equal compensating change in the sum of all other preference ratios, for the sum of all the preference ratios must be equal to unity: i.e.,

$$r_a + r_b + \ldots + r_z + r_m = 1 \qquad (14)$$

It follows that a change in price which is due to a change in *preference*, as opposed to a change in the quantities of goods or money, must be accompanied by opposite changes in other prices, unless it is counterbalanced by an equal and opposite change in liquidity preference or in quantities. Thus if the *preference* of the market for commodity A increases, without there being any change in the preference for money or in the quantities held, there must be not only a rise in the price of A but also a fall in the price of other commodities.

The mathematically inclined reader will not find it difficult to derive the general formulæ relating the price of each commodity to the individual preference ratios of each marketer for each commodity and for money. A general formula for the quantities exchanged can also be developed for the many-commodity case. As these formulæ involve complex and unresolvable determinants, however, they are of no practical value that I can discover, and are omitted.

The implications of the above analysis for economic theory are, I believe, profound. It is, in the first place, a powerful instrument for the unification of many

---

[1] It will, of course, lower the price level in so far as its own price is lowered.

parts of our existing theoretical structure which hitherto have been rather unrelated. It unifies, for instance, the theory of general prices and the theory of particular prices. As we have seen, if P is the general price level, W the total stock of all valuta, excluding money, R_w is the general commodity preference ratio and R_m the liquidity or money preference ratio, we have a formula for the general price level exactly analogous to equations (13) and (5):

$$P = \frac{MR_w}{WR_m} = \frac{M(1 - R_m)}{WR_m} \tag{15}$$

This price-level formula has an important contribution to make to the understanding of the crisis of late capitalism in which we seem to be living. The most striking feature of the past twenty years has been the strength of the deflationary forces in the western world. Equation (15) gives an important clue to this mystery. We see immediately that the total *value* of the stock of goods (PW) is equal to the quantity of money, M, multiplied by the " preference factor ", R_w/R_m. It follows that if the quantity of money and the preference factor are constant, the total value of the stock of goods cannot change, for every increase in the quantity of goods will result in a proportionate decline in their price. In such a case investment, in the financial sense, is absolutely impossible, for by investment we mean the *increase* through time of the total value of goods. (By " goods ", of course, we mean all physical capital.) Investment is only possible if either the quantity of money increases or liquidity preference declines, no matter how rapid the accumulation of physical capital. The rate of investment therefore depends, paradoxically enough, directly on the monetary situation, and only indirectly on the rate of accumulation of goods. It follows immediately that if there is no change in the preference ratios the rate of investment is equal to the rate of growth of the monetary stock. In the absence of a growth of the monetary stock or a fall in liquidity preference the accumulation of physical capital must inevitably result in a deflationary movement of prices.

The commodity preference ratio is likely to fall and the liquidity preference ratio to rise on the expectation of falling prices, for when prices are falling the purchasing power of stocks of money is continually increasing while the money value of a given stock of commodities is declining. This in itself is sufficient to account for the self-justifying nature of price anticipations: if people expect a fall in prices, R_m will rise and R_w will fall and P will fall in the absence of counterbalancing changes, whereas if people expect a rise in prices R_m will fall and R_w will rise and a rise in prices will ensue.

There is no reason to suppose also that commodity preference will decline and liquidity preference increase as the total stock of goods increases. There is no point in piling up stocks for ever, and in the course of accumulation the time must come when further accumulation becomes less and less desirable. This will be reflected in a declining rate of profit, which will make the holding of goods less attractive relative to the holding of money. When accumulation has proceeded to the point where stocks of most physical goods are large there will be a deflationary force operating due to the decline in commodity preference. This will be reinforced by the expectation of declining prices ; hence even if money stocks keep pace with stocks of goods, there will still be a powerful deflationary force operating. In such a period a rapid increase in money stocks will be necessary to keep the price level constant. The equilibrium of the price system, however, will be difficult to maintain because of the expectational factor.

The present analysis also enables us to see the so-called " liquidity preference " theory of interest as merely a special case of equation (13). The true money rate of interest to be expected from a security is determined at any moment by the price of that security. The higher the price of the security, the lower the rate of interest assuming that the future payments accruing to the owner of the security do not change, There is no such thing, strictly, as a " market rate of interest "—it is not the rate of interest that is determined in the market, but the price of securities—i.e., of expected future payments-series. The rate of interest itself is not a price, like the price of wheat: it does not have the dimensions of price. It is merely a certain mathematical property of a series of expected payments and their present price. The price of securities is not determined by the rate of interest; the expected rate of interest (and all rates of interest are expected) is determined by the security's present price. The price of a security is determined by the same factors that determine the price of any commodity—the quantity of money in the market, the quantity of the security in the market, the liquidity preference ratio and the security preference ratio (the proportion of total resources which the market wishes to hold in the form of the particular security). Thus if S is the quantity of the security held, R_s the security preference ratio, the price of the security is given by equation (13): $P_s = \dfrac{MR_s}{SR_m}$. We see therefore that the price of a security will be increased, and the rate of interest will therefore be lowered, by an increase in the quantity of money, by a decrease in the quantity of the security, by an increase in security preference or by a decrease in liquidity preference.

A formal explanation of the difference in apparent yields of various classes and terms of securities can be given in terms of the " security preference " concept. Where a security or other item of property has certain desirable qualities apart from its monetary return—such as, for instance voting privileges, or a high degree of salability, or a certain prestige value, its " security preference " will be high, its price high and the rate of return correspondingly low.

The extension of the principles of this paper to the theory of the firm, to the labour market, and to the theory of monopoly and imperfect competition must wait for another paper. Instead of treating the firm primarily as a profit and loss account, as is done in the usual marginal analysis, it can be treated as a balance sheet, and its decisions described in terms of their effects on the balance sheet rather than on the income account. Thus a purchase of anything, whether it be raw materials, equipment, or labour, involves an asset transfer—a reduction in illiquid assets and an increase in illiquid assets. Similarly a sale involves a reduction in illiquid assets and a gain in liquid assets. The willingness of firms to buy and sell can therefore be explained partly in terms of their preferred liquidity ratio. This aspect of a firm's behaviour is strictly analogous to the type of analysis we have employed in this paper. There is, of course, an additional complication that firms buy and sell not merely to change the form of their assets, but to increase their net worth. This is the sole assumption behind the refined marginal analysis. Thus it is assumed that a firm will extend its purchases of each factor of production until the discounted marginal productivity of the factor is equal to its marginal cost. The discounted marginal productivity, however, is what the purchase of the factor adds to the illiquid assets of the firm; its marginal cost is what the purchase of the factor subtracts from the liquid assets. We can rephrase the marginal productivity condition, therefore, and say that a firm will extend its purchases of any factor as long as there is a net addition to its assets. It will be seen immediately that the marginal productivity analysis assumes that the firm is quite indifferent as to the *form* of its assets—i.e., has an infinite number of preferred liquidity ratios. This assumption is very far from the truth, and changes in the liquidity preference of firms, as well as the composition of their assets, may have profound effects on their demand for factors of production. This is a factor that has been largely neglected in the theory of the firm, although it is implicit in much recent monetary analysis. The effects of an increase in liquid balances on the demand for labour and on the level of employment can hardly be explained without some reference to the liquidity preference factors in the demand for input.

This " asset-transfer " type of analysis provides, I believe, the most useful stepping-stone to the analysis of dynamic problems. Not only does it provide us with an " instantaneous " picture of price determination which can then serve as a basis for the " moving picture " technique of describing dynamic changes, but it also gives us a parameter which can reflect all the forces operating from the side of the future: viz., the preference ratios. Not only, therefore, have we separated out of the chaos of causes the price-determining and the quantity-determining factors; in the price-determining factors themselves we have distinguished between those that operate from the results of the past and those that operate from the expectations of the future. The quantity of money and of goods are given to us as a result of past events. The preference ratios are in part determined by future expectations. It would be difficult to devise a more suitable dichotomy for the analysis of the well-nigh inconceivable fluxes of reality.

THE INCIDENCE OF
A PROFITS TAX

American Economic Review, 34, 4 (Sept. 1944): 567-572.

THE INCIDENCE OF A PROFITS TAX

It is generally assumed in economic analysis that a tax on profits, whether proportionate or progressive, cannot be shifted. This assumption follows from a further assumption: that the policy of an enterprise is directed toward maximizing its profits. This further assumption is a very rough first approximation. Indeed, it may well be that conclusions drawn from it, such as the above, are so far from the truth as to be positively misleading. It is the purpose of this note to develop a technique for analyzing the behavior of the firm on a rather more realistic assumption, and to use the analysis to prove—what has been asserted by business men as vigorously as it has been denied by economists—that profits taxes may have some effects on the prices and outputs of an enterprise.

The "classical" theory of the incidence of a profits tax is illustrated in Figure 1. Profits are measured on the vertical axis, while output—or some parameter representing the scale of enterprise—is measured on the horizontal axis. It is assumed that the profits curve, ABC, reaches a maximum at some output OD. OD is then the most profitable output; from this the prices of the product or products and of the inputs can be determined, if they are not already given. If now a proportional tax on profits is imposed—say, 50 per cent—the profits curve after the tax is deducted will be AJB'C, and though the amount of profits at the maximum is smaller than before, the output at which profits are a maximum (OD) is unchanged. Even if the tax is progressive, so that a higher rate falls on large profits than on small, the shape of the profits curve will be flattened—*e.g.*, to AGB'C, but the maximum will still be at the same output, OD. This must always be true as long as the tax remains below 100 per cent on a marginal unit of profits. If the tax is so progressive that an increase in gross profits results in a decrease in net profits at high levels, the net profits curve would exhibit two maxima, but this case is so unlikely to occur that it is of theoretical interest only.

It should be noticed that the inability to shift a profits tax is only found in an industry where entry is restricted. Under either perfect or imperfect competition, where the least profitable firms are making zero profits, a profits tax on a single industry will eventually result in the winding-up of marginal firms, a decline in production, a rise in the price of the product and possibly a fall in the price of the factors of production. The tax is thus shifted in part to the consumer and to the factor-owner. It has been argued that a general profits tax, however, will not be shifted even in competitive industry, because the profitability of all industry will be reduced equally and, hence, there will be no inducement to shift from one industry to another. This argument, however, like that relating to a single firm, assumes that *whatever* the level of profit, however low, firms will continue to produce at a level of output at which profits are maximized.

This assumption of the universal maximization of profits neglects altogether the vital fact that enterprise—the task of making profits—is itself a factor of production that is not only scarce (probably very scarce) but also is not perfectly elastic in supply. The supply of enterprise is a difficult concept to quantify because of the difficulty of *measuring* the "quantity" of enterprise. Nevertheless it is clear that something like it exists, and is important.

The assumption that business men are solely interested in maximizing the profit of their enterprises contains the further assumption that they are quite indifferent about the scale of their enterprises, except in so far as it affects the total profit. This assumption is almost certainly not true. If we suppose, for instance, that a business man has the choice of a substantial range of outputs all of which yield him the same profit,[1] it is fairly certain that he will prefer one output to all the others. If he is extremely ambitious, anxious to be the "captain" of a large and important concern, interested in the prestige and power that come from the control of a large business, it is probable that up to a point he would wish to expand his business even at the cost of smaller profits. If on the other hand he does not care very much for the stress and strain that comes from the management of large enterprise; if he has wide interests outside his business, and begrudges the time given to it, he might well prefer a smaller output to a larger even at the cost of a smaller profit. In the first case we might say loosely that the supply of enterprise was

[1] This assumption might not be far from reality in many cases, if the top of the profits curve is "flat"—*i.e.*, if the marginal costs and marginal revenues are equal over a certain range of output. Recent statistical studies indicate that this situation may be quite common.

negatively elastic, and in the second case that it was positively elastic. There is an analogy here between the "backward sloping" and "forward rising" supply curves of labor, as indeed we might expect, enterprise being only a specialized form of human activity.

These considerations can be expressed graphically in the convenient form of a system of indifference curves[2] on the profits-output diagram. Thus in Figures 1 and 2 these indifference curves are shown by the dotted lines. They are likely in general to have a U-shape, indicating that at low outputs the business man would be willing to expand his business even at the cost of a certain diminution in profits, whereas at high outputs an expansion of the business is troublesome and risky, and even if higher profits result from the expansion, it may not be considered worth the trouble. The position of the minimum points of the indifference curves depends, of course, on the psychology of the business man. If he is venturesome, ambitious for business power, and lacking in outside interests—in other words, a Ford or a Carnegie—the minimum point of his indifference curves will lie far to the right, at a high level of output, though even with the most absorbed man of affairs there must surely come some point beyond which he begins to prefer leisure to activity and a quiet life to power and dominion. If, on the other hand, he is less venturesome, has many outside interests and is interested in life rather than wealth, peace rather than power—in other words, a John Woolman—the minimum point of the indifference curves will be at a low output, and they will soon slope sharply upwards.

The business man will seek to get on to the "highest" indifference curve open to him, which will be the one that touches the profits curve. Thus in Figure 1, if ABC is the profits curve the most preferred position on that curve will be E, the most preferred output will be OF and the preferred level of profits will be FE. It will readily be seen that if the indifference curves have a positive slope, E will be to the left of B; i.e., if the "supply of enterprise" is positively elastic, the enterprise will produce at a smaller output than that at which the profits are greatest—OF rather than OD. This is what we should expect: if the earning of profits is troublesome and risky, we should expect the business man to stop short of the point at which profits are a maximum, for the trouble and risk of earning the extra profits are not worth the gain. If on the other hand, as in Figure 2, the indifference curves have a negative slope in the relevant region, indicating a "captain of industry" psychology, the preferred position, E, is to the right of B, indicating that where the management of enterprise is a positive delight, the output is likely to be greater than that at which maximum profits are earned, for the pleasures of power are worth some pecuniary loss.

The case in which profits are maximized now appears as a special case in which the indifference curves are horizontal, i.e., in which the supply of enterprise is perfectly elastic. The extent to which this quite unwarranted assumption underlies the mass of economic analysis, and the extent to which it has led to false conclusions, particularly in the field of the theory of taxation

[2] I am indebted to my colleague, Professor Gerhardt Tintner, for this construction.

and employment, is insufficiently recognized. The problem of the incidence of a profits tax is but one among many. It is clear from the above construction that a profits tax will affect output unless the supply of enterprise is perfectly elastic. The direction of the effect, however, depends on the sign of the "elasticity of supply" of enterprise.

In Figure 1, where the indifference curves are positively sloped, a tax results in a decline in output. Even a proportionate tax will cause output to decline from OF to OK, J being the point where the net profit curve AJB'C is touched by an indifference curve. A progressive tax will cause an even greater decline in output to OH, G being the point where the net profit curve AGB'C is touched by an indifference curve. The effect of a progressive tax is to "flatten" the net profits curve, as the deduction is proportionally greater at higher profits. It is necessary to move back along it further, therefore, before the point of tangency is reached.

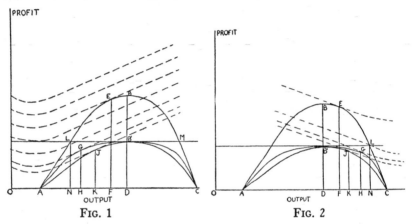

FIG. 1   FIG. 2

These results, of course, assume that the indifference curves have approximately the same slope within the significant range. If there is a pure 100 per cent excess profits tax—*i.e.*, if all profits above NL are taxed away—the net profits curve will be ALMC, and the point of equilibrium will be L, ON being the equilibrium output. All these conclusions hold in Figure 2, except that the movement is now the other way: a proportionate tax will increase output a little (OF to OK); a progressive tax will increase it more, to OH; and a 100 per cent excess profits tax will increase it still more, to ON.

Because of these changes in output, of course, there will be changes in the price of the product and of the inputs, unless the firm is operating in perfect markets. In imperfect markets the tax will normally raise the price of the product and lower the prices of inputs if the supply of enterprise is positively elastic, and will lower the price of the product and raise the price of inputs if the supply of enterprise is negatively elastic. In the former case some of the burden of the tax will be shifted to consumers and to the factor-owners. In the latter case the tax apparently has no burden, only benefits! By the mysterious alchemy of human nature, not only is the whole burden of the tax absorbed by the business man, but he drives himself to further efforts that positively benefit the rest of us: the burden is a carrot in front of his nose rather than a load on his back.

The above analysis holds strictly, of course, as far as incidence is concerned, only to the case where the tax is placed on one enterprise alone. If the tax is universal on all enterprises the case is much more difficult to analyze. It seems reasonable to suppose, however, that if the supply of enterprise in general is positive, a profits tax will lessen the willingness of business men generally to engage in business and provide employment at any given level of profits. Just as it is dangerous to argue from the supply curve of labor of an individual to the supply curve for labor as a whole, however, so is it dangerous to draw conclusions from the analysis of a single business and apply them generally. Thus the supply curve of labor from an individual may easily have a negative elasticity; but this does not mean that the total supply curve of that kind of labor has a negative elasticity, for the elasticity of total supply depends more on new entrants to the occupation than on the work from each individual. Similarly, though the elasticity of supply of enterprise from a particular individual may be negative, this does not mean that the supply of enterprise in general would be negative, for the supply of enterprise in a competitive industry depends more on new entrants and liquidations than on changes in the output of individual firms.

It is of the greatest importance from the point of view of public policy to know something about the sign of the elasticity of supply of enterprise. I am aware of no empirical work on this problem; indeed, there seems to be little awareness that it even exists. One further consideration may be adduced, however, which indicates that the positive elasticity of supply (Fig. 1) is by far the most likely case. This is the "principle of increasing risk" pointed out by Mr. Kalecki.[3] If a firm expands its scale of operations with borrowed capital, the greater the proportion of borrowed capital to its own equity the greater the risk of loss of equity. Thus if a firm with $100,000 of its own capital and $100,000 of borrowed capital suffers a loss of 5 per cent on the total, this amounts to 10 per cent of the firm's own capital. A firm on the other hand with $100,000 of its own and $900,000 of borrowed capital that suffered a 5 per cent loss on the total would lose 50 per cent of its capital.

An expansion of output with exactly the same actuarial value in terms of expected profit will, therefore, look much more attractive at small outputs than at large. In other words, the larger the output, the greater must be the expectation of profit in order to induce further expansion. This risk factor, therefore, unless the business man has a complete gambler's temperament and positively prefers risk, is likely to give the indifference curves of our diagrams a positive slope. It would follow that the deleterious effects of profit taxation are more likely than the beneficial, if the tax is proportioned in some way to the amount of the profits.

A further conclusion may be drawn from the above analysis: that the least objectionable form of profits tax is probably the straight "franchise" where the

[3] M. Kalecki, *Essays in The Theory of Economic Fluctuations* (London, 1939).

amount of the tax is independent of the amount of profit earned. The effect
of such a tax would be to lower the whole profits curve by a fixed amount,
the *slope* of the curve remaining the same at each point. If the slopes of
the indifference curves at each output are the same, there will be no change
in the most preferred output under such a tax, no matter what the slope of the
indifference curves. Thus in Figure 3, ABC is the profits curve before the
tax, DEF the net profits curve after a flat tax is deducted. The preferred
output, ON, is the same in both cases, provided that the slope of the
indifference curves is the same at E as at B. The possibility of a flat-rate

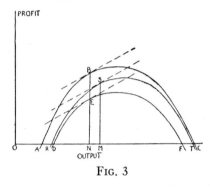

FIG. 3

tax coupled with a subsidy, or rebate
from taxation varying with output, or
some other measure of scale of operations (*e.g.*, total sales revenue),
should not be left out of account.
Such a tax system would have an
output-increasing effect even under a
positive elastic supply of enterprise.
Thus under such a system the net
profits curve (Fig. 3) might be RST,
and the preferred output would rise
from ON to OM. In a day when unemployment (*i.e.*, an inadequate

amount of enterprise) is likely to be the most pressing problem of the future,
these considerations, abstract as they are, may be worth the attention of the
policy maker.

THE CONSUMPTION CONCEPT IN ECONOMIC THEORY

American Economic Review, 35, 2 (May 1945): 1-14.

THE CONSUMPTION CONCEPT IN ECONOMIC THEORY

Ever since Adam Smith's celebrated dictum that "consumption is the sole end and purpose of production,"[1] the consumption concept has played a significant role in economic theory. It gave its name to one of the four provinces of the subject, in the days when the subject had provinces. It gave a title to a Book in Marshall's principles, and constituted the apparent ground from which the marginal utility school took its theoretical flight. Under the stimulus of the emancipation of women and the development of faculties of Home Economics, Consumption Economics almost threatens to become a separate science. And finally, a concept labeled "consumption" plays a vital role in the Keynesian theory of the macroeconomic process.

One would suppose that with so long a history the meaning of the term would be moderately clear. Unfortunately this is not so. It is only a slight exaggeration to say that the classical economists, up to and including Marshall, had a fairly clear concept of consumption but no adequate theory of how consumption fitted into the whole economic process. In spite of Adam Smith, Say, and Malthus, in whose writings there is at least the germ of a theory of consumption, the influence of Ricardo switched the line of development of economic thought for over a century towards production, distribution, and exchange. Marshall, for instance, having defined consumption fairly accurately, immediately leaves the subject and devotes the rest of his Book III to a discussion of the related, but by no means identical, topic of Demand. It was not until the development of the Keynesian system that a consumption concept took its place in the theory of the whole economic process. Unfortunately, however, while the Keynesians had a fairly good *theory* of consumption, they worked with a very inadequate and confused *concept,* and to this fact must be attributed many of the quite unnecessary difficulties and confusions of Keynesian economics.

Up to the time of Marshall the meaning of the word "consumption" was fairly clear. It meant, what it literally means, the destruction of

[1] *Wealth of Nations*, Book IV, Ch. 8 (Vol. II, Cannan Ed.), p. 159.

commodities—i.e., of valuable things—in the way in which they were intended to be destroyed. Not all destruction is consumption; the destruction of a loaf of bread by digestion, or of a suit of clothes by abrasion, is presumably somewhat different in character from the destruction of a building by fire, though even in this case, taking the society as a whole, it would be reasonable to call every *insurable* destruction consumption, as being part of that destruction which is necessarily incidental to the carrying on of life. As above defined there is, of course, no particular virtue in consumption. It is, unfortunately, a necessary incident in the business of living. We cannot eat without destroying food; we cannot walk without destroying shoes; we cannot drive without destroying gasoline, tires, and cars; and so on. Were we possessed of unbreakable china, widow's cruses, waters of life, undying fires, immortal garments and inexhaustible energy we would presumably be better off, economically, though what we would do with all these riches is, of course, another question. Any discovery which renders consumption less necessary to the pursuit of living is as much an economic gain as a discovery which improves our skills of production. Production—by which we mean the exact opposite of consumption, namely, the creation of valuable things—is only necessary in order to replace the stock pile into which consumption continually gnaws.

Production and consumption are related through what I have called the "Bathtub Theorem"—not so much because bathtubs, as Archimedes discovered, and as I can testify myself, are admirable places for discovering theorems, as because the bathtub is itself a simple example of its operation. The theorem is that the rate of accumulation is equal to the rate of production minus the rate of consumption. In the economic bathtub the total stock pile of all valuable things represents the water in the tub. Production is the flow from the faucet; consumption is the flow down the drain. The rate of accumulation is clearly equal to the difference between these two flows. In this simple theorem lies the key to the understanding of much that is puzzling about economic life. It is the key, for instance, to the problem of postwar reconstruction in the devastated areas. War is the great consumer; during war destruction and consumption by far exceed production, for a large part of productive resources are diverted into tasks of destruction. At the end of a war, therefore, the world's stock pile is likely to be very much depleted, and the main task of the ensuing years is that of rebuilding the stock pile. This can only be done by widening the gap between production and consumption, or, in the case of a single country or region, by obtaining a surplus of imports over exports. The struggle of depleted countries to diminish their internal consumption and to increase their net imports was almost the whole drama of reconstruction after the first World War, and probably will be so after the second. It is a struggle that in extreme cases almost inevitably leads to inflation, which, as long as it is not anticipated, contributes materially to the restriction of internal consumption and to the finance of imports.

The Bathtub theorem likewise is the first step in the understanding of the long-run crises of capitalism—the deflationary pressures of a mature society and its intractable unemployment. This is what Mr. Robertson has so aptly called the "worm" at the heart of capitalism— the dreadful shadow of the stationary state. It is clear that accumulation cannot proceed for ever. The day must come, in the course of economic development, when income can grow but capital cannot. In the case of raw materials we reach that stage very quickly. It is all too easy to accumulate two years' supply of wheat in the warehouses, and there is practically no sense in accumulating beyond that point. Even in the case of fixed capital the productive powers of modern society are so great that it does not take us long, even after a great and destructive war, to accumulate fixed capital to the point where the advantage of accumulating more scarcely outweighs the risks. That is to say, as the stock pile accumulates the *rate* of accumulation must eventually decline, and decline to zero. There is only one way of doing this, and that is by reducing the gap between production and consumption. This can be done in two ways: either by consumption rising, or by production falling. If consumption does not rise in these circumstances, then production must fall. The mechanism by which a decline in production is achieved is through deflation, which makes enterprise unprofitable and thereby creates unemployment. In a situation where the owners of the stock pile are unwilling to increase their holdings beyond a certain rate, in the absence of an increase in consumption, employment and production must decline until the difference between production and consumption is equal to the rate of accumulation which capitalists are willing to allow. This, I take it, in a nutshell is the main Keynesian contribution to economic thought, and a very important contribution it is.

Unfortunately, however, the Keynesians have confused their own arguments and other people's minds almost beyond reason by defining consumption as "consumer's expenditure." This definition has led them into all sorts of difficulties, especially in the concepts of income, saving, and investment. Similar confusion has resulted from their definition of Investment in terms of net business expenditure. The receipt or the spending of money is in itself merely an act of exchange; i.e., an asset transfer. It results in the first instance only in a redistribution of assets among the individuals of a society, and while it may have indirect effects on income and consumption, it does not constitute either income or consumption. Thus if I buy a loaf of bread the transaction itself consists only in a redistribution of the liquid and nonliquid assets of society. I have decreased and the baker has increased liquid holdings by eleven cents, and I have increased and the baker has decreased nonliquid assets to the extent of one loaf of bread valued at eleven cents. The transaction itself is not consumption: consumption does not take place until I eat the loaf of bread, for then my assets actually decline by a value of eleven cents. Similarily the transaction is not income to the baker, for it does not add to the total value of his assets, but merely exchanges an illiquid asset for a liquid asset of the same value. The baker's act of producing income took place earlier, when he made the loaf and so added something to his assets. In like manner the receipt of a pay check is not income, but merely the exchange of one form of assets (a claim on the employer), for another form of assets (a claim on society in general). Income accrues as the claim on the employer is built up; it is not created merely at the moment when this claim is exchanged for money at the pay clerk's window.

The confusion about consumption and income is very apparent in the "savings-investment" controversy. Everyone agrees that saving means the difference between income and consumption. The difficulties arise over the definition of income and of consumption. If income is defined as the value of production then in value terms, saving, both for an individual and for society as a whole, is equal to the difference between the value of production and the value of consumption. But this is the same thing as the value of the increment of the total stock; i.e., the value-rate of accumulation, which presumably is what is meant by investment.[2] The classical definition of consumption and income leads immediately, therefore, to the identity of saving and investment, both consisting in the net growth of assets. This identity in itself, of course, is not particularly useful, as the important question is not so much the rate of accumulation as the level of production and consumption at which a given rate of accumulation is established, but it serves to dispel certain possible illusions; e.g., that an individual can consume a smaller value than he produces, or save, without this resulting in any increase in the value of the stock pile; i.e., in investment.

The relationships between money receipts and outlays, production and consumption are not difficult to clarify. Consider first an individual economic unit. Let T_0 be the total value of the assets of the individual at the beginning of the year, equal to A_0 worth of real assets and M_0 of money. Suppose that during the year the individual produces assets valued at D and consumes assets valued at C. Then the total assets at

[2] Difficulties due to changes in prices are treated later.

the end of the year $T_1 = T_0 + D-C$. That is to say, the change in total assets depends only on production and consumption, and is equal to the difference between them, and does not depend on the extent of money transfers. The change in real assets or in money will, however, depend on the amount of money transfers. Let Y be the money received and X the money expended during the year. If M_1 is the money held at the end of the year, then $M_1 = M_0 + Y - X$. Real assets held at the end of the year, $A_1 = A_0 + D - C - Y + X$.[3]

Consider now a society with two organisms, I and II. Then with the symbols having the same significance as in the previous paragraph, but identified as pertaining to organism I by the superscript $'$ and as pertaining to organism II by the superscript $''$ we have:

for organism I

$$T_1' = T_0^1 + D' - C' \tag{1a}$$
$$M_1' = M_0' + Y' - X' \tag{1b}$$
$$A_1' = A_0' + D' - C' - Y' + X' \tag{1c}$$

for organism II

$$T_1'' = T_0'' + D'' - C'' \tag{2a}$$
$$M_1'' = M_0'' + Y'' - X'' \tag{2b}$$
$$A_1'' = A_0'' + D'' - C'' - Y'' + X'' \tag{2c}$$

If the society consists of only two organisms, the receipts of one are the same thing as the outlays of the other. That is,

$$X' = Y'' \tag{3a}$$
$$X'' = Y' \tag{3b}$$

Adding equations (1a) and (2a), (1b) and (2b), (1c) and (2c), we have, if the symbols without superscripts represent the total quantity for the whole society,

$$T_1 = T_1' + T_1'' = T_0 + D - C \tag{4a}$$
$$M_1 = M_1' + M_1'' = M_0 \tag{4b}$$
$$A_1 = A_1' + A_1'' = A_0 + D - C \tag{4c}$$

---

[3] We know that
$$T_1 = A_0 + M_0 + D - C \tag{1}$$
$$\text{and} \quad M_1 = M_0 + Y - X; \tag{2}$$
from which it follows that the real assets at the end of the year, $A_1 = T_1 - M_1$; but
$$T_1 - M_1 = A_1 = A_0 + D - C - Y + X \tag{3}$$
obtained by subtracting the right-hand member of equation (2) from the right-hand member of equation (1).
If we rewrite (3) as
$$A_1 = A_0 + D - C - (Y - X), \tag{3.1}$$
it is clear that the real assets at the end of year 1 equal the money value of the real assets of the beginning of the year plus the money value of production minus the money value of consumption, *and minus the money savings,* for in order to get these money savings the savers had to give up in exchange real assets of the same money value as the savings.

Equations (4) show that if the quantity of money in the whole society is constant, as we have assumed, not only is the increase in total assets equal to the difference between production and consumption, but the increase in real assets is likewise equal to the difference between production and consumption, and does not depend directly upon the extent of monetary transfers. These propositions are clearly true no matter how many units comprise the society, as the algebraic sum of the money transfers is zero.

It is interesting to contrast these concepts of "real investment" (increase in assets) and "real saving" (difference between production and consumption) with the monetary flows concept used by the Keynesians. If we suppose that in our example organism I represents "individual consumers" and organism II represents "businesses," then X'—the money outlay of consumers—is presumably what the Keynesians call "consumption" and Y', the money receipts of consumers, in what the Keynesians call Income. The Keynesian Saving, then, is the difference between Income and Consumption, or $Y' - X'$. Investment, in the Keynesian sense, presumably means the net outlays of business, or $X'' - Y''$. Then from equations (3) it follows immediately that the Keynesian Saving equals the Keynesian Investment. It also follows that the total Income, Y', is equal to Consumption plus Investment, or $X' + X'' - Y''$. These relationships are, of course, formally valid. One wonders, however, whether it is altogether justifiable to give the name Investment and Saving quantities which have nothing directly to do with the creation of real assets, however great their indirect effect may be.

The Keynesian definition of Consumption inevitably leads to a concept of Saving which equates it with the increase in the cash balance of consumers, and a concept of Investment which equates it with the decrease in the cash balance of businesses. It is obvious that if the operations of government are left out of account, and if the quantity of money is unchanged, that these must be equal, but this equality has very little to do with the equality of "real" saving and "real" investment. Indeed it would be perfectly possible for businesses to be gaining and consumers to be losing cash—i.e., for dissaving and disinvestment to be taking place in the Keynesian sense, at the same time that real saving and real investment were strongly positive.

In fact, the whole dichotomy between "consumers" and "businesses" is not particularly relevant to the Keynesian concepts of Saving and Investment. The Keynesian Saving might better be called the net budget surplus of consumers, and the Keynesian Investment the net budget deficit of business. Now for the economy as a whole, if there is no creation or destruction of money, over any period of time the algebraic sum of the budget surpluses $(+)$ and deficits $(-)$ of all economic organisms is zero. The budget surpluses represent increases in the cash balances of the organism enjoying them, which increases must be exactly equal to the budget deficits, or the decrease in cash balances, of the other organisms. If now we divide the organisms of the economy into two arbitrary groups, if the sum of the budget surpluses of one group is positive, that of the other group must be negative and equal in amount. The equality of Savings and Investment in the Keynesian sense, therefore, applies to any arbitrary division of the economy, and has nothing particularly to do with the distinction between "consumers" and "businesses," although of course it applies to this division as well as to any other.

Similarly the Keynesian description of the mechanism by which a net desire to "save"—i.e., to accumulate money—results in a decline in Income, and a net desire to "invest"—i.e., to decumulate money— results in a rise in Income has nothing *directly* to do with "real" saving or investment, nor with the division of the economy into "consumers" and "businesses." The way the argument usually runs is as follows: suppose that businesses plan to "invest" more than consumers plan to "save." Businesses, that is to say, decumulate money by expanding their money expenditures. These money expenditures are the receipts of consumers and hence consumers find themselves, willy nilly, accumulating the money that businesses are decumulating through a rise in their investments. The realized Saving of consumers is equal to the Investment of business. If, however, consumers are obdurate in not wanting to "save"—i.e., to accumulate money—they will react to their increased receipts by increasing their expenditures. The expenditures of consumers, however, are the receipts of business, and business now finds its receipts expanding and its investment declining to the amount of consumers' "savings." If business remains obdurate in its plans it expands its expenditures still more, which expands consumers' receipts, which expands consumers expenditures, which expands business receipts, and receipts and expenditures rise until somebody gets exhausted and either consumers become willing to accept the money which business is set on disgorging or until business accepts the money that consumers are intent on disgorging, and the sum of the planned budget surpluses is equal to zero. A similar process in the reverse direction, with receipts and expenditures declining, will take place if the sum of planned budget surpluses is positive; i.e., if people as a whole are trying to accumulate money.

It is evident that this process represents something real and important in economic life. It is, in fact, only an old friend in modern dress—

namely, a description of what happens when there is a decrease or an increase in the "demand for money"—or to put it in other words, when there is an increase or a decrease in the velocity of circulation. It is also evident that the description of the process in terms of "consumers" and "businesses" in quite arbitrary, and that any two groups— e.g., American and non-American, rural and urban, smokers and non-smokers—which divide the whole economy between them would do just about as well. Hence the Keynesian terms Saving and Investment really mean very little; indeed, it is perfectly possible, and indeed common, for "consumers" to be "investing" and for "businesses" to be "saving." If the terms "budget surplus" and "budget deficit" were used not only would much confusion of terminology be avoided, but also the intimate relation of the budget deficits and surpluses of private organisms to the budget deficits and surpluses of government would become clear, and the effect of governmental receipts and expenditures on private expenditures and receipts would become clearer.

The confusion between consumption and expenditure, income and receipts, "real" saving and investment and budget surpluses and deficits has had other unfortunate consequences. It seems to have led to a neglect of the concept of consumers' capital, both in theoretical and empirical studies. In all the many investigations of consumption there is hardly one that even interests itself in the problem of consumers' stocks. The main interest of the consumption economists, that is to say, is in consumers' expenditures and receipts, and the last thing they seem to be interested in is consumption. I know of no attempt to estimate the total value of consumers' capital; yet this total value is very considerable; it must be of the same order of magnitude as industrial capital, even if it does not amount to as much. Even more important there has been little attempt to estimate *changes* in consumers' capital, or the part played by consumers' capital in the business cycle, except in the case of large single items such as automobiles. Yet it would seem that the number of shirts in the drawer and of suits in the closet is a matter of very vital concern to the textile industry. It may be even that the age distribution of consumers' capital is of great importance in interpreting and in forecasting fluctuation in consumers' demand. It should not be too difficult to direct investigators towards these problems. Indeed, it would seem to be easier on the face of things to investigate consumers' capital, which after all can be observed on the spot, than to investigate consumers' budgets, which, if my own is any criterion, contain large elements of surmise.

The other element in the economic process which has been neglected in consequence of the neglect of the real consumption concept is the *direct* effect of consumption on production occasioned by the fact that the replacement of inventories[4] is an important motivation in production itself. The usual analysis of the relationship between consumption (by which is usually meant consumers' expenditures) and production is conducted in terms of a complicated chain of events operating through incomes, expenditures, profits, interest rates, prices, expectations, disappointments, windfalls, and the rest. The complex chain of inflation and deflation unquestionably operates. The focusing of attention on the complex chain, however, has led to the neglect of a much more simple and direct connection, resting on the assumption that production is stimulated by a decline in inventories and retarded by the growth of inventories. Then consumption operates on production directly by its effect on inventories. If we suppose as a first approximation that all prices are fixed by law and are not within the control of businessmen, and that the object of the economic policy of businesses and consumers is to maintain inventories intact, then the relationship between production and consumption would be a direct and equal proportionality. If the consumption, of shirts, say, increased, consumers would find their stocks depleted and would buy shirts from the retailer. This would deplete the stocks of the retailer, who would buy from the wholesaler, who in turn finding his stocks depleted would order from the manufacturer an amount just equal to cover the consumption of consumers. Similarly it is when the consumer finds his drawers and closets full that he stops buying; the retailer then finds his shelves bulging and he stops buying; the wholesaler finds his warehouses full and he stops ordering; and production shuts down.

We can now relax the assumption that inventories are simply replaced (which excludes investment or saving) and suppose that there is net accumulation on the part of both businesses and consumers. This has exactly the same effect as consumption; i.e., from the point of view of its effect on production, the development of a willingness to hold an increased quantity of goods is equivalent to their consumption. Production, then, must equal the sum of consumption and investment; we assume the purpose of production is to increase the total stock of goods by certain amount; this desired increment is what we mean by "planned" investment. Then production must replace the stock that has been consumed and must also add to the stock by an amount equal to the investment that people wish to make. Thus if consumers decide to hold 600 million shirts instead of 500 million, and if the consumption of shirts is 2,000 million a year, production must be equal to 2,100 million if the inventories of business are not to change. Or if

---

[4] The argument applies of course not only to inventories in the narrow sense but to the total stock of all real assets.

wholesalers decide to increase their inventories by 100 million in the above case orders for shirts and therefore production will amount to 2,200 million.

If now we relax the assumption that prices are constant, the relationships between consumption, investment, production, and budgets become much more complicated, and we cannot hope to describe them in a short paper. The equations 1-4 assume that there is no change in prices from one period to the next. If there is an increase in prices, then the value of real assets can rise not only because of the increase in the physical quantity of assets, but because each unit has a higher money value than before. Let a_0, a_1, be the physical quantity of assets at times 0 and 1. Let d be the physical production, c the physical consumption—assuming that these can be measured in some homogeneous units. Then we have the "bathtub theorem,"

$$a_1 = a_0 + d - c \qquad (5)$$

If the same price p_0 prevails in both periods, we have $A_1 = p_0 a_1$, $A_0 = p_0 a_0$, $D = p_0 d$, $C = p_0 c$, and multiplying through equation (5) by p_0 we obtain immediately equation (4). If, however, there is a rise in prices to p_1 on the last moment of the period, we have $A_1 = p_1 a_1$, and equation (4c) no longer holds. That is, we seem to have a bathtub in which water generates itself spontaneously while lying in the tub! We have

$$A_1 - A_0 = p_1 a_1 - p_0 a_0 = a_1 (p_1 - p_0) + p_0 d - p_0 c \qquad (6)$$

Thus instead of investment $(A_1 - A_0)$ being equal to saving $(p_0 d - p_0 c)$, it is equal to saving plus the appreciation due to the rise in price. The only way to restore the equality of saving and investment would be to define income as including the appreciation of assets due to price changes; i.e., as $a_1 (p_1 - p_0) + p_0 d$. There is something to be said for this definition of income; it is in fact that commonly used in the business world; however, we have the uneasy feeling that a rise in income due to increased "earnings"—i.e., addition to real assets —is in some way different from a rise in the price per unit of existing assets. The difficulty is mainly a terminological one, but it may cause some confusion. Similarly the value of production or of consumption may rise either because physical production or consumption rises, or because prices or wages rise.

The relation of consumption to prices and production is a complex one when prices can change. The competitive market price, as I have shown in a previous paper,[5] is equal to the ratio of the quantity of money to the stock of the commodity, multiplied by the preferred

[5] *Economica*, May, 1944, p. 62. If P is the price, M the quantity of money held by the marketers, Q the quantity of commodity, r_m the preferred liquidity ratio; i.e. the proportion of total assets which people wish to hold in the form of money, and r_q the preferred

commodity ratio and divided by the preferred liquidity ratio. Consumption, therefore, operates on the market mainly by its effect on the stocks held. An increase in the consumption of any commodity, or of all commodities, other things remaining the same, will reduce their stocks and therefore augment prices. This rise in prices will reinforce the direct effects on production noted before, for when prices are rising it becomes more profitable to hold goods than to hold money. Hence investment, in both the real and the Keynesian sense, is likely to increase, and production is increased beyond what is necessary to replace the consumed stocks. Moreover, the general desire to get rid of money will increase money receipts and expenditures, and will also contribute further towards the rise in prices, as commodity preference (r_q) increases and liquidity preference (r_m) declines. The increase in money receipts may change consumption patterns in an upward direction, which will reduce stocks and lead to still further increases in prices, money receipts, and real consumption; so the spiral may go on until (a) the total of planned budget surpluses and deficits is zero, and (b) physical production is equal to physical consumption plus "planned" physical investment. Similarly a decline in consumption, leading to the accumulation of stocks, may lead to a deflationary spiral of prices, receipts and expenditures, and consumption and production. It is evident that the introduction of flexible prices makes the whole system much more unstable than under fixed prices.

The place of consumption in determining the long-run equilibrium of prices is easy to determine in the case of a single commodity, but is much more difficult in the case of the system as a whole. In the case of a single commodity such as wheat the price can be regarded as the regulator of the "bathtub." If c is the long-run rate of consumption we can assume a long-run demand curve, $c = C(p)$, and if d is the long-run rate of production we can assume a long-run supply curve, $d = D(p)$, where p is the average long-run price. Then if there is no long-run increase in stock (investment), we have $c = d$ in equilibrium, and from these three equations the price can be determined. Or, if there is a long-run rate of investment, e, then $c + e = d$ and the problem is still soluble.

In applying this concept to the system as a whole, however, we run

commodity ratio, or the proportion of total assets which people wish to hold in the form of commodity, and if T is the total value of assets, then:

$$r_m = \frac{M}{T}, \quad r_q = \frac{PQ}{T}, \text{ whence, eliminating } T, \text{ we have:}$$

$$P = \frac{Mr_q}{Qr_m}$$

into serious difficulties. Let us suppose, for instance, that there is a persistent tendency in the system for production to outrun consumption by an amount greater than the preferred rate of investment. That is to say, stocks are piling up at a rate which is greater than owners are willing to absorb. The result of this situation, as in the case of a single commodity, will be that owners will try to get rid of the unwanted stocks by selling them, causing prices to fall. In the case of a single commodity the fall in price tends to re-establish equilibrium by encouraging consumption and discouraging production .This effect only takes place, however, because the fall in price is relative to that of other commodities. If the price of wheat falls, other prices remaining the same, then production will be diverted from wheat into other things and consumption will be diverted from other things to wheat. But if the price of everything else falls, obviously the fall in the price of wheat will be useless in restoring equilibrium. A general fall in prices, while it is going on, is likely to discourage both production and consumption. But there is no reason to suppose that there is any low level of general prices, incomes, wages, etc., at which equilibrium is restored. There is no particular reason why we should consume more or produce less or invest more at a low general level of prices, incomes, wages, than at a high level. Hence while a disequilibrium in the general production, consumption and investment relationship will produce movements in the general monetary level, these movements of prices, etc., will not lead to the restoration of equilibrium. In the case of output as a whole, that is to say, the law of supply and demand breaks down. The equilibrium of supply and demand applies only to relative prices; it does not apply to general prices.

The long-run "aggregate demand curve"—i.e., the curve showing the relation between total consumption and general prices—is perfectly inelastic. That is, assuming that relative prices are unchanged, there is not the slightest reason to suppose that consumption will be greater at one general level of prices than at another. Similarly the long-run aggregate supply curve, which shows the relation between total production and general prices, is also perfectly inelastic. If now the horizontal distance between these two curves happens to be equal to the preferred rate of investment, monetary equilibrium is possible at any level of general prices, the actual level being set by the quantity of money and the demand for it; i.e., the velocity of circulation. If, however, the horizontal distance between the curves is not equal to the preferred rate of investment, no monetary equilibrium is possible at any level of prices; equilibrium can only be established by shifts in the curves themselves, towards or away from each other. This may take place temporarily through the dynamic effects of price and income changes, but these effects are not only undesirable in themselves but also offer no permanent solution.[6]

Thus the long-run situation in which the Western World is placed today is one in which there is a persistent tendency for production to be larger than consumption plus preferred investment. There is a long-run tendency to accumulate stocks beyond what investors are willing to hold; hence there is a long-run deflationary pressure, checked by wars and new inventions but always reasserting itself in time of peace. In periods when the deflationary pressure operates fully, as in the thirties, the fall in prices and money receipts and expenditures, by making enterprise unprofitable, moves the long-run aggregate supply curve to the left; unemployment also moves the aggregate demand curve to the left; but probably not as much; there are certain physical limits on the contraction of consumption; hence prices will fall and depression will deepen and unemployment grow until the relatively fast-moving supply curve catches up with the slower-moving demand curve and an equilibrium is reached at a low level of employment and output. The establishment of this equilibrium between production, consumption, and investment, however, deplorable as it is, may necessitate a perpetually falling price level! If the price level stops falling, enterprise becomes more profitable, and production may increase more than consumption, and unless the willingness to invest likewise increases a new disequilibrium will result.

It is no exaggeration to say that consumption is the most important and intractable problem of a mature capitalism. As the total stock of real assets grows, the time must come when the rate of accumulation—i.e., of investment—must decline, and eventually indeed must decline to zero. There is no continuing future for investment; its demise may be put off for a long time by new discoveries, by wars, by the opening up of new fields, but the more investment there is, the more surely does it sign its own death warrant. Hence in the development of economic life, saving—the gap between production and consumption—must likewise decline. There is no sense in a decline in production from present levels, though production like investment has its limits, and eventually technical improvements will be taken out increasingly in leisure.[7] The great problem of the modern age, therefore, is how,

---

[6] This argument assumes that the price-income level adjusts itself to the quantity of money and the liquidity preference function; i.e., that any change in the price level is the result of changes in the monetary situation. If we assume the general monetary situation fixed and then draw aggregate demand and supply curves, they will not be perfectly inelastic; with a fixed quantity of money and fixed liquidity preference, a low price level may encourage both consumption and investment.

[7] Leisure can, of course, be regarded as a form of production analogous to "services" in which production and consumption are simultaneous and therefore equal. The shift of production from goods to services and leisure is thus one method of diminishing saving.

eventually, to increase consumption to the point where full production can be maintained. Unfortunately the only respectable method of consumption on a large scale is war, and it is to this that the nations resort, apparently, when the burden of abundance becomes too great. The world now sits on the prongs of a monstrous dilemma of its own making: to expand consumption through war, or to diminish production through depression and unemployment. Unless the consumptive powers of the state can be used for raising the standard of life rather than for destruction and waste, I see no escape from this dilemma; for the price system, as I have shown, is utterly unable to solve the problem. While there may be much to be said for relative price adjustments, a general "low price policy" cannot encourage consumption sufficiently to create full employment. Whether relative price adjustments and a redistribution of income could do so is a question to which we do not know the answer; there is no reason why attempts should not be made along these lines. But there is no point in relying exclusively on such policies when their results are so much in doubt, when we have in the consumptive powers of the state a weapon powerful enough for our purposes. It is a dangerous weapon, for danger is a necessary corollary of power. But unless we become skilled in its use, I see no future whatever for a free economy or a free society, and we must resign ourselves to an ever increasing degree both of economic and political tyranny.

IN DEFENSE OF MONOPOLY

Quarterly Journal of Economics, 59 (Aug. 1945): 524-542

IN DEFENSE OF MONOPOLY

Ever since Adam Smith let off the first thunderous broadside, the attack on Monopoly has been a favorite occupation of economists. It cannot be claimed, however, that the attack has been particularly successful; indeed, it seems to have produced more smoke than shot. For coincident with the attack there has been a great growth of the very institution attacked. The forces of free trade have been completely routed, and even Great Britain, the last citadel, has fallen to the protectionists. In business, in labor, and in agriculture combinations of a more or less monopolistic nature have grown until they have become the normal state of affairs. And government, far from discouraging this movement, in most cases actively promotes it, in spite of some small libations to the competitive ideal in the shape of anti-trust acts.

This universal disregard of the advice of the economists should, perhaps, have the effect of calling its soundness into question. It is the main thesis of this paper that the drive towards monopoly is not only the result of original sin and human selfishness, but is also a desperate and rather misguided attempt to solve a problem that the economists have rarely recognized as important — the problem of deflation. I do not argue that monopoly is a desirable or necessary solution to the problem, nor that the fear of deflation is the only motive for monopoly. I maintain, however, that in the absence of a more adequate solution of the problem (which I believe to be possible through governmental fiscal and monetary policy), monopolistic organization and restriction of some kind is the only device which is available to particular groups within society to isolate themselves from the deflationary pressure characteristic of any economy in an advanced stage of capitalistic accumulation.

There are two arguments generally brought by economists against monopoly. The "classical" argument, which stems directly from Adam Smith, concerns itself mainly with the effect of monopoly on the distribution of resources between different employments and on the distribution of income between individuals. It regards the main task of economic organization as that of dividing resources among a number of competing employments. If there are costs of transfer between employments, the social product is greatest when the difference between the value of a marginal unit of resources in one employment and in another is equal to the cost of transfering the unit from the less to the more advantageous use. The case against monopoly is that it creates artificial "costs of transfer" between the rest of society and the monopolistic employment, and hence leads not only to a maldistribution of the social product — the monopolist getting too much and the rest of us too little — but also to a diminution of the product, due to the fact that resources which might be more advantageously employed in the monopolistic occupation are forced artificially to remain outside. Monopoly may be shown to be present, and harmfully present, if for artificial reasons there are workers who would prefer to work in a certain occupation, but cannot, or capitalists who would prefer to employ their capital in a certain occupation, but cannot.

It is important to stress that the resistances to these transfers must be in some sense *artificial*. There may be wide differences in the marginal return to resources in different occupations due to the real costs of occupational or geographical transfer. Such differences are not evidence of monopoly. It is only when the hindrances to the transfer of resources are created by some act of deliberate human organization, and do not involve the expenditure of real resources having alternative uses in the production of a product, that monopoly is in evidence.

With the general principles of the classical case against monopoly there can be little quarrel, once its limitations are understood. It is, of course, like almost all classical theory, "static" in the sense that it deals with the ends towards which the economy is moving, rather than with the process of movement towards those ends. Hence any practical conclusions for public policy which are drawn from the theory must be directed towards rather long-run objectives of society, and are especially subject to judgment by criteria drawn from outside the sphere of pure economics. In drawing political conclusions from the argument, certain practical difficulties also arise which are worthy of mention. There is a certain difficulty in deciding what hindrances to the movement of resources are "artificial" and what are "natural." We may feel fairly safe in identifying a tariff barrier as an artificial increase in the cost of transport between two places, and hence in condemning it as a monopolistic institution. We may feel a little more doubtful about the status of trusts, cartels, agricultural coöperatives, marketing agreements, and labor unions. We may be still more doubtful about such institutions of social life as the professional exclusiveness of medical associations, the Ph.D. obstacle race of the professors, the licensing of barbers and plumbers, high pressure advertising, and the legal protection of patents, trade-marks and brand names.

It is evident that there is a sphere of "natural" monopoly where the only possible remedy is regulation or administration by somebody responsible to the whole community. These policies have generally been applied only in the field of public utilities and transportation, but they may be capable of much wider application — for example, to the regulation of land rents or of the rent of ability. There are also important cases where a regulated monopoly is actually preferable to the situation that would emerge in the absence of regulation. The practical alternative to monopoly is usually not perfect competition, but imperfect competition is one of its many forms. Imperfect competition usually results in certain social wastes, which in theory at least could be avoided by substituting a regulated monopoly, as in house-to-house deliveries. There are also situations where the alternative to monopoly is a highly unstable oligopoly, characterized by alternative periods of destructive price-cutting and quasi-monopolistic agreement. Industries where a few sellers produce a fairly homogeneous product are likely to fall into this category: the steel and cement industries are good examples. In such industries, in the absence of some sort of concerted action, an aggressive seller will be tempted to cut prices, hoping that the others will not follow suit and that he will be able to attract a large volume of business from them. The other sellers, however, are forced sooner or later to try to recapture their market by cutting their prices also, whereupon the original price cutter may cut his prices still further.[1] This process may go on until the whole industry is unprofitable, when the temptation to come to some agreement or combination is almost irresistible. Thus it is no accident that the basing-point system, which effectively restricts price competition, is characteristic of industries where a few firms produce similar or identical products.

Another limitation on the classical case against monopoly is the danger that innovations will not be made unless the innovator is protected, either by law or by laziness, from too rapid imitation of his innovation: otherwise the profits of innovation will be immediately swallowed up by a host of imitators. This is the principle which underlies the patent and copyright laws. It follows from the theory of economic progress rather than from that of static distribution, and hence must be regarded as a limitation of the classical case against monopoly due to its static character. There are difficult theoretical problems involved in considering how much legal protection of monopoly should be given in the interests of innovation. Questions such as the length of time for which patents should be protected, or whether the protection given to trade-marks and brand names should also be of limited duration, seem to be capable as yet of no theoretical answer.

It is not, however, the main purpose of this paper to discuss the limitations on the long-run classical case against monopoly. I wish to consider a neglected phase in the motivation and origins of monopoly, and to answer a criticism of monopoly based, not on long-run, static considerations, but on short-run considerations of price policy and full employment. The neglected phase in monopoly theory is the part played by the pressure of deflation in the formation and encouragement of monopolistic organization and legislation. The unjust criticism is that monopoly causes unemployment by preventing the downward movement of the prices both of commodities and of factors of production in times when these downward movements are held to be necessary.

It has been particularly evident in the past two or three

1. It is worthy of note that under certain circumstances the unorganized labor market also may exhibit the phenomenon of oligopoly. Although it is not customary for the worker to "undercut" wages, as it is usually the buyer (employer) in this case who quotes the price of labor, yet the worker who is willing to accept a cut in wages in order to retain his job may force all competing workers to follow suit.

decades that powerful deflationary forces are at work in the capitalist world—forces which even the great budget deficits of two wars and an unprecedented flow of gold from the mines have failed to check more than temporarily. These deflationary forces underlie almost every major social and economic problem in our society, yet they have been little heeded by economists. The root cause of this deflationary pressure is the ever-increasing stock of goods, resulting from the failure of consumption to keep pace with the productive powers of a technical society. I have shown elsewhere[2] that in a purely competitive market the price of any commodity is given by the formula

$$P_a = \frac{Mr_a}{Ar_m} \tag{1}$$

where A is the total stock of the commodity in the market, M is the total quantity of money in the hands of the marketers, r_m is the "preferred liquidity ratio" — the proportion of the total value of assets which people wish to hold in the form of money, and r_a is the "preferred commodity ratio" — the proportion of their total assets which people wish to hold in the form of the commodity. This formula also holds for the general price level of storable goods, A in this case being the total quantity of goods in existence and M being the total quantity of money.

It is clear from Equation (1) that if the stock of goods (A) increases without any changes taking place in the quantity of money or in the preference ratios, r_a and r_m, prices must decline proportionally. If prices are to remain constant in the face of an increase in the total stock of goods, there must be either an increase in the quantity of money or an increase in the commodity preference ratio (i.e. an increase in the willingness to hold commodities), or a decline in the liquidity preference ratio (i.e. a decline in the willingness to hold money). It also follows that a rise in the physical stock of commodities will not cause a rise in the *value* of that stock $(P_a A)$, unless M and r_a increase, or unless r_m falls. A rise in the value of the stock, however, is what

2. Economica, May 1944, p. 55. A simple proof is as follows. Let the total value of all assets be T. The value of the stock A is $P_a A$. Then by definition,

$$r_m = \frac{M}{T} \quad \text{and} \quad r_a = \frac{P_a A}{T}$$

Eliminating T between these two equations gives us equation (1) above.

is meant by "investment," in the financial sense of the word.
Such investment is impossible unless there is an increase in the
quantity of money or a favorable change in the preference ratios.
Otherwise any increase in the physical stock of goods would be
counterbalanced by a proportionate fall in their prices, and the
"dollar value" of the total stock could not be increased by increasing its physical quantity. Thus, if a rise in the stock of wheat
from 100 to 101 million bushels led to a decline in price from one
dollar to ninety-nine cents, the total value would fall from 100
to 99.99 million dollars, and there could not be any net total
investment in wheat, even though some individuals could increase
the value of their holdings at the expense of others. If this situation is general for all goods, any net attempt to save (i.e. to increase
the total money value of assets) will simply result in a decline in
production through unemployment.

Throughout the nineteenth century the deflationary force of
the accumulation of goods was largely counterbalanced by a great
increase in the quantity of money (i.e. liquid assets), in small
part due to increased production of gold, but for the most part
due to the development of systems of banking and paper money.
Even in the nineteenth century there were serious deflationary
periods — e.g. the years after 1815, and again after 1870, and it
is noteworthy that they gave substantial stimulus to the growth
of combinations, both in business and in labor. Thus in Britain,
the post-Napoleonic deflation coincided with a great burst of
trade-union activity, as did the deflation of fifty years later in
both Britain and the United States. The rise of business combinations also is substantially a phenomenon of great deflationary
periods — so much so that in the N. R. A. the movement even
received legal sanction. In agriculture, also, the "Union" movements have been characteristic of deflationary periods — the
Grangers and the Populists of the '80's, the Farm Bureau and
Farmers Union of the 1920's and 1930's. It is, indeed, impossible
fully to appreciate the significance of unionism — using that term
in the broadest sense to cover all combinations for joint economic
action, whether of workers, businessmen, or farmers, unless we
see it against the background of deflationary forces.

The prime error of the economists in the interpretation of
unionism and protectionism has been to assume that the only
purpose of monopolistic combination is to divert a larger pro-

portion of a fixed total output to the possession of the "union." In a static society with full employment this would, of course, be true — an increase in the price of a monopolized product would presumably mean a gain for the monopolist, solely at the expense of the other sections of society. It must also be confessed that one aim of most combinations is indeed that of maintaining a position of privilege at the expense of the rest of society. Nevertheless, if this were the whole story, the universal support which is found for monopolistic combinations among all the most active sections of society could not be explained. In the field of labor most trade unionists will support the wage-maintenance policies of other unions, even to their own detriment. This is seen clearly in the "label trades," which are mainly concerned with the manufacture of wage goods. Most unionists support the Union Label, even though, according to the usual theory of monopoly, the gains of unionists in the label trades would be made, for the most part, at the expense of unionists outside these trades, through the rise in the price of the union-label product. Among businessmen there is much moral support of monopolies in general, even while lip-service is paid to "free enterprise." It is not so much part of our mores to approve monopolistic combinations in business, as it is in the field of labor; hence the "solidarity" of business is to be seen more openly in the almost universal support given to another monopolistic device — the protective tariff. Businessmen will support a tariff on someone else's product even to their own hurt, simply because they feel that protection is in some way a "good thing." Farmers, as Adam Smith pointed out, are perhaps least subject to the "wretched spirit of monopoly"; but that judgment might have to be modified substantially today, in view of the universal support in agricultural circles for restrictive legislation, for agricultural cartels, and for governmental assistance.

The support of monopoly *in principle*, and not merely as a means for feathering one's own nest, is undoubtedly an expression of an almost unconscious but very strong fear of deflation on the part of the world of practical men. Workers, businessmen, and farmers know from experience that periods of falling prices and falling money incomes are disastrous to all concerned. Hence, they have been entirely unreceptive to the blandishments of economists, who have based their arguments against monopoly .on the ground that it prevented prices from falling, and who have tried to persuade people that the remedy for falling prices was to make prices fall still faster and more furiously. In this the wisdom of the ignorant may have been sounder than the folly of the learned. It is becoming apparent that "price flexibility," far from being the golden recipe for prosperity, may lead us into disastrous or even bottomless deflation.[3] The world has never experienced a hyperdeflation, as it has experienced hyperinflation, though there was a moment in 1932 when it almost seemed possible. It is only the inflexibilities in the system, however, that prevent such a bottomless deflation: if all prices were immediately adjustable to every shift of demand or liquidity preference, if the quantity of money were likewise adjustable, as it would be under a pure banking system where bank deposits were the only liquid assets, and if there was perfect flexibility in people's ideas of what the price level "ought" to be, so that the elasticity of expectations was independent of the absolute price level, then there would be no endogenous causes operating to stop a deflation once it had begun.

It is odd that the supporters of price flexibility seldom apply their doctrines to the case of inflation. Applying the usual argument in reverse, one might say that if an excess of consumption over production (e.g. in war) leads to sharp declines in the stock of goods, then the remedy would seem to be a rise in prices. The rise in prices would choke off consumption, would prevent shortages, and would restore equilibrium. The fallacy is obvious; a rise in price of any commodity or group of commodities for which the demand is relatively inelastic will raise the money incomes of the producers of the dearer commodity. This rise in incomes causes an increase in demand for other goods, leading to a further increase in prices, and if the demand for these goods is relatively inelastic, to a further increase in incomes. So we run into the familiar "inflationary spiral." It may be, of course, that when the inflation has reached a certain point the redistribution of purchasing power which it causes will so reduce consumption that further inflation is unnecessary, and the "spiral" becomes a "circle." This point, however, may be at a very high level, and may even be at an infinite level, as in the case of "hyperinflation." It is now almost universally recognized that other methods of

3. See Hicks, Value and Capital, Chapter XX.

restricting consumption in a period of inflation — such as rationing — are greatly to be preferred to a sharp rise of prices.

It should be equally obvious that deflation works in a very similar way, and that "gluts" are likely to lead to a deflationary spiral, just as "shortages" lead to an inflationary spiral. If prices are flexible, falling prices may lead to falling incomes, which lead in turn to falling demands and a further fall in prices. Just as administrative restrictions on consumption are generally preferable to serious inflation as a means of dealing with shortages, so the administrative encouragement of consumption should be preferred to serious deflation as a means of dealing with gluts.

The "spiral" effect, whether inflationary or deflationary, depends on the assumption that the demand for the commodity whose prices are changed is relatively inelastic. Otherwise, in the case of a commodity with a relatively elastic demand a fall in price has an inflationary and a rise in price a deflationary effect on incomes and on other demands and prices. The elasticity of demand for any commodity or group of commodities depends, however, on the proportion of the total output (or income) which the commodity or group represents. The larger the proportion which the output of a given commodity or group bears to total output, the less elastic is its demand likely to be. The demand for all commodities together would be perfectly inelastic, if behavior was rational and the money supply flexible: there is no reason why a similar change in *all* prices should appreciably change consumption or purchases. To put the same matter in another way: the elasticity of demand for any commodity or group of commodities depends on the degree to which substitutes are available. The larger the group, the less likely is it to have substitutes, and the more inelastic the demand: the totality of commodities has no substitutes, and has a perfectly inelastic demand. Price changes are a cure for gluts or scarcities, then, only in the case of groups of commodities the output of which is small enough in relation to the total to permit an elastic demand. When we reflect that even a commodity such as wheat, which has fairly good substitutes in consumption and which accounts for only about one per cent or less of the total value of output, almost certainly has a relatively inelastic demand, it will be seen that a commodity or group will have to have excellent

substitutes and account for a very small proportion of total output
before its demand can be relatively elastic.

The full discussion of this problem would go far beyond the
scope of this paper; we may, however, develop the analysis a
little further in the field of labor. It should be theoretically
possible, in any given situation, to divide occupations into two
groups — those in which a fall in wages will raise employment
as a whole, and those in which a fall in wages will lower employment as a whole. The dividing line will be somewhere along the
range of elasticities of demand for labor: in those occupations in
which the demand for labor is highly elastic a fall in wages, by
bringing a large increase in employment, will raise incomes in
that group, raise the expenditures of that group and therefore
raise the incomes of other groups and increase employment elsewhere in the system. If wages are lowered, on the other hand,
in occupations where the demand for labor is inelastic, incomes
in that occupation will decline, and unemployment is likely to
increase elsewhere in the system. This increase in secondary
unemployment may more than compensate for the fall in primary
unemployment in the occupation concerned. The elasticity of
demand for labor in any particular occupation which would make
a change in wages have no net effect on total employment may
be called the "null elasticity." An occupation is "employment-
increasing" if the elasticity is greater than the null elasticity, and
is "employment-decreasing" if the elasticity is less than the null
elasticity. It is shown in the footnote below[4] that the null elasticity, on certain reasonable assumptions, is equal to the proportion which the employment outside the particular occupation
bears to total employment. Unless the particular occupation is
a large part of the economy, therefore, the null elasticity will be
only slightly less than unity. Thus, even for an occupation which
accounted for 10 per cent of total employment, the null elasticity
would be as great as 0.9. A demand for labor more inelastic than
this would put the occupation into the "employment-decreasing"
category, in which a fall in wages would have an adverse effect
on total employment.

4. Let w be the wage, q the amount of employment in a particular
occupation. Let r be the amount of employment in the rest of the system.
Then total employment, $E = q + r$. We have then, if $r = Nq$, and μ is the
elasticity of demand for labor in the particular occupation,

The same formula holds, approximately, for prices as well as wages. Thus a cut in farm prices amounts to the same thing as a cut in farm wages, and will have an employment-increasing effect only if the elasticity of demand for farm products is above its "null elasticity" — say about 0.9. This is most unlikely to be the case, from what we know of the elasticity of demand. Thus the resistance of business groups and farm groups to a cut in prices, and of labor groups to wage cuts, makes a good deal more sense, even as a matter of public policy, than economists have usually allowed, especially in view of the fact that so many demands are in fact relatively inelastic.

In fact, when people talk and write about the "evils of competition," what they are usually referring to, all unconsciously, is the process of deflation. Thus the classic description of the "higgling of the market" given by Sidney and Beatrice Webb in Industrial Democracy, on which they base their main theoretical defense of trade unionism, is nothing more nor less than a quite unrecognized description of the process of deflation, whereby the deflationary pressure operates, first on the retailer, then on the wholesaler, then on the manufacturer, then on the worker, leading to a perpetual pressure for lower money prices and lower money wages all down the line. The Webbs conceive unions — and indeed monopolies in general — as "dams" to hold back the flood of deflation, though they fail completely to recognize the essentially *monetary* nature of the phenomenon.

$$\frac{dE}{dw} = \left(\frac{dq}{dw} + \frac{dr}{dw}\right) = \left(\frac{dq}{dw} + N\frac{dq}{dw} + q\frac{dN}{dw}\right) = \frac{q}{w}\left(\mu(1+N) + w\frac{dN}{dw}\right)$$

If now $\frac{dE}{dw} = 0$, i.e. if a change in wages is to produce *no* effect on total employment, we have

$$\mu_0 = -\frac{w\frac{dN}{dw}}{1+N}$$

If we assume that employment in the rest of the system is a constant proportion K of the income in the particular occupation, so that $r = Kwq$, the formula can be further simplified, for then $\frac{dN}{dw} = \frac{d(Kw)}{dw} = K$, and we have

$$\mu_0 = -\frac{N}{1+N} = -\frac{r}{q+r}$$

μ_0 is the "null elasticity." It will be seen that it must be less than 1, but will not be much less than 1 unless the particular occupation is a large part of the system.

Why, then, is deflation so disastrous and so much dreaded by all economic groups? The unimportance of the absolute level of prices, provided that relative money values are unchanged, has been recognized from the days of Adam Smith. It has long been recognized also that the *process* of deflation or inflation inevitably distorts the relative price structure and causes grave injustices as between debtor and creditor. Less clearly understood, perhaps, has been the intimate and necessary connection between deflation and unemployment, these indeed being essentially part of the same phenomenon — the desperate attempt of a gorged economic system to slacken the rate of accumulation, in the face of a strong net desire to accumulate on the part of its members. The rate of accumulation — i.e. the rate of increase of the total stock of goods — is equal to the rate of production minus the rate of consumption. As accumulation proceeds, the time eventually comes when the *rate* of accumulation must slacken, for there is no point in mere accumulation for its own sake, no point in merely piling up stocks forever, when the only ultimate purpose of these stocks is to assist the processes of production and consumption. There are only two ways to lessen the rate of accumulation; one is to increase consumption, the other is to diminish production. The sensible solution would seem to be to increase the consumption of those goods which give rise to wholesome pleasures and a high standard of life. This solution is either too simple or too sensible for us: we prefer either to increase the consumption of materials of war or to diminish production through unemployment. The crisis of our time can be explained rather simply on the assumption that the closing of the frontier, the decline in the growth of population, and the absence of any great equipment-using inventions in the western world have brought us to the point where the rate of accumulation *must* decline substantially, but where we are apparently unwilling to accept the sensible solution (i.e. a very substantial rise in the standard of consumption) and are therefore thrust against the horns of an intolerable dilemma — war and full employment or peace and unemployment. This crisis is always threatening in a rich society with great productive powers. It was postponed during the nineteenth century, because the opening up of new lands, the growth of population, and the discovery of great capital-using inventions such as the railroad made necessary an unprecedented increase in the total stock of goods, and therefore permitted a rate of physical accumulation equal to, or even at times exceeding, the "preferred" rate of accumulation.[5]

In the presence of a strong desire to save (i.e. to increase the total value of assets) a decline in the rate of accumulation will come about mainly through deflation, unemployment, and a decline in production. The mechanism is as follows. Abstention from consumption leads to a piling up of inventories and a consequent decline in prices. The decline in prices makes production unprofitable, for profits are obtained through a *rise* in the value of assets: if prices generally are falling, the fall in the prices of assets will tend to counterbalance the increase in the quantity and quality of assets which takes place in the transformations of the productive process: hence money profits will decline, or even disappear, for profit consists in the rise in the net worth of assets. The rise in inventories and the decline in profits both cause a decline in production. The rise in inventories has a direct effect, in that "orders" usually originate in a desire to replace inventories that have been consumed, while the decline in profit, or rather in profit anticipations, will diminish the amount of "enterprise" — i.e. the profit-making, employment-giving, goods-holding activity. When prices are falling, it may be more profitable to hold assets in the form of money than in the form of goods. There is a strong temptation, therefore, for the capitalist to transfer his assets from the goods-form to the money-form. This means that he will wish to sell rather than buy; supply curves all move to the right, demand curves to the left, and the deflationary pressure is all the more increased. Since the act of giving employment is one in which a liquid asset (money) is exchanged for a non-liquid asset (the product of labor), the volume of employment depends very largely on the extent to which the administrators of capital are willing to hold it in the form of non-liquid assets. In time of deflation this willingness is bound to decline.

5. The "preferred rate of accumulation" is the sum of the rates at which the members of an economic system wish individually to increase their total "real" assets. ("Real" assets have to be measured by dollar assets divided by the price level of assets.) The actual rate of physical accumulation is determined mainly by technical opportunities, though of course political factors affect these opportunities, and the over-all monetary situation likewise affects production. Thus inflation may for a time increase, or deflation may decrease, the rate of accumulation above or below what is technically the most desirable.

Price flexibility is no answer to the problem, because it leads to further and further deflation. In terms of equation (1), an expected decline in prices leads to a decline in commodity preference (r_a) and to an increase in liquidity preference (r_m), and hence to a further decline in prices. This will go on as long as prices and supply of money are perfectly flexible: it is only when the chin of inflexible prices bumps up against the foot of inflexible money supply that the monetary Alice ceases to shrink.

The weakness of most economic analysis of the monopoly problem has been the failure to distinguish between *competition* and *deflation*. Competition, in the sense of the ability of superior processes and resources to displace inferior processes and resources, is an essential condition of economic progress, both from the point of view of the development of new techniques and from the point of view of the best allocation of existing resources. This is true whether the economy is individualistic or collectivistic: in an individualistic system the competition is more strictly "economic" — i.e. the sanctions which are employed to get resources out of the less desirable occupation consist mainly in economic disadvantages relative to other occupations. In a collectivist system the sanctions are more likely to be direct and political in nature — e.g. the "liquidation" of the Kulaks — but they still retain the essential character of "competition."

In an unregulated capitalism, however, "competition" is constantly threatening to produce "deflation" — a process which hinders economic progress and operates to prevent the fruits of "competition" from being enjoyed. The whole "protectionist" movement — using that term to cover the growth of monopoly, of industrial combinations and labor unions, of barriers to trade and of restrictionist policies of government — has two aspects, one beneficial, one malevolent. As the destroyer of competition, the protector of privilege, the preserver of the status quo against the innovator, it is, of course, almost wholly undesirable — I say "almost," because a case can be made against a too rapid rate of economic progress in terms of its social cost. But as a dyke against deflation the movement has much more justification. The movement cannot be dealt with, therefore, by mere exhortation or by pleas for a return to laissez-faire, unless a *better* method for tackling the problem of deflation can be devised.

Two illustrations may complete this part of the argument.

A deplorable feature of the economic history of the past eighty years has been the growth of protectionist commercial policies on the part of national states. The economist is apt to see this merely as a movement against competition — as indeed in part it is; a move on the part of vested interests to prevent a readjustment of the use of resources which might injure them while benefiting the whole. But were protectionism *merely* this, it would not be so universally popular. A study of the protectionist movements of the 1870's and of the 1930's indicates clearly that the greatest and most disastrous growth of protectionism (including such items as quotas and exchange control) came as a desperate attempt to isolate the national state from the deflationary floods which were engulfing the rest of the world. It is hardly an exaggeration to say that in the absence of deflation the protectionist movement in international trade would no longer be an unmanageable problem, for the strength of the opposition to Free Trade rises more from the fear of deflation than from any other source.

The second example is that of the "standard rate" of trade unions. It is one of the principal objects of Trade Union policy to establish a single wage rate for a given job over the whole competitive area, and to prevent the undercutting of this rate. It is true, as Dr. Simons points out, that this policy *may* lead to protection of special privilege and exploitation of the non-union or the less efficient worker, particularly where it is supported by the restriction of entry to a trade. But this is not the whole story. Restrictionism is not, quantitatively, an important aspect of trade union policy, though it exists and should be curbed. The standard rate, on the other hand, draws its support from workers and employers alike, because it is a bulwark against "destructive competition" — i.e. deflation.

One further argument should be noticed — one which has been used both in attacking and in defending combinations. It has been frequently observed that when price competition is restrained by combinations, it is replaced by "services" or "quality" competition, or by competitive advertising. There is something of a tendency among economists to denounce non-price competition and to praise price competition. We have already noted that price competition, when it leads to deflation, has serious social disadvantages. It remains to observe that the effect of non-price competition depends on its nature. Where the competition takes the form of quality differentials there is much to be said for it, particularly in the field of labor. The "standard rate" can frequently lead to an ever-increasing quality of workmanship, where wage competition leads to a decline in productivity. It is not perhaps altogether an accident that relatively high price and money wage levels tend to go along with high standards of life and high real wages. The observation of Malthus that the backwardness and poverty of many areas was to be explained in terms of the limitation of the market, rather than in terms of population pressure, is well worth our attention, in spite of a hundred years of neglect. To what extent, for instance, have the highly flexible and competitive labor and commodity markets of the warm-temperate and tropical regions actually hindered their development by restricting the growth of internal consumption? It is not perhaps possible to give outright answers to these important queries; but one might well hesitate before recommending to the Southern States, for instance, a continuation at all costs of their supply of cheap non-union labor. Indeed, it is probable that the flexible wage rates of the South, far from enabling that unhappy region to raise its standard of life in competition with the high-wage, high-productivity regions of the North and West, have actually entrapped it in a treadmill of low wages, competitive belt-tightening, malnutrition and low productivity.

In the commodity field the case against competition in quality or services rather than in price is perhaps stronger. The eloquence of the consumption economists against unnecessary gadgets, superficial streamlining, and unwanted services is by no means vain, though one wonders sometimes how much of it is due to a streak of misplaced puritanism. It must not be forgotten, also, that technical progress to a great extent involves the creation of a better article, rather than the production of an old article for a cheaper price. It would almost seem sometimes as if the purists of price competition would rather ride in very cheap stagecoaches than in expensive pullmans! The problem of price versus services competition is often posed as if the only thing at issue were the maintenance of the *relative* price, or purchasing power, of the article in question. This, however, is by no means the whole story. Another question is also involved: whether the increased consumption which technical progress permits should come about through a fall in prices, incomes remaining constant, or through a rise in incomes, prices remaining constant, or through some combination of the two. The case for rising incomes, as opposed to falling prices, is a strong one: a fall in prices is dangerous, in that it lowers profits while it is going on and also has a strong tendency to be cumulative. Rising money incomes, on the other hand, are almost universally favorable, both to consumption and to investment. I should not be prepared to argue, of course, that monopoly is the best way to protect society against falling prices, but it is folly to suppose that this protection is not needed.

The case for and against advertising must be judged in like terms. It may be argued with some force that advertising is an expensive, wasteful, and misleading way of expanding consumption. It should not be maintained, however, that there is no problem in the expansion of consumption, nor that the problem could be solved by putting the money spent on advertising to reducing prices. It is very probable that the fall in prices which might result if advertising were abolished would not of itself expand consumption sufficiently to prevent deflation and unemployment. Price cutting, therefore, as a general measure is no substitute for salesmanship, even from the point of view of society as a whole. Consequently, unless we have some alternative to advertising other than price cutting, the case against it largely falls to the ground. Advertising, that is to say, is but another aspect of the problem of the limited market, and the case against it is not that it performs no function, but that there may be better ways of performing the vital function than it serves.

It is not the purpose of this paper to expound in detail a general solution to the problem of deflation.[6] The lines of the solution are by now almost a commonplace among economists, for it is clear that any deflationary movement can be stopped by placing in the hands of the public, through the operation of the fiscal system, a sufficient volume of liquid assets. The main problem before us is how to translate this solution into politically respectable terms. It would almost seem as if two sets of reasons for any practical policy must be discovered — the right ones and the convincing ones. There is coming to be rather broad agreement among economists as to the necessity for a vigorous long-run anti-deflation policy. The reasons for such a policy have not, however, been translated into terms which sound reasonable to

6. I have outlined a possible solution to this problem in The Economics of Peace (New York, 1945).

the average voter or politician, and here is a real task for our middlemen of the intellect.

If we suppose, however, that a successful anti-deflation policy can be inaugurated, one of the main *economic* reasons for the monopoly and protectionist movement will have ceased to exist, and the attack on the "vested interest" or "special privilege" aspects of monopoly is likely to be much more successful. Take, for instance, the problem of free trade. The experiences of the war show that vast readjustments of resources between industries can take place relatively easily, if there is an inflationary movement going on at the same time. Hence the argument that the introduction of Free Trade will cause serious dislocations and transfers of resources falls to the ground, if only it is admitted that the introduction of Free Trade should be accompanied by an inflationary budget policy sufficient to offset the deflationary effects of tariff removal. It is only because the removal of a tariff leads to deflation that the "dislocation" argument has loomed so large. If there are other jobs to go to, the individuals displaced by the removal of a tariff have little cause for complaint; but when there are no other jobs to go to, when the removal of a tariff increases unemployment in general, as it would do in the absence of counterbalancing inflationary measures, then the case for protection remains unanswerable.

It must not be supposed, of course, that the removal of the specter of deflation would result in the collapse of the combination movement, whether in business, labor, or agriculture. The combination movement has broad sociological as well as economic roots. The associative process is important in its own right, for it is through association with others that an individual gains status. In the progress of society, moreover, the "skill of association" develops along with other skills, and the division of labor eventually produces the specialized "promoter" — the missionary, the paid secretary, the labor organizer, the lobbyist, the farm politician, the cartel promoter — whose principal task is the development of organizations, almost for organization's sake. The very fact that these promoters are successful, however, indicates that they are peddling a product which satisfies some basic human need — call it the herd instinct or what you will. Even if an anti-deflation policy removed the narrower economic functions of combinations, they would not thereby become functionless. Thus, even if it were no longer necessary for labor unions to prevent wage deflation, they would still have important tasks to perform. They give a feeling of status and security to the worker. They are an essential element in industrial government, in the day-to-day adjustment and negotiation of the complex elements involved in the labor bargain. They are in part an outgrowth of the "domestic" character of the labor contract — a contract which owes its peculiar difficulties to the fact that it shares both the psychological subtleties of the marriage contract and the economic rigorousness of the commercial contract. The very complexity of the labor contract, therefore, almost necessitates some form of collective bargaining and industrial democracy in the settlement of grievances, and it is difficult to see how this end can be accomplished without free labor unions.

The monopoly problem, therefore, resolves itself into two elements: first, how to prevent deflation, and so undermine the principal economic justification for monopoly; second, how to distinguish in practice between the legitimate social functions of economic associations and their illegitimate, exploitive functions. It is clear that mere anti-trust policy is much too crude an instrument for dealing with so complex a problem; its failure to deal with the problem of the exploitive practices of certain labor unions, for instance, is not merely due to a whim of the courts but to a basic weakness in the anti-trust law. We cannot deal with the monopoly problem on the theory that all that is necessary is to break up combinations and restore the benevolent sway of atomistic competition. The associative forces in society too strong to permit the break-up of combinations, and the rule of atomistic competition, moreover, is by no means as benevolent as the neo-Benthamites would have us believe. It is evident that the solution lies with the prohibition of restrictive practices, rather than with the prohibition of organization as such. By contrast the older anti-trust policy would seem like an attempt to solve the problem of domestic quarrels by prohibiting marriage!

The problem of what practices to prohibit and how to prohibit them is a thorny one, to which no clear theoretical answer seems to emerge at present, but towards which the practical politicians have been blindly striving. It might be better for economists to attempt to clarify the problem of regulation instead of merely making deprecatory anti-trust noises on the sidelines.

THE CONCEPT OF ECONOMIC SURPLUS

American Economic Review, 35, 5 (Dec. 1945): 851-869.

THE CONCEPT OF ECONOMIC SURPLUS

Economic surplus may be said to be present whenever a seller makes a sale for a sum greater than the least sum for which he would have been willing to make the sale, or whenever a buyer makes a purchase for a sum smaller than the greatest sum for which the buyer would have been willing to make the purchase. If I am able to sell an article for $10 which I would be willing to sell for $8.00, then $2.00 represents economic surplus. Likewise, if I am able to buy an article for $10 for which I would be willing to pay $13, then $3.00 represents the economic surplus. This concept of an economic surplus has played an important part in economic theory, whether in a simple or in an extended form. It is the basis of the Ricardian theory of economic rent and of the Marshallian theory of consumers' surplus, and is an important concept in welfare economics. It lies at the root also of the Marxian theory of surplus-value.

Economic surplus can arise only where there are differences among the various buyers or sellers of an identical article in respect of their willingness to buy and sell. What is the same thing in other words, it is a phenomenon necessarily associated with less than perfectly elastic demands and supplies. If all the sellers of a given commodity were willing to sell it at a price of $10, the supply would be perfectly elastic within the range of sellers, and no matter what the demand within this range the price would always be $10 and there would be no economic surplus for the sellers. Similarly, if all buyers were willing to buy a commodity at a price of $10, the demand would be perfectly elastic within the relevant range and, no matter what the supply, the price would always be $10 and there would be no economic surplus for the buyers. Suppose, however, that some sellers are willing to sell at $9.00, some at $10, and some at $11. If the demand is such that the $9.00-sellers can supply all that is necessary, the price will be $9.00 and there will be no economic surplus. If, however, the demand rises so that the amount which the $9.00-sellers are willing to supply is insufficient to satisfy the buyers at that price, the price must rise to $10 in order to attract the $10-sellers into the market. Then the $9.00-sellers receive an economic surplus of $1.00, for they would be willing to sell for $9.00, but in fact receive

$10. If the demand rose still further, so that the $11-sellers had to be brought into the market, the price would rise to $11, the $9.00-sellers would have an economic surplus of $2.00 and the $10-sellers of $1.00.

Similarly in the case of demand, if there are some buyers willing to buy the commodity for $11, some for $10 and some for $9.00, and if the supply is so small that at a price of $11 all that sellers will offer will be taken by the 11-dollar buyers, the price will be $11 and there will be no economic surplus on the buyers' side. If, however, the supply is larger, so that the price must be brought down to $10 in order to attract the $10-buyers, the $11-buyers will receive an economic surplus of $1.00. If the supply is still larger, so that the price falls to $9.00 in order to bring the $9.00-buyers into the market, the $11-buyers will receive $2.00 economic surplus and the $10-buyers will receive $1.00 economic surplus. Economic surplus on the sellers' side may be called "sellers' surplus" and on the buyers' side, "buyers' surplus."

The principle is illustrated in a familiar diagram in Figure 1. The "buyers' curve," $B_1 \ldots \ldots b_n$, shows what quantities buyers are just willing to buy at various prices. Thus, at a price OB_1 there are buyers just willing to buy B_1b_1; at a price ON_2, there are buyers just willing to buy an amount B_2b_2; and so on. The total amount that will be bought at the price ON_2 is, of course, $B_1b_1 + B_2b_2$, or N_2b_2, and, as the same principle applies all the way down the curve, the "buyers' curve" is also the demand curve. The demand curve is essentially the *cumulative frequency distribution* of the amounts that people are just willing to buy at various prices. Similarly the "sellers' curve," $S_1 \ldots \ldots s_n$, shows what quantities the sellers are just willing to sell at various prices. It is the cumulative frequency distribution of the amounts that people are just willing to sell at various prices.

The equilibrium price, ON, is that at which all sellers can find buyers for the amounts desired—*i.e.*, at which the quantity offered is equal to the quantity sold. Then the total buyers' surplus at the equilibrium price is measured by the area NB_1P and the total sellers' surplus by the area S_1NP. The buyers' surplus measures the difference between the total amount actually paid by the buyers ($ONPM$) and the total amount which they would have been willing to pay if perfect price discrimination could have been practiced—(*i.e.*, if each unit had been sold at the highest price that anyone was willing to pay for it)—which would be the area OB_1PM. The sellers' surplus measures the difference between what the sellers actually receive ($ONPM$) and the least sum for which the amount OM could be obtained under perfect price discrimination—*i.e.*, if each quantity were to be paid for at a rate only just sufficient to induce the seller to part with it. This is the area

OS_iPM. The sellers' curve is similar to what Marshall called the "particular expenses curve." It is identical with the supply curve only if changes in the willingness to supply due to external economies can be neglected.

This is essentially the "classical" theory of economic surplus. The Ricardian theory of rent appears as a special case: if rent is that which is paid for the "original and inexhaustible powers of the soil," then clearly rent is being paid for something that is perfectly inelastic in supply. In the case of any commodity the supply of which is perfectly inelastic at all prices, the whole payment for the commodity is economic surplus; for the commodity would be supplied even if nothing were paid for it.

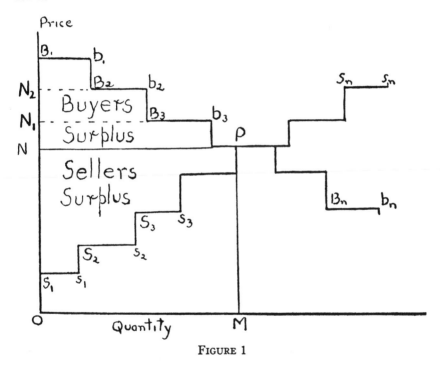

FIGURE 1

Thus in Figure 1, if the sellers' curve were MP, the whole area $ONPM$ would be sellers' surplus—*i.e.*, economic rent. The question of whether any such commodity exists, of course, is a doubtful one: certainly most of the services of land, with the possible exception of the great river-bottoms, are neither original nor inexhaustible. Even the element of *location*, which might seem at first sight to be perfectly inelastic in supply as land cannot be other than where it is, nevertheless is significant only in relation to the location of the human population, which is perfectly capable of shifting. If, however, there exists any commodity with a perfectly inelastic supply there can be no doubt that the whole payment received for it by its owners would be economic rent.

The exposition is considerably complicated, although not changed in essence, when we consider that demands or supplies may be less than perfectly elastic for two reasons: first, because *individual* buyers and sellers will buy or sell different quantities in response to different prices; and, secondly, because a change in price may affect the *number* of buyers or sellers. This is the distinction between what used to be called, rather vaguely, the "intensive" and the "extensive" margins. In the illustration of the $11, $10 and $9.00-buyers or sellers, it was assumed that the variation in quantities offered or demanded with change in price came solely from changes in the number of sellers or buyers. In fact, of course, a rise in price may not only attract new sellers, but may also encourage each individual seller to sell more; likewise a fall in price may not only attract new buyers, but may also encourage each individual buyer to buy more. This fact is not excluded by Figure 1, where the buyers and sellers curves refer to *quantities*, not only to individuals.[1] Thus the quantity B_2b_2, which would just be bought at the price ON_2, may represent an addition to the purchases of existing buyers as well as the purchases of new buyers; and the quantity S_2s_2 likewise may represent an addition to the sales of existing sellers as well as the sales of new sellers.

For a complete analysis of the problem, then, we must consider the demand curve of an individual buyer and the supply curve from an individual seller. Fortunately, much that was previously obscure in this matter has been cleared up in recent years through the indifference curve analysis. In Figure 2A we show the indifference curves, M_0I_0, M_1I_1, etc., for a single marketer (buyer or seller, depending on the circumstances), showing his preferences between money and the commodity marketed. Quantity of money is measured along the vertical, quantity of commodity along the horizontal axis. Any one indifference curve shows those combinations of money and of commodity to which the marketer is indifferent. Any point on indifference curve M_1I_1 is preferred to any point on M_0I_0: generally, any point on M_nI_n is preferred to any point on $M_{n-1}I_{n-1}$.

We suppose that the marketer has in his possession a quantity OR_0 of commodity and a quantity R_0P_0 of money. The point P_0, therefore, represents his initial position. The problem is: Given a "market"—*i.e.*, a situation in which he can buy or sell any amount of the commodity at a given price—to what point will he move? The line showing what

_____

[1] Marshall does not seem to be quite clear on this point in drawing his particular expenses curve.

FIGURE 2A

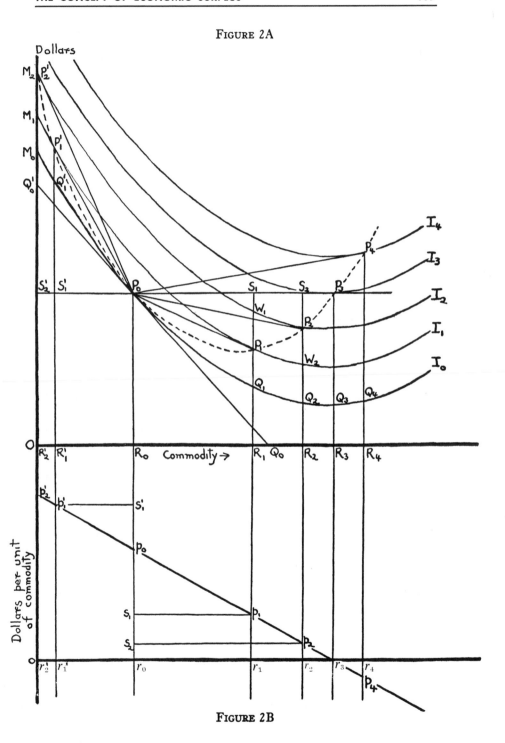

FIGURE 2B

combinations of money and commodity are open to him through exchange is his "opportunity line." At a constant price it is a straight line through the point P_0, the slope of which is equal to the market price. Thus if the price is $\dfrac{P_1S_1}{P_0S_1}$ the opportunity line will be P_0P_1. Moving to the right along an opportunity line means that the marketer is buying —i.e., giving up money for commodity. Moving to the left means selling—giving up commodity for money. The marketer will move along his opportunity line as long as the line is cutting indifference curves, for this means that he is progressing to higher and higher indifference curves—i.e., more and more preferable positions. When the opportunity line ceases to cut, but instead *touches* an indifference curve, the marketer has reached the best possible position with the given price. Thus, when P_0P_1 is the opportunity line the marketer will move along it until he reaches P_1, where the line P_0P_1 touches the indifference curve M_1I_1. He will not go beyond this point because, if he does, he will be passing to lower—i.e., less preferred—indifference curves.

If the market price is equal to the slope of the indifference curve at P_0, the marketer will neither buy nor sell. His opportunity line will be $Q'_0P_0Q_0$, but no matter in which direction he moved along it from P_0 he would move to lower indifference curves. He will, therefore, sit tight at P_0: the price $\dfrac{OQ'_0}{OQ_0}$ ($= r_0p_0$ in Figure 2B) is his "null price." If the price is lower than the null price, he will buy: if the price is higher, as represented by the opportunity lines $P_0P'_1$, $P_0P'_2$, etc., he will sell. The locus of the points of equilibrium at various prices is the dotted line $P'_2—P_0P_1P_2—P_4$. This may be called the total revenue-outlay curve. From P_0 to P_3 it is a total revenue curve, showing the total amounts of money measured from the line $P_0S_1P_3$, that the marketer will receive for the sale of various amounts of commodity, measured from the line P_0R_0. Thus the point P_1 shows that at a price $\dfrac{P_1S_1}{P_0S_1}$, the marketer will give up an amount S_1P_1 of money and will receive in exchange P_0S_1 of commodity, leaving him with R_1P_1 of money and OR_1 of commodity. From P_0 to P'_2 the line is a total outlay curve, showing what amounts of money will be received for the sale of various amounts of commodity.

The total outlay-revenue curve can easily be turned into the marketer's demand-supply curve in Figure 2B, where the horizontal axis is identical with that of Figure 2A, and the vertical axis measures the ratio Money/Commodity. For each quantity of commodity represented by r_1, r_2, etc., we calculate the price, $\dfrac{S_1P_1}{P_0S_1}$, $\dfrac{S_2P_2}{P_0S_2}$, ($= r_1p_1$, r_2p_2, etc.) and plot the line $p'_2p_0p_4$ accordingly. The segment p_0r_3 is the marketer's *demand curve:* it shows how much he will buy at each price. The segment p'_2p_0 is the marketer's *supply curve:* it shows how much he will sell at each price. The segment of the outlay-expenditure curve P_3P_4, and of the demand-supply curve r_3p_4 represents a situation (extremely unlikely to occur in a commodity market) where the price is negative—*i.e.*, where the marketer can increase *both* the amount of money he has and the amount of commodity at the same time. In this case the commodity has become a discommodity, as is shown by the positive slope of the indifference curves: at points such as P_4 an increase in the quantity of commodity is so distasteful that it must be compensated for by an increase in the quantity of money.

In Figure 2A the indifference curves have been drawn vertically parallel—*i.e.*, the whole system can be mapped out by moving one of the curves parallel to itself in a vertical direction. It follows that, for each quantity of commodity, the slopes of all the indifference curves are identical. The slope of an indifference curve is called the marginal rate of substitution of money for commodity: it is the amount of money which must be substituted for one unit of commodity if the individual is to feel no gain or loss. Thus, if the marginal rate of substitution (for short, MRS) is \$3.00 per bushel, then if a bushel is subtracted from the marketer's stock of commodity, \$3.00 must be added to his stock of money in order to leave him as well satisfied as he was before. If now the indifference curves are parallel, the MRS of all the indifference curves at any given quantity of commodity is equal to the price of the commodity. Thus at a quantity of commodity OR_1, the slopes of the indifference curves at Q_1, P_1, W_1, etc., are the same, and are also equal to the slope of the line P_0P_1—*i.e.*, to the price of the commodity—as P_0P_1 is tangent to the indifference curve at P_1. The MRS of all the indifference curves at the quantity OR_1 is therefore equal to r_1p_1 in Figure 2B. That is to say, when the indifference curves are parallel, the MRS curve corresponding to each indifference curve is the same as the demand-supply curve.[2]

---

[2] This condition of "parallel indifference curves" is essentially similar to the condition that the marginal utility of money should be constant, assumed by Marshall in his analysis of consumer's surplus. It is, however, somewhat broader than Marshall's assumption. The MRS at any point on an indifference curve is the ratio $\dfrac{\text{Marginal Utility of Commodity}}{\text{Marginal Utility of Money}}$ (see Boulding, *Economic Analysis*, p. 663). Marshall assumed that for a given quantity of commodity the marginal utility of the commodity would be independent of the amount of money, and that the marginal utility of money was likewise independent of the

FIGURE 3A

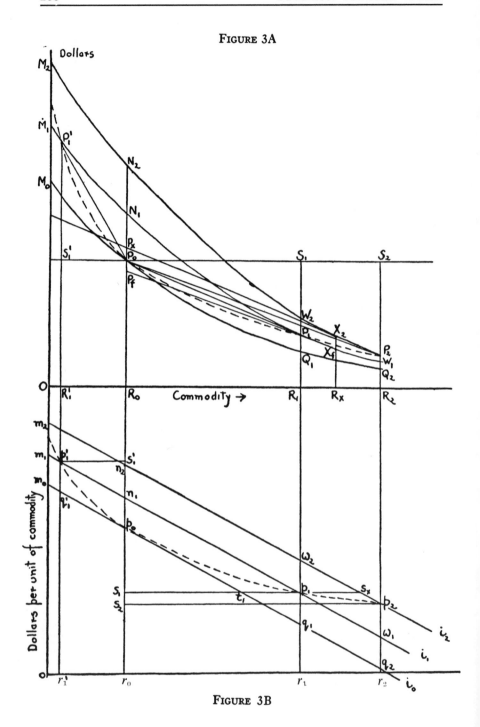

FIGURE 3B

There are several concepts of economic surplus which can be derived from this construction. Perhaps the simplest is the "buyer's surplus" and "seller's surplus," analogous to the Marshallian "consumer's surplus." The buyer's surplus is the difference between what the buyer pays for a given quantity of the commodity under the conditions of a uniform price, and what he would have paid under the least favorable conditions of differential pricing. Thus in Figure 2A the curve P_0I_0 shows the path the marketer would follow under perfect differential pricing: at a price just a little less than r_0p_0 he will buy one unit; at a slightly smaller price he will buy another unit; and so on down the curve $P_0Q_1 \ldots \ldots I_0$. Under perfect differential pricing, therefore, he will pay S_1Q_1 for a quantity R_0R_1; under uniform pricing he would only pay S_1P_1. The buyer's surplus, therefore, is P_1Q_1. Similarly, if the marketer buys an amount R_0R_2 at a uniform price r_2p_2, the buyer's surplus is P_2Q_2. It can easily be shown that the buyer's surplus is also equal to the triangular area under the demand curve. Thus, at a quantity R_0R_1 ($= r_0r_1$) the total amount which the marketer would have to pay under perfect differential pricing is the area $r_0p_0p_1r_1$ in Figure 2B. This is equal to the line S_1Q_1 in Figure 2A. The total amount paid under uniform pricing is the area $r_0s_1p_1r_1$ in Figure 2B ($= S_1P_1$ in Figure 2A). The buyer's surplus in Figure 2B, therefore, is $r_0p_0p_1r_1 — r_0s_1p_1r_1 =$ area $s_1p_0p_1$.

An exactly analogous concept of "seller's surplus" can be derived from the supply curve $p_0p'_2$ in Figure 2B, and the corresponding part of Figure 2A. Thus the marketer will sell an amount $P_0S'_1$ for an amount $S'_1P'_1$ under uniform pricing. Under perfect differential pricing he can be made to sell this amount for only $S'_1Q'_1$. The seller's surplus —the difference between these two amounts—is $P'_1Q'_1$. It can easily be shown that this is also equal to the area $s'_1p_0p'_1$ in Figure 2B.

The next problem is to remove the limitation of parallel indifference curves. Figures 3A and 3B show a situation in which, for each quantity of commodity, the MRS increases as the quantity of money increases: as we move upward along any vertical line in Figure 3A we cut indifference curves of successively steeper slopes. The system of indifference curves do not now reduce to a single MRS curve, but in-

amount of money. This last assumption could only be even approximately true over small ranges. On these assumptions, of course, the MRS would likewise be independent of the quantity of money for each quantity of commodity. The MRS may also be constant, however, if both the marginal utility of commodity and the marginal utility of money change in the same proportion as the quantity of money changes. Thus as we proceed upward along any vertical line in Figure 2A, the marginal utility of money is likely to fall, as the quantity of money increases, following the familiar law of diminishing marginal utility. It is possible that the marginal utility of the commodity will also fall as the quantity of money increases, even though the quantity of commodity is held constant. This will happen if the commodity is "competitive" with money.

stead each indifference curve has its own MRS curve: in place of the single MRS curve of Figure 2B we now have a system of such curves as in Figure 3B: m_0i_0, m_1i_1, etc., corresponding to the indifference curves M_0, M_1, etc., of Figure 3A. Then at a price equal to the slope of the opportunity line P_0P_1 in Figure 3A ($= r_1p_1$ in Figure 3B) the amount bought will be R_0R_1, P_1 being the point of tangency of P_0P_1 with the indifference curve. If in Figure 3B a perpendicular from r_1 cuts the MRS curve m_1i_1 in p_1, r_1p_1 is the price at which the amount r_0r_1 will be bought — being equal to the slope of the indifference curve at P_1. Similarly r_2p_2, p_2 being on the MRS curve m_2i_2, is the slope of the indifference curve at P_2, and is the price at which r_0r_2 will be bought. The dotted line $p_0p_1p_2$ is, therefore, the demand curve, which is not now identical with any one of the MRS curves, but has a flatter slope. Similarly, $p_0p'_1$ is the supply curve, derived from the outlay curve $P_0P'_1$. The supply curve in this case has a steeper slope than the MRS curves. It is easy to show that if the slopes of the indifference curves at a given quantity of commodity *fall* with increasing quantity of money, the MRS m_1i_1 will lie below m_0i_0, m_2i_2 will lie below m_1i_1, and so on. In this case the demand curve will have a steeper slope than the MRS curves and the supply curve a flatter slope.

The buyer's surplus does not, in this more general case, equal the triangular area under the demand curve. Thus, in Figure 3A the buyer's surplus at the quantity R_0R_1 is P_1Q_1 ($S_1Q_1 - S_1P_1$). Corresponding to S_1Q_1 in Figure 3A, we have the area $p_0q_1r_1r_0$ under the MRS curve m_0i_0: corresponding to S_1P_1, we have—as before—the rectangle $r_0s_1p_1r_1$. The buyer's surplus, then, is equal to $r_0p_0q_1r_1 - r_0s_1p_1r_1$ which is equal to the triangle $s_1p_0t_1$ minus the triangle $t_1p_1q_1$. This is clearly less than the "demand triangle" $s_1p_0p_1$, which in this case has no meaning whatever. Similarly in the case of supply: the seller's surplus, at a quantity $R_0R'_1$, is equal to the quadrilateral area $s'_1p'_1q'_1p_0$. This is *greater* than the "seller's triangle" $p_0p'_1s'_1$. If the MRS became smaller as the quantity of money increased, the relations would be reversed: the buyer's surplus would be larger than the buyer's triangle, the seller's surplus would be smaller than the seller's triangle.

There is another important concept which is associated with the idea of economic surplus. This is the concept of a "compensating payment": *i.e.*, of the sum of money which would be sufficient to compensate a marketer for a given change in the price of the commodity. Thus, in Figure 3, suppose that there is a rise in price from r_2p_2 to r_1p_1. The opportunity line shifts from P_0P_2 to P_0P_1: the buyer shifts from the position P_2 to the position P_1. P_1 is on a lower indifference curve than P_2—*i.e.*, the buyer is worse off because of the shift in price. The question is, What sum of money, given to the buyer, would just compensate him for the rise in price—*i.e.*, would enable him to get back again to the indifference curve M_2? This is the sum P_0P_x, where P_xX_2 is drawn parallel to P_0P_1 to touch the indifference curve M_2 in X_2. If he had a sum R_0P_x to start with, and if the price were r_1p_1, the opportunity line would be P_xX_2, as the slope of this line is equal to that of P_0P_1: with this sum of money and at this price he will proceed to X_2, where he is just as well off as he was at P_2, X_2 and P_2 being on the same indifference curve. The amount he would buy under these circumstances is in between the amounts he would buy at P_1 and at P_2.

If the indifference curves are parallel it can easily be shown that the compensating payment is equal to the change in the buyer's surplus due to a shift in price: under this circumstance X_2 coincides with W_2, as the slope of the indifference curve at W_2 is equal to the slope at P_1. The change in buyer's surplus is $P_2Q_2-P_1Q_1 = W_2P_1=P_0P_x$. If the *MRS* increases with increases in money, as in Figure 3A, the compensating payment is larger than the change in the buyer's surplus.[3] It can be shown that, in terms of Figure 3B, the compensating payment for a change from p_2 to p_1 is the area $s_1s_2p_2s_x$: the change in the buyer's surplus is the area of the complex polygon $s_1s_2p_2q_2q_1p_1$. It should be observed that the compensating payment in the case of a fall in price from r_1p_1 to r_2p_2—*i.e.*, the tax which a buyer would have to pay in order to bring him to the indifference curve I_1 when the price is r_2p_2—is less (in Figure 3A) than the compensating payment in the case of a rise in price. If P_tX_t is drawn parallel to P_0P_2 to touch M_1W_1 in X_t, P_0P_t is the tax which will just balance the gain to the buyer resulting from a fall in price from r_1p_1 to r_2p_2. This is equal to the area $s_1s_2s_tp_1$ in Figure 3B. If the indifference curves are parallel, of course, the compensating payment is the same whether the movement of price is a rise or a fall.

Consider now what the payment must be to compensate the marketer for the entire loss of the market—*i.e.*, for the prohibition of buying or selling. In that case he will not be able to move from the position P_0. If the original price was r_2p_2, the payment which would be necessary to compensate for the loss of the market would be P_0N_2. This will bring the marketer up to the indifference curve to which he could have attained had he been free to buy at the price r_2p_2. P_0N_2 is equal to the

[3] For a fuller discussion of the "Compensating Payment" concepts see the following:

J. R. Hicks, *Value and Capital* (Oxford, 1939), pp. 38-41; and "The Rehabilitation of Consumer's Surplus," *Rev. Econ. Stud.*, Vol. 8 (Feb., 1941).

A. Henderson, "Consumer's Surplus and the Compensating Variation," *Rev. Econ. Stud.*, Vol. 8 (Feb., 1941), p. 117.

A. Kozlik, "Note on Consumer's Surplus," *Jour. Pol. Econ.*, Vol. XLIX, No. 5 (Oct., 1941), p. 754.

area $p_2s_2n_2$ in Figure 3B. It will be observed that this area is larger than the "demand triangle" $p_2s_2p_0$. In the case of a seller, if the price had originally been $r'_1p'_1$, the sum needed to compensate the seller for the loss of the market is P_0N_1, equal to the area $p'_1s'_1n_1$ in Figure 3B. This area is smaller than the "supply triangle," $p_0p'_1s'_1$.

We can apply this analysis to the consideration of the "gain from trade"—*i.e.*, the total payment which would be necessary to compen-

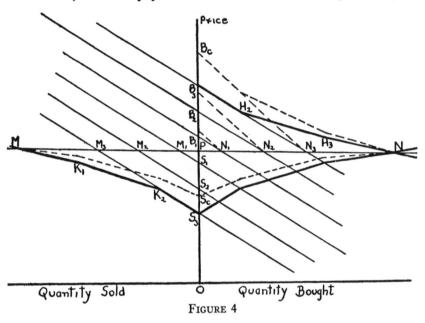

FIGURE 4

sate all the marketers for the loss of a market. In Figure 4, a group of individual demand-supply curves is shown, cutting the price axis in S_3, S_2—B_2, B_3. The market demand curve is obtained from these demand-supply curves by summing the total quantity bought at each price—*i.e.*, by adding horizontally that part of the curves to the right of the price axis: it is the curve $B_3H_2H_3N$. Similarly, the market supply curve, $S_3K_2K_1M$, is obtained by adding horizontally those parts of the demand-supply curves which lie to the left of the price axis. The market price is OP, where $PN = PM$—*i.e.*, the total quantity demanded is equal to the total quantity offered. If now the indifference curves of the marketers are parallel, so that the "demand triangle" measures the compensating payment for each buyer, the total compensating payment to buyers is the area $PN_1B_1 + PN_2B_2 + PN_3B_3$, which is equal to the area PNB_3. Similarly, the total payment which would compensate sellers for the loss of the market is the area PS_3M. If now we draw S_3N the mirror image of S_3M, we get the familiar supply and demand figure, and the total compensating payment is the area S_3NB_3.

It is not difficult to introduce an adjustment to take care of the case where the marketers' indifference curves are not parallel. The curve B_cN is obtained by summing horizontally the MRS curves of each buyer passing through N_1, N_2, N_3, (shown as dotted lines in Figure 4). B_cN is an aggregate MRS curve for the buyers: the total compensating payment is, therefore, the area PB_cN. Similarly, MS_c is the aggregate MRS curve for the sellers: the total compensating payment to sellers is PS_cM. If NS_c is the mirror image of MS_c, the total payment which would compensate both buyers and sellers for the loss of the market is the area B_cNS_c. Unless conditions are very peculiar, the area B_cNS_c is not likely to differ very greatly from the area B_3NS_3, as the corrections lie in the same direction. While the assumption that the MRS increases with increase in the quantity of money makes the buyers' compensating payment larger, it makes the sellers' compensating payment smaller, so that the total is not much changed. If we assumed that the MRS declined with increase in the quantity of money, the effect would be to diminish the buyers', but to increase the sellers' payment.

We can apply the above analysis to the well-known theorem in the field of taxation, to prove that, if a tax is laid on a commodity, the total tax revenue is less than the "loss" to the marketers, as measured by the compensating payment. That is to say, even if all the revenue from a commodity tax were to be returned as a lump sum to the taxed marketers, the marketers would be worse off than before. This is shown in Figure 5, where BP, SP are the market demand and supply curves. If a tax equal to N_sN_b is placed on each unit of the commodity, when the market is in equilibrium buyers will pay ON_b, sellers will receive ON_s. The total tax revenue is $N_sN_b \times N_sP_s =$ the area $N_sN_bP_bP_s$. If indifference curves are parallel, the sum that would have to be paid to buyers to compensate them for the rise in price is NN_bP_bP: the corresponding sum for sellers is NPP_sN_s. The total payment required to compensate for the tax is $N_sN_bP_bPP_s$: this is greater than the total tax revenues by an amount equal to the area P_sP_bP. If now we introduce a correction for increasing MRS, PH_b and PH_s are the aggregate MRS curves for buyers and for sellers, and the total payment required to compensate for the tax is $N_sN_bH_bPH_s$. This is greater than the total tax revenues by an amount equal to the complex area of the polygon $P_sP_bH_bPH_s$. This area will not differ greatly from the area P_sP_bP.

Up to this point we have considered the concept of economic surplus only in relation to the pure market phenomenon in which there is no production or consumption, only transfers of money and commodity among the marketers. The application of the concept to long-run problems is beset with many difficulties, largely because it is impossible to treat such cases realistically without reference to uncertainty. A distinction can be made between those surpluses (or deficits) which are the results of uncertainty—*i.e.*, the result of the "disappointment"

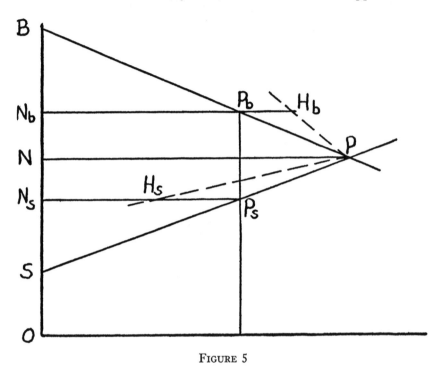

FIGURE 5

of expectations in a favorable or unfavorable direction—and those which are in some sense part of the permanent structure of economic life. This seems to be the basis for the Marshallian distinction between "true"—*i.e.*, permanent—rents and "quasi-rents." Marshall observed that a supply curve which was highly elastic in the long run might be quite inelastic in the short run. Hence for limited periods the rewards of a factor such as durable equipment might be much diminished, or even completely taken away, without affecting the output of its services. Such a reward has something of the nature of a surplus, or "rent." Because, however, the services of the factor would not be forthcoming indefinitely at low or zero rewards, Marshall called its return a "quasi-rent."

Quasi-rents, however, can exist only because the future is uncertain:

if, for instance, the potential owners of a durable good knew at the outset that the returns were going to be lower than the long-run supply price, the good would not be produced. Disappointment, therefore, is of the essence of a quasi-rent. What we know too little about, however, is the relation of a succession of disappointments to the long-run supply price itself. Long-run supply and demand curves are a useful cloak to cover up a vast complexity of inter-temporal relationships and, while they may enable us to perceive the broad shape of these complexities more clearly, they frequently hide the real dynamic structure of the system. Thus the application of the economic surplus concept to long-run demand and supply curves is beset with difficulties, and may not be very fruitful. The concept cannot be used, certainly, to justify the thesis of Marshall and Pigou regarding taxing industries of increasing supply price to subsidize industries of decreasing supply price—quite apart from the question of whether these categories are "empty boxes."

Nevertheless, as applied to a particular "industry" or sector of economic life, the concept has some meaning: in fact, several possible meanings. We may ask ourselves, "What is the greatest amount that could be extracted from this industry by price discrimination, without change in output?" Thus by price discrimination consumers could be forced to pay more for the present output, and producers could be forced to receive less. The economic surplus, in this sense, represents that theoretical maximum which the state might get out of an industry by discriminatory taxation, without affecting output. Another possible meaning of economic surplus in this case is the sum of money which would be just sufficient to compensate the individuals of society for the loss of the industry. These correspond to the two concepts already described. There is small likelihood, however, that these concepts will coincide, or that either of them can be measured by the area between the demand and supply curves.

The problem of applying the economic surplus concept to the economy as a whole is of the utmost importance, yet tantalizingly difficult. The "compensatory payment" concept here is quite meaningless: obviously no sum of money, or purchasing power, could compensate for the loss of the whole volume of production. The alternative concept, however, of the amount that might be extracted from the society without a diminution of output is of very great importance, for it represents that part of the total product which is "available"— either for redistribution, or for the extravagance of the state or for the pursuit of military power. For Marx, of course, the whole produce of society above the subsistence of the working class was "economic surplus" (i.e., surplus-value); for by the labor theory of value the subsistence of the working class is all that is necessary to call forth the total product. Marx undoubtedly went too far in this, for the process of production is not merely a mechanical transformation of acts of labor into product, but is a subtle complex affected by innumerable institutional and psychological factors. How much can be expropriated from society without destroying productive activity depends a great deal on the manner of the expropriation. Thus the economic surplus of the whole economy is not a very clear concept. There are indications that in modern industrial society it may be very large, and the experience of the war shows what a great proportion of current output can be diverted to "unproductive" uses without any serious impairment of productivity.

The indifference curve analysis used earlier can throw some light on this problem. In Figure 6 we show, for an individual, indifference curves between money and a factor of production. We will suppose, to fix our ideas, that the factor is labor: then OR_0 is the amount of labor at the person's disposal—say, 24 hours per day; R_0P_0 is the amount of money in his possession at the beginning of the day; P_0P_1 is the opportunity line at zero wages (as we have drawn the indifference curve with a positive slope at P_0, indicating that in small quantities labor is positively pleasurable, the individual will give up an amount P_0P_1 of labor even at zero wage). P_0P_2, P_0P_3, etc., are the opportunity lines at successively higher hourly wage rates: the locus of their points of tangency with the indifference curves, $P_0P_1P_2$ . . . . is the total receipts curve, measured from the line P_0P_1. From this curve, the supply curve for labor can be derived just as the supply curve was derived in Figure 2. It will be observed that the curve is re-entrant: *i.e.*, above a certain wage, represented by the slope of P_0P_3, an increase in the wage results in a decline in the amount of labor offered. This is the familiar "backward sloping" supply of labor.

Suppose now that a flat-rate income tax is laid on the individual when his wage was equal to the slope of P_0P_4. The result of the tax is simply a reduction in the effective hourly wage: the opportunity line less tax falls to, say, P_0P_3. Because the supply is negatively elastic in this region, there is actually a rise in the amount of work done because of the tax, from R_0R_4 to R_0R_3. The gross income earned is then $S_3P'_4$: the total tax collected is $P_3P'_4$. If the tax were laid in a region where the supply was positively elastic, as between P_3 and P_2, it would cause a fall in the amount of work supplied.

Some interesting conclusions can now be drawn as to the theory of progressive or regressive taxation. A progressive tax is one where the proportion of income paid in taxes rises with rise in income. The opportunity line after tax therefore bends downwards—*i.e.*, its slope becomes less and less with increasing work done. Where the tax rate increases by "brackets" of income, the line will be a series of straight lines of diminishing slope. Thus P_oT represents the opportunity line

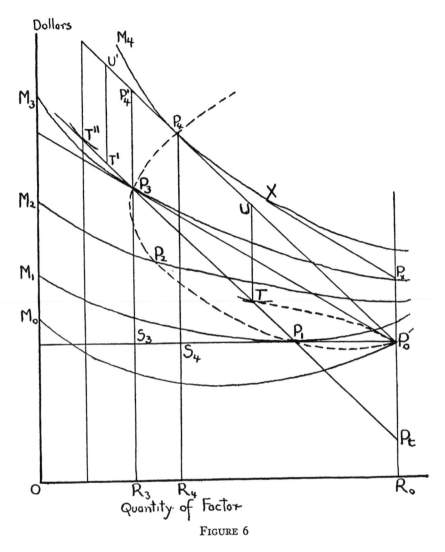

FIGURE 6

after a progressive tax is deducted from the income of P_oP_4. It touches an indifference curve at T, and has been drawn so that the total tax paid, TU, is equal to the tax paid under a flat rate tax, $P_3P'_4$. It will be seen that the effect of raising a given revenue from an individual by a progressive rather than a flat-rate tax is to lower the amount of work done, to lower net income after tax, and to make the individual relatively worse off, as may be seen by comparing the position at T with the position at P_3. Raising the same revenue by a regressive tax, on the other hand, results in an expansion of output and of income, and makes the individual relatively better off, as may be seen by comparing T' with P_3, T' being a point where a net opportunity line from P_o after a regressive tax (not shown on figure) touches an indifference curve. A regressive tax has somewhat the same effect as "overtime" pay—*i.e.*, it increases the marginal return, and so spurs the individual to greater effort. It is interesting to note that an even better way of collecting a given amount of taxes from an individual is to assess him a lump sum which is independent of his income. His net opportunity line is then $P_tTT'T''$, which touches an indifference curve at T''—the highest indifference curve attainable to the individual, whose gross income opportunity is given by the line P_oP_4 and who has to pay a tax equal to P_oP_t.

It is interesting to note that, under the assumptions of Figure 6, the compensating payment would be less than the tax paid in all cases except that of the fixed tax. Thus under the proportionate tax discussed above, $P_3P'_4$ is the amount of tax paid. If now XP_x is drawn parallel to P_oP_3, touching the indifference curve M_4 at X, P_oP_x is the "compensating payment"—*i.e.*, is the lump sum which, if given to the taxpayer, would make him just as well off as he was before the tax. P_oP_x, under the conditions of Figure 6, is less than $P_3P'_4$. It must be observed that this conclusion depends on the assumption that the MRS increases with increase in the quantity of money. The backward-sloping supply curve also can only exist on this assumption.

Some conclusions for tax policy follow from this analysis. If there is no serious unemployment problem we can assume that the objective of policy is to increase production by all possible means. Then the deleterious effect of progressive taxes on the supply of factors must be taken into consideration. A desirable situation would be one in which taxation was progressive as between individuals, but regressive for each individual. The best system—if it were administratively possible—would be one in which each individual had to pay a lump sum tax based on his "wealth"—*i.e.*, on his earning *power*—but independent of his income—*i.e.*, independent of the degree to which he put his earning power to use. To some extent the property tax is of this nature; and, although one hesitates for political reasons to advocate extending the principle of the property tax to the property that we have in our minds and bodies, real economic benefits might follow.

In the presence of an intractable unemployment problem, however, it is by no means certain that a "property tax" would be even theoretically the most desirable. In such a condition we might wish to repress the labor supply rather than encourage it, and there might then be a case for diminishing the labor force through progressive taxation, even though this might seem a counsel of despair.

The moral of this analysis would seem to be that the concept of economic surplus, while it can be defined to have a good deal of meaning, is not a sufficiently accurate analytical tool for the solution of problems of policy. As an instrument for the analysis of welfare problems it is much inferior to the more general device of indifference curves. It is a concept capable of much ambiguity and, in hands that are not highly skilled, its use can easily lead to false or misleading results. Nevertheless, it is a useful expository device and has a long and interesting history. Even if it occupies a relatively subordinate place in modern economics compared with the central position it once occupied, it is by no means to be discarded. And the student who appreciates its full significance will understand a great deal about the problems which both the classical and the modern economics seek to solve.

A NOTE ON THE THEORY
OF THE BLACK MARKET

Canadian Journal of Economics and Political Science,
13, 1 (Feb. 1947): 115-118.

A Note on the Theory of the Black Market

ONE of the most striking economic developments of the war and post-war periods has been the rise of black markets. It may be of interest, therefore, to turn the techniques of economic analysis on to this problem. The term "black market" usually refers to those transactions which take place illegally at prices higher than a legal maximum. Essentially the same phenomenon is observed when the illegal transactions take place at prices below a legal minimum (e.g., in the case of contraventions of a minimum wage law). However, as it is the former case that at present is most in the public eye, we may begin the analysis by supposing that there is a legal maximum price for some commodity which is fixed below the "normal" price, i.e. the price that would exist in a free market. A black market can only develop, of course, if the legal maximum is below the hypothetical free market price, so that at the legal price more is demanded than will be supplied. The situation is illustrated in the figure. $S'S$, $D'D$ are the normal (free market) supply and demand curves for the commodity in question. PN is the price that would obtain in a perfectly unregulated market. Now suppose that the price control authority sets a legal maximum price equal to OR. At this price only RH will be supplied, but RK will be demanded. If there is no further regulation a "shortage" will develop as stocks are being taken off the market faster than they are being replaced. Once the cushion of stocks has gone, the quantity bought will be forced into equality with the quantity forthcoming (RH) not by the restrictive action of higher prices but by some form of rationing, formal or informal. A black market will develop if some buyers and sellers can be found who are willing to buy or sell at prices higher than the legal maximum in spite of the penalties involved. We can therefore draw black market supply and demand curves, HS_b and GD_b. If we take H as the origin, HG, HK as the price and quantity axes, any point on the black market supply curve HS_b represents the excess of the black market over the legal price at which the corresponding quantity will be supplied in the black market. Similarly any point on the black market demand curve GD_b represents the quantity demanded in the black market at the corresponding excess of black market over the legal price. If we refer to O as the origin, the curve $S'HS_b$ shows the total quantity supplied in both legal and black markets at each legal price below OR and at each black market price above OR. A similar interpretation can be given of the total legal-and-black market demand curve, GD_bKD. The black market supply curve HS_b has been drawn rising from H more steeply than the free market supply curve HS. This is because there are certain costs and risks of operating in the black market in excess of what would be found in a free market: these costs must be expressed by a higher supply price for each quantity, or, what is the same thing, by having a smaller quantity supplied at each price in the black market (plus the legal market) than would be supplied at that price if the market were entirely free.

The more severe the penalties, the greater the moral obloquy, the more effective the law enforcement in regard to the black market sellers, the steeper
will be the black market supply curve, and the further will it diverge from the
free market supply curve.   In the limiting case where the penalties are so
great and so well enforced that nobody will venture into the black market at
all the black market supply curve becomes perfectly inelastic (HG).   Similarly

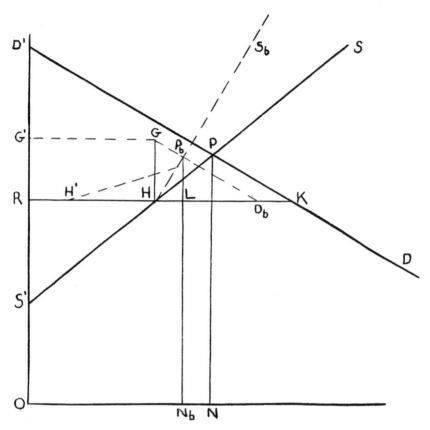

the black market demand curve, GD_b, will lie to the left of the free market
demand curve because of the penalties and moral obloquy involved in purchasing in the black market: at each price there will be a smaller quantity
demanded in the legal and black markets together than would be demanded
at that price if the market were perfectly free.   The black market price will
then be P_bN_b, where P_b is the point of intersection of the black market demand and supply curves: the quantity bought and sold in the black market
will be HL, the total quantity bought and sold in both legal and black markets
together will be RL.

Some interesting conclusions follow from this analysis.   The first is that the black market price may easily be lower than the price which would have obtained in the absence of all regulation. Even if the black market price is higher than the "free" price PN, it is very unlikely that the average price in the legal and black markets together would be higher than the free price. Only if the black market demand and supply curves are extremely inelastic will the black market price rise so high as to make the average legal-plus black market price greater than the free price. Another interesting conclusion is that the greater the penalties laid upon black market buyers the further to the left will the black market demand curve lie and the lower will be both the price and the quantity in the black market. The greater the penalties laid on sellers in the black market the further to the left and the more inelastic will the black market supply curve be, hence the higher the black market price. It follows that if our main concern is with the *price* in the black market, the less we penalize sellers and the more we penalize buyers the better: it is the housewife, not the grocer, that the law should frown upon. Penalizing either buyers or sellers, of course, diminishes the quantity sold in the black market, but penalizing the buyers has the added advantage that it lowers the price, whereas penalizing the sellers has the added disadvantage that it raises the price. In practice, of course, the political and legal difficulties of penalizing the buyers may make it necessary to concentrate the punitive effort on sellers, but other things being equal it is clearly better to penalize buyers.

In the above analysis it has been assumed that the existence of the black market has not affected the willingness to sell of those sellers who would sell in the free market at the price OR: we have assumed that these sellers constitute the "legal" sellers, selling an amount RH, and that the black market sellers are those who would not have been willing to sell except at prices above OR even in a free market. In fact, however, the existence of the black market may affect the willingness to sell of the "legal market" sellers. When this happens there is a tendency for the black market to encroach on the legal market: less and less comes forward for sale in the legal market, more and more is diverted to the black market. The result of this encroachment is that the black market supply curve begins to rise at a point further to the left—say at H'. Unless the "encroachers"—those sellers attracted into the black market out of the legal market—are only willing to transfer their supplies at prices above the existing black market price, encroachment will not raise the black market price: the new supply curve is $H'S_b$, which still intersects the black market demand curve at P_b. If however some of the encroachers are only willing to go into the black market at prices above the prevailing black market price the result may be a rise in the black market price. If on the other hand the result of the encroachment is to increase the output of the producers, under the stimulus of the higher black market price, the result may be a decline in the black market price. But, however much the black market price declines under the stimulus of encroachment, it will never fall to the legal price: hence there will always be a further stimulus to encroachment.

The above analysis throws some light on a problem which besets the economy of any communist or near-communist country where there is a "legal" black market, i.e. where there are two sections to the economy, an "official" section where prices are kept low by authority, and a "free" section where prices are allowed to find their own level.   In such a case it is evident that the temptation to "encroachment," i.e. the transfer of supplies from the low-price official market to the high-price free market—is likely to be very great, and unless it is checked by some form of producer-rationing or taxation in kind, encroachment will go on until the official economy disintegrates into a completely free market.   It is interesting to notice that the experiments of communist governments with differentiated prices for producers represent an attempt to extract producers surplus or "economic rent," very much as differentiated prices for consumers represents an attempt to extract consumers surplus.   The success of these experiments especially in the long run depends on the long-run elasticity of supply, i.e. on the immobility of the factors of production involved.   A logical consequence of price-differentiation policies therefore is an attempt to create inelastic supplies capable of discriminatory exploitation by introducing legal and institutional obstacles to mobility.

ECONOMIC ANALYSIS AND AGRICULTURAL POLICY

Canadian Journal of Economics and Political Science,
13, 3 (Aug. 1947): 436-446.

ECONOMIC ANALYSIS AND AGRICULTURAL POLICY

B Y "agricultural policy" I mean the pattern of those acts of government, especially of national governments, which specifically concern the agricultural segment of society. The discussion of agricultural policy, like that of any other social problem, involves all the social sciences, perhaps one should say all the sciences. Economic analysis, dealing as it does with a limited range of abstractions, cannot pretend to give an "answer" to any social problem, agricultural policy included. Sociological, political, legal, historical, psychological, technical considerations obviously enter into the discussion. Nevertheless it may be useful to ask what are the insights yielded by economic analysis, as a discipline of thought and as a system of related propositions, in approaching a problem of this degree of generality. The case for economics, or for any other discipline of thought, is the case for specialization. The problems involved in the study of even so relatively simple a problem as agricultural policy are beyond the wit of any single mind to explore fully. To appreciate the problems of agriculture fully one would need to be an economist, sociologist, political scientist, social psychologist, biologist, chemist, physicist, botanist, zoologist, and much more; and in these days no one man can hope to be expert in all fields. The only way in which we can even begin to encompass any problem is by specialization; but, according to what is almost the first proposition in economics, specialization is useless without exchange. The aim of this paper is a little intellectual trade, a small offering of an economist to other disciplines, in the hope perhaps of some enlightenment in return.

I am not unaware of a doubt in some minds as to whether economic analysis exists at all, whether there is anything by this name which can properly be called a "discipline," in view of the notorious failure of economists to agree among themselves. This doubt I shall endeavour to assuage in the course of the paper, but it may be appropriate to outline at the start what seem to be the subject matter and special skills of the economist. The subject matter of economics consists of economic quantities and their relationships. Within the universe of quantity, that great continent of knowledge which responds to the name of More-or-Less and of which the capital city is How-Much, there are a good many kingdoms—chemistry, physiology, geography, and many more. Of these economics is one. It is true that, as in the human world, there are many quantities whose exact citizenship is not easily determined and which may even have dual or multiple citizenship. Nevertheless quantities sort themselves roughly into groups which form the subject matter of the separate sciences, and just as the height of Mount Everest is a geographical quantity, a blood count is a physiological quantity, and the number of atoms in a given molecule a chemical quantity, so prices, wages, incomes, interest rates, inputs, outputs, productions, and consumptions are economic quantities, and economic analysis is mainly concerned with their definition and relationships.

As the nature of its concepts has become clearer economics has developed two main branches, which may be called "Microeconomics" and "Macroeconomics." Microeconomics deals with particular firms, particular households, particular markets, particular commodities, and particular prices. Its problems, and even to some extent its methods, are not unlike those of the astronomy of complex planetary systems; the economic system is regarded as a complex of related "economic organisms" (firms, households, governments) each of which has certain "laws of motion" or principles of reaction of its own, and each of which is determined in its own course by the courses of all the other organisms to which it is related. The general theory of microeconomics has been developed from the equations of Walras; its weakness is that much of it turns out to be purely formal and incapable of yielding useful conclusions, especially where the problem of the whole economy is concerned. Perhaps because of this there has developed another less secure but perhaps more useful attack on the problems of the whole economy which may be called "Macroeconomics." This is the part of the subject which deals with large aggregates of economic quantities, with price levels, output levels, wage levels, and the broad relationships of classes, industries, and nations. Analysis of this kind is not easy, and is subject to error because of the fact that the aggregates with which it deals are not strictly homogeneous. Hence it is bound to assume relationships between these aggregates which are too simple, and it is always in danger of overlooking happenings *within* its aggregates which are of more significance than the relationships between the aggregates. Nevertheless Macroeconomics, of which the late Lord Keynes was perhaps the greatest exponent, is both necessary and useful, for aggregates (nations, classes, groups) rather than individuals, are the objects of social policy and hence unless we can discuss the relationships of aggregates, social science will not provide adequate means for discussion of the most acute problems of the day.

Let us consider first what contribution "Microeconomics" can make to the study of agricultural policy. A great deal of microeconomic analysis is concerned with the theory of the firm, or more generally of the individual economic organism, the "atom" of choice or decision. This branch of economics is of great importance in farm management; it is not perhaps of great direct importance in policy questions except in so far as the conclusions of other parts of the analysis are based on it, though in so far as this theory throws light on the forces which determine the size of the firm it is important where farm size is an important question of agricultural policy. Thus there is a clear relationship between the scale of the farm enterprise and the perfection or imperfection of the farmers' market for output, and if the non-economic considerations of social policy seem to make a restriction of farm size desirable, the economist can point out that artificially created imperfections in either output or input markets form the basis for any attempt to effect such a restriction. On the other hand a farm size too small for efficient operation may be the result of imperfections in input or output markets which might be in some degree alleviated by state intervention (e.g., provision of credit institutions, easier land transfer on the input side, co-operative marketing organizations on the output side).

Over most of North America at least the size of the farm is not a burning question at present, and perhaps the most significant contribution of micro-economics to agricultural questions lies in the theory of particular prices and of the *function* of the price system. The price system, i.e. the whole system of *relative* prices of all commodities and all factors of production, has two functions in the economy. One is to allocate the resources (factors of production, i.e., land, labour and capital) among the various industries and occupations of the economy. The other is to allocate the product, or claims on the product ("income"), among the owners of different types of resources.

The relation of the price system to resource allocation is so familiar that it seems almost unnecessary to stress it. Nevertheless it has been so much neglected in the past by the propagandists of agricultural policy that it has become one of the main interests of the newer school of agricultural economics centring around T. R. Schultz which may perhaps still be called the "Ames School," in spite of its partial movement to Chicago. A high price for any particular commodity, high, that is, relative to other prices, will normally encourage its production; a low price will discourage its production. Hence we cannot interfere with the price system without either creating changes in the relative outputs of different commodities, or establishing alternative and more direct and dictatorial methods of production control. Recent economic history is full of the record of schemes such as Brazilian coffee, Malayan rubber, United States cotton, international sugar and wheat which have run on the rocks for lack of cognizance of the above proposition. A mere list of such experiments in price regulation would take almost the whole paper. It is perhaps as a result of these experiences that the "Ames School" is so insistent upon the close relationship between relative prices and relative production, and upon the necessity for planning price policy, if we are to have it at all, around the socially desirable distortions of the relative structure of outputs (e.g., towards protective foods) and not around the socially desirable distortions of the income structure. It is this point of view which lies behind the celebrated "Marriage of Agriculture and Nutrition" and the remarkable discovery, made, I think, by the League of Nations in 1936, that the main purpose of agriculture is not to provide agriculturalists with income but to provide everybody with food.

This trend in agricultural economics is realistic and healthy. However, it has not yet penetrated very far into the thinking of agricultural organizations and agricultural politicians, among whom "parity" is still a war-cry. It is perhaps one of the most important tasks of economists to expose the weaknesses of the "parity" doctrine, and indeed of the whole school of thought which it represents. I need not go into the argument in great detail, for it is a familiar one. The "parity" doctrine centres around the "terms of trade" of agriculture, i.e., the ratio of agricultural to industrial prices, and sets up some past ratio (in the United States that of 1909-14) as an ideal of agricultural policy. The power of this doctrine must be explained by the political scientists rather than by the economists, for it has no rational foundation; it provided, however, a pseudo-intellectual rationalization for a good many deep seated agricultural emotions.

The emotional drive behind agricultural policy has been the feeling of farmers, especially of the more well-to-do farmers, that they have not received "justice" in the distribution of the product.   There are, as we shall see, real grounds for this feeling, but it has undoubtedly had a deleterious effect on the analysis of the problem and even on the remedies proposed.   Of course, the trouble with the "parity" doctrine is that it pays no attention to relative changes in alternative costs which rapidly make any "parity" ratio obsolete.   If, for instance, productivity in agriculture is improving more rapidly than productivity in industry, the parity price would be too high; if the reverse is the case, the parity price would be too low.   Worse than this, the doctrine has led to an emphasis on the relative price structure within agriculture as it existed in the base period, a structure which rapidly becomes out of date because of the different pace of technical improvement in the production of various commodities.

Too much agricultural policy in the past has been based on an essentially false syllogism.   The major premise, with which most of us would agree, is that the Poor should be helped.   However, the minor premise and the conclusion— farmers are poor, therefore farmers should be helped—are open to searching question.   The truth is that *some* farmers are poor, and we might well conclude from this that some farmers should be helped.   But some miners and some garment workers and some retailers and some unemployed workers are poor also, while some farmers are by no means poor.   Hence, policy which is directed towards "helping farmers" on the ground that farmers are poor has no foundation in justice.   It is unjust to help poor farmers when we do not help poor retailers, and it is unjust to help rich farmers.   One cannot help suspecting that a great deal of so-called "aid to agriculture" is, in fact, a great political bluff engineered by the wealthier farmers who are, of course, the more politically active.   They obtain general support for the policy on the grounds that farmers are poor, but the assistance goes not specifically to the poor farmers but to all, indeed, in many cases it has gone to the rich farmers rather than to the poor.

Thus political support for agricultural assistance has been obtained by invoking the laudable ideal of justice, but in fact the ends of justice have been thwarted because we have tried to do justice to commodities or to occupations instead of to people.   The extent to which agricultural policy, especially in Europe, has been dominated by the idea of "doing something for Wheat" is one of the most extraordinary chapters in political pathology.   Especially is this true of the French, to whom "le blé, c'est une chose sacrée," and who have sacrificed both their agriculture and their power on the altar of this estimable condiment.   The British, after passing through a brief period of rationality after 1846, finally succumbed to the prevailing agricultural mythology after the First World War.   In fact, all European countries with the possible exception of Belgium and Denmark have turned their backs on the magnificent opportunities provided by cheap imported grain for improving the composition of the home agricultures and the nutrition of their peoples, all in the interest of something that can only be described, to misquote a phrase of Marx, as a "fetishism of commodities."

The degree to which agricultural policy has been dominated by the idea of "justice" to a depressed industry makes of peculiar importance the question why agriculture is thus depressed. Economic analysis throws a good deal of light on this historical phenomenon. The explanation rests on two propositions. The first is that as the products of agriculture are for the most part basic necessities, "means of subsistence," with very inelastic demands, an improvement in agricultural techniques results only in a limited increase in agricultural output, and manifests itself mainly in a transfer of resources, especially of labour and capital, out of agriculture into other occupations. Hence in a technically progressive society, and especially in a society in which agricultural techniques are improving, the proportion of total resources devoted to agriculture continually falls. The past two hundred years have seen a most striking demonstration of this great interpretative principle. The second proposition is that in order for resources to be transferred from one occupation to another, the relatively declining occupation must be less attractive than the relatively expanding one. No matter what form of society we have, this relative unattractiveness of a declining industry is achieved through the system of relative prices; the "terms of trade" of the declining industry, i.e. the ratio of what it gets for what it gives, must be such as to make the resources employed in it look longingly at the other side of the fence.

These two propositions are of great importance in the interpretation of economic history. It is hardly any exaggeration to say that economic progress, and especially industrial development, depends more than anything else on labour-saving improvements in agriculture, or more generally, in the "subsistence industries." The proportion of its population which a closed society can afford to have in the "luxury" trades depends clearly on the productivity of labour in food-getting: in savage societies one man can only just produce enough food for his own family, and no specialized industry, no cities or towns can exist. If one food-getter can produce enough food for two families, only half the population need be employed in food-getting, and the other half can produce the conveniences and luxuries of life. In our society we are rapidly moving towards the day when one man can produce food for perhaps twenty or even a hundred families, and we may only need to have 5 or even 1 per cent of the people in food-getting, and the other 95 or 99 per cent can be released for other things.

It is no accident, therefore, but a necessity of economic development, that all industrial expansions have been preceded by, or have gone hand in hand with, a period of agricultural improvement. The cathedrals of Europe were built by the labour liberated from agriculture by the introduction of the three-field system and the horse-collar. The so called "industrial revolution" was not created by a few rather unimportant technical changes in the textile industry; it was the direct child of the agricultural revolution based on turnips, clover, four-course rotation, and livestock improvement which developed in the first half of the eighteenth century. It is the turnip, not the spinning jenny, which is the father of industrial society.

We have therefore a strange paradox, that labour-saving techniques in agriculture are of supreme importance to society at large but are a distinct source of embarrassment to agriculture itself. The fruits of our scientific farming and our agricultural colleges are found on the tables of the masses, not in the pocketbooks of the farmers. A relatively prosperous agriculture is a sure sign of economic retrogression: witness, for instance, the movement back to the farm during the depression, or the agricultural prosperity which vulture-like fattens on the distress occasioned by a great war. Agriculture will be most prosperous in a society in which agricultural techniques are stagnant or declining, and in which industrial techniques are advancing rapidly, for after all, the greater part of the real income of the farmer consists of the product of industry.

The moral of this argument is not that we should abandon agricultural research, burn our agricultural colleges, and go back to scrabbling the ground with a stick, though a strong pursuit of "justice to agriculture" might lead us to this alarming conclusion. Rather is it that we should endeavour to assist agricultural poverty in its purpose, or rather, to find swifter and less painful ways of accomplishing this purpose. In other words, the *economic* answer to agricultural poverty is mobility: the easier the "flight out of agriculture," which is the inevitable accompaniment of agricultural progress, the less unattractive will agriculture have to be relative to industry in order to accomplish the object of the relative unattractiveness—to drive resources out of agriculture.

One thing should be said in modification of the above conclusion. As techniques improve and society gets richer the composition of agricultural output changes: some of the shift towards "luxuries" takes place within agriculture itself. The development of livestock production, meat and milk, vegetables and fruits are all signs of advancing productivity and mitigate the relative decline of the whole agricultural industry. This development is advantageous not only for agriculture but for society at large—diets become more varied, nutrition improves, health and productivity improve, and so on. An agricultural policy which is devoted to preserving a large proportion of resources in basic crops (e.g., cereals) defeats the very object of technical progress even within agriculture.

I should pause here, to avoid misunderstanding, to indicate that the problem of agricultural poverty is a much more complex one than is suggested above; it has deep sociological as well as economic roots. It should also be pointed out that agricultural poverty looked at as a world problem is a matter of too slow advance in techniques, not of too rapid progress. The mass of the agricultural poor in India, China, Eastern Europe, Africa, South America, even the Southern States, are poor not because they are exploited (i.e., not because they produce a lot and have their product taken away from them), but simply because they are miserably unproductive and produce so little. The greatest social problem of the world is how to spread the techniques of the productive tenth to the unproductive nine-tenths; only thus will the curse of the world's poverty be removed. Nevertheless it is not the sharecropper, the pauper-peasant or the ryot who instigates agricultural policy or for whom, for the most part, agricultural policy is designed. It is rather the progressive, "industrialized" relatively rich and productive farmer of the western world who observes that, rich as he is, his brother in the city is richer, and who therefore exercises his political power to obtain "aid to agriculture." It is to this type of farmer and this type of agriculture that the analysis of the preceding paragraphs applies.

The problem of the "unproductive nine-tenths" arises partly from the fact that agriculture more than any other occupation is "land using." That is to say, the total output of agriculture is limited as much, if not more, by scarcity of land as by scarcity of labour; this is much less likely to be true of industrial processes as such, except in so far as industrial output also is limited by the scarcity of its raw materials. Hence arises the "Malthusian Spectre," still a very real one for the greater part of the world's population. We need constantly to be reminded that for most of the world economics is still the "dismal science," puncturing the myth of Godwinian perfectability in which most of us still believe in this favoured spot. If only misery can check the growth of population all improvements are ultimately worse than vain, for they merely permit a larger population than before to live in misery. Nevertheless "land-saving" improvements, resulting in higher food yields per acre, may be highly significant in the historical process, in that they give populations which are close to the subsistence level a breathing spell in which perhaps the magic adjustment to an economically minded and controlled population may be achieved. We tread here at the edge of an unknown country; the economist can offer suggestions about what cake we cannot have and eat too; but we need the combined wisdom of mankind to make even an attempt at a solution. The possibility, however, that the public health officer and the agricultural improver may be great multipliers of human misery is grim enough and real enough to turn every economist into something of a Malthusian missionary. No other field of human inquiry is perhaps so important for the ultimate lifting of the curse of poverty than an examination of the obscure forces—economic, sociological, psychological, religious—which determine the movement of population. And I should emphasise once again that the economist alone cannot pass judgment. It may well be, for instance, that in our own brittle and highly urbanized society there are strong reasons for wishing to preserve a larger proportion of the population in rural areas than the naked forces of economic and technical change would permit. Agriculture produces not only food but the men to eat it and to work in the cities; this less visible and unpriced product should unquestionably enter into our social accounting and may be used to justify some form of agricultural policy. But even here let us not jump too hastily to the conclusion that a subsidized or technically unprogressive agriculture is the solution to the problem of rural life. It may well be that the social virtues of rural life are not indissolubly tied up with the practice of agriculture as an occupation, and that we shall do well to look to some divorce of rural life from agriculture, and encourage industrial decentralization rather than agricultural stagnation. Here, however, we move in a world of prejudice, fancy, oratory, and public passion, and the economist is not sorry to turn the problem over to his tougher *confrères* in sociology or politics.

The problems which we have been discussing lie close to the boundary between "micro-" and "macro-" economics. I shall conclude with a brief glance at the contributions which may be made to this discussion by "Macroeconomics" proper, i.e. by the theory of employment, price levels, inflation and deflation, business cycles, etc. Perhaps the main contribution which can be made at this level of analysis is to point out the extent to which problems which are frequently regarded as "agricultural" problems are in fact "monetary" problems, i.e., problems which concern the whole system of exchange relationships and which are common to the whole society. The cyclical fluctuations in output, prices, and incomes which make up what is rather inaccurately called the "business" cycle constitute one of the greatest problems of agriculture, as of any other segment of the economy. It is not the intention of this paper to go deeply into the causes and cures for this phenomenon; my main intention is simply to point out that solutions cannot be found within any one industry, but must be developed over the whole economy. To a very large extent the "agricultural problem" is not an agricultural problem at all, but a problem of the instability of the price-income system. In agriculture, fortunately for society at large, the cycle mainly takes the form of a price-income rather than an output-income cycle. Agricultural output is remarkably stable over the cycle: there is even some evidence of a slight movement counter to the movement of output as a whole. In the depression of the nineteen-thirties, for instance, agricultural output seems to have risen slightly at a time when industrial output was drastically curtailed. As a result of this stability in physical output there is, of course, great instability in agricultural prices. Income is the value of output, i.e., the quantity of output multiplied by its price. In both agriculture and industry income is subject to fluctuations—this is the basis of the cycle in both cases. In agriculture, however, the fluctuation of income manifests itself by stable outputs and fluctuating prices while in industry, roughly, the cycle manifests itself in stable prices and fluctuating outputs. Of the two, of course, the agricultural type of cycle is much to be preferred. The really damaging cycle is the cycle in output; it is this cycle that manifests itself in unemployment and unnecessary poverty. Price cycles are inconvenient, but as long as they do not produce cycles in output there is even something to be said for them, in moderation. Price cycles contribute powerfully to the social mobility of property and of classes, and it can be argued that they perform a most valuable social function—that of disinheriting the inefficient inheritor! If we succeed in stabilizing the monetary cycle we may discover some quite unexpected and perhaps not wholly welcome consequences. Stability, like any other good, has to be paid for, and we know far too little about its price, and far too little about the difference between stability and stagnation. Nevertheless my doubt as to whether we would really want stability if we could buy it is considerably exceeded by my pessimism about the likelihood of finding a shop where it may be bought, so that it may well be that these slightly gloomy asides are quite irrelevant to any situation in which we may find ourselves.

I do not wish to be understood as defending seven-cent corn or the *débâcle* of 1929-32. There is no excuse for deflations of this magnitude, and we now know perfectly well how to avoid them by a sufficiently courageous fiscal policy. It is obviously necessary to introduce a "governor" into the monetary system which will exert an inflationary force in periods of deflation and a deflationary force in periods of inflation. It is clear also that the only force powerful enough to act as such a governor is the budget of government. It is, in fact, the prime, but most neglected function of government to act as a governor; what we need is not a "planned," but a "governed" economy. What we must avoid, however, at all costs is an attempt to solve the problem of income fluctuations on an industry-by-industry basis; most of all, we must avoid any attempt on the part of agriculture to emulate industry and turn its income cycle into an output rather than a price cycle. Such a policy, if successful, would be utterly disastrous for society. As it is now, agriculture is the one bright spot in the output-employment cycle, largely because of the relatively competitive nature of its output markets and the difficulties of controlling (i.e., restricting) the output of its millions of small producers. We suffer in a depression because of the houses that are not built, the conveniences and luxuries of life which could be made but which are not; but we eat just about as well in depression as in boom, thanks to the blessed instability of agricultural prices and the stability of agricultural outputs. The reason why the farmer is worse off during a depression is the same as the reason why practically everybody is worse off—the decline in the output of industrial goods. It is true that the farmer's "terms of trade" (which consist of the ratio of the agricultural surplus, i.e., the food, etc. not consumed within agriculture, to the industrial surplus, i.e., the industrial products not consumed by the industrial population) are likely to worsen relatively to industry in a depression. It is evident that in a depression, when industrial output shrinks but agricultural output does not, the industrial surplus will decline relative to the agricultural surplus and the farmer's terms of trade will worsen—hence the cry for "parity." However, it should be noted in passing, that even with this worsening of the farmer's terms of trade, the movement from industry back to agriculture which is noticeable in a severe depression indicates that in terms of actual welfare the industrial population is probably worse hit by depression than the agriculturalists.

The solution to this problem lies, of course, not in the restriction of agricultural output but in the expansion of industrial output; not in the emulation by agriculture of the deplorable practices of industry, but rather in the emulation by industry of the admirable price-cycle of agriculture. Could we but turn the whole cycle into a price cycle rather than an output cycle, we would at once turn the cycle from a tragedy of waste to a comedy of inconvenience. Let me hasten to say, however, that I do not advocate such price flexibility as a solution to the problem; I regard it as politically impossible and economically unnecessary. It is far better to eliminate the income cycle altogether, though even then I suspect that we shall not have solved the problem altogether since even within a stable national income, great fluctuations in output and price in opposite directions could take place. The worst of all possible worlds, however, is to have an income cycle and have it take the form of an output cycle rather than of a price cycle. This, I fear, is the objective of a good deal of recent agricultural policy, from Mr. Wallace's plowed-under pigs to the Canadian Wheat Agreement.

The problem of the relation of the agricultural price cycle to the agricultural debt problem should perhaps be noticed, though it is a familiar one. A great many of the difficulties of agriculture in a price-depression arise not so much through the worsening of the current terms of trade of agriculture as through the effects on the balance sheets and the equity position of farm enterprises. Farmers, as a result of a long process of natural economic selection, acquire a genius for getting into debt at the wrong time. Those who have the genius for getting into debt at the right time, i.e., the entrepreneurial geniuses, tend to leave agriculture where the opportunities for unusual entrepreneurial ability are not very great, and devote themselves to trading of one sort or another. Consequently those who are left tend to be those whose contribution to society lies in the transformation of physical rather than of financial assets, and they are not unnaturally characterized by a certain financial naivety. In particular, there is a strong tendency in the agricultural community to project current situations too far into the future: hence at the peak of the price cycle land values are inflated and farmers borrow to acquire farms at these inflated prices, only to lose their equity when the price cycle reaches its lower levels.

It is clear that the problem of agricultural debt and ownership cannot be settled inside agriculture, and that it depends for its solution on the whole economic apparatus of society.

In conclusion, I may perhaps say a word concerning the attitude of mind which is generated by the study of economics, and which the economist inevitably brings with him to the study of any particular problem. From long looking at the intricate relationships of the multitudinous units of a whole society, the economist comes to have two prejudices: one a prejudice in favour of the general interest and against special pleading for particular groups within society, whether nations, classes, or occupations, and the other a certain prejudice against government and against political expressions of social solidarity. These two prejudices may seem somewhat contradictory—to preach the General Interest on the one hand and to scoff at its main organ of expression, government, on the other. Nevertheless, the prejudice against government which almost any economist acquires is perhaps a result of his scepticism as to the ability of political organizations to carry out the general will. He not only sees the world absurdly divided into strutting sovereign states, lacking any sense of responsibility for human welfare as a whole; he sees even within the national state the political power of the group as against the general interest, and almost despairs of establishing political institutions, even more a political frame of mind, in which a conscientious search for general good will prove more powerful than clever play for group advantage. Nevertheless government in all its many forms is here, and the economist cannot fail to be concerned with its proper functioning. The economist's conclusion is not, therefore, that the less agricultural policy the better, although he might perhaps be accused of saying that the less agriculture, or at least the fewer agriculturalists, the better off we are, provided that it is for the right reasons, i.e., improving agricultural productivity. Rather, since the economist's attention is focussed upon society as a whole, his interest is not in preserving agriculturalists as a group, but rather in speeding the improvement of productivity and the migration out of agriculture which that improvement necessitates. He is suspicious of the political power of the agricultural interest, seeing as he does that a strong "group feeling" on the part of agriculturalists may prove most detrimental to the interests of society at large, and that agricultural policy in practice is all too often an expression of this group feeling and not the result of a concern for the general welfare.

At this point therefore the economist may well hand the subject over to his fellow inquirers: to the political scientist, who should study how agricultural policy is in fact formed and executed, and should be interested in the more normative aspects of his science such as how to establish institutions which will suppress the expression of group interest and facilitate the expression of the general interest. The sociologist also should have his say in studying the virtues and vices of the whole complex of rural life with a view to effecting some possible separation of the two. And some day we might even find a philosopher who can occupy the vacant throne of the vast empire of modern knowledge and bring our scattered and so often dissipated labours under his benevolent sway.

SAMUELSON'S FOUNDATIONS:
THE ROLE OF MATHEMATICS
IN ECONOMICS

Journal of Political Economy, 56, 3 (June 1948): 187-199.

SAMUELSON'S *FOUNDATIONS*: THE ROLE OF
MATHEMATICS IN ECONOMICS[1]

THE appearance of Paul Samuelson's *Foundations of Economic Analysis*[2] —a brilliant and important work by an unusually gifted author in the general field of mathematical economics—is a suitable occasion for some further examination of the role of mathematics in economics. The question is one of great importance for the future of the science; it is, for instance, a very practical question for graduate schools which are training the future generation of economists. Is economics an essentially mathematical science? Must the student of economics become proficient in the use of the higher mathematical analysis before he can qualify to be called an "economist"? What is the basic minimum of mathematics which must be required of all students of economics? The conflict between the mathematical and the so-called "literary" economists still rages in our schools and can only be resolved, apparently, either by victory for one side or the other or by some agreed division of labor.

I

I would like first of all to develop some considerations which, while much too elementary for Dr. Samuelson's work, should be made quite clear before attempting an appraisal of the significance of his (or other similar) works. At this date mathematical economics is too ubiquitous to allow any question as to whether economics is a "mathematical science." Mathematics is a technique for the exposition and discovery of relationships among quantities.[3] Economics clearly deals with quantitative concepts —prices, wages, outputs, incomes. In so far as it deals with quantity, it must therefore be a mathematical science. The question does not quite rest there, however. Quantitative or qualitative concepts are common to all the subject matters of human discourse; there is

[1] I am much indebted to Professor Gerhard Tintner for his criticisms and suggestions in writing this article. I accept sole responsibility, however, for the errors which it may contain.

[2] Harvard University Press, 1947. Pp. xii+447. $7.50.

[3] I use the word "quantity" here in the broadest possible sense to include any concept which has a quantitative aspect. Mathematics is not, of course, confined to the discussion of extensive magnitudes; any concept which can be said to be "more or less" may be said to be quantitative.

never any escape from the dominion of "more or less." What, then, is the characteristic of a subject of study which makes it "mathematical" in character? We observe in practice that mathematics is essential to such studies as astronomy or physics; that it is perhaps slightly less significant, though still vitally important, in chemistry, biology, and economics; that it is used much less in political science and sociology; and that it is used hardly at all in history or in literary and artistic criticism.

It has sometimes been suggested that the mathematical character of a subject of study depends on whether it deals with "quantities" or with "qualities"—that is, whether the magnitudes with which it is concerned are extensive or intensive magnitudes. The development of a calculus of intensive magnitudes (e.g., the indifference-curve analysis in economics) has made it clear that mathematical methods are by no means confined to extensive magnitudes and that qualitative differences are equally subject to mathematical analysis. It is not, therefore, the fact that astronomy deals with extensive magnitudes (e.g., mass and distance), and literary criticism with intensive magnitudes (such as lyric quality and dramatic force), that makes astronomy a mathematical subject and literary criticism nonmathematical. Rather is it the fact that the magnitudes of astronomy are themselves internally homogeneous, whereas the magnitudes of literary criticism are internally heterogeneous, consisting of aggregates and structures of innumerable interrelated parts, the significance of any part being determined only by its relation to the whole. Thus it makes sense to say, "Let X equal the distance from the earth to the sun," since distance has no internal structure that is particularly significant—one mile is very much like another. But it makes very little sense to say, "Let *Hamlet* equal H and *Macbeth* equal M," for *Hamlet* and *Macbeth* are extremely complex structures, the significance of which lies in their structure and not in any aggregation of their parts. Word-counting is a very low form of literary criticism.

To this apparent delimitation of his field, the mathematician may perhaps object that the only reason why literary criticism is not mathematical is that the mathematics of literary structures has not yet been written. One would certainly hesitate to put it beyond the wit of mathematicians to invent a calculus of literary criticism—for all I know it may even have been done.[4] Nevertheless, such a calculus would not replace, even though it might assist, literary studies in nonmathematical language.

The key to this problem of the bounds of mathematics may perhaps be found in the quotation from J. Willard Gibbs's *Mathematics Is a Language*, with which Samuelson has adorned his title-page. Any language is a symbolic abstraction from reality designed for the purpose of communicating experience from one person to another. Mathematical symbols clearly fall into this category. Nevertheless, perhaps it is an overstatement to say that mathematics is a language, for, while it is probably true that all mathematical expressions can be translated into "literary" language if we are prepared to be sufficiently long-winded, it is not true that all "literary" expressions can be translated into mathematics. The expression, $dC/dq = dR/dq$, can be translated into English as "Marginal Cost equals Marginal Revenue." I know of no

[4] There is, for instance, George Birkhoff's work, *Aesthetic Measure* (Cambridge: Harvard University Press, 1933).

mathematical expression for the literary form, "I love you." It is clear that, though mathematics is a language of sorts, it is not a complete language. If the word did not have unfortunate emotional overtones, one might describe it as a "jargon"; that is, it is a way of talking about certain things but not about all things. The very fact that mathematics itself cannot be written without a certain literary sentence structure is evidence of the limits of mathematical discourse. These limits are set by the fact that the "universe of discourse" of mathematics consists essentially of relationships between internally homogeneous variables and the operations which may be performed upon them. It is true that, in advanced analysis (e.g., in matrix theory), symbols are used which describe a multiplicity of operations on a complex of variables; nevertheless, these symbols are essentially a "shorthand" and represent a series of operations rather than a single operation. Mathematics operates at the level of abstraction where any heterogeneity or complexity in the structure of its basic variables may be neglected. This fact constitutes at once the strength and the weakness of mathematics as applied, say, to economics—strength because, by abstraction from the internal structure of variables, certain basic relationships may be seen more clearly and inconsistencies exposed; weakness because mathematical treatment distracts attention from the actual complexity of the internal structure of the variables concerned and hence is likely to lead to error where this structure is important.

Good examples of the above principle can be found in the mathematical treatment of the Keynesian system of macroeconomic relationships. Samuelson gives a brilliant mathematical analysis of the dynamics of the Keynesian system (pp. 276–83). His skill in analyzing the variables of this system did not, however, enable him to avoid very substantial errors in forecasting when he tried to apply the system to problems of the transition.[5] It is no discredit to Samuelson to have had the courage to commit into print what most economists of his school (myself included) thought and said privately. But it is a question of acute importance for economics as to why the macroeconomic predictions of the mathematical economists have been on the whole less successful than the hunches of the mathematically unwashed. The answer seems to be that when we write, for instance, "let i, Y, and I stand, respectively, for the interest rate, income, and investment," we stand committed to the assumption that the internal structures of these aggregates or averages are not important for the problem in hand. In fact, of course, they may be very important, and no amount of subsequent mathematical analysis of the variables can overcome the fatal defect of their heterogeneity. Thus it may well be that the composition of income, or of the capital stock, may have more effect on the volume of consumption or of investment than the aggregate size of income or capital. The judgment as to *what* variables are significant, what aggregates are homogeneous enough to be treated as variables, what basic assumptions are reasonable about the nature of assumed functional relationships—these involve the exercise of a faculty of mind which is more akin to literary criticism than to mathematical analysis.

We cannot pursue these matters very far without becoming deeply involved in the psychology and sociology of knowledge. However, one may tentatively sug-

[5] *New Republic*, CXI (1944), 297 and 333.

gest that there are two broad types of mental operation by which knowledge is gained: one is the faculty of judgment, or insight; the other is the faculty of logical manipulation. Mathematical analysis as such clearly belongs to the latter rather than to the former, though one would hesitate to deny altogether the place of insight in mathematics. Mathematics, that is to say, is a branch of logic—or perhaps one should say these days that logic is a branch of mathematics! It consists of a framework of hypothetical propositions—if this, then that. In this framework the distinction between axioms and conclusions is not very important; it is the framework that matters, not the order in which the framework is followed. Any subject such as economics which is "empirical," in the sense that it is interested in the interpretation of actual human experience, must have two parts: the construction of logical frameworks (the "pure" subject) and the interpretation of reality by fitting the logical framework to the complex of empirical data (the "applied" subject). In economics we have "pure" economics which is simply a structure of hypothetical propositions; in "applied" economics we fit such a structure to various points of the mass of real experience and see how well the structure then fits other points. "Pure" economics, however—like the "pure" part of any subject—is never quite pure, because of the fact that we are interested in hypothetical frameworks not for their own sake alone but because of their usefulness in interpreting reality. There is an infinite number of possible economic "models," all of them consistent logical frameworks. The task of "judgment" in economics is to select, out of the many possible .frameworks, those which have interpretive value when applied to reality.

If now we ask what it is that gives a logical framework interpretive value, two elements seem to emerge: one is the homogeneity of the variables of the framework, the other is the stability through time of the functional relationships assumed to exist among these variables. As far as we know now, there is no *manipulative* way of discovering what variables are homogeneous and what relationships are stable. The homogeneity of variables and the stability of relationships in any *given* system can perhaps be *tested* by empirical and statistical research; but the decision of "what to test" rests on the faculty of judgment or insight rather than on that of manipulation. Insight (judgment) and logic (mathematics) are strictly complementary goods. Logic without insight has no content; insight without logic has no form. Logical, mathematical, manipulative ability is a necessary but not a sufficient condition for the development of good economics.

Having admitted the necessity of mathematics in some form in economics, the problem now arises, "What kind of mathematics is most useful?" Two questions may be raised here. One is perhaps a question of exposition, as to where the analytic (algebraic) or the geometric methods should be used. The other is more fundamental and is the question of which type of mathematics is more suitable for economics: the essentially Newtonian mathematics, which is primarily adapted to the study of particular functions and of relationships "in the small"; or the newly developing topological mathematics, which studies the relationships of general functions "in the large." The two questions are, as we shall see, related.

The simplest form of analysis of the relationships of variables is, of course, the graphical or geometrical analysis of the elementary textbook, which is no less mathematical because of its almost universal use. It can indeed be said that today there are no nonmathematical economists; there are only those whose principal tool is geometry and those whose principal tool is algebra, including the calculus and higher forms of analysis. However, when the term "mathematical" is employed in its more esoteric sense, the connotation is usually that of the analytic method rather than of the geometrical. Both methods are in essence different ways of saying the same thing; both, however, have certain advantages and disadvantages. The geometric method has the advantage that it is more vivid and that it is an excellent way of dealing with relationships of which we know some properties but not the exact form. When we draw a demand curve, for instance, we express, in a general way, a relationship between price and quantity demanded which would require several expressions to describe in analytic terms, involving, say, first and second or even third differentials, limits, etc. The geometrical method is also a very convenient way of dealing with functional discontinuities, the description of which is very awkward in analytical terms. One need only compare, for instance, (1) the geometrical proof that the effect of a change in demand on price and quantity depends on the relative slopes of the supply and demand curves with (2) Samuelson's analytical treatment of the same problem (p. 260) to see how much more simple and even more general, at a two-dimensional level, is the geometrical treatment. Nevertheless, there is among mathematical economists a certain feeling (from which Samuelson is by no means exempt) that there is something a little childish and elementary about geo-

metrical treatments and that analytical treatment is the only ultimately satisfactory method.

There are real grounds for this feeling in that the geometrical method, superior as it is when we are dealing with two or three variables, cannot easily be extended to problems involving many variables, owing to the inability of the human mind to picture a space of more than three dimensions. We may perhaps make four-dimensional models by means of coloring, contouring on three-dimensional surfaces, or some other device, but it would require a very exceptional mind to handle even five variables simultaneously by means of geometric methods. Hence, in problems involving many variables—and in principle almost all economic relationships do so—there is no escape from recourse to the methods of the higher algebra, in spite of their inherent difficulties and disadvantages.

Nevertheless, the question must be asked how important, for economics, is the gain in generality which comes from extension of the analysis to an indefinite number of dimensions? It is clear that there is gain as we move from analysis involving fewer dimensions to that involving more. To a surprising extent, the classical analysis was carried on with analytical concepts that implied only one dimension, in which the equilibrium concepts were discussed mainly in terms of the variation of a single variable above or below some "normal" value. The development (around the time of Marshall) of graphic techniques in two dimensions represented a substantial step forward; if we compare, for instance, Book I, chapter 7, of the *Wealth of Nations* with Marshall's discussion of supply and demand curves, we can see that there is a great gain in discussing the problem in terms of two-dimensional supply and demand functions rather than in terms of a one-dimensional "effective demand." Similarly the development of the indifference curve analysis, isoquants, and similar "contour line" methods are significant mainly because they provide a convenient way of extending graphical analysis to three dimensions, and this extension results in a further gain in the range of problems which can be tackled. Nevertheless, it is significant that, even though he worked mainly with the limited techniques of one-dimensional analysis, Adam Smith was able to erect virtually the whole conceptual framework of economic theory. Indeed, in re-reading Smith, one continually marvels at how little (except perhaps in monetary theory) has really been added to this framework in spite of our refined techniques—we have added walls, partitions, furniture, and ornaments to his edifice, but the skeleton is still his. Similarly, while the extension of graphical analysis from two to three dimensions greatly improves the marginal analysis, all of its most essential propositions can be developed within the simple framework of two dimensions. It is evident, therefore, that the adding of dimensions to our analysis runs into a law of diminishing returns: the step from zero to one dimension is the step from no science at all to a substantial science. Moving from one dimension to two gives form, and moving to three gives elegance; moving to four, five, or more dimensions will add further elegances, and may even unearth minor propositions which would not otherwise have been discovered, but will not affect the fundamental conceptual framework. So we find that the n-dimensional analyses of Samuelson and his confreres add much to the aesthetics of economics but surprisingly little to its substance. I would be prepared to defend

this proposition even in the case of general equilibrium analysis. There is undoubtedly real value in the formal solutions of the general equilibrium problem (e.g., the Walrasian solution). The closer we get to generality, however, the more difficult it is to obtain significant propositions, even of a qualitative character, from our relationships. One wonders whether a student will not get a better understanding of the realities of "general equilibrium" from a study of Wicksteed's account of the consequences of his gift to Indian relief than from the most beautiful mathematical system.

A much more fundamental problem than that of geometry versus analysis—which may be, as Poincaré has pointed out, to some extent a matter of the temperament of the student—is the question of "topological" versus "infinitesimal" analysis. The mathematical structure which has been used in economics to date has on the whole been of the latter variety; it is the mathematics of Descartes, Newton, and Leibniz with a little shorthand added. It is most adept at dealing with the relationships of variables suffering infinitesimal changes "at a point"; it is not well adapted to dealing with the *general* relationships of variables "in the large." This is not to say that the infinitesimal mathematics is altogether incapable of dealing with problems involving functions "in the large" (indeed, Samuelson has an interesting, if not altogether satisfying, section on the calculus of finite variations). Within its dimensional limitations geometric methods are much more suited to dealing with functions "in the large" than the analytic methods: a "curve" is a symbol for the whole shape of a relationship; a differential is a symbol for a property of a relationship at a point. It is only in very simple cases—such as linear, exponential, quadratic, or cubic forms—that the whole shape of a relationship can be expressed analytically in a form simple enough to handle. A very interesting question for economists is whether the topological mathematics now being developed (e.g., at Princeton) is capable of application to economic problems. It may be that the work of Morgenstern and Neumann is a step in this direction. Since the problems of economics frequently are, in essence, "topological" rather than "infinitesimal," it would seem on general grounds that the newer mathematics should prove to be very useful. The present reviewer, however, is too much of an amateur in this field to make any solid judgment; it does not seem, however, that Samuelson has given adequate attention to this problem.

II

With these considerations in view, let us now turn to the *Foundations* to see what it has to offer. According to Samuelson, these foundations consist of two pillars: the theory of maximization and the theory of difference equations. The first is familiar to all economists in the guise of the marginal analysis. Samuelson's treatment of it seems to be practically complete; nevertheless, it illustrates very well the difficulties which an analysis based fundamentally on infinitesimal variations may encounter. The use of the calculus results in inadequate attention being given to two problems of some practical importance in economics: the problem of functional discontinuities and the problem of the *maximum maximorum*. A simple example will illustrate both problems. Suppose that, instead of the usual continuous demand or sales curve which is used in the theory of the firm, we assume a "stepped" demand curve (Fig. 1). This is by no means an un-

likely case—e.g., a commodity may have a number of different uses, in each of which the demand is highly inelastic. Here the marginal revenue curve shoots down to minus infinity and back at each

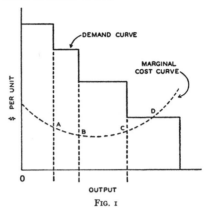

FIG. 1

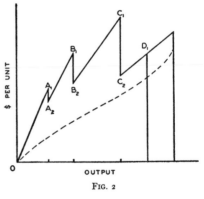

FIG. 2

"step"; the marginal cost curve cuts the marginal revenue curve at a number of points (A, B, C, etc.), each of which represents both a maximum and a minimum. The situation is clearly represented in Figure 2, where the jagged, solid line is the total revenue curve and the dotted line is the marginal cost curve. There are four relative maxima of net revenue, at the points A_1, B_1, C_1, and D_1; there are three relative minima also at A_2, B_2, and C_2. The firm is in equilibrium "in the small" at each of the relative maxima, where all the marginal equalities are fulfilled. "In the large," however, the firm will, if it has sufficient knowledge, select that relative maximum at which the net revenue is absolutely the greatest. The marginal conditions throw no light on this problem.

This discussion throws light also on the stability of equilibrium under conditions of discontinuous functions. It is clear that the position of each relative maximum is likely to be fairly stable. In Figure 1 or Figure 2 it would take a very substantial movement of the cost curve to effect any change in the relative maximum. As far as relative maxima are concerned, therefore, Samuelson is right in stating that discontinuities make equilibria more stable and the problem of the firm easier. Nevertheless, a change in underlying conditions (e.g., in the cost curves of Figs. 1 and 2) may easily cause the *maximum maximorum* to skip from one relative maximum (say C_1) to another (say B_1). In the small, the firm is very stable indeed; an olive does not have to be very nearsighted (Samuelson, p. 80) to perceive that it is cozily ensconced at the bottom of a conical paper cup. In the large, however, the firm may be affected profoundly by quite small changes in its environment, as these lead to one relative maximum supplanting another. Far from being a snug olive, the firm may well be a cat on hot bricks, leaping wildly from one relative maximum to another in response to quite small changes in market conditions or in production functions.

Before leaving the theory of maximization, there are some more fundamental doubts which should perhaps be raised concerning the significance of maximiza-

tion theory for economics. As the theory of maximization is the foundation of the marginal analysis—and therefore of the larger part of present-day "microeconomics"—it may seem somewhat rash to question its importance. Nevertheless, many economists are increasingly wondering whether the theory of maximization has not reached the limit of its usefulness, and whether further development toward a more realistic theory of an economic or social organism does not lie along other lines. It is observable, for instance, that in macroeconomic theory very little use is made of the theory of maximization. The theory is based on certain simple "empirical" functions ("propensities") which are not necessarily derived from any maximization principle. The "propensity to consume," for instance, is not derived from utility analysis, at least in any direct way, and the "propensity to invest" likewise is not assumed to be derived from profit maximization. Liquidity preference likewise is simply an assumed function, not derived necessarily from any maximization principle. In the theory of the individual economic organism itself there are signs of search for principles other than that of maximization. In the attempt to construct a model of a trade-union, the principle of maximization has proved to be singularly useless. The conclusion is being forced on labor economists that a trade-union does not maximize anything, except (in a purely formal sense) "utility," and the most fruitful models seem to be those constructed on the assumption of certain propensities (e.g., toward self-preservation).[6] In the theory of the firm likewise there are pronounced rum-

[6] Arthur M. Ross, "Wage Determination under Collective Bargaining," *American Economic Review*, XXXVI (December, 1947), 793.

blings of dissatisfaction,[7] and the principle of organizational preservation may here also be more fruitful than the maximization principle. It is always true, of course, that the equating of marginal values is *formally* a condition of maximization. However, the question is whether we know more about the "Maximand Function" (i.e., the function relating the variables of the organism to the parameter, such as "utility," which is maximized) or more about the direct relationships of the other variables. The maximization principle yields its most fruitful results when the maximand is an *objective* variable such as profits; as we push toward reality, we find that we are forced to abandon objective maximands, so that the theory of maximization becomes more and more formal. It is something of a question, therefore, whether the very beautiful and elaborate theory of maximization—on which Samuelson seems practically to have said the last word—is not a monument to economics rather than a foundation.

I do not, of course, advocate the abandonment of the marginal analysis; it is a most useful analytical tool and produces valuable results at the level of first approximation. I suspect, however, that it does not produce valuable results *beyond* the level of first approximation. This is because the theory of maximization should be viewed as a special case of a more general theory of selection. Any theory of an economic or social organism involves two elements: a description of the *opportunities* or *choices* among which selection may be made and a *principle of selection* according to which the choice is

made. In the marginal analysis the opportunities are described normally by continuous functions (e.g., production, market, cost, and revenue functions in the case of a firm), and the principle of selection is that of selecting the point on the opportunity function at which some related maximand (e.g., profits) is maximized. But continuous opportunities and the maximization principle are merely special cases, and it is quite possible to construct models of economic behavior which have, for instance, discontinuous opportunities or other principles of selection. A very simple theory of the individual economic organism (firm or household) can, for instance, be constructed by assuming that consumption is a function of the existing stock of capital and that the principle of selection is that of maintaining the existing stock of capital intact. This type of model involves no maximization, except in the most formal sense, yet it is very fruitful, especially in macroeconomics.

The second pillar of Samuelson's *Foundations* is the theory of difference equations. The theory of maximization is in principle familiar to all economists; difference equations are much less familiar, though most economists have probably met them without recognizing them, and it may be useful to explain very briefly what they are. A difference equation is a functional relationship between successive[8] values of a single variable. Suppose, for instance, that we assume that the output of one year (Q_t) is functionally related to the output of the preceding year (Q_{t-1}). Then, if we are given the value of the variable for any given year, we can immediately deduce

[7] See the controversy around Lester's article, "Shortcomings of the Marginal Analysis for Wage-Employment Problems," *American Economic Review*, XXXVI (March, 1946), 63; cf. *ibid.*, XXXVI, 519; XXXVII, 135, 645.

[8] The succession does not have to be succession in time, as Samuelson seems to suggest; succession in space may also be economically important.

what will be the values for all other years. Suppose, for instance, that Q_t and Q_{t-1} are related according to the equation

$$Q_t = 100 + 0.5Q_{t-1}. \qquad (1)$$

Then, if we are given the value of Q for any one year, we can deduce the value for all other years. Thus, if $Q_0 = 128$, we have $Q_1 = 100 + 0.5Q_0 = 164$; $Q_2 = 100 + 0.5Q_1 = 182$; $Q_3 = 191$, $Q_4 = 195.5$; $Q_5 = 197.75$, etc. Similarly, if we had $Q_0 = 240$, we would have $Q_1 = 220$, $Q_2 = 210$, $Q_3 = 205$, $Q_4 = 202.5$, etc. In this example it is clear that, no matter what the figure from which we start, the value of Q approaches 200 with the passage of time. This value is the "solution" of the difference equation (1). If $Q_0 = 200$, then clearly we have $Q_1 = Q_2 = Q_n = 200$; the value of the variable is stable through time.

There are two aspects to the solution of a difference equation: one is the "path" of the variable through time; the other is the equilibrium value which is approached asymptotically by this path. Of course, the path may not approach a solution at all, except at infinity. We may also have solutions which are unstable, in the sense that a slight divergence from the equilibrium value leads to a path departing from it. There may also be cyclical solutions in which the path retraces a certain course continually. Consider, for instance, the difference equation

$$Q_t = Q_{t-1} - Q_{t-2}. \qquad (2)$$

This is a difference equation of the third order, relating three successive positions of the variable instead of two. If we know any *two* successive values of Q, we

can find all the others. Suppose that we have $Q_0 = 5$, $Q_1 = 10$. Then we have:

$$
\begin{array}{llr}
Q_2 = Q_1 - Q_0 & = & 5 \\
Q_3 = Q_2 - Q_1 = -Q_0 & = & -5 \\
Q_4 = Q_3 - Q_2 = -Q_1 & = & -10 \\
Q_5 = Q_4 - Q_3 = -Q_1 + Q_0 & = & -5 \\
Q_6 = Q_5 - Q_4 = Q_0 & = & 5 \\
Q_7 = Q_6 - Q_5 = Q_1 & = & 10
\end{array}
$$

It is evident that, as $Q_6 = Q_0$ and $Q_7 = Q_1$, we must have $Q_8 = Q_2$, $Q_9 = Q_4$, and so on indefinitely. The value of Q tramps forever round the circle of six values and never reaches a single position of equilibrium. In the above example this is true no matter what values of Q_0 and Q_1 we start from; in other cases this may not be so, but we may still approach circular paths at particular values.

An equilibrium solution of a difference equation is obtained by putting the various values in the equation equal to each other. Thus, in equation (1), if $Q_t = Q_{t-1} = Q$ (the equilbrium value), we have $Q = 100 \div 0.5\,Q$, or $Q = 200$. In equation (2) the only equilibrium values "in the small" are $Q_0 = Q_1 = 0$. It should be noticed that equations (1) and (2) both represent possible economic "models." Equation (1) is the simplest difference equation underlying the Keynesian system. Equation (2) implies that production plans are determined, not by the previous absolute level of production, but by the *change* in output between the two preceding periods.[9] We

[9] It should be observed that the "topological problem" arises in the case of difference-equation analysis as well as in the theory of maximization. Samuelson's analysis mainly consists of infinitesimal analysis—that is, the discussion of the nature of the equilibrium of difference equations "in the small" (i.e., at a point). He recognizes (p. 390) the problem involved in circular solutions such as the above; but the "Leontief solution," as he himself recognizes, is little more than a statement of the problem. Here again we have a problem which geometry can solve very easily but in which the fruit-

can construct more complex systems as we will.

What, then, is the significance of these difference equations for economics? It is clear that they are the very stuff and substance of dynamic economics and of its offshoot, economic forecasting. Any kind of forecasting, in fact, is based on the discovery of *stable* difference equations relating past variables to future. The reason for the success of astronomical (as opposed to either meteorological or economic) forecasting is that, in astronomy, the planets move in orbits or systems of orbits, which can be described by stable, if complex, difference equations.[10] In meteorology and economics the complexity of the relationships is so great that the difference equations ("laws") which have been discovered are not stable enough to provide for more than rough forecasting. In economics also we have the distressing fact that the economist is part of the universe which he studies, and hence the very fact of discovering stable difference equations might unstabilize them! The *art* of economics is very largely that of discovering difference equations which are stable enough to be instruments of analysis. The success of the Keynesian economics is largely due to the fact that many of the relationships which it assumes (e.g., the consumption function) are based on moderately stable difference equations.

Samuelson points out also—and this is perhaps his most important single con-

ful generalization of a geometrical solution to more than three dimensions seems to present great difficulties.

[10] In fact, of course, the movements of the planets, being continuous, are described by differential equations. A differential equation, however, is essentially the limiting case of a difference equation as the intervals between successive values of the variables approach zero.

tribution—that difference equations are necessary to the study of the *stability* of static equilibrium.

This principle may be illustrated briefly with reference to that most familiar of economic principles—the equilibrium of supply and demand. The "static equilibrium" price is that at which the excess-demand quantity (quantity demanded minus quantity offered) is zero. In order to discuss the stability of this equilibrium, we must make some assumptions regarding the excess demand and the change in price. It is usually assumed that a positive excess demand leads to a rise, and a negative excess demand to a fall, in price. These assumptions usually lead to a difference equation in price with a stable equilibrium. If the excess-demand function is $D_t = D(p_t)$, and if the function relating excess demand to price changes is $D_t = F(p_t - p_{t-1})$, by substitution we get immediately a difference equation for the price, $D(p_t) = F(p_t - p_{t-1})$. We know that, when $p_t = p_{t-1}$, $F(p_t - p_{t-1}) = 0$, so the solution of this difference equation is $D(p) = 0$, which is the same as that of the excess-demand function itself.

The stability of the whole system clearly depends on the nature of the functions. Three cases may be distinguished, illustrated in Figure 3. D and S are the supply and demand curves. In Figure 3, A, we suppose that the change in price as a result of excess demand or supply is not sufficient to "overshoot" the equilibrium point. Starting from OP_0, the excess demand S_0D_0 leads to a price OP_1 in the next period, which creates an excess demand S_1D_1, which in turn leads to a price OP_2 in the next period, and so on toward the equilibrium price OP. In Figure 3, B, the excess-demand, price-change function is more responsive, so that a cyclic movement is set up with excess supply alternating with excess demand; the excess demand S_0D_0 creates so great a change in price (to OP_1) that, at this price, there is an excess supply, D_1S_1; this sends the price back to OP_2, at which there is an excess demand, etc. In this case, however, the equilibrium is still stable. In Figure 3, C, the equilibrium is unstable; the cyclic movement is explosive instead of damped. An unstable equilibrium is also found in the somewhat unlikely case where an excess demand produces a fall in price and also in the case where a fall in price diminishes the excess demand.

can only be mentioned in this brief treatment. There is, for instance, what he calls the "correspondence principle." Most of the propositions of economics concern themselves with the *qualitative* effects of a change in the determinants of equilibrium on the magnitude of the equilibrium variables. Thus we assert, for instance, that a rise in demand, with supply remaining the same, will raise price and output if the supply is positively elastic and if the elasticity of demand is less than that of supply. Samuelson points out that there is a close connection between the derivation of propositions of

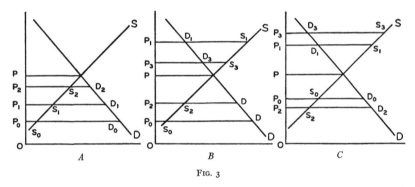

FIG. 3

It is also possible to have cyclic solutions that are "neutral" or self-perpetuating; thus suppose in Figure 3, B, that an excess demand of S_2V_2 gave rise to a price OP_1 in the next period, which produced an excess supply D_1S_1, which in turn produced a price OP_2 in the next period. The cycle would clearly go on forever in the absence of any change in the functions. An "exploding" cycle, as in Figure 3, C, will usually reach such a "neutral" position.

Enough has been said, perhaps, to illustrate the significance of difference equations for the discussion of static equilibrium as well as for dynamic economics. There are many other matters of great interest in Samuelson's book which

this nature and the derivations of the stability conditions of the equilibrium itself. This "correspondence" again seems only to hold "in the small"; for changes of a topological nature it is less clear.

One can also do no more than mention Samuelson's chapter on welfare economics, which, in a sense, forms a separate essay not very well integrated into the rest of the book and consisting, for the most part, of a generalized restatement of existing doctrine. Here again one feels that the infinitesimal analysis fails to answer the important, and much neglected, topological questions in welfare economics—the problems that arise because of discontinuities in outputs, factors, and factor combinations. Welfare economics can perhaps tell us what toll we should charge on a bridge once it is built; it has remarkably little to say about whether we should build it or where we should put it!

One may perhaps conclude this review with some remarks on the problem of "communicability" raised so eloquently by J. M. Clark.[11] Mathematics is only part of the foundations of economic analysis; its other foundations lie in philosophy, in the other social sciences, and even in art and literature where that essential but nonmathematical quality of critical judgment is developed. There is a place for specialization in economics between more-mathematical and less-mathematical economists; indeed, in view of the limitations of the human mind, there must be this specialization. If economics becomes a preserve of the higher mathematicians, it will lose its essentially humanistic and empirical quality. There is not time, in the average life, to acquire *both* the higher mathematics and the critical judgment. For the exceptional mind this may be possible; for the general run it is not. Hence the great importance of communicability and the serious consequences that will flow if mathematical economists become a "sect," shut up in their own wonderland of abstraction and generality. This problem of communication, oddly enough, is to a considerable extent a moral one. The danger of sectarianism is that it leads to a certain pride in the sect's "mysteries" and to a lack of will to communicate. Much injury has been done to the economist's profession in the past by the pride of "literary" economists who, from wilful egotism, have refused to acquire that modicum of mathematical training which yields clearly in-

creasing returns. It may be that today the greatest danger is from the other side. The mathematicians themselves set up standards of generality and elegance in their expositions which are a serious bar to understanding. Conventions of generality and mathematical elegance may be just as much barriers to the attainment and diffusion of knowledge as may contentment with particularity and literary vagueness. One may perhaps lay down a general rule that, in exposition, pedagogical virtue is always to be preferred to logical aesthetics and that pedagogical virtue (ease of understanding) is usually best served by the exposition of particular and simple cases first, leading up to a final generalization. The mathematician always seems to prefer to generalize first and to develop his particular cases from the generalization, which, while no doubt the logical order, contributes substantially to incommunicability.

The *Foundations* is an important book. It should be studied not only by the mathematically baptized but also by those who, like myself, hang on to n-dimensions by the skin of their teeth. No economist who studies it can fail to profit by it. Nevertheless, the present reviewer cannot help feeling a certain sense of rapidly diminishing marginal productivity in the application of mathematics to economics. There is an elusive flavor of John Stuart Mill about the *Foundations* which makes it seem less like a foundation than a coping stone, finishing an edifice which does not have much further to go. It may well be that the slovenly literary borderland between economics and sociology will be the most fruitful building ground during the years to come and that mathematical economics will remain too flawless in its perfection to be very fruitful.

[11] "Mathematical Economists and Others,' *Econometrica*, XV (April, 1947), 75.

IS ECONOMICS NECESSARY?

Scientific Monthly, 68, 4 (Apr. 1949): 235-240.

IS ECONOMICS NECESSARY?

Being an economist, I can hardly be expected to answer "No" to the question that forms the title of this paper. My thesis is, however, that economics is necessary, not merely for the support of economists, but for the development and perhaps even for the survival of science in general and the civilization that supports it. I propose to consider particularly what justification there is for a separate discipline of economics, and what contribution this discipline makes to the general advancement of knowledge.

The social sciences are reputed, at least in popular imagination, to be less "successful" than the physical sciences. The "success" of a science is judged mainly by its ability to predict or to control future events in its field. For the common man, as for the operational philosopher, knowledge is identified with power, and knowing with know-how. By this standard even economics, which has a certain reputation as the most successful of the social sciences, makes a poor showing compared with the prediction of eclipses, the certainties of chemistry, and the miracles of genetics. This, we hasten to explain, is a result of the difficulties of the science, not of the inadequacies of the scientist. We sympathize with the wayward universe of the meteorologist even as we chafe at the waywardness of his predictions, and, if the predictions of the economist are even more wayward, it is because of the complex and unstable nature of the universe with which he deals. Moreover, the social scientist faces a problem which normally does not bother the nonsocial scientist, in that he is himself part of the field of his investigation. If the heavenly bodies were themselves moved by astronomers, or even if they were moved by temperamental angels who guided their behavior by the astronomers' predictions, the astronomers would find themselves in just as bad a fix as the economists. The bacteriologist who must stain his bacteria in order to see them would be in even worse trouble if his bacteria blushed when they were observed. Of course not even the astronomer seems to be exempt from observer trouble in these days of relativity, but in the case of the social sciences the trouble develops long before we approach the speed of light. Nowhere is the positivistic fiction of a dispassionate, objective observer wholly removed from the field of his observation more absurd than in the social sciences. The difference between the social and the other sciences, however, is merely one of degree, and as the nonsocial sciences run increasingly into observer trouble it may be that not merely the results but the methods also of the social sciences may be of interest to other scientists.

Economics has a certain reputation—not, I think, wholly undeserved—for being the most scientific of the social sciences. It does possess, I think, a larger body of analytical propositions that are widely accepted by competent persons than either sociology or political science. It also exhibits the marks of the history of a true science, in that it exhibits an orderly development toward greater and greater generality. The older theories—i.e., of the classical economists—can easily be formulated as special cases of the more general modern theory. This very internal consistency and success, however, has developed in some economists a certain spiritual pride which has injured the development of social science as a whole, and I think the profession is coming to realize more and more the necessity for trade among the various disciplines if further specialization is to be fruitful. We are reaching out on all sides today toward a unified social science—a regional federation, as it were, which must be accomplished before we can proceed to that great federation of all knowledge that is the ultimate task of the inquiring spirit. All the social sciences have much to learn from one another, and the same might be said of sciences of any kind.

I

Economics, like any other science, has two closely related parts— the pure science and the empirical science. Pure economics is a branch of logic or of mathematics (in these days there does not seem to be much distinction between them). It attempts to construct systems of hypothetical propositions, mainly of a qualitative nature (if A rises, B falls) relating certain "economic quantities" such as prices, wages, outputs, interest rates, etc. Such a system is called a "model," and the construction of such models is, of course, the characteristic activity of the "pure" part of any science. The nature of the models themselves, however, is determined mainly by the empirical content of the subject matter of the science. Thus, even though the model is an abstraction, not depending on any correspondence with empirical reality for its self-consistency, yet the act of model-building—except perhaps in pure mathematics—is not unrelated to the empirical interests of the model builder, and the usefulness of a model depends on the degree to which it helps in interpreting the complexities of the empirical world. The Keplerian theory of a single planet revolving around a sun is a good example of an "astronomical" model. It has no exact counterpart in reality, at least in our solar system, yet it derives interest and significance from the fact that it helps to interpret (by being capable of extension and generalization) the movements of the actual solar system. Similarly in economics the marginal analysis of the individual economic unit (planet!) or the Walrasian system of equations of general equilibrium of the price system under perfect markets (which corresponds somewhat to the Laplacian system in astronomy) is a "model" which derives interest from the light it throws on the workings of the intolerable complex of social relationships. Models which do not apparently abstract from an empirical universe may be called "non-Euclidian" models from the analogy with non-Euclidian geometry. Thus it would no doubt be possible to construct models of planetary systems assuming different laws of gravitational attraction, of momentum, etc. than those which seem to prevail in our system; indeed, I have no doubt this has been done. Nor are these non-Euclidian models mere idle exercises of an overactive mind; they may turn out to have more than an aesthetic value, as witness the significance of non-Euclidian geometries in modern physics. In economics also there is something to be said for model-building for its own sake, and there is no need whatever to stick to the assumptions of the elementary textbook. Economics is in no way bound to such assumptions as profit maximization; there never has been an economic man even in economics, except as a very first approximation, and by means of the indifference curve analysis economics has increasingly liberated itself from any narrowness of assumption. The *methods* of economic analysis would apply just as well to a Franciscan economy as to a Benthamite! Nevertheless, the *interests* of the model builder are likely to be determined to a considerable extent by the empirical world in which he lives, and even by the practical problems he faces. It is no accident, for instance, that the depression of the thirties was the scene of a great deal of theoretical activity centering around the problem of unemployment. Similarly, in the elementary theory of the firm, the assumption is made that the firm selects that position of the variables under its control which results in the maximization of some measure of money profits. As a first approximation, this assumption yields useful results. But it is quite possible, and indeed necessary, to go beyond it, and to take account of more complex motivations, such as the desire to be important, or to be well regarded, or to obey the dictates of conscience, or even to be liquid.

It is not generally realized, I think, how far economics has gone in the direction of becoming a generalized theory of choice. Economics begins as an attempt to explain the magnitudes and movements of certain quantities, such as prices, wages, outputs, sales, and so on. Very early in its development it became clear that these quantities cannot be treated as an independent world of their own, for they are thrown up as a result of the whole complex of human choices operating within the strait jacket of a niggardly natural environment. Thus even in Adam Smith we find the explanation of wage differences in terms of what might be called the nonmonetary advantages of the various occupations; and little more than a hundred years later we find Wicksteed illustrating the principles of value theory with reference to the problem of how high a cliff one would dive off to save a mother-in-law, or how much family prayers should be shortened to speed a parting guest to the train—problems that are a long way from what is usually thought of as economic. Nevertheless, it is an inevitable logic that has turned the study of prices into a theory of value, for the price system is simply one reflection of the general problem of "scarcity," and the choice between nuts and apples differs only in its simplicity from the choice between income and leisure, between freedom and security, between love and power, between color and form, or between better and worse. Value, in the sense of what we have to give up of one thing in order to get a unit of another—i.e., as a "transformation ratio"—is a phenomenon we meet in every conceivable branch of human activity, for wherever there is limitation, wherever there is choice, wherever we cannot have our cake and eat it, there the value phenomenon pops up. The novelist balancing up his chapters, the painter balancing his picture, the general apportioning his troops, the preacher arranging his service, the professor preparing his course, the cook planning a menu, the government formulating a policy, are all of them facing essentially the same "economic" problem as in the apportionment of time or the spending of money. Wherever resources are limited, choice is necessary and value raises its earthy head. It may be, as Wordsworth says, that "High Heaven rejects the lore of nicely calculated less or more" (i.e., economics), but, even if this is the case (and Wordsworth's authority is by no means unimpeachable), it is merely because High Heaven is presumably possessed of unlimited resources. In some fields the "less or more" may be less nicely calculated than in the market place, though one sometimes wonders after studying the exotic behavior of banks, corporations, and labor unions whether these phenomena could not be profitably studied with the techniques of the cultural anthropologist. Custom, habit, tradition, and ritual play an important part in the day-to-day activity of the most solemnly economic and ostensibly money-making institution. On the other hand, the balancing of advantage against disadvantage which is the mark of the "economizing" process is found among the most primitive tribes, the most careless bohemians, and the most other-worldly saints. Indeed, it may well be that the saint—who knows what spiritual goods he wants and who goes after them regardless of how many norms of conventional behavior he shatters—is closer to the pattern of economic man than is the frock-coated banker whose watchword is respectability (a thoroughly primitive, anthropological concept) and whose walk of life is hedged about with innumerable barriers of established custom.

Economics is significant, then, not merely because it investigates an important slice of life in the market place, but because the phenomena which emerge in a relatively clear and quantitative form in the market place are also found in virtually all other human activities. Hence, economic life itself, in the narrow sense of that part of human activity that is concerned with buying, selling, producing, and consuming, is a "model" of the whole vast complex of human activity and experience, and the principles which are discovered in a clear and quantitative form in the market may be applied to the understanding of apparently quite unrelated phenomena in biology, art, religion, morals, politics, and the whole complex structure of human relationships. I do not mean, of course, that economic principles are *sufficient* to the understanding of the complex universe of reality; but they are, I believe, a necessary implement in the inquirer's tool chest.

It is also true, of course, that principles which come to the clearest expression in the study of other subject matters are of great importance in the interpretation of so-called "economic" phenomena. The concept of an ecological system, which was developed first in the biological sciences—i.e., of a system of populations of various things, in which the equilibrium size and the movement of each population are dependent on the size of other populations—is an interpretive principle of the utmost value in the social sciences. Just as a pond develops an equilibrium population of frogs, fishes, bacteria, algae, and the like, all in subtle competitive and cooperative relationships with one another, so society is a great pond, developing equilibrium populations of Baptist churches, post offices, gas stations, families, counties, states, wheat farmers, chickens, and so on, which also exhibit complex co-operative and competitive relations one with another. The concept of mechanical equilibrium, both static and dynamic, has also had an immense impact—indeed, too great an impact—on the social sciences. Wherever we find a potential difference producing a current or flow by overcoming a resistance, we find something like Ohm's law, exhibited in its purest form in the study of electricity, but valuable as an interpretive principle when we study the flow of goods or of resources in response to price differences (economic potential) against the resistance imposed by costs of transport. In the theory of electrical circuits we may find clues to some baffling phenomena connected with the circuit flow of money.

Within the social sciences themselves, concepts which have been developed in anthropology, such as systems of ritualistic and customary behavior, and concepts which have been developed in sociology and social psychology, such as the crisis-adjustment patterns in family relationships, are all applicable to the subject matter of economics.

Indeed, I see the great empire of human knowledge, not as a conglomeration of independent and perhaps even warring kingdoms, each cultivating its own little field of subject matter by its own methods and each living wholly on its own produce, but as a great Republic of the mind, comprised, it is true, of subdivisions such as Physics, Chemistry, Economics, Botany, and the like, the boundaries of which are, like the boundaries of political states, partly the result of historic accident and partly the result of the lay of the land, but all uniting and cooperating in a common task of producing and exchanging the most precious of all commodities, and, indeed, exchanging not only the results of their labors, but exchanging also the tools which the special requirements of each field have perfected.

II

I propose to devote the remainder of this article, therefore, to a brief discussion of the contribution which the methods of economics may be able to make to other fields.

Recent developments in economics in the theory of oligopoly have an important bearing on problems of political science. It is perhaps significant that there was no representative from political science in this symposium. In a day when civilization itself is threatened by our inability to solve an essentially political problem (the abolition of war), it is tragic that so little fundamental thinking is being done in political science. Even the World Federalists—the only group who seem to be intellectually active in this field at all—seem to have got little further than the eighteenth century. It may well be that a significant revival in political thought will come out of the economics of oligopoly, where we are concerned essentially with problems of *strategy*—i.e., situations in which the choices of each person or organization involved depend upon their expectations regarding the choices of the others. It may be that the present bankruptcy of the national state, which can provide us with neither security, justice, peace, nor honor, is closely associated with the duopolistic character of international rivalry. There are marked similarities between the power struggles of oligopolistic firms and the power struggles of states: price wars and sales wars exhibit in a simplified form many of the essential problems of that most destestable of sciences, military science. There is no more striking contrast than between the resourcefulness and inventiveness which is shown in dealing with the "war" problem in the business world, with its multitudinous forms of agreement and federation, and the sterility and ritualistic rigidity of the political world.

Economics can also make an important contribution to those sciences in which general equilibria or a great multiplicity of interconnected relationships are characteristic of the subject matter. In economics, as in astronomy, the experimental method is almost impossible. We cannot simplify our universe, as the chemist or the physicist does, by the artificial creation of conditions in which virtually all factors but the ones we are investigating are excluded. We cannot take a businessman or a household and expose them first to one set of prices and then to another set to see what happens. Our subject matter is presented to us in a manner that is for the most part not within our control; there is no recipe for unscrambling in fact the magnificent omelette of social experience. We are always faced with an overwhelming and baffling multiplicity, and because of the very dominance of the problem we have been forced to devise methods for handling it.

These methods fall into three groups. There is first the *ceteris paribus* approach, identified mainly with the name of Marshall, which is in a sense a method of intellectual experiment, involving the isolation of a single problem by the assumption that all variables other than those investigated are held constant. This method has yielded valuable results in a limited sphere, and is a necessary prerequisite to the solution of more difficult problems. Nevertheless, it also has its dangers, especially the danger of overgeneralization from the particular to the general case. Thus the fact that a fall in the wages of carpenters is likely to lead to a rise in the amount of employment offered to them by no means implies that the remedy for general unemployment is general wage reduction. It is easy to fall into fallacies of composition when using this method, but in spite of its dangers it remains a necessary implement in the economist's, and indeed in any scientist's, tool bag.

The second method is one that is familiar in the physical sciences, the method of simultaneous equations. In economics this is associated chiefly with the name of Leon Walras and the Lausanne school. It is based on the proposition that any system of n variables, each of which can be written as a function of all the others, yields n of these equations which may be capable of solution to yield values of the variables each of which is consistent with every other. The difficulty of the method is that unless we know a good deal about the form of the assumed functional relationships we cannot be positive that the system has a "real" solution, or that it does not have many real solutions. It may even have solutions that are mathematically correct but economically meaningless, such as negative prices. Consequently, if we except the pioneering work of Leontieff at Harvard, the method has not been particularly fruitful of results in economics, in spite of its superior elegance and generality.

The third method is that associated with the name of Keynes, now frequently called that of "macroeconomics." This consists essentially in using large aggregates of economic variables as the basic parameters of simplified models, the exact properties of which can be fairly easily determined. In a sense this combines the simplicity and fruitfulness of the Marshallian approach with the generality of the Walrasian. Marshall's method is admirable in discussing the forces that determine the price and output of, say, limburger cheese, but it cannot deal with the problems of the system as a whole. Walras deals with the system as a whole, but at such a level of generality and abstraction that practically nothing can be said about it except that it exists. Keynes, by taking the system as a whole, but ruthlessly lumping it into large aggregates, the relationships of which he explores, affects in a sense a combination of the virtues of both the other methods. The macroeconomic models are simple enough to be handled, and yet cover the whole system. Not that the macroeconomic method is without its own dangers. Aggregates like "the national income," or "the level of employment," or "the price level" are all heterogeneous conglomerations, and there is danger, particularly for the more mathematical and less philosophical users of the technique, of neglecting the *structure* of these aggregates. It is fatally easy to write "Let the National Income be Y and the Price Level be P" and straightway to get so deliciously involved in the manipulation of our Y's and P's that we forget that they are not simple aggregates but have a complex structure which may well be relevant to the problem in hand. This "fallacy of aggregation" is a common one; it is at the root of most of the fallacies of Marxism, with its assumption of homogeneous classes; of Nationalism, with its assumption of homogeneous nations; and it even accounts for the spectacular lack of prophetic success among the brighter young economists. Nevertheless, for all its dangers, the macroeconomic method has led to a revolution in economic thought, the end of which is by no means visible, and it creates a discipline and habit of mind which might easily create revolutions in other sciences as well. I suspect that the natural scientists are also subject to both the fallacy of composition and the fallacy of aggregation; that they are much too uncritical of their basic taxonomic systems, much too prone to generalize on the basis of particular experience, and too little sensitive to the abominable interrelatedness of things! It would be a valuable experience for any scientist to familiarize himself thoroughly with what may be called the "macroeconomic paradoxes"—the propositions which are true in individual experience but which are quite untrue for society as a whole. Thus an individual can increase his money stock by "hoarding"—i.e., spending less money than he receives: but the attempt on the part of all individuals to hoard does not result in general "hoarding;" it merely decreases the total volume of money payments. An individual can get rid of money by spending it: a society cannot. For an individual, expenditure and receipts are two very different things: for society they are exactly the same thing, every expenditure being another person's receipt. An individual can "save"— i.e., increase his net worth—by not consuming as much as his income. If everyone tries to do this the result may not be an increase in society's capital but a decline in income and employment. In distribution these paradoxes abound. A trade union may raise the wages of its members: it is very doubtful whether trade unions as a whole can raise wages as a share of the total income. Profits are determined by the level of investment, not by the wage bargain; the more business distributes in dividends, the greater will be the profits out of which dividends can be paid. The macroeconomic world is a Wonderland full of widow's cruses and Danaïd jars, where nothing is what it seems, where things do not add up, where the collective result of individual decisions is something totally different from the sum of these decisions. Moreover, this is the real world: yet it cannot be understood by any generalization from individual experience; it can only be understood through the kind of intellectual discipline which economics provides. Moreover, it is not only in economics that this topsy-turviness prevails. In politics prohibiton leads to drunkenness, the quest for national security leads to national destruction, the more literate we make people the less educated they become, and the conquest of nature by the physical sciences leads to ever-increasing misery, fear, and degradation.

III

I have not attempted in this paper to defend economics by reference to the importance of its subject matter, as that can hardly be a matter of question. Was Marx right in supposing that capitalism has an inherent contradiction in it? What is the necessary minimum of governmental intervention into economic life? Can inflations and depressions be remedied? How far can the distribution of income be equalized without destroying the roots of economic progress? These and like questions cannot possibly be answered without serious study, and the name of this serious study is economics. One needs no more reminder of its necessity. It is trite, but frighteningly true, to say that the survival of this present civilization depends, not on the further development of natural science, but on the solution of certain serious intellectual problems in the social sciences.

In conclusion, I should like to urge the necessity for the study of economics not only for its conclusions and methods, but also for the state of mind it produces. In the old Cambridge tripos, economics—or, to give it its grander title, political economy—was listed as a Moral Science. For all the attempts of our positivists to dehumanize the sciences of man, a moral science it remains. Its central problem is the problem of value: and value is but a step from virtue. Every science, like every craft, imposes certain of its marks on its practitioners. I would hesitate to suggest, especially to members of the AAAS, that geologists grow like their rocks, chemists like their smells, or even astronomers like their heavens. I cannot forbear, however, from quoting from Professor Robbins, of the London School of Economics: "It is not an exaggeration to say that, at the present day, one of the main dangers to civilisation arises from the inability of minds trained in the natural sciences to perceive the difference between the economic and the technical." In the lurid twilight of science in which we live, when it has gained the whole world and lost its own soul, when it is everywhere prostituted to special interests, whether of the dairy farmers, the steel industry, or the national state, when the search for truth is subordinated to the lust for power, it is not altogether an accident that it is in the social science departments that the occasional voice crying in the wilderness is most likely to be heard. In a world of technicians, it is the economist who raises the cry that the technically most efficient is not necessarily, or even usually, the socially most efficient; that the best cow is not the one that gives the most milk; the best business is not the one that makes the most profits; the best army is not the one that creates the most havoc; and, above all, that the best training is not the best education. In a day when self-interest, nationalism, totalitarianism, militarism, and a dreadful pride threaten our very existence, economics points always toward the general interest, looks toward a free-trading world society, claims that the business of living even in a complex society can be accomplished with a small minimum of police coercion, urges that plenty is the source of power and war the greatest enemy of plenty, and by its very failures induces that humility for lack of which we perish.

INCOME OR WELFARE

The Review of Economic Studies, 17 (1949-50): 77-86.

Income or Welfare

The concept of income may seem at first glance to be one of the most simple and innocuous in economics. On deeper reflection, however, it turns out to be one of the most difficult and confusing concepts. It is well known that the principal weakness of classical economics was its failure to distinguish clearly between income and capital concepts. The confusion between funds and flows foreshadowed in the opening sentence of the *Wealth of Nations*[1] and flowering into the manifold confusions of the wage fund theory is an ever-present weakness in the classical system. We owe the clarification of the dimensional problem mainly to Irving Fisher, and there is not much danger to-day of repeating the classical error of confounding stocks with flows. It is the purpose of this paper, however, to demonstrate that another serious error, which also goes back at least to Adam Smith, still persists in modern economics, and renders a great deal of thinking and writing on the subject of income both wrong and harmful.

The error in question is the identification of income, either in the form of production or consumption, with economic welfare, or perhaps it would be more accurate to say the use of income as a measure of economic welfare. So ingrained is this identification into our thinking that the assumption passes almost unquestioned, not only in the economics of the neo-classical school as represented by Pigou, but also in the more fashionable Keynesian economics. Whether we are looking at income microeconomically in the case of an individual, or macro-economically in the case of a whole society, the same assumption is made—the more income, the more welfare, at least up to the point of marginal equality between the income-producing and income-consuming uses of time (work and leisure). It is this assumption that I wish to question.

It is necessary first to examine closely the true significance of the concept of income itself. One or two minor confusions may be cleared out of the way first. There is some confusion, in the Keynesian literature especially, between income and receipts. By receipts I mean in-payments of money to the account of an individual. There is an even more dangerous confusion between expenditure and consumption. A receipt or expenditure of money normally represents an exchange or an asset-transfer. It is reflected in the balance sheet of the individual receiving the money by an increase in his money stocks and an equal decline in some other asset which was " sold " or exchanged for the money. Correspondingly, in the balance sheet of the individual spending the money, there is a decline in money stocks and an equal increase in some other asset representing the thing bought. In both cases there is no change in the *total* of assets as an immediate result of the receipt or expenditure, for it is a fundamental accounting convention that in exchange equal values are exchanged. A receipt or an expenditure merely represents a change in the *form* of assets—from non-liquid to liquid in the case of a receipt, from liquid to non-liquid in the case of an expenditure. This is clearly true where the receipt results from the sale of a material object or commodity, or where the expenditure results from the purchase of a commodity. It is a little less apparent, but none the less true, when the assets transferred are non-material claims. A wage payment, for instance, is no more " income " than a payment for an old cupboard dug out the attic and sold to a neighbour. A wage payment also represents a transfer of assets—in this case, the transfer of a claim on an employer into liquid assets of some kind. If the wage payment is effected by cheque it represents simply a transfer from a claim on an employer to a claim on a bank.

[1] " The annual labour of every nation is the fund which originally supplies it with all the necessaries and conveniences of life which it annually enjoys."

If, then, receipts are not income, what is income ? The example of the wage payment provides a clue.   Income is earned as the wage-claim on the employer is built up, day after day, by the productive activity of the worker. Similarly, the receipt of money on clipping a coupon is not income : it is the building-up of the interest-claim on the bond issuer that constitutes income.   Income, in other words, is the gross growth in, or addition to, assets.   Receipts merely represent the transfer of assets from one form to another.

The income concept exists in two main forms—money income and real income. Money income is the money *value* of the gross growth in assets. Real income is the gross growth in assets in physical terms. Real income is, of course, a list of hetero-geneous items : it can only be reduced to a homogeneous measurable form by evaluating each item of the list according to some constant price weight. There is some ambiguity in the concept of money income because of the fact that the total value of assets may change, not only because of a change in the physical quantity of assets, but also because of a change in the prices at which durable assets are valued. The rise in the value of assets due to a rise in their price is usually termed " capital gains," and there is some doubt as to whether capital gains should be included in income. We may perhaps distinguish between " accounting income," which includes capital gains, and " productive income " which does not.

Corresponding to the income concepts there are the consumption concepts. Real income is the gross addition to real assets : real consumption is the gross subtraction from assets. Corresponding to the money income concept there is the " money out-go " concept, which is the value of consumption—i.e. the money value of assets consumed. Just as there is some doubt whether capital gains should be included in money income, so there is a question whether capital losses (declines in the value of assets because of a decline in their prices) should be counted as " money out-go." Perhaps the most satisfactory method of treating this problem is to regard out-go as consisting only of the value of assets consumed, analogous to " productive income " as defined above, and to treat capital losses as deductions from " productive income " necessary in order to reach the figure for " accounting income " : i.e. capital losses would in this sense simply be regarded as negative capital gains and would be considered as negative " accounting income."

The above concepts enable us to clarify the concepts of saving, investment, and hoarding. There are two processes on the part of individuals which must be distin-guished : one is the process of not consuming as much income as we produce, and thereby adding to the total of assets. The other is the process of not spending as much as we receive, thereby adding to the total of liquid (money) assets. The term " saving " has frequently been applied to both these processes, distinct as they are, and the confusion between income and receipts and between out-go and expenditure has led to a corresponding confusion between the process of increasing total assets and the process of increasing liquid assets. The process of increasing total assets by not con-suming as much as we produce may perhaps most properly be called " saving," as we have another word—"hoarding"—for the process of accumulating liquid assets by not spending as much as we receive. The distinction between these concepts may be seen clearly if we reflect that it frequently happens that an individual is hoarding and dis-saving, or dis-hoarding and saving, at the same time. When an individual's purchases consist of a high proportion of durable goods (e.g. automobiles, houses, furniture), and his sales consist of a high proportion of non-durables (e.g. labour), he may easily be " dis-hoarding " and " saving " at the same time. Consider, for instance, an individual with an income of $5,000 per annum from labour : he adds to his assets—at first in liquid form—$5,000 during the year. Suppose that his consumption (subtraction from assets) amounts to $4,000. He will have " saved "—i.e. increased his net worth—by $1,000 during the year. In the same year, however, he may have sold an automobile for $1,000 and bought a house for $10,000 : his receipts may then be $6,000 and his expenditure $14,000 : he will have dis-hoarded $8,000. If we suppose that at the beginning of the year his balance sheet contained the items Money, $10,000, Other Assets, $20,000, Total $30,000 : at the end of the year his balance sheet will read Money, $2,000, Other Assets, $29,000, Total $31,000. In general, if Y is income, C is out-go, R is receipts, E is expenditures, S is saving, and H is hoarding, we have :

$$S = Y - C \dots\dots\dots\dots\dots\dots\dots\dots\dots\dots\dots\dots\dots\dots\dots\dots (1)$$
$$H = R - E \quad \dots\dots\dots\dots\dots\dots\dots\dots\dots\dots\dots\dots\dots\dots\dots (2)$$

One hesitates to name any concept " investment " in view of the protean meanings of the word : nevertheless it would seem that the concept of the increase in non-liquid assets would qualify fairly well for the title, as we need a word for this concept and it corresponds fairly well to the meaning of investment in ordinary speech. If then we call the increase in non-liquid assets I, we have, as the increase in total assets must equal the increase in liquid plus the increase in non-liquid assets,

$$S = H + I \dots\dots\dots\dots\dots\dots\dots\dots\dots\dots\dots\dots\dots\dots\dots\dots (3)$$
whence $$I = S - H = Y - C - R + E \dots\dots\dots\dots\dots\dots\dots\dots\dots\dots (4)$$

In the above equations we have neglected capital gains and losses : if Y stands for accounting income it will be equal to $Y_p + G$, where Y_p is productive income and G is capital gains.

Many confusions of the saving-investment controversy can be straightened out with the aid of the above very simple, but surprisingly neglected, analysis. Equations (1) to (4) can all be aggregated so that the symbols represent the aggregates for society as a whole. Equation (1), then, states the Keynesian " Savings = Investment " identity in its most accurate form : that the net addition to total assets is equal to the gross addition less the gross subtraction. Equation (2) in its aggregate form is likewise a very important proposition : that the difference between money receipts and money expenditures must be equal to the amount by which the total money stock has increased. Equation (3) states another important proposition : that the total increase in individual net worths must be equal to the increase in money stocks plus the value of the increase in real capital.

I have pursued the implications of these distinctions further in another article,[1] and it is not the intention of the present paper to pursue them further. My task now is to call attention to an even more dangerous confusion in income theory than the confusion between income and receipts. This is the confusion between income and " utilisation." There is a very general assumption in economics that income (or out-go) is the proper measure of economic welfare, and that the more income and out-go we have, the better. In fact, almost the reverse is the case. Income consists of the value of production : out-go is the value of consumption. Both income and out-go are processes involved in the maintenance and expansion of the capital stock. I shall argue that it is the capital stock from which we derive satisfactions, not from the additions to it (production) or the subtractions from it (consumption) : that consumption, far from being a desideratum, is a deplorable property of the capital stock which necessitates the equally deplorable activities of production : and that the objective of economic policy should not be to maximise consumption or production, but rather to minimise it, i.e. to enable us to maintain our capital stock with as little consumption or production as possible. It is not the increase of consumption or production which makes us rich, but the increase in capital, and any invention which

[1] " Professor Tarshis and the State of Economics," *American Economic Review*, March, 1948, Vol. XXXVIII, p. 92.

enables us to enjoy a given capital stock with a smaller amount of consumption and production, out-go or income, is so much gain.

The illusion that consumption—and its correlative, income—is desirable probably stems from too great preoccupation with what Knight calls " one-use goods," such as food and fuel, where the utilisation and consumption of the good are tightly bound together in a single act or event. We shall return to the problem of one-use goods later. In the meantime let us direct our attention towards many-use goods, such as houses, automobiles, furniture, crockery, clothing, machinery and tools, buildings, roads, bridges, etc. It is quite clear that the consumption of these goods (which necessitates their production) is something quite incidental to their use and frequently not even closely connected with the degree of use. We want houses, not because they depreciate, get dirty, sag, crack, disintegrate and need repairs : we want houses because we can live in them, and the living in them is in no way bound up with their consumption. If we had houses that would not depreciate, walls that would not get dirty or require painting, roofs that would never leak, foundations that would never sag, furniture that would not wear out, crockery that would not break, footwear that never needed repair, clothing that never got ragged or unpressed, we should clearly be much better off : we would be enjoying the services of these things without the necessity of consuming or producing them. Coming now nearer to the one-use goods, consider fuel : it is clear that there is no virtue in consuming fuel—that the consumption of fuel for domestic heating merely arises because of the depreciation of warmth by poor insulation ; any economy in the consumption of fuel that enables us to maintain warmth or to generate power with lessened consumption again leaves us better off. Much as the reader may accept the desirability of unconsumable houses, clothing and furniture, or even unconsumable fuel, he may perhaps revolt at the thought of unconsumable food. Even here, however, though the connection between consumption and utilisation is strong, the two concepts are separable in thought. Food has two aspects, a nutritional and a psychological. In so far as food is simply fuel for the body it has the characteristic of any other fuel : an economy in consumption makes us better off. If discoveries in nutrition enable us to maintain the health and energy of the human body with less intake of food than before, we are better off on that account, just as we are better off if we can economise fuel consumption. In regard to the psychological aspect of food consumption—the pleasure that is derived from eating—it may be admitted that there are cases in which satisfaction seems to be derived from consumption itself. Our impression that satisfaction is derived from consumption merely arises, however, from the fact that it is not easy to imagine an improvement which will increase the efficiency of consumption in the case of food. We might imagine the development of a longer-lasting flavour in the gum, but a longer-lasting steak might not be so desirable. It must be admitted that there are certain cases in which satisfaction seems to be derived from consumption itself rather than from utilisation. Many of these cases, however, border upon the pathological : the satisfactions of the potlatch and of incendiarism border on the sadistic, and one wonders also whether the satisfaction derived from the consumption of food is not of a somewhat similar order. Certainly these cases comprise only a small part of satisfaction : in the case of the overwhelming mass of commodities it is not consumption but utilisation which is the source of satisfaction.

A related problem arises in the consideration of production. There are certain satisfactions which arise from the act of production itself, and these do not seem to have the slightly morbid connotations of satisfactions derived from acts of consumption. There is a healthy pleasure in " making things " which is derived from a fundamental " creative urge " in human nature. This may express itself in ways as diverse as philo-progenitiveness, knitting, fishing, woodworking, writing, painting, or perhaps even thinking. Consequently, a world which had reached a truly " stationary state " in cultural and intellectual as well as in physical capital would be very dull. If we were so well supplied with poetry, pictures and music, as well as with permanently durable goods of all kinds, that no further production of anything was necessary, we might be rich, but it is doubtful whether we should be happy. The problem of stagnation is much wider than the narrowly economic : it is a problem which faces every civilisation as its cultural capital increases. The fact that so much good poetry has been already written makes it increasingly difficult to write anything that has not been equally well done before ; the same problem applies to all the arts. Consequently, as cultural capital increases the creative urge is apt to take unhealthy forms ; in the struggle to produce something new, novelty comes to be appreciated more than beauty, and a civilisation expires in a cancer of morbid art forms engendered by a horror of imitation and a craving to be original and creative at all costs.

It may well be, therefore, that there is a value in consumption quite apart from any direct satisfaction which it produces, in that consumption may be necessary in order to clear the ground for productive activity. There is a kind of grim comfort in these times in the reflection that even disaster frequently clears the ground for fresh creative effort. The destruction of Athens gave us the Parthenon ; the Great Fire of London gave us St. Paul's. These considerations, however, underline further the proposition that there is no great value in consumption itself. In so far as we want the satisfactions of utilisation, consumption is a nuisance, a real " cost " of maintaining the stock of goods. In so far as we want the satisfactions of creativity, consumption is merely a means to creating conditions favourably to creation. Consumption is the death of capital, and the only valid arguments in favour of consumption are the arguments in favour of death itself. The stock of humans is as much part of real capital as the stock of sheep or of automobiles, and the consumption of humans by death is subject to much the same principles of evaluation as the consumption of any other form of capital. It is clear that death is at the same time a tragic waste and a magnificent opportunity—a waste because it represents the loss of painfully acquired human capital and the break-up of an intricate pattern of human relationships, and an opportunity because it is the prerequisite for birth. Without death, birth would soon become impossible, for the world would be choked with its own fecundity. It is clear that with any given system of valuation functions there must be an optimum length of human life. If, for instance, the average age at death was only thirty years, so much effort would have to be put into the task of maintaining the population that there would be little energy left over for any form of creativity other than procreation. There are populations to-day—e.g. in the Far East—where this condition is approximated. If on the other hand the average age at death was Methuselah's nine hundred and sixty-nine, assuming that the vigour and creativity of the individual persisted throughout the long life and the maturity was reached in the twenties as at present, the scarcity of children, the insignificance of family life, and the absence of the thousand-and-one interests that in our society centre around procreation would create a situation so different from our present society that it is difficult for us to imagine it. One suspects that such a society of Methuselah's would be forced to seek refuge from the boredom of the sensate in flights of contemplation which would make them quite incapable of procreation, and that in spite of Mr. Bernard Shaw's propaganda there is really no equilibrium point between a society of men and a society of immortals. Even the prolongation of life which the scientific age has created has brought with it grave social problems. A further prolongation—say to 100 or 150 years—would compel us to re-cast our whole social structure.

What is true of the human population is equally true of the population of commodities. The consumption (i.e. death) of commodities is at once a waste of capital and an opportunity for productive activity. If the life span of commodities is too short too much energy must be devoted to the sheer mechanics of economic reproduction. If the life span is too long the joys of dynamics and the satisfactions of creativity would have to give way to a stationary nirvana of unchanging and, therefore, probably unappreciated and unconscious bliss. There should be, therefore, some optimum " period of production " at which the joint satisfactions of creation and utilisation are at a maximum.

In the case of commodities, however, the problem is complicated by the existence of what may be called " geological capital " ; the stores of coal, oil, minerals, metal ores, etc., which have been accumulated in the earth over the long process of geological time. To a considerable extent the process of economic production is a process of material diffusion and deconcentration—a kind of increase in economic or material entropy. The geological history of the earth, for some reason which I confess I fail to understand, has resulted in a very imperfect diffusion of the elements through the earth, and particularly, an imperfect diffusion through the earth's skin, so that instead of finding iron, copper, sodium, and so on, diffused equally through the earth, we find the astonishing phenomenon of " mines "—mountains of iron ore, of copper, veins of gold, and so on. Man, however, in his economic busyness, is on the whole an agent of diffusion. The iron that he digs from the Mesabi range rusts away in countless dumps and deposits. The carbon that he digs from coal pits burns away into the chemically featureless and homogeneous atmosphere ; the phosphorus and potash that he extracts in his crops runs down his sewers into the equally featureless and homogeneous sea. This process is clearly not self-perpetuating, and to an alarming extent our " production " consists of the squandering of our geological capital. We are apt to point with pride at the achievements of our technology in increasing " output," without reflecting that this is not necessarily a symbol of health, but of a wasting disease. In some cases we have extracted more minerals from our mines, and perhaps even from our soils, in the present century, than our forefathers did in the whole course of recorded history, but far from being a source of pride this should perhaps be an occasion for shame and dismay. Our economy is not merely one of high consumption— it might almost be described as an economy in a state of galloping consumption. We may be squandering our geological capital of ores, fuels, and soils, that it has taken the whole of geological time to accumulate, on such frivolities as war and a high standard of life at a rate which bodes ill for much permanent future for the human race.

There are, however, a few more hopeful straws in the wind. In some instances modern technology has reversed the usual process of diffusion and man is acting as an agent of concentration. The two principal cases are the fixation of nitrogen from the air and the extraction of magnesium from the sea. The ancient process of extracting salt from the sea by evaporation is another example of a reversal of diffusion. In spite of these exceptions, however, the fact remains that a large part of productive activity is of a diffusionist, non-repeatable nature, and that it represents, from the long-run point of view, the decumulation of capital. We must not infer, of course, that capital decumulation of this kind is necessarily irrational. It would be just as foolish to shiver on top of unused coal deposits for fear of using them up as it would be to mine them without ever giving thought to their irreplaceability. From a short-run point of view the " optimum " rate of use of exhaustible resources depends on our time preference and the " horizon of expectations." From a long run point of view, however, we may well regard the geological capital with which man has been favoured as a fund which gives him a chance, but no more than a chance, to pass from a low-level ecological system of natural reproduction and circulation based on unconscious chemical processes to a high-level ecological system based, perhaps, on conscious atomic transformations. As long as we are confined to purely chemical processes the diffusion and dissipation of the elements involved in most processes of production is a critical problem from the point of view of the long-run survival of humanity. The " nitrogen scare " of last century would have been perfectly justified by history had not the process for the fixation of nitrogen been discovered. As long as we are confined to purely chemical processes, however, a twentieth-century Crookes might well work up a " potash scare " or a " phosphorus scare." Both these elements are as essential to plant growth as nitrogen. Both of them are being " squandered " by the dissemination of geologically accumulated deposits. Neither of them exist appreciably in the atmosphere, where nitrogen is present in such an enormous and inexhaustible quantity. The only chemical reservoir of these elements is the sea, where they exist in such minute proportions that the problem of chemical or physical extraction presents grave difficulties. It would not be difficult, therefore, to visualise a day when the none-too-plentiful natural deposits of potash and phosphates will be exhausted and the high-output agriculture which depends on their application to the soil will be impossible. The only hope for a permanently high-level agriculture would seem to be the development of methods of production of scarce elements by atomic transmutations.

There are important implications of the above analysis, both for economic theory itself and for the policy conclusions which stem therefrom. In the first place it is necessary to separate more clearly than hitherto the concept of income, output, or gross national product from the concept of economic welfare. There may be, and usually is, a correlation between the level of income and of welfare. But this connection is by no means invariable, and it would be most rash to suppose that an increase in income always means an increase in welfare. Irving Fisher saw this forty years ago, when he coined the phrase " psychic income " : psychic income is that which is derived from the possession or use or capital, and is the significant welfare concept. " Real " income or " output," on the other hand, is significant only because of the power which it gives us to increase our capital stock, and hence our psychic income. It is by no means an unrealistic model to suppose that the volume of consumption is determined mainly by the size and character of the existing stock of capital, each item of capital consuming itself at its own technically determined rate. This model is not quite accurate, as within limits the rate of consumption of existing capital can be modified— e.g. by more or less intensive use : these limits, however, in many cases, are quite narrow. In such a model accumulation is determined by output, and hence the more output, the more accumulation, with a *given* capital stock. It is because of the power which it gives us to accumulate and maintain capital (spiritual as well as physical) that output is desirable.

These considerations have many implications for the theory of economic progress. We cannot simply assume that output, or output per head, is a measure of economic progress. An increase in output, statistically measured by a weighted index of physical outputs, may easily be accompanied by a decline in economic welfare if the increased output is necessitated by a declining durability of capital or by declining efficiency of utilisation. If we produce twice as many shirts of only half the durability as before we are clearly no better off, but the increased output of shirts will be reflected in increased total output and income. It may perhaps be argued that in this case the price of the less durable shirts will be less than that of the more durable shirts, and hence the increase in the number of shirts produced will not affect the index of physical output because of the decline in the price " weight." Thus a million shirts valued at $4.00 would have the same weight in the output index as two million valued at $2.00.

There is no reason to suppose, however, that price is directly proportional to durability. Moreover, as it is relative prices only that are significant in weighting output indices, if all commodities suffered a decline in durability the output index would unquestionably reflect an increase which was quite spurious from the point of view of welfare. The same principle applies to the interpretation of output (income) statistics of various countries or regions. To get a true picture of the relative economic power or welfare of different countries we must have some notion of their total capital stock and of the durability of its components.

The concept of income developed above also throws a good deal of light on the significance of " national income " estimates. In particular it is useful in interpreting the significance of the " gross national product " versus the " national income," or " net national product " concepts. The gross national product is equal to the net national product plus the depreciation of industrial fixed capital. Unfortunately the confusion between the money-flow (receipts-expenditure) process and the income-out-go process noted earlier has bedevilled national income analysis and made its conceptual framework much less clear than it should be. Both the gross and the net product concepts are output concepts, not money flow concepts. There are two aspects to the distinction. One is to regard it as an attempt to derive the net national income as a welfare concept. Depreciation is part of consumption, but it is regarded as in some way not contributing to welfare. There is not much to be said for the distinction on these grounds. The depreciation of household capital contributes no more to welfare than the depreciation of industrial capital, and if we are trying to get a net income concept as a measure of welfare by deducting some forms of consumption from gross income, then there is no logical stopping place short of deducting all consumption, for as we have seen from the welfare point of view there is no marked difference between one-use goods that are " consumed " and many-use goods that " depreciate." The truth is, of course, that there is no simple way of passing from any output or consumption concept to that of " psychic incomes," and we certainly do not want to define net income as equivalent to net accumulation, as we would have to do if we deducted *all* consumption from gross output.

There is, however, a certain justification for the distinction because of the " double counting " problem. As we have seen, some commodities are consumed in the production of others, and it is quite legitimate to regard the difference between the gross output and the consumption necessitated by it as the " net output " of the process in question. Thus when milk is made into cheese, the net addition to assets is not the cheese, but the cheese less the milk, and if we included both the milk and the cheese in our output index it is clear that there would be " double counting " in some sense. If, therefore, the depreciation of industrial fixed capital can be regarded as transformation of the industrial capital in some sense into finished products, then the consumption of industrial fixed capital would in no way differ from the consumption of milk in the cheese industry, and the " net natural product " would be a more significant measure of output than the gross product. There are some very real difficulties, however, in the concept of " net " product. In the first place much of the consumption which goes under the head of depreciation takes place whether the goods in question are used or not. Thus factories and machines depreciate, very often, just as fast, or even faster, when they are not being used as when they are used in the production of further output. There is not the direct connection, therefore, between the consumption (depreciation) of a factory and the production of its product that there is in the case of the consumption of a raw material and the production of the product into which it is transformed. There is a further difficulty in the case of labour : a certain part of consumption by humans (food, shelter, medical care, etc.) may be regarded as contributing to the production of further output. There is a real sense in which that consumption which is necessary to keep the individual alive and in health is a " cost of living "—the " maintenance " of human capital, which is no more part of the net product than, say, the oil which is used to oil a machine. This maintenance is in some sense a mechanical necessity, and is not part of the conscious purposes of a society. Perhaps the best definition of " net income " is that part of the product of a society which it is free to devote to its purposes—e.g. to war, to luxury, or to welfare. A " poor " society is one in which the effort to maintain its capital, both human and material, requires the major part of its energies, and which cannot devote much of its resources to purposive activity. This is essentially the Ricardian concept of " net revenue."

It is clear that there are several concepts of national income or output, each of which is suitable for a particular purpose. If we want a measure of economic power, then perhaps the extreme " net " concept—net of human maintenance—is the significant quantity. If we want a measure of output which is closely correlated with employment, however, the gross concept is in the main superior. The superiority of the gross national product as a measure of the degree of employment depends on the assumption that the consumption of fixed capital is independent of its use. If that is the case, then if there was no employment at all, the gross national product would be zero, but the net national product (gross product minus depreciation) would be negative. An increase in employment increases both gross and net product equally in absolute terms, on this assumption, but a given proportional increase in employment produces a proportional increase in the gross, but not in the net product. Thus suppose depreciation—assumed to be independent of the product—were $20. At zero employment gross product would be zero, net product would be − $20. If every man employed adds $1 to the product, a doubling of employment—say from 50 to 100 men—doubles the gross product, from $50 to $100, but more than doubles the net product, which goes from $30 to $80. If depreciation were exactly proportional to use, net product would also be zero when employment was zero, and would rise proportional to employment, though at a lower rate than the gross product.

There are certain implications for economic policy which arise out of the above analysis, and which are worth a brief mention. It is clear that a certain conflict may emerge between policy directed towards full employment and policy directed to economic progress. The volume of employment is closely related to the total of consumption, and where unemployment is a problem the encouragement of consumption seems to be an obvious remedy. On the other hand, from the point of view of economic progress it is not the encouragement but the economy of consumption that is desirable. The conflict between the two aims is to some extent only an apparent one ; the economy of consumption in particular lines is quite consistent with an overall expansion. Nevertheless, we should beware of regarding full employment as an end in itself, and short-run policies directed towards full employment through increasing consumption may well conflict with the long-run objective of economic progress.

These considerations are closely related to the problem of *conservation*. In its more familiar aspect conservation consists essentially in economy in the consumption of geological capital : in its very long-run sense it is the problem of the maintenance of capital. It may be—and this is a disquieting thought—that all civilisations have been maintained only by the expenditure of irreplaceable capital—i.e. by " mining," both of the soil and of mineral deposits. In this regard any economy of consumption increases our power of ultimate survival. It seems likely that not enough attention has been given, by theorists and policy-makers alike, to the problem of the conservation of industrial and domestic capital. It may well be that one of the deepest conflicts between private and public interest lies right here, in the "impatience" of the individual, whether as householder or as producer, which leads him to prefer goods of durability less than is socially desirable. It may be that the regulation of the quality of goods by the medieval guilds is a policy which needs a modern counterpart. How to do it is another question, and one which the present writer does not feel competent to solve. But the problem remains, and merits serious consideration on the part of the makers and inspirers of policy.

COLLECTIVE BARGAINING AND FISCAL POLICY

American Economic Review, 40, 2 (May 1950): 306-320.

COLLECTIVE BARGAINING AND FISCAL POLICY

The study of industrial relations has now spread so far beyond the limits of economics that the economist in these days has considerable difficulty in persuading students of labor that his discipline has anything to contribute to their studies. It is not enough for him to confess —as in all honesty he should—that economics comprises no more than about 20 per cent of the subject, and that the rest is sociology, social psychology, individual psychology, psychiatry, anthropology, law, engineering, political science, etc., with perhaps an occasional dash of philosophy, ethics, and even physics to improve the flavor. There is a strong (and to my mind a deplorable) tendency among the bright young labor specialists not merely to let economics go by default out of ignorance, as was customary among the older generation of writers on this subject, but to cast it out of the window bodily, with shrill cries of jubilation. One can hardly pick up a new book on labor nowadays without finding the author jumping gleefully on what he thinks is the corpse of Demand-and-Supply, or proclaiming with trumpets, "The Labor Market is Dead, Long Live Human Relations." In the interests of continuing certain valued friendships, I refrain from mentioning names, even at the cost of some bibliographical respectability, but the phenomenon is too obvious and widespread to have to be annotated.

This animosity displayed toward economics may perhaps be explained by the Oedipus complex (economics being in some sense the father of the new discipline of industrial relations), and while it may on that account be forgiven it is nonetheless to be deplored, if only because any animus is an obstacle to learning. I have wrestled in committee for a whole year with a psychiatrist who thought that industrial relations not only began but ended with the love life of foremen, and I have had similar difficulties with psychologists who think that industrial relations is no more than the science of "how to push people around and make them like it." I hasten to add, lest I be accused of the very animus that I deplore (and I confess to as much animus as a worm turned) that by far the most important contributions to industrial relations in the past few years have come from outside economics. Even the most hardened economist must now realize that purely economic models of trade unions in terms of maximizing behavior are not very realistic, and that the interpretation of union behavior in terms of power structures, considerations of prestige, relative advantages, and so on is extremely illuminating. Similarly, the Mayo studies and others like them have revealed the immense importance of the factor of status and human significance in the industrial relationship and have rightly centered interest on the "human relations" aspect of the wage bargain.

Up to a point, therefore, the shift of interest in the labor field away from economics is entirely justified. The focus of interest of economics as a separate discipline is not men but commodities. The focus of interest of students of labor is, quite properly, men. It does not follow, however, that because economics is not the whole story or is even a small part of the story in the study of labor that it has nothing to say. I will concede 80 per cent to the other disciplines; but they try to take over the remaining 20 per cent at their great peril. Economics enters this field because labor is bought and sold and has a price (its wage); it is, that is to say, in spite of the Clayton Act, the ILO and the Federal Council of Churches, a commodity. It is, of course, a human commodity, and therefore around the circumstances of its purchase and sale there gathers a large and significant penumbra of human relations. It must not be thought that labor is unique among commodities in this regard: all exchanges, even in the stock market or the wheat market, have a certain social-psychological environment; this, in a sense, is what we mean when we say that all competition is in some degree imperfect. Nevertheless it is certainly true that the social-psychological penumbra is much more important in the case of labor than in the case of any other commodity, and it is this fact that makes labor a peculiar commodity, deserving of highly special treatment. But to say that it is peculiar does not mean to deny that it is a commodity, or to deny that the wage bargain is, among other things, an act of exchange.

I would argue, furthermore, that the commodity or exchange aspect of the industrial relationship is much more central to the understanding of the problem than most labor specialists are prepared to admit. The general character or "tone" of industrial relations in any period is determined to a large extent by what is happening in the world of commodities—whether, for instance, there is an inflation or a deflation in the general price-wage level, whether the level of employment and of income is rising or falling, is "high" or "low," and so on. Sociology and psychology may have a good deal to say about the effects of unemployment, for instance, on groups or on personalities; they have practically nothing to say as to its causes; that is the field of economics, and a field in which it can claim a great deal of success. I would hesitate to argue that happiness is a function of the national income, but I am pretty sure that misery is! And the national income in real terms is simply the total output of commodities; in money terms, the value of these commodities. Given a severe deflation or even a severe inflation, no amount of industrial psychology or sociology will save us from severe dislocations in the industrial relationship; nor can the best industrial psychology or sociology save us from inflations or deflations, if the world of commodities is producing them.

I am not arguing, of course, that the world of commodities operates independently of the world of men. The economist, in his better moments, is aware that it is not commodities that behave, but men; that commodities move not of themselves, like the planets, but are moved by men; and that every exchange involves two people or groups of people as well as two commodities. He rightly bears this information at the back of his mind, however, rather than at the front, because his very skill as an economist depends on his ability to abstract from the complexity of human behavior those aspects which concern commodities and to summarize these aspects in fairly simple functional relationships among commodity variables. Thus he is somewhat in the position of the astronomer who can neglect the problem of whether angels move the planets, because whether they do or not their behavior toward the planets is perfectly regular, and therefore predictable, and hence any other quirks of motive or character which they possess can be neglected. I say "somewhat" because the men who move commodities are much less regular in their behavior toward them than are the angels, if any, toward the planets, and hence the economist cannot regard the universe of commodities quite without regard to the men who move them and are moved by them. Nevertheless, the behavior of men toward commodities is regular enough and simple enough to justify as a first approximation the concept of a universe of commodities following its own laws. This is what the economist means when he speaks of "impersonal market forces"—and it must not be thought that this impersonality applies to the extreme case of perfect competition.

An example will perhaps clarify my meaning. During the past few years the level of money wages as well as of prices in the United States has approximately doubled. The fundamental reason for this is not the development of superior skills on the part of trade unions or of management, nor changes in "bargaining power," nor power or prestige struggles, nor backyard-wall comparisons, nor price or wage leadership, nor any of the thousand and one noneconomic complexities which motivate the actual behavior of individuals. The rise can, without much exaggeration, be put down to a single cause: the growth in private liquid assets as a result of the public methods of war finance. Compared with this great single cause all the noneconomic factors shrink into insignificance. When the tide rises, the exact movement of waters and even the exact levels in the innumerable creeks and estuaries depends on their particular local configurations; but the water in them rises because the tide rises, not because there is a channel here or a sandbank there. This is what the economist means when he affirms that there is such a thing as a labor market. A rise in the quantity of money or in its velocity of circulation creates an economic tide which will eventually filter into every creek and cranny in the economic system; it will create "shortages" at existing prices and wages which create a pressure for higher prices, whether that pressure is exercised through price and wage leadership, through the increased bargaining power of sellers, or the increased competition of buyers, and whether it is exercised in competitive or in noncompetitive markets. As a result of local power configurations (the channel here and the sandbank there) the tide may run a little higher in some places than in others, but the empirical evidence suggests that the differences so created are secondary in magnitude, especially when the tide is running in. At ebb tide it seems to be true that the dams of monopoly power can hold back a certain amount of the retreating income, but even these advantages seem to be only temporary.

I have used the metaphor of the tide advisedly, because it is precisely the "tide in the affairs of men" known as the business cycle which is the main problem of fiscal policy. The word cycle, with its implications of pendulum-like regularity, is perhaps a misnomer, but whether we are dealing with true cycles or not there is no doubt about the phenomenon of fluctuations in many important economic variables—especially output and employment and, to a less significant extent, in prices and values. The fluctuation which concerns us most, of course, is the fluctuation in output and employment, if only because any operation of the system below its proper "capacity" (i.e., ideal output) is almost pure loss. Price fluctuations are less serious—indeed, in moderation there is even something to be said for them as making for social mobility and for the dislodgment of vested interests—but beyond a certain point even price fluctuations are a serious inconvenience and create a good deal of haphazard injustice.

The principal task of government in this connection is to act as a "governor"; that is, to introduce a mechanism into the system analogous to a thermostat in a heating system or a governor on an engine. There are many reasons in theory, as well as in experience, for supposing that an unregulated free market system would be subject to marked fluctuations in payments, prices, incomes, and outputs. Dr. Wiener has coined the word "cybernetics" (from the Greek for "steersman") to denote the study of these stabilizing mechanisms,[1] of which there are innumerable examples in physiology (the homeostasis of the body), engineering, and ecology. The alternate chills and fever to which an ungoverned market economy seems to be subject is a familiar

[1] Norbert Wiener, *Cybernetics* (New York: John Wiley & Sons, 1948).

symptom of an inadequate cybernetic mechanism. The provision of such a mechanism is clearly a task of government; no other agency of society has the power, even if it had the will, to throw sufficient forces into the system to check movements away from the optimum position. It has been the inability of governments to govern, in this sense of the word, which has led to many quite improper extensions of government activity in the protection of special interests injured by general fluctuations; e.g., in agriculture and commercial policy. The principal instrument of governmental cybernetics is the fiscal system—by which we mean the whole system of governmental purchases, sales, receipts, and expenditures. Hence most economists regard "fiscal policy" as the principal weapon in the control of economic fluctuations. This point of view is a relatively new one in economics, but its acceptance is so wide that it can safely be described as orthodox. There are two ways in which government can have an impact on the magnitude of the economic system: it can have an indirect influence through affecting the behavior of private individuals, and it can also have a direct influence through its own transactions and transfers. Indirect influences consist mainly of prohibitions which limit the legal behavior of individuals (e.g., the minimum wage law); though they may also include propaganda devices for encouraging certain desired forms of behavior. The cybernetic aspects of these indirect influences are not altogether to be neglected, and occasionally (e.g., in the case of price-wage control) may be of very great importance. Nevertheless, for the most part they are not suitable for use as cybernetic mechanisms; they pertain rather to the long-range regulation of society rather than to its year-by-year stabilization. For the main instruments of a stabilization policy, therefore, we must turn to the direct influences (i.e., the transactions and transfers) of government. Of these the tax system is probably the most powerful in principle, especially if "negative taxes" (subsidies) are included, even though there are serious political obstacles to flexibility in taxes. Government purchases also are a powerful potential instrument of stabilization, though there are important physical as well as political obstacles to rapid changes in the volume of public works. Of less importance, but again not to be neglected, is the government financial system, including that of the central bank; by the management of the public debt and of central bank portfolios the composition of private assets can materially be affected. This is what is usually understood by "monetary" as opposed to "fiscal" policy, though the name is somewhat inappropriate, as the stock of liquid assets in private hands is determined much more by the fiscal system than by the financial or banking system.

If now we were concerned merely with the stabilization of a single variable, the cybernetic problem would be relatively simple: it would consist merely in finding means of increasing the unruly variable whenever it was decreasing and of decreasing it when it was increasing. Thus in the control of temperature by a thermostat a mechanism is set up which turns on the heat when the temperature falls below the desired level and turns it off when the temperature rises above the desired level. An analogous mechanism in economic life would be the stabilization of the total volume of payments by means of an adjustable tax plan, such as I have proposed in my *Economics of Peace*.[2] Any reduction in the total tax bill will have a direct effect in increasing the total volume of private payments. It is also practically certain to have a strong indirect effect in the same direction because by increasing the government cash deficit it increases the amount of money in private accounts. Similarly an increase in the total tax bill will almost certainly diminish the total volume of payments. Government expenditure is here assumed constant, so that an increase in the tax bill automatically diminishes the deficit (or increases the surplus). This being so, if tax rates were linked automatically with a statistically determined total volume of payments, so that any rise in payments above the "standard" level brought a fall in taxes and any fall in payments below the standard level brought a rise in taxes, the fluctuations of the actual value of payments about the "standard" level could be reduced to any desired amount, depending on the sensitivity of the automatic reaction.

The total volume of payments is not, however, what we really want to stabilize. The critical instability in an unregulated economy is the instability in output—particularly as reflected in the periodic decline of output below its "ideal" level. Payments can fluctuate independently of output for two reasons: because of fluctuations in prices and because of fluctuations in the turnover of commodities. Fluctuations in the rate of turnover of commodities—i.e., in the ratio of total purchases (or sales) to total output—does not present a serious cybernetic problem except perhaps in local cases of extreme speculative hysteria, such as the Florida land boom and occasional bull (or even bear) markets in stocks or commodities. Fluctuations in price, however, present a very serious cybernetic problem. Thus suppose that by means of cybernetic controls in the tax system we succeeded in stabilizing not merely total payments but the national income, in money terms. This could probably be done, as the national money income is reasonably sensitive to changes in the budget deficit or surplus. It would still be possible to have wide fluctuations in "real income" (i.e., output) and therefore to have wide fluctuations in employment, with corresponding fluctuations in price levels in the opposite direction. Thus if Y is the national money in-

[2] K. E. Boulding, *The Economics of Peace* (New York: Prentice-Hall, 1945).

come, R is the national real income and P is the price level of that real income (R and P being measured by indices which are consistent), we have

$$Y = RP$$

Clearly within a stable Y it is possible to have indefinite fluctuations of R and P in opposite directions. Conversely it is possible to have a fluctuating Y with a stable R, provided that P fluctuates proportionately with Y. It follows that if the problem of stabilizing Y cannot be solved, then we have a certain choice between fluctuating prices and fluctuating outputs. Clearly of these the former is much to be preferred, remembering always that it is R (real income, or output) which is the principal object of any stabilization policy.

In dynamic terms, any attempt to increase R by increasing Y will be frustrated if the increase in Y runs off into price-wage increases. As long as output is very much below capacity there is every reason to suppose that there will be little pressure for price or wage increases, and that therefore an increase in Y—brought about, say, by fiscal policy—will almost certainly increase output and employment. As output rises towards capacity, that is, as the level of employment rises towards full employment, conditions for a rise in the price-wage level become more favorable. At low levels of output all supplies are likely to be highly elastic, for increased output can come simply from the employment of unused resources. Under these circumstances a rise in money demand-curves produced by a rise in payments or in private money stocks will not raise prices but will simply raise outputs. As we approach capacity, however, supplies in one field after another become less elastic; instead of merely absorbing unemployed resources in some fields, the limit of easily available specialized resources may be reached, and further expansion of output must then overcome the resistance of actual transfer of resources from one gainful occupation to another. When this point is reached in any industry a further increase in demand is bound to be reflected in price increases: we have reached the "inflation threshold." The nightmare of the fiscal policy enthusiasts is a situation in which the inflation threshold is reached over large sections of the economy long before the rise in output has brought the system to "capacity." If this is generally the case, then full employment cannot be attained without perpetual, and perhaps even accelerating, price inflation. The only available remedy would seem to be price-wage control. This is the wartime recipe for full employment, and experience shows that it works: highly inflationary public finance coupled with tight price-wage control to prevent the inflation going off into prices. Whether this recipe can be applied in peacetime, as a normal part of the system, is highly doubtful in the present state of administrative techniques. Up to now we have not been able to develop an administrative technique of price-wage control on anything more than a strictly temporary basis: the recipe here is to freeze an existing situation and then to set up elaborate mechanisms of procrastination such as the OPA and the War Labor Board. Procrastination, however, while admirable as a short-run policy, will simply not do for the long run. Eventually the pressures become too great, the absurdities of the politically determined price structure become too patent, enforcement becomes too difficult, and the controls break down under the weight of their own absurdity. Unless we can improve the administrative regulation of the relative structure of prices, therefore, to the point where it can do even half way as good a job as the free market, price-wage control in a democratic society would seem to be out of the question as a permanent part of the economic apparatus. This being the case the question of the "inflation threshold"—at what level of output does it appear and what determines this level—is of prime importance for the success of any full employment policy.

It is at this point in the argument that the "state of the market"—competitive, monopolistic, oligopolistic—and therefore the development of collective bargaining becomes relevant to the problem of fiscal policy. Are we more likely to reach the inflation threshold at undesirably low levels of employment with perfectly competitive markets, with monopolistic markets, or with any of the varieties of monopolistic competition? Here, perhaps, is a point where the indirect aspects of governmental policy—its encouragement or discouragement of competitive markets, for instance—may be of great importance. Unfortunately, however, the question of the exact impact of market forms on the inflation threshold is by no means easy to answer. We certainly cannot assume, for instance, that if all markets were highly competitive there would be no problem of the inflation threshold. Highly competitive markets are notoriously subject to speculative price movements which may be set off by very slight occasions, and which up to a point have the power of self-perpetuation. It is not the elasticity of supply of the output of the commodity which is significant here but the existing stocks of assets (including money) and the asset preferences.[3] Hence a budget deficit, leading to increased holdings of liquid assets in private hands, might easily set off speculative price movements in the organized commodity and security markets long before full employment was reached. There is some evidence that this took place, for instance, in 1936-37. Such speculative price movements are less likely to be felt in labor

[3] K. E. Boulding, "A Liquidity Preference Theory of Market Prices," *Economica*, May, 1944, p. 55.

markets, of course, because of the non-storable nature of the commodity involved, but there is a great deal of evidence to show that unorganized labor markets respond rapidly to increases in the money holdings of the public, especially of employers.

Monopolistic markets, on the other hand, react much more slowly to inflationary or deflationary forces. The reasons for this may be more sociological than economic: monopolistically determined prices tend to be determined more "visibly" than prices in competitive markets. The "social visibility" of price determination in monopolistic markets is seen very clearly in the labor market. Wages of unorganized labor—e.g., agricultural workers or domestic servants—rise imperceptibly, but surely, in an inflationary situation. Each bargain is like the wavelets of the tide, so small that it raises no fuss, gets into no papers, calls for no editorials; but if there is an acute labor shortage at existing wages, each bargain represents a slight advance, imposed on the employer by the necessity of dragging labor away from his neighbor. When the tide rises against the sluice-gates of a union contract, however, there is pressure, discussion, violent spraying, and a final dramatic surge as the gates yield. All this is news, and is vividly before the public eye. When there are only four "rounds," the "fourth round of wage increases" becomes a topic of national importance. When there are a million "rounds," nobody notices any one of them and is not even particularly conscious of the whole movement. Similarly a rise in the price of steel or of automobiles makes the papers. Much greater changes in the price of wheat can pass almost unnoticed.

All this means, however, that monopolistic organization of the market is no hindrance but a positive help to a full employment policy in the short run. Unions, paradoxically enough, in an inflationary period become devices to prevent money wages rising as fast as otherwise they might have done—a paradox to which the war experience is a clear testimony. It is also true, of course, that in deflation, monopolistic prices fall more slowly than competitive prices. All that we are saying, in fact, is that monopolistic organization makes for greater stability of prices than a competitive organization. When the monopolistic organization takes the form of collective bargaining, this proposition is reinforced. It may well be that the most significant thing about collective bargaining is not that it is collective but that it is bargaining. Bargaining, as a method of price determination, has been largely superseded in commodity markets—especially in retail markets—by the custom of the quoted price, by organized brokerage, or by the auction sale. There are good reasons for this. Bargaining, for most people, is a disagreeable, time-consuming affair, of necessity involving an unsatisfactory, even unethical, type of personal relationship between the bargainers. Hence once a bargain has been struck there is a certain unwillingness to reopen the negotiations. This is a fact of great importance in collective bargaining, whether of unions with employers or of milk producers with distributors. A peculiarity of the collective bargain is that it sets the terms upon which the individuals represented may trade, and sets these terms usually for an appreciable period in the future—months, a year, or even two years. Once the terms have been set there are strong institutional and psychological obstacles to changing them before the prescribed period. Having gone through the disagreeable experience of bargaining, we have no great urge to repeat it.

There are no such obstacles to changes in quoted prices, because the quoting of the price or accepting the quoted price in a transaction is not an act disagreeable in itself, nor surrounded with any publicity or effective penumbra. If a retailer finds that a certain standardized product is not selling, there is very little to prevent him cutting the price. Only in cases where there is strong differentiation of the product and hence the price comes to have an emotional significance created by advertising, etc., do we find any of these obstacles to changes in the case of quoted prices. Bargaining, therefore, and especially collective bargaining because it results in a contract extending into the future, acts as a strong price stabilizer. The growth of unions has led to a great increase in palaver, and palaver is a great friend of procrastination. We can see the significance of this for price-wage flexibility if we imagine that we had to spend a week of impressive argument bargaining with the milkman about the price at which he was to deliver milk during the ensuing year. Such an arrangement would introduce a marked inflexibility into the price of milk, even under strong inflationary or deflationary conditions! Even the fact that union officials are specialized in bargaining is not sufficient to offset the ponderousness of the bargaining procedure.

In the short run, therefore, we must unquestionably reckon collective bargaining as a friend of fiscal policy. The economist, however, usually has a bad conscience about the long run. Even though we—the present company—will be dead in the long run, the society of which we are a part will continue, and in spite of the fact that heredity has done precious little for us we cannot wholly divest ourselves of the desire to see our society perpetuate itself. And it may well be that policies and institutions which make things easier in the short run turn out to have cumulative effects which make things harder in the long run. The long-run worry about collective bargaining is, of course, whether it involves us in long-run inflation; i.e., in a persistent upward trend of the price level. The inflexibility in the price system which collective bargaining engenders may have excellent results on the upswing, when money income is rising. It does mean, however, that we simply cannot afford ever to let money income decline, for a decline in money income can only come about through decreased output and employment, not through decreased prices and money wages. With a highly flexible price-wage system, fluctuations in payments or money incomes are not so important, simply because they result in changes in price levels rather than in output levels. With an inflexible price-wage system downward movements in payments or money incomes cannot be permitted, and hence upward movements cannot be corrected. This clearly leads to an inflational bias in the system. How serious this is, of course, depends on its magnitude. It is conceivable that money wages might rise just about as fast as the rise in productivity; so that the price level of commodities would be approximately stable. As far as the trend is concerned, this was the case in the United States between, say, 1800 and 1940. This long-run stability in the trend, however, has only been achieved at the cost of several severe deflations and depressions. In periods of full employment the price level has always risen. Even if the secular trend of the price level amounted to only 5 per cent per annum a substantial revolution would have taken place in the economic structure. This would amount to a thirty-fold rise in the price level during the lifetime of a single individual. It would make most of our present pension and insurance schemes practically worthless, would create an acute social security problem, and would necessitate a sharp rise in money rates of interest. We might, of course, adjust ourselves to such a condition, but the problems of such an adjustment have been given very little thought.

Whether the development of collective bargaining necessitates secular inflation or not, there can be no doubt that an inflationary situation makes collective bargaining easier. The collective organization of the labor market invests the determination of wages with an atmosphere of sport, and substitutes for the cold calculation of the market place the hot enthusiasms of the football field. The parties that face each other across the bargaining table are not negotiating a commercial agreement so much as fighting a battle. Each side goes in to "win"; each side has its invisible "rooters"—the vociferous ranks of union members on the one side, the more decorous but still powerful ranks of the capitalists on the other. It is, however, much more important for the union leaders to "win" than it is for the management, if only because union leaders are much more liable to lose their jobs if they lose. There is a world of difference between the regretful shrug of a capitalist and the raucous displeasure of a worker. Thus the union leader is under tremendous pressure to "bring home the bacon," even if what he brings home is something which the workers would have got even without his assistance. It may well be that the "football psychology" engendered by the stress on competitive athletics in our educational system may be a serious handicap to a society geared to negotiation rather than to warfare. The battle of capitalism is more subtle than the battle of Waterloo and may well be lost on the playing fields. Whatever the causes of this phenomenon, there can be no doubt about its consequences. Even a mild deflation will produce sharp internal strains in labor organizations and is almost certain to result in a marked intensification of industrial strife. A fall in money wages is something for which the union gets blamed, as a rise is something for which it gets praised. A fall in real wages due to price increases cannot be laid directly at the union's door; neither can a rise in real wages due to price declines. Hence in an inflation the union gets credit for the rise in wages but does not take the blame for the rise in prices; in a deflation it gets the blame for the fall in wages but gets no credit for the fall in prices. The interest of unions in at least a gentle inflation is all too clear.

It is important to inquire, therefore, whether anything can be done to mitigate the danger of secular inflation under a "liberal" regime, without going over to the other extreme of Republican stinginess. Several lines of policy are worth consideration. There is first the possibility of recurrent but temporary price and wage control to effect a rapid scaling down of the whole price-wage level. We have already rejected any permanent price-wage control as administratively impossible in the present state of knowledge. It might be possible, however, to replace the long, slow, painful deflations of the pre-Roosevelt era by short, sharp, and consequently relatively painless deflations. If when deflation and unemployment threaten the economy the regulative powers of the state are used to effect a sudden—indeed, an overnight— reduction in all quoted or contractual wages and prices, the effect from the point of view of the consumption function would be virtually the same as an increase in the quantity of money in private accounts. By this means we might be able to avoid the great dilemma of deflation— that while low money wages and prices, with a given money stock, are conducive to a high consumption function and hence high employment, falling money wages and prices are extremely destructive of profits and of investment, and lead to low levels of employment. Consequently, it is the long, slow deflations, such as took place in the seventies or the thirties, that are associated with severe depressions and slow recoveries, while the short sharp deflations, as of 1857 or 1919, produce only mild depressions and rapid recoveries. Almost the only alternative to the "instantaneous" deflation proposed above, if a full employment policy is rigorously followed, is continual budget deficits and increase in privately held money stocks whenever employment slackens. Such would inevitably give us a secular inflation.

The possibility of controlling price levels in the stable commodity markets through the composite commodity standard proposed by Benjamin Graham[4] should also be considered seriously in any scheme for controlling secular inflation while preserving a full employment policy. We have already noticed that it is not the monopolistic but the competitive markets which are likely to give most trouble to the economic stabilizer in the short run. A speculative inflation in commodity markets, by its impact on the worker's cost of living, is also likely to increase the pressure for wage increases; so that the control of the wholesale price level is by no means irrelevant to the problems of the labor market. The advantage of the Graham standard—under which, it will be recalled, the government stands ready to buy or to sell a fixed "bundle" of commodities at a standard price, somewhat like Marshall's old "symmetallism" proposal applied to many commodities—is that the "cybernetic mechanism" involved plays directly on the markets concerned. An inflationary move in the markets is met immediately both by an increase in stocks of commodity and by a decline in stocks of money held by the speculators. There is every reason to believe, therefore, that such a plan—properly co-ordinated with other elements of economic policy—would be successful in stabilizing the price level of the standard commodities, while permitting any amount of change in the relative price structure. Under severe pressures—e.g., resulting from inflationary war finance—the standard would have to be abandoned; but this, of course, is true of any "standard" as the history of the gold standard abundantly demonstrates.

Another scheme may be mentioned, not because it is in any sense practicable at the moment, but because if all else fails it suggests a possible remedy to be held in reserve. This is the "wage money" plan, by which wages would be paid in a special kind of "wage money," which would have to be exchanged into ordinary money for making purchases, the rate of exchange between wage money and ordinary money being set by the government. The struggle for relative advantage in the labor market could then be conducted in terms of wage money, but if this treatened a general inflation of prices in ordinary money, the value of wage money could be lowered. Thus it might be possible to have a perpetual inflation in wage money, with all the consequent advantages, without producing any inflation in ordinary money —every rise in the wage level in wage money being counterbalanced by a fall in the value of wage money. I am not, of course, suggesting this seriously as a practical proposal, but any proposal, however impractical, which will set people thinking about the problem is worth making.

[4] B. Graham, *Storage & Stability* (New York: McGraw-Hill, 1937).

Finally, there are certain lines of regulative policy which may be followed to reduce the demand for inflation created by collective bargaining. Legislation like the Taft-Hartley Act, which is aimed at weakening "union security" and making the labor leader more dependent on the rank and file, is likely to increase the demand for inflation, and the more bacon he has to bring home the more vigorous will be the pursuit by the labor leader. Conversely any strengthening of the internal security of the labor leader is likely to diminish his aggressiveness. The extreme of such divorce of leaders from the led is to be seen in the Russian trade unions, which have become almost entirely a device to prevent the workers from exercising any force in the direction of higher wages! I do not suggest, of course, that this extreme is desirable, but those who wish to move to the other extreme must be prepared to offer alternative solutions to the problem which will inevitably arise.

Something may be done, also, not merely to lessen the response of union leaders to pressure from below, but also to diminish that pressure. Much of the pressure which may be translated into a demand for wage increases arises, as we well know, from the more strictly "human relations" aspect of the problem, and any steps toward the solution of these problems of status, respect, personal relationships, and the like are likely to ease the demand for money wage increases. Often, as every labor student knows, it is the condition of the toilets rather than of the pocketbook that creates dissatisfaction with the worker's lot. Something can be done also by means of a definite "wage policy" on the part of government, such as the Little Steel Formula, which sets up a standard of public policy by which particular bargains can be judged. To be effective such a formula must be well enough accepted and understood so that it can at least provide union leaders with a satisfactory excuse when the members put pressure on them. It is difficult to see, however, how such a wage policy could be effective in the absence of an elaborate mechanism for the regulation of wages, but the possibility of "wage ceilings" based on employment or price movements is not to be despised.

A different, and much neglected, problem is that of the distribution of incomes, especially of wage incomes, according to the age of the worker. It is quite possible for the wage of every individual to be constantly rising as he gets older, even while the average wage remains unchanged, simply because oldsters are constantly dying off and youngsters taking their place. The contentment of the individual, and hence of the group, may be quite noticeably a function of the extent to which his income rises with age. If the age distribution of incomes is fairly even, so that a man reaches his maximum wage while he is relatively young and has no prospect of advancement thereafter, and *a fortiori* if wages decline with advancing age, the worker is likely to feel personally frustrated, to feel that he is not "getting anywhere," and this individual frustration may be reflected in group pressures. On the other hand, if wages rise with the age of the worker, the individual can advance even though the group does not, or in any case advances more rapidly than the group; hence he is less likely to be frustrated, and the group is less likely to be dissatisfied. It is evident, then, that the morale of the worker group may be a significant function of the distribution of labor income according to age, and will be higher the more steeply income rises with age. Unfortunately one consequence of the increasing length of life and the increasing numbers of older people is that age loses its scarcity value, and the age-distribution of income is likely to tip away from the older toward the younger groups, with consequent decline in the morale of the population. Something might be done to correct this through the tax system, if taxes were adjusted according to the age of the taxpayer, but this would not particularly contribute to union morale. Unions themselves have a certain tendency to build up privileges for older members—e.g., through seniority—but if the demand for people of various age groups tends to be inelastic, it is very difficult to prevent a change in the age distribution of the population from shifting the distribution of income according to age.

In conclusion, what of the general title of this discussion: "Can Capitalism Dispense with Free Labor Markets?" If by "free" is meant perfectly competitive, the answer is that it always has done so. If by "free" is meant "free from union or employer organization," the answer is that it has done so pretty well up to now. Nevertheless, there are grounds for some slight tempering of optimism in this regard. The labor movement is unquestionably a sociological necessity, and a free (from government domination) labor movement is a strong political support to a liberal capitalism. Economically, however, the labor movement is a slight embarrassment, not because of its impact on the distribution of income, which over the long pull is almost negligible, but because of its impact on the flexibility of the whole price structure. With a strong labor movement we cannot afford to have deflations; and this may mean that we cannot escape a secular inflation. It has been indicated that this problem is not intrinsically insoluble. We shall be deluding ourselves if we think we have solved it.

ASSET IDENTITIES IN ECONOMIC MODELS

In: *Studies in Income and Wealth,* National Bureau of Economic Research, Conference on Income and Wealth, 14 (1951): 229-247.

Asset Identities in Economic Models

In the various 'models' or determinate systems of economic variables which are such an important feature of macroeconomic analysis, identities play an important, perhaps even an essential role. These identities are obtained by equating two different breakdowns of a single aggregate or by equating a breakdown of an aggregate to the aggregate itself. A simple example is the 'savings equals investment' identity, which in its most significant form is based on the breakdown of total output, Y, into the part that is consumed, C, and the part that is not consumed and is therefore accumulated, A. Since $Y \equiv C + A$,

$$A \equiv Y - C, \tag{1}$$

where A is 'investment' and $Y - C$ is 'savings', or income minus consumption. Irving Fisher's equation of exchange likewise results from the division of a single aggregate, total payments, into two products: price multiplied by the quantity of the exchangeables for which payment is made and the total quantity of money multiplied by its average velocity of circulation.

Naturally, an identity must be true. It may or may not be interesting, and there is no sense in formulating uninteresting identities. The interest of an identity depends upon whether its components have enough homogeneity, independence, and connectedness to be related in a set of functional equations sufficient to determine them. Thus the savings-equals-investment identity is of some interest because its components can be related in functions that make some sense, at least at the level of first approximation. In the simplest possible model of a 'Keynesian' system we assume a consumption function,

$$C = F_c(Y) \tag{2}$$

and an investment function,

$$A = F_a(Y) \tag{3}$$

or, if we like, assume A to be given by exogenous factors: these two equations together with the identity (1) are sufficient to determine the three unknowns, Y, A, and C. The value of such a model of course depends entirely upon whether the functional relations it assumes are reasonably stable. Their stability in turn depends upon whether the relations rest upon some stable attributes of human behavior and whether the variables are homogeneous enough to justify the neglect of their parts and structure.

Little has been done with identities involving assets, yet these are actually more fundamental, and frequently more illuminating, than the income identities commonly used. Income quantities, such as output, consumption, savings, expenditures, and receipts, are essentially *changes* per given period (gross or net) in asset quantities. The income identities, therefore, are obtained by the differentiation of the asset identities with respect to time.

The most fundamental asset identity, the balance sheet identity, is based upon a twofold division of the total value of resources controlled by a firm or other social organism: into a classified list of the resources controlled (the assets side) and into the distribution of this total value among the various types of claimant to it (the liabilities side). The breakdown can be as fine or as coarse as the nature of the problem requires. For the purpose of constructing economic models a very convenient breakdown rests upon the assumption that all accounts in the system can be classified under three heads — businesses, households, and government. For any business, then, we can classify the items in its balance sheet into assets and liabilities. Any item in the balance sheet can be classified under one or another of these headings although, as in all taxonomic structures, there may be doubtful cases which must be resolved in more or less arbitrary fashion. Bank deposits, for instance, are strictly classified under k_{bb} and government money under k_{gb}, but for many purposes we may wish to classify them under m_b or perhaps as a separate item.

BUSINESS BALANCE SHEET

Assets		*Liabilities*	
Money stock	m_b	Debts to businesses	k_{bb}'
Value of physical capital	q_b	Debts to households	k_{bh}'
Debts from businesses	k_{bb}	Debts to government	k_{bg}'
Debts from households	k_{hb}	Net worth	g_b
Debts from government	k_{gb}		

The balance sheet identity for a single business then reads:

$$m_b + q_b + k_{bb} + k_{hb} + k_{gb} \equiv k_{bb}' + k_{bh}' + k_{bg}' + g_b \tag{4}$$

The balance sheets of all businesses can now be added. If we use capital letters to represent the aggregate quantities, $M_b \ (= \Sigma m_b)$ is the total money stock of all businesses, $Q_b \ (= \Sigma q_b)$ the total value of real capital held by businesses, and so on. The aggregate balance sheet identity may then be written:

$$M_b + Q_b + K_{bb} + K_{hb} + K_{gb} \equiv K_{bb}' + K_{bh}' + K_{bg}' + G_b \tag{5}$$

When the balance sheets of all businesses in a closed society are added, however, the sum of all debts from businesses to other businesses, K_{bb}, is obviously the same quantity as the sum of all debts to businesses from other businesses, K_{bb}', as each inter-business debt appears twice in the aggregate of balance sheets — as a liability in one balance sheet and as an asset in another. We can therefore rearrange and rewrite identity (5) as the *aggregate business net worth identity:*

$$G_b \equiv M_b + Q_b + (K_{hb} - K_{bh}') + (K_{gb} - K_{bg}') \tag{6}$$

Highly significant income identities can be derived by differentiating (6) with respect to time. If by dG_b, dM_b, etc. we mean the changes in the quantities G_b, M_b, etc. in a given period, we have:

$$dG_b \equiv dM_b + dQ_b + dK_{hb} - dK_{bh}' + dK_{gb} - dK_{bg}' \qquad (7)$$

Each quantity in this identity has economic significance; dG_b, the total change in business net worths, is closely related to what the Department of Commerce calls 'undistributed profits'. However, because of a certain ambiguity in this term, which is used also to designate a certain part of the total net worth of business in the balance sheet statement, 'business savings' seems preferable. It represents the net addition to net worth, i.e., the part of profits (gross additions) that has not been distributed in interest or dividends. Identity (7) may therefore be called the *aggregate business savings identity*.

dM_b is the increase in the money stock held by businesses. For the purposes of this exposition bank deposits and government currency are assumed to be included under the money category and correspondingly excluded from the debt categories to which they would otherwise belong. This item may be divided still further into the balance of payments of businesses with households, X_{hh}, the balance of payments of businesses with government, X_{bg}, and the portion of net additions to the money stock that remains in the accounts of businesses, dM_b'. The balance of payments of businesses with households is the excess of money receipts of businesses from households over the money expenditures of businesses to households. Neglecting government and changes in the money stock for the moment, we can visualize the money stock of society as a shifting cargo, now shifting into business balance sheets as households spend more toward businesses than businesses are spending toward households, now shifting toward household balance sheets when the reverse takes place. The positive balance of payments of businesses of course equals the negative balance of payments of households. We would ordinarily expect X_{bh} to fluctuate between positive and negative magnitudes, being positive when money surges into business balances, negative when it surges out into household balances. The longer the period the more these alternate positive and negative values will cancel, and the smaller this item will be in relation to the other magnitudes of the economy: in the long run, that is to say, X_{hh} approaches zero.

The balance of payment of businesses with government, X_{hg}, is likewise the excess of money receipts of businesses from government over money expenditures by businesses to government. The first item consists of payments for goods and services or securities purchased from businesses by government, plus subsidy or other transfer payments; the second consists of tax payments and payments for goods, services, or securities purchased from government by businesses. Because of the peculiar power of government to create money, there is no necessity for this item to approach zero in the long run, though under conservative canons of public finance its long run value is presumably small. War inflation is likely to render it perennially positive. dM_b' represents mainly the increase in bank deposits. For the purposes of our model we include banks under government and regard bank deposits as part of the public debt. For some purposes it is desirable to set up a separate account for the banking system.

From identity (7) an identity for total profits can immediately be derived. Total profits, V, must equal business distributions out of profits in net business taxes, T_b, and in dividends and interest, D plus business savings, dG_b. We have therefore:

$$V \equiv T_b + D + dG_b \equiv dQ_b + (D + X_{bh} + dK_{hb} - dK_{bh}')$$
$$+ (X_{bg} + T_b + dK_{gb} - dK_{bg}') + dM_b' \qquad (8)$$

A similar identity can now be constructed for total wages. First, we construct a balance sheet for a household. Again representing the sum

HOUSEHOLD BALANCE SHEET

Assets		Liabilities	
Money stock	m_h	Debts to businesses	k_{hb}'
Value of physical capital	q_h	Debts to households	k_{hh}'
Debts from businesses	k_{bh}	Debts to government	k_{hg}'
Debts from households	k_{hh}	Net worth	g_h
Debts from government	k_{gh}		
Net worths of businesses	g_{bh}		

of the various items in all household accounts by capital letters, we find on adding the balance sheets of all households that $K_{hh} = K_{hh}'$, and we have a *household net worth identity:*

$$G_h \equiv M_h + Q_h + K_{bh} + K_{gh} - K_{hb}' - K_{hg}' + G_b \qquad (9)$$

As will be observed, in the household balance sheet we included an item, g_{bh}, on the assets side, representing the part of the net worth of businesses that is owned by the household. The entire net worth of businesses must theoretically be allocated among households, as a business is a fictitious 'person'. The actual allocation of this net worth may, of course, be somewhat arbitrary. Nonprofit institutions such as universities and churches present some difficulties: they may either be regarded as 'households' in themselves or their assets may be allocated to the individual households or persons benefiting from their existence. The sum of all these allocations must equal the sum of business net worths: i.e., $G_{bh} \equiv G_b$.

The household net worth identity also may be differentiated, the prefix

d being used as before to indicate the change during a fixed period in the variable so modified:

$$dG_h \equiv dM_h + dQ_h + dK_{bh} + dK_{gh} - dK_{hb}' - dK_{hg}' + dG_b \quad (10)$$

This may be called the *household savings identity,* as dG_h, the increase in household net worths, is the amount saved by households, which is the same thing as total savings. It may be objected that as household savings, on this definition, included business savings, which are not directly under the control of households, it is improper to say that the increase in household net worths is the amount 'saved' by households. As far as business savings are reflected in household balance sheets, however, households will rightly regard such savings as income, i.e., additions to net worth, and may, if they wish, offset them by consumption. Here we have a problem of the *form* in which an increase in net worth manifests itself — whether, for instance, in liquid or in nonliquid form — and the effects of the form on individuals. But at the level of approximation of this paper such complications may be neglected. The household savings identity then identifies household savings with the increase in the money stock of households plus the increase in the physical capital of households plus the increase in the net debts of business and of government to households plus business savings. If identities (7) and (10) are combined we have:

$$dG_h \equiv dM_h + dM_b + dQ_h + dQ_b + dK_g \quad (11)$$

where dK_g is the increase in net government debt to both households and businesses. When both business and household balance sheets are added, all inter-business and inter-household debts cancel: $dK_{hb} \equiv dK_{hb}'$, $dK_{bh} = dK_{bh}'$, and we are left with the identity that household savings equal the increase in the money stock of society plus the increase in the value of total physical capital plus the increase in net government debt.

Household savings consist also of household income minus household consumption, C_h, minus household taxes, T_h. Household income consists of wages, W, business distributions, D, and business savings, dG_b. We have therefore:

$$dG_h \equiv W + D + dG_b - C_h - T_h \quad (12)$$

The increase in the money stock of households may likewise be analyzed into three parts: first, the positive balance of payments of households with business, i.e., the excess of household receipts from business over household expenditures to business, which is exactly the same as the negative balance of business payments, $-X_{bh}$. The second part of dM_h is the positive balance of payments of households with government, X_{hg}; the third part is the new money that finds its way into the balances of households, dM_h'. We have therefore:

$$dM_h \equiv X_{hg} - X_{bh} + dM_h' \quad (13)$$

Combining identities (10), (12), and (13) we get an identity for *total wages:*

$$W \equiv (C_h + dQ_h) - (D + X_{bh} + dK_{hb} - dK_{bh}')$$
$$+ (X_{hg} + T_h + dK_{gh} - dK_{hg}') + dM_h' \qquad (14)$$

It will be observed that

$$D + X_{bh} + dK_{hb} - dK_{bh}' \equiv T \qquad (15)$$

occurs in both the total profits and the total wages identity. It may be called the *transfer factor.* The items

$$(X_{bg} + T_b + dK_{gb} - dK_{bg}') \equiv V_g \qquad (16a)$$

and

$$(X_{hg} + T_h + dK_{gh} - dK_{hg}') \equiv W_g \qquad (16b)$$

represent government contributions to total profits and to total wages respectively. Equations (8) and (14) can then be written in simple form:

$$V \equiv dQ_b + T + V_g + dM_b' \qquad (17a)$$
$$W \equiv (C_h + dQ_h) - T + W_g + dM_h' \qquad (17b)$$

Adding these two identities we obtain a familiar identity for *national income:*

$$Y = V + W = dQ_b + (C_h + dQ_h) + (V_g + W_g) + (dM_b' + dM_h') \qquad (18)$$

dQ_b is 'business accumulation' or 'investment'. $C_h + dQ_h$, total household purchases or absorption, corresponds to the Keynesian 'consumption'. The third item, the net government contribution to national income, and the fourth item, the increase in the money stock, will be analyzed later.

Suppose for the moment that we neglect the third and fourth items. The identities then indicate that the *distribution* of national income between wage and nonwage income is related to the *composition* of national income by business investment and household absorption through the transfer factor, T, which added to business 'investment' yields total profits and subtracted from household absorption yields total wages. Figure 1 illustrates the concept: national income is divided first into business investment, AC, and household absorption, CB, and second into total profits,

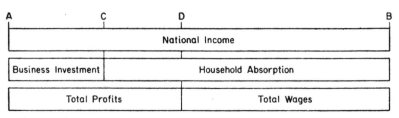

Figure 1

AD, and total wages, *DB. CD* is the transfer factor. The concept of a transfer factor would, of course, be meaningless unless it could be shown that it is related to certain aspects of human behavior. But identity (15) analyzes the transfer factor into four items, each of which is a rough 'parameter of behavior' and can, therefore, be profitably used in economic models. The first item, *D,* depends upon the dividend policy of corporate businesses and, in the case of unincorporated businesses, on entrepreneurial withdrawals. In the short run we can regard the interest and contractual rent items in *D* as constant, determined by the structure of debt and financial contracts, so that any fluctuation in *D* can be attributed to dividend policy. Unfortunately it is not at all clear what determines dividend policies, and in the absence of much detailed study there must be some doubt concerning what should be put into a 'dividends function' in an economic model. But there is little doubt that past profits are a major item in it, and also perhaps the liquidity position of businesses. There are, however, certain institutional, conventional, even fashion-determined elements in dividend policy that may undermine the stability of any dividends-function postulated.

The second item, X_{bh}, is the positive balance of payments of businesses toward households or, what is the same thing, the negative balance of payments of households toward businesses. The excess of household payments to businesses over business payments to households is, as already noted, likely to fluctuate between positive and negative values. In the short run, however, it may be an important contribution to (or subtraction from) profits: a 'surge' of several billion dollars into or out of business balances is not impossible in short periods. This is one of the big gaps in our statistical information, and a continuous series showing the distribution of liquid assets between business and household accounts would be instructive. The chief determinants of this item are the relative liquidity preferences of households and businesses. If both are trying to decumulate or to accumulate money at the same rate, or with the same degree of intensity, neither will succeed. But if the liquidity preference of one declines faster, or increases more slowly, than the other, liquid assets will 'surge' into the accounts of the one with the relatively weaker liquidity preference. Parameters for liquidity preference can be set up in terms of relative velocities of circulation: in simple models, however, the balance of payments item itself may be used as an irregularly fluctuating, exogenous variable, or it may be related in the short run to such variables as dividend or wage payments. Thus an increase in wage or dividend payments may well cause an initial surge of the money stock into household and out of business accounts. But in the long run the balance of payments item approaches zero and may be neglected.

dK_{hb} is the increase in household indebtedness to business, i.e., mainly in consumer credit, book or instalment. Since it represents the equity of businesses in household goods (automobiles, household equipment, furniture, clothing, etc. held by households), it can increase continuously with household capital. But it is likely to fluctuate considerably, and there is nothing to prevent its being negative. Like the balance of payments, it may be expected to swing between positive and negative values if the average volume of consumer credit is constant: a secular rise in total consumer credit will, of course, make the positive values of dK_{hb} predominate over the negative values. However, an increase in consumer credit that exceeds the secular trend is almost certain to be followed by a decline, i.e., by a shift from a positive to a negative value for dK_{hb}. To that extent a rapid increase in consumer credit is almost certain to set up cyclical movements in the transfer factor. The problem of a 'consumer credit function' in economic models presents great difficulties. Income is probably the main determining factor, yet the relation is certainly not linear. Consumer credit per household reaches a maximum at middle or high-middle income levels. Other factors, such as household liquidity, may also be important, and factors on the business side influencing the willingness to grant consumer credit. The structure of household capital itself is also important, as consumer credit is closely related to household accumulation, dQ_h, and distortions in the age distribution of household capital are likely to lead to fluctuations in replacements and additions, as in the case of business capital.

The fourth item in the transfer factor, dK_{bh}', is the increase in debts due households from businesses. These debts include a rather heterogeneous aggregate of unpaid wage claims and accrued but unpaid interest or rent, but consist chiefly of business securities held by households. We thus get the paradoxical proposition that the sale of bonds by businesses to households actually diminishes total profits, the other variables being constant. Again there is considerable question regarding the variables to be included in a 'securities function': naturally it is likely to be related to both business investment and dividend policy. Certain special problems also related to equity financing and to the creation of new businesses are postponed at this stage.

What has emerged from the analysis of asset identities, then, is the outline of a macroeconomic theory of the distribution of national income into labor and nonlabor income. The absence of such a theory has been a great weakness of the Keynesian, indeed of all, economics. The identities clearly show that the distribution structure is not a result of the productive process but is in the main attributable to investment and financial processes and decisions. Investment itself is the chief determinant of profits, and is in turn determined in part by expected profits. It would not be surprising if under these conditions the economic system was markedly unstable. The identities indicate also that the distributional pattern is largely independent of the money wage bargain, except as far as the wage bargain affects indirectly the significant determinants, such as dividend or investment policy. From the identities we get some important clues about the future of the distributional shares — the question that so greatly interested the classical economists and has been so important in Marxian economics but seems to have dropped into the background recently. From the business savings identity, (7), it is clear that there cannot be any business savings in the stationary state, unless the national debt perpetually increases, for investment, dQ_b, will cease, and we can hardly expect a permanent rate of increase in the money stock or in consumer credit. The disappearance of business savings, however, does not necessarily involve the disappearance of profits, for as long as businesses are willing to distribute profits, profits will return to them to distribute. This is the 'widow's cruse' effect foreshadowed, for instance, by Keynes in his *Treatise on Money* (Book 1, p. 139). Hence there is a curious indeterminancy in the distributional pattern, and our models give results more akin to the economics of J. S. Mill than to that of J. B. Clark. The apparent distributional determinism that resulted from the marginal productivity theory (which, by allying the laws of distribution with those of production, apparently removed distribution from the sphere of human influence) may be shown to be due to an illegitimate extension of microeconomic principles to the macroeconomic field. The marginal productivity theory is a theory of the demand for input from a particular enterprise: it cannot be generalized to the economy at large.

We now return to consider in more detail the contribution of government to output as a whole and to the distributional shares. Consider first equation (16a). The balance of payments of businesses with government, X_{bg}, can be analyzed further into payments for net purchases of government from businesses, i.e., government expenditure for goods and services bought from businesses, E_{gb}, minus net business taxes, i.e., taxes minus subsidies, T_b, minus business payments to government for securities, S_b.

$$X_{bg} \equiv E_{bg} - T_b - S_b \qquad (19a)$$

Similarly for households, if E_{hg} is the net payment by government to households for goods and services, T_h is net taxes, paid out of household accounts, and S_h is net payments of households to government for securities,

$$X_{hg} \equiv E_{hg} - T_h - S_h \qquad (19b)$$

We have therefore, from equations (16a and b), further identities for the contribution of government to profits and to wages:

$$V_g \equiv E_{bg} - S_b + dK_{gb} - dK_{bg}' \qquad (20a)$$

$$W_g \equiv E_{hg} - S_h + dK_{gh} - dK_{hg}' \qquad (20b)$$

The total contribution of government to national income, Y_g, is given by:

$$Y_g \equiv V_g + W_g = E_{bh} + E_{hg} \qquad (21)$$

as the total net payment to government for securities $(S_b + S_h)$ must equal the net increase in government securities held $(dK_{gb} - dK_{bg}' + dK_{gh} - dK_{hg}')$, if we neglect income arising from changes in the price of securities already in private balance sheets. That is to say, the government contribution to national income equals the total government absorption of goods and services from both households and businesses.

For many purposes the significant variable is not 'total' but 'available' income, i.e., income after the deduction of taxes. If V' represents available profits and W' available wages, we have:

$$V' \equiv dQ_b + T + V_g' + dM_b' \qquad (22a)$$

$$W' \equiv C_h + dQ_h - T + V_g' + dM_h' \qquad (22b)$$

where

$$V_g' \equiv E_{bg} - S_b - T_b + (dK_{gb} - dK_{bg}') = X_{bg} + (dK_{gb} - dK_{bg}') \qquad (23a)$$

$$W_g' \equiv E_{hg} - S_h - T_h + (dK_{gh} - dK_{hg}') = X_{hg} + (dK_{gh} - dK_{hg}') \qquad (23b)$$

The two balance of payments factors for businesses, X_{bh} and X_{bg}, and for households, X_{bh} and X_{hg}, are likely to be closely related. If liquidity preferences are stable, a shift in the distribution of the total balance of payments of government (the cash deficit or surplus) between business and household accounts — occasioned, for instance, by a shift in the distribution of total taxes between business and household taxes — will be offset by a corresponding shift in the balance of payments between businesses and households. Thus suppose there is an increase in business taxes and a corresponding decrease in household taxes. The initial effect is to shift money out of business into household accounts, as more money in taxes is taken out of business accounts and less is taken out of household accounts. If, however, the liquidity preferences of business and households are unchanged, this shift in money stocks will be offset immediately by a shift in the business-households balance: in order to recoup their depleted money stocks, businesses will spend less toward households, and households will spend more toward businesses as they find themselves with larger money stocks in consequence of the decline in household taxes.

We may expect, therefore, that the quantities

$$X_b = X_{bh} + X_{bg} \text{ and } X_h = -X_{bh} + X_{hg} \tag{24}$$

will be fairly stable in the absence of changes in attitudes toward money. If then we take X_{bh} out of the transfer factor and write $T' = T - X_{bh}$, we can rewrite the available profits and wages identities as follows:

$$V' \equiv dQ_b + T' + (X_b + dM_b') + (dK_{gb} - dK_{bg}') \tag{25a}$$

$$W' \equiv (C_h + dQ_h) - T' + (X_h + dM_h') + (dK_{gh} - dK_{hg}') \tag{25b}$$

dM_b' and dM_h' need some comment. As government creation of money is taken care of in the factors X_b and X_h, $dM_b' + dM_h'$ represent the private creation of money. In a commodity-money economy this would represent simply the distribution between households and businesses of the total amount of money-commodity, e.g., gold, produced. In a bank-money economy the problem is more complicated: if banks are included in private businesses, bank deposits should strictly be regarded as debts. Since we include banks with government, we put bank deposits under government debt. To take account of these complications adequately would require a four-part model, i.e., adding the banking system to the three-part model already constructed. Such a model is rather beyond the scope of this paper, and as the general principles can be indicated without it the dM_b' and dM_h' factors will be neglected in what follows. It may be assumed roughly that the nongovernment increase in money stocks will be distributed in the same proportions as the general money stock.

An interesting conclusion with respect to the incidence of taxation follows from equations (25a) and (25b): if the investment, consumption, liquidity, and debt behavior patterns are stable, available profits and wages are quite independent of the distribution of the total tax burden between business and household taxes. That is, if these other factors are constant, a shift from household toward business taxes will be exactly compensated by a rise in profits before taxes and a fall in wages before taxes. In practice, a shift in the tax structure is likely to affect business and household decisions somewhat, and hence contribute to changing available incomes. This change, however, is a result of the effect on private decisions, not of the tax directly. The history of the last few years indicates that profits after taxes are markedly stable despite changes in taxes.

It seems to follow also that the available national income itself is independent of the tax load. This is the very agreeable 'widow's cruse' theory of taxation, that an increase in taxes always creates an equal increase in national income with which to pay them, and hence leaves income after taxes unchanged! But this proposition is subject to many qualifications.

It assumes first that the budget deficit does not change, so that the tax increase actually represents an increase in government absorption of product: it implies also that private absorption does not change, and that unemployed resources are available, so that the increase in government absorption produces an equal rise in the product. This condition can be fulfilled only at low levels of employment.

An indefinite variety of models can be constructed from these identities by assuming various types of relation among their components. Merely by way of illustration, one of the simplest models is based on the assumption that household absorption, $H = dQ_h + C_h$, business accumulation $B = dQ_b$, and the transfer factor, T, are functions of the relative distribution between wages and profits, neglecting the government variables: Then we have three equations: $H = F_h\left(\dfrac{W}{Y}\right), B = F_b\left(\dfrac{V}{Y}\right), T = F_t\left(\dfrac{W}{Y}\right)$; and three identities: $Y \equiv W + V \equiv H + B$ and $T \equiv V - B$ (or $T \equiv H - W$). The six equations determine the six unknowns: $H, B, T, W, V,$ and Y. This model is susceptible to simple graphic analysis, as in Figure 2. The base line WV shows the relative distribution, W representing 100 percent wages and V 100 percent profits. Intermediate points such as K represent a proportion WK going to profits and KV going to wages. CC_o and I_oI are the 'consumption' (household absorption) and 'investment' (business accumulation) functions. Investment is measured from WV downward, so that at any point, K, on WV, KC_k is consumption, KI_k is investment, and therefore C_kI_k is consumption plus investment, i.e., national income. YY_mY is the national income curve — in this figure exhibiting maximum at Y_m. We now divide the line C_kI_k at the point S_k, where $\dfrac{C_kS_k}{S_kI_k} = \dfrac{KV}{WK}$. Then C_kS_k is the absolute amount of wages and S_kI_k the absolute amount of profits when the ratio of wages or profits to national income is given by the point K. The locus of S_k is the dash line I_oC_o which, measured from the base line WV, is the $V - B$ curve: $KS_k = S_kI_k - I_kK = V - B$ ($= KC_k - C_kS_k = H - W$). We now postulate a T curve, T_oET, showing the value of the transfer factor T at each relative distribution. T is likely to rise with an increasing proportion of profits, as dividends will be larger: consumer credit also may be larger. The point of equilibrium is where the T curve cuts the $V - B$ curve at E. When the T curve is above the $V - B$ curve, decisions will be made at any given relative distribution that will raise profits above the given proportion; when the T curve is below the $V - B$ curve, decisions will be made that will lower profits below the given proportion. This is shown by the arrows. The equilibrium E is obviously stable; the equilibrium at E' would be unstable. The possibility of a very high 'shiftability' of equilibrium in this model is all too apparent; i.e., a slight change in the functions involved may bring about a large change in the position of equilibrium because of the similarity in the slopes of the curves T_oT and I_oC_o. Indeed, a relatively slight shift upward of the curve T_oT might produce a situation in which there was no equilibrium, and profits would increase indefinitely at the expense of wages until some sort of subsistence level was reached: this is the 'Marxian' case. On the other hand, a shift downward in the line T_oT until it lay entirely below I_oC_o would produce a situation in which wages increase indefinitely at the expense of profits until the economy broke down in unemployment. There is a suggestion of this kind of collapse in the debacle of 1929-32.

In this model it is interesting to note that a rise in the investment function (represented in Fig. 2 by a shift in the line I_oI downward) will increase the proportion going to profits in equilibrium, as the line I_oC_o is also pulled downward and E moves to the right. Similarly, a rise in the consumption function pulls the line I_oC_o upward and moves the equilibrium toward a higher proportion of wages.

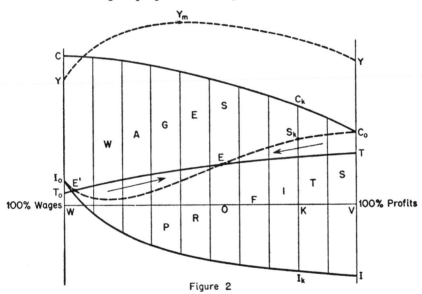

Figure 2

Other possible models will come readily to the reader's mind. Thus the more general model involving the equations $H = F_h(W,V)$; $B = F_b(W,V)$; $T = V - B = F_t(W,V)$; and $H + B \equiv W + V$ has many interesting properties, and exhibits in general the same kind of 'shiftability' as the simpler model.

The approach through general equilibrium models and comparative statics is not, of course, the only method of approaching macroeconomic relationships. The movements of these variables can be explored directly in a true dynamic approach by means of postulating difference equations connecting consecutive time-values of the variables. Thus if we assume that the magnitude of each component of an identity is determined by certain magnitudes of the identity in the preceding period (or even in many preceding periods), the time-course of the variables can be traced out and if the system yields an equilibrium, the equilibrium position will be successively approximated, regardless from what values we start. This method has the advantage also that it is susceptible to graphic analysis, no matter how complex the fundamental identity, as long as the difference equations relate only two, or at most three, variables.

The method is illustrated for a very simple case in Figures 3-5. We suppose that the transfer factor is constant, that there is a business investment function $B = F_b(V)$ (Fig. 3), and a household absorption function $H = F_h(V + W)$ (Fig. 4). Then the identities $T \equiv V - B \equiv H - W$ give us four equations to solve for the four unknowns, H, B, V, and W. We interpret the investment and household absorption functions as difference equations, so that we should strictly write $B_{t+1} = F_b V_t$ and $H_{t+1} = F_h(V_t + W_t)$. The graphic solution of the equilibrium position is not difficult: in Figure 3, OS is measured downward from the origin equal to the transfer factor T (assumed constant), and a 45° line drawn from S to cut the investment curve in B_e; $V_c B_e$ is the equilibrium level of investment ($B = V - T$). Now in Figure 4 we draw OR downward from the origin equal to $V_e B_e$ in Figure 3, and draw a 45° line from R to cut the household absorption curve in H_e; this gives the equilibrium value of national income.

Now suppose that we start with any arbitrary magnitudes of the four variables represented by the line $A_o B_o C_o D_o$ in Figure 5: $B = A_o B_o$, $H = B_o D_o$, $V = A_o C_o$, $W = C_o D_o$, and $T = B_o C_o$; national income, $(Y) = A_o D_o$. We then make OV_o in Figure 3 equal $A_o C_o$ in Figure 5, and find the corresponding value of B, $V_o B_1$ in Figure 3; on a new line in Figure 5 we draw $A_1 B_1 = V_o B_1$. Similarly, we draw OY_o in Figure 4 equal to $A_o D_o$ in Figure 5, get the value of H, $Y_o H_1$, and draw $B_1 D_1$ in Figure 5 equal to $Y_o H_1$ in Figure 4. This gives us all the variables for time t_1. Repeating the process we get lines $A_2 B_2 C_2 D_2$, $A_3 B_3 C_3 D_3$, and so on, each line being derived from the one above it. In this case it is evident that we are approaching a stable equilibrium rather rapidly: with other functions, of course, the difference equations might lead to an explosive solution. This method of attack can be employed even when the fundamental identity is too complicated to allow a graphic solution of the equilibrium position. The possibility of statistical attack by this method needs further exploration.

Neither the identities nor the models mentioned so far have included

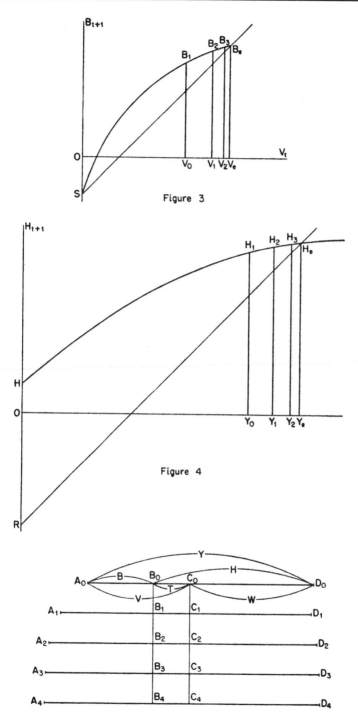

Figure 3

Figure 4

Figure 5

prices explicitly, though a price structure is implicit in the valuation of real assets. The 'real capital' items Q_b and Q_h are value items, and can be divided into some index of physical quantity of assets multiplied by some index of their prices. Likewise, the investment items dQ_b and dQ_h can be divided into two parts, one of which represents the increase in physical assets at constant prices, and the other the rise in the dollar value of existing assets as a result of a rise in their prices. From the viewpoint of national income the latter portion may be regarded as 'spurious': from the viewpoint of individual or sectional group incomes, however, it is not entirely spurious as it represents a redistribution of income, those who hold the assets that are rising in price benefiting at the expense of those whose assets are not rising. Models of the Keynesian type have never, to my knowledge, succeeded in incorporating prices and price levels as explicit variables of the system. This is a great weakness, as it means in effect that the models are valuable only at low levels of employment: as the system approaches capacity and price changes begin to be important, the functional relations assumed in the models break down and become too unstable to use. The models do not give an explicit picture of how the system behaves as it begins to approach capacity output, and in particular do not treat the mechanism of price-wage inflation explicitly. Nor is there any analysis of the impact of 'exogenous' changes in prices or money wages on the other variables in the system. I do not propose in the remaining space of this paper to eradicate this defect or even to attack a problem that has hardly even been stated: the effect of monopolistic and imperfectly competitive market conditions on aggregate economic activities. Nevertheless, there are indications that asset-analysis will throw a good deal of light on this problem.

In 'A Liquidity Preference Theory of Market Prices' (*Economica*, May 1944) I have shown that market price in a competitive market can be expressed in terms of money stocks, commodity stocks, or some other 'priced' exchangeable, and two 'parameters of behavior' reflecting the psychological attitude toward these assets (preferred asset ratios). Thus if p_a is the market price of any exchangeable, M the stock of money held by the marketers, A the stock of the exchangeable, and if r_m, the preferred liquidity ratio, is the desired proportion of money to total assets and r_a is the desired proportion of the value of the exchangeable to the value of total assets, then

$$p_a = \frac{Mr_a}{Ar_m} \qquad (26)$$

For, if T is the total value of all assets held by the marketers, by definition $r_m = \frac{M}{T}$ and $r_a = \frac{p_a A}{T}$; eliminating T between these identities gives us (26). The preferred asset ratios of the market are complex averages of the preferred asset ratios of the individuals in the market, and changes in them reflect a change in the 'state of mind' of the market as a whole. The liquidity preference theory of interest is a special case of this formula where the 'exchangeable' is fixed-interest securities.

The inference may be drawn from this identity that if the price structure is to enter explicitly into the macroeconomic models stocks of assets also must enter as given. There are also very convincing reasons for including asset stocks in investment and consumption functions, as Lawrence Klein shows in his paper. Consumption is consumption of assets, hence the larger the stock of assets the higher may the rate of their consumption be expected to be. Indeed, it is not wholly preposterous to assume that each asset consumes itself at its own rate, irrespective of use, and that consumption therefore is primarily a function of the composition of the asset stock. Similarly, investment, being itself an addition to real assets, should depend largely upon the size and composition of the existing stock. But the difficulties of analysis here seem to lie in the fact that the composition of the stock may be much more important than its over-all magnitude, and it is not at all easy to see offhand which breakdowns are significant. Asset quantities, however, are significant not merely because asset identities are the basis for significant income identities but also because they must enter explicitly into the models. The task of constructing such models is beyond the scope of this paper.

DEFENSE AND OPULENCE: THE ETHICS OF INTERNATIONAL ECONOMICS

American Economic Review, 41, 2 (May 1951): 210-220.

DEFENSE AND OPULENCE:
THE ETHICS OF INTERNATIONAL ECONOMICS

One of my favorite half-truths is that there is no such thing as the theory of international trade. There is, of course, a theory of trade-in-general. There is a theory of the location of economic activity. There is a general theory of the balance of payments (i.e., of monetary circulation). There is a theory of comparative advantage, which is, after all, merely a special case of the general theory of specialization. There is a theory of exchange rates, which is merely a special case of the general theory of exchange and markets. There is a theory of the geographical mobility of economic resources. None of these topics fits comfortably into what is usually termed "international trade." The theoretical parts of textbooks on this subject are a hodgepodge of stuff taken from monetary theory, location theory, exchange theory, and so on. Indeed, from the point of view of the pure economist international trade can almost be regarded as little more than a very bad statistical sample of the total volume of trade—a sample which happens to be collected at national frontiers. A shipment which goes from Detroit to Windsor is international trade; a shipment which goes from Detroit to California is not. If a world state were established tomorrow all international trade would disappear immediately. Practically all the problems connected with international trade would remain. It is evident that we are dealing with an arbitrary and almost meaningless segment of the universe, much as if we had set up a Study of Things Beginning with P, and written textbooks around peanuts, politeness, and peculiar people.

The trouble with half truths, however, is the other half. International trade is a by-product of the existence of the national state—an institution which may, to the economist, be arbitrary, but which is none the less real and which becomes more and more noticeable all the time. The economist's attitude towards the national state is symbolized in the fact that he calls its activity "intervention." The national state, that is, is not really part of the economist's universe. It is conceived as a capricious, though frequently as a benign, *deus ex machina* "intervening" in the "natural" world of private economic institutions and relationships with tariffs, taxes, quotas, price regulations, labor laws, and so on, but not really forming part of any larger universe. There is nothing in economics resembling a "theory of the state" in the way that there is a

"theory of the firm." Unfortunately there is very little theory of the
state anywhere in social science, not even in political science, which
seems to be in much the same position today that economics might be
in if there had never been anything but institutional economics since
Aristotle. Consequently, the study of international relations (of which
international trade is a part) is still almost entirely conducted at the
level of high-class journalism, or at best history, without either theoretical foundations or empirical superstructure. The appalling nature
of this gap in social science can be seen vividly if we contrast the kinds
of answers which social scientists are able to give to the questions of
how can be avoid depression and how can we avoid war. To the first
question economists can give some kind of answer. By the second, social
scientists are, or should be if they have any decent humility, struck
dumb.

Nevertheless, Adam Smith brazenly called his great work "An Inquiry into the Nature and Causes of the Wealth of Nations," and almost half the work is given over to a discussion of the "Sovereign or
Commonwealth" as an economic entity. Theories of defense, justice,
public works, education, religion, the "dignity of the sovereign," taxation and public debt—all find their place. It is perhaps one of the great
misfortunes of social science that the innumerable hints and suggestions in Adam Smith's superb Book V were never systematized into a
"discipline" in the way that succeeding generations of economists perfected his more "pure" economics. A hint of a "theory of the nation"
is given in the famous passage on the navigation acts from which I
have taken my title: "As defence, however, is of much more importance
than opulence, the act of navigation is, perhaps, the wisest of all the
commercial regulations of England." The prime object of the policy of
any nation is not the welfare of man, even of its own citizens, but is its
own preservation. The welfare objectives are important mainly as the
servants of defense. Any organization which obviously and clearly
makes no contribution, or a negative contribution, to the welfare of
those on whom it relies for support will not ultimately be defended.
Hence over a large range of human activity "opulence" and "defense"
are complementary rather than competitive goods. Nevertheless the
nature of this relationship needs to be examined.

The concept of defense is important not only in the theory of the
nation-state but also in the theory of all other organizations. We are
beginning to realize in economics that a theory of the firm (or union
or household or any other organization) which fails to take into account the political nature of all these organisms is seriously deficient
for many purposes. Newer interpretations of business behavior, such
as that of W. W. Cooper, which make the concept of "retaining con-

trol" central are closely allied to the theories of defense. It is not unreasonable to say that the main objective of the businessman is to stay in business, of the politician is to retain office, of the union leader is to keep his job, and of the saint is to maintain his sanctity—as long as these roles are satisfying to the individual performing them and no more alluring alternative role seems possible. The maximization of the welfare of the "clientele"—whether this is seen as the maximization of stockholders profit, of national welfare, of benefit to union members, or of the welfare of the church—is behaviorally significant mainly as it becomes part of the role which the executive sees himself playing. Even the exceptions to the above principle serve to underline its significance. The businessman who sacrifices his business to some high principle, the politician who would "rather be right than president," and the labor leader who sacrifices his union for a cause are themselves defending what in their eyes is a superior role to the one in which the world has placed them. The significance of organizations rests in the persistence of the roles which they create. Indeed, an organization might almost be described as a bunch of roles tied together with red tape. The role persists despite change of person (the king is dead—long live the king!) and it is the role that is defended rather than the particular incumbent who happens to be playing the part.

The concept of defense, therefore, is in no way peculiar to the national state but applies in some degree to all organizations. Nevertheless, the methods of defense of the national state raise acute welfare problems. The national state is almost the only organization, apart from criminal organizations, which employs violence as a regular and essential instrument of its defense. The defense of most organizations, such as businesses, universities, families, and churches, involves the maintenance of "attractive" power; i.e., the ability of the organization to draw people into relationships with the organization and away from competing organizations. Businesses live by their ability to produce goods which they can sell at prices sufficient to enable them to hire resources. Very rarely do they employ violence, and the occasional "Pink" and thug is exceptional. Normally businesses can survive only by their ability to attract both customers and employees. The same is true of families, universities, and churches. The competition of these organizations is therefore in a very real sense competition in the satisfaction of human desires; that organization which can best satisfy these desires in its whole scheme of operations is most likely to survive. For this reason, "economic" competition has been for the most part highly beneficial, whether this has been the competition of businesses, universities, churches, or even of families, and tends to move the character of these organizations constantly in the direction of a better satisfaction of human need. There are some important possible exceptions to this principle, of course, most of which arise, I suspect, because of ignorance; i.e., an inadequate learning process. The patent medicine peddler, the sophistical cult, the parasitic family—all exist in the interstices of a noncoercive society. The principal characteristic of all these less desirable organizations is the ability to create the need which they satisfy—usually through the semicoercive device of arousing fears—so that it represents in a sense a partial breakdown of the principle of defense by attraction.

Defense by coercion enables organizations to survive which are inimical to the welfare of man, in that the ability to defend an organization by coercion releases it from the necessity of defending itself by attracting voluntary support. Nevertheless, there are reasons for supposing that defense by coercion cumulatively diminishes the attractive power of an organization, and that it is therefore unstable in the long run, for coercion always has its limits. No organization can survive without some vestiges of attractive power, for men will not coerce merely for the sake of coercion. Unless they feel that the organization which they are defending is in some sense "worth" defending, the morale of the defenders will be undermined. Consequently the more coercion is used, the less sense there becomes in using it. Finally the organization simply withers away because of its inability to attract even the coercers—and somebody must always do the coercing. It has been said that someday somebody will give a war and nobody will come! The history of religious persecution is a good case in point. Coercion so undermines the attractive power of the persecutor that it eventually collapses from the sheer inability of anybody to get excited about the ideas which they are supposed to be defending.

It is highly probable that in our day the national state is similarly threatened with destruction because of its unstable reliance on coercive defense. Coercive defense has become increasingly unstable in modern society for several reasons. In the first place the maintenance of the security of a number of competing organizations by means of coercive defense implies the set of inequalities in which each organization be stronger than any reasonable combination of the others. Even in the two-organization case, this system is highly unstable. Strictly speaking, the inequalities—A is not weaker than B and B is not weaker than A—can only be satisfied by $A = B = 0$; i.e., by total disarmament. The only conceivable stable solution to a two-organization individual defense system is in a spatial system where the distance between the organizations is great enough so that each can be stronger than the other in its own backyard. This equilibrium depends on the proposition that the strength of any organization varies inversely with the distance from "home" at which it is conducting its coercive operations. Thus in 1900 it may well have been true that America was stronger than Japan in the East Pacific and Japan was stronger than America in the West Pacific. By 1945 this solution was clearly impossible, owing to the enormous reduction in significant distance. In a similar way, of course, social or economic distance may contribute to the stability of a defense system. This is probably the main reason for the development of caste systems.

The instability of national security in a world where distances are as small as they are today inevitably leads to an arms race and to war. Indeed, war may well be regarded as the normal relationship among nations. Because of the technical revolution, however, war is steadily undermining the ability of the national state to attract voluntary service and loyalty. In the eighteenth century it may be doubted whether war ever absorbed more than 10 per cent of national incomes. In the twentieth century a major war absorbed up to 50 per cent of national incomes. The reason for this change is, first, the tendency of any system of national defense, because of the essential instability of the national security system, to be "insatiable," up to the limit which the system can support, and, second, the constantly increasing proportion of the social product which represents "economic surplus" which is available for social purposes, whether for welfare, fecundity, waste, or war. Even in the eighteenth century it took 90 per cent of a nation's resources simply to keep it going. In the twentieth century we can keep ourselves going with less than half our resources, and hence can spare—and in a system of national defense will be forced to spare—half or more of our resources for defense. Consequently war, which even in the Napoleonic era could almost be regarded as a peripheral phenomenon (we recall that the novels of Jane Austen were written in the midst of the Napoleonic Wars) except for those areas where the battles were actually fought, in the twentieth century has become an institution which reaches down into the lives of almost every individual in the society. Defense on this scale, however, cannot be undertaken without the development of the coercive power of the state against its own citizens. Military conscription is the entering wedge; industrial conscription, both of labor and capital, follows; and in the interests of its defense a society transforms itself into a coercive society in which the market is abolished, in which the carrot of incentive is everywhere replaced by the stick of coercion, and in which fear rather than hope becomes the ruling motive. We saw this happen in Germany and Russia. We are watching it happen in America before our own eyes. It is a strange paradox that the American Legion, with its ideology of "toughness" and its faith in the power of fear, is probably one of the principal agencies making for an American version of the communist state, for once the principle of internal coercion is accepted in military conscription, the major barrier to the conscription of both capital and ordinary labor in the interests of national defense has fallen.

One thing coercion cannot command, however, and that is affection. Because the coercive organization does not have to rely on the power of attraction, it loses that power; and because it fails utterly to serve human needs and human welfare, eventually nobody can be found to play the roles which it creates and it collapses, to be replaced by organizations which have greater power of contributing to human welfare. It is only in the short run, then, that defense is more important than opulence. In the long run defense without opulence defeats itself—opulence, that is, in the sense of "ophelimity" or welfare.

What has all this to do with either ethics or international economics? Ethics is concerned primarily with the "good" (i.e., with the ultimate standards for judging welfare) or "profit" in the sense of "what shall it profit a man to gain the whole world and lose his own soul." The ethical parameter—that quantity which is increased when things get "better" and decreased when things get "worse"—is not to be identified with any other single parameter—neither with wealth nor power nor peace nor glory nor even survival. There is no reason to suppose, in the language of ecology, that the "best" system is the climactic ecosystem, and it may be that an essential ingredient of the defense of the "best" is an occasional catastrophe, just as the southern pine forests must be cut down every so often if they are to persist! The ethical parameter (goodness) is a function of a large number of other subordinate goods and bads. Whether this function is an objective reality is beyond the scope of this paper to investigate. Nevertheless, the function is neither purely arbitrary, nor is it merely a matter of taste. It is a proper subject of discussion, and that discussion can be fruitful, even though it is unlikely to result in universal agreement.

My contention is that the principal ethical confusions into which we seem to have fallen in the past hundred years are due to a confusion of the public-private value scale with the coercive-noncoercive value scale. The world has become extremely sensitive to the virtues of "publicness." There are good reasons for this. Virtually all religious systems denounce selfishness. A devotion to the general welfare is properly regarded as high in the scale of virtue. Consequently, organizations which are public rather than private such as the state are perceived with an aura of approval which private organizations, especially businesses, do not possess. The Coca-Cola corporation may in fact go around the world quietly doing good—cleaning up water supplies and providing people with moderately innocent refreshment. It is almost inconceivable that men should fight or die for it; it inspires amusement rather than respect, at best tolerance rather than affection, at worst an active resentment. National states rampage around the world noisily doing evil—destroying the innocent and ravaging the earth. Nevertheless they command the love and devotion of millions, and inspire self-sacrifice and martyrdom on a scale unknown even to religion. The tragedy of the twentieth century has been that the moral force which is generated by the appeal to publicness has to a large extent reinforced the growth of coercive rather than noncoercive organizations. On the whole privateness has gone with noncoerciveness and publicness with coerciveness. It has been the failure to realize this connection which has led us steadily towards the trap of a coercive society, whether communist or military. Public coerciveness has grown because it has been able to take advantage of its public nature and has kept its coercive nature hidden. Private noncoerciveness has declined because it has failed to exploit the moral advantage of its noncoerciveness and has been undermined by the moral weakness of its privateness. Worse still, private organizations have allied themselves with the coercive and have thereby rendered them utterly vulnerable to ethical attack. The private-coercive stands at the very bottom of the ethical scale! The alliance of business with military power and ideology is the factor more than any other which has made a private society untenable and has undermined the ideological foundations of capitalism.

In hardly any other sphere are these principles more apparent than in the field of international economic relations. In a noncoercive world society the proposition that there was no such thing as international trade would be a whole truth. Probably the closest approximation to this condition was found in the nineteenth century—a period which in this age of terror evokes almost a nostalgia for a golden age. It was an age when moderately economic men went quietly about the earth improving communications and spreading improved techniques, providing employment, and taking risks by building railroads, dredging harbors, planting tea, selling little things that little people wanted, without any more pernicious ulterior motive than private gain—a motive which compared with the subtle and sinister motives of national states seems remarkably high on the ethical scale. It was an age even when the gold standard represented a real modification of national economic sovereignty in the interests of a world order. It is easy, of course, to paint too rosy a picture of any golden age, and it is true, also, that the nineteenth century, by failing to evolve an ethical ideology which could sustain it, produced the discontents which destroyed it. The tariff represents an ancient alliance between the private interest and the coercive state. Economists have always been able to show that a tariff could be in the national interest. The case for free trade has always been a moral one and has rested ultimately on the ideal of a noncoercive society. Once the principle is admitted that the coercive power of the state can be used to protect a private interest against other private interests, there seems to be no logical resting place short of a coercive society in which the competition of organizations in the satisfaction of human needs and the attraction of human loyalties is replaced by the struggle to capture the instruments of coercive power. In this regard the utter failure of conservatives to conserve what is worth conserving is one if the depressing spectacles of human history.

The days in which the tariff was the main instrument of coercive power in this field, however, really belong to the golden age itself. A tariff, as Bastiat pointed out, is little more than a negative railroad— a device to increase the cost of transport (one way) between two places as a railroad is a device to diminish it. There is even a general-interest case for tariffs on the grounds that people can be too close to each other for satisfactory relationships, and that there is some sort of optimum social or economic "distance" in terms of the kind of strains and extreme specializations which "closeness" brings. The quota or quantitative restriction is, as all economists know, a more pernicious device, based as it must be on a historical base and tending to freeze ancient and out-of-date relationships. More significant than this, however, is the growth of state trading and investment itself. We are rapidly approaching the day of the complete socialization of international trade, when it will consist wholly of barter, gifts, or investment between nation-states, and will become almost indistinguishable from warfare. The nightmarish possibilities of unstable oligopolistic competition which such a prospect opens out are familiar to all students of the theory of competition.

Lest I be accused of being either an anarchist or a complete pessimist, I will conclude the paper on a note of faint hope. The way out of our present impasse seems to be surprisingly clear. It lies in the development of organizations of both public and noncoercive character. There is no necessary reason why the scale of possible organizations should stretch only from the public-coercive to the private-noncoercive corners of the field. We know that it is possible to have private-coercive organizations (gangs). It is possible also to have public-noncoercive organizations. The public character of an organization depends on the extent to which the population with which it is concerned conceives itself as "belonging to" or in some sense "inside" the organization or, looked at from the point of view of the organization itself (which is not quite the same thing), on the extent to which those most immediately participating in the activity of the organization regard themselves as responsible to, or representative of, the less active participants. Thus the significance of the development of democratic institutions is that on the whole the national state has become more public and as a result we have moved from *L'état c'est moi* to *L'état c'est nous*. This is a real gain. Nevertheless, from the point of view of the world at large the national state remains a largely private institution —even the democratic state. In spite of the fact that the policy of the United States, for instance, profoundly affects the welfare of almost the whole of humanity, neither the government nor the people of the United States feel much ultimate concern or responsibility for the welfare of non-Americans, nor do non-Americans feel much sense of participation in the activities and policies of the United States. There are hopeful signs, however, that a rapid extension of publicness beyond the boundaries of national states is in progress. This is reflected, not only in the development of international organizations, but also in the development of such institutions as the British Commonwealth, the "Good Neighbor" policy, the Marshall Plan, and Point Four. These involve something a little more than defense, though it is true that they generally have to be sold under that label. They represent a dim recognition of the genuinely public (i.e., world-wide) responsibilities even of organizations like national states, which are organized essentially on a private (i.e., a limited) basis of political franchise. The main difficulty with these movements so far is the weakness of the political institutions through which they are carried out. It is not enough to feel responsible *for*. One must be responsible *to,* otherwise the very feeling of responsibility is apt to corrupt the relationship of responsibility into either appeasement or condescension. In this respect the Marshall Plan, for instance, and Point Four represent a considerable retrogression from the excellent principles of UNRRA.

There is hope, also, that as public organizations become more truly public they will become less coercive. It is another prime virtue of the democratic process that insofar as it promotes genuine discussion (a process which involves listening as well as talking) it also promotes consensus and therefore consent. Government, then, is not necessarily synonymous with coercion. Coercion, indeed, may properly be regarded as a breakdown of discussion (you cannot argue with these people!) and hence as a breakdown of political process. There are several indications that we may be on the verge of important discoveries in the techniques of political process. From fields as diverse as group dynamics, child psychology, and industrial relations evidence is accumulating in regard to successful noncoercive techniques of human relationships. If we can begin to apply some of these techniques to international relations, where we are still committed to a blind toughness, there may yet be some hope of redeeming the national state in a blessed union of defense and welfare. Failing these discoveries, the national state, which can at present provide neither peace nor welfare, nor security nor honor, would seem to be doomed as being just too expensive to keep up. Under those circumstances the only alternative might well be a world tyranny of one complexion or another, where international economic relations become largely a matter of naked exploitation. Even a new Rome, however, would not last for ever, and it is not unreasonable to hope for a noncoercive, public world order being hammered out of the present time of troubles, however prolonged.

APPENDIX

The ethical theory of this paper can be illustrated by means of an indifference-curve analysis. In Fig. 1 we measure some index of "publicness" or "privateness" along one axis, and some index of coerciveness or noncoerciveness along the other. In this field we can draw a set of contours of an ethical-parameter function, G_1, G_2, etc., each repre-

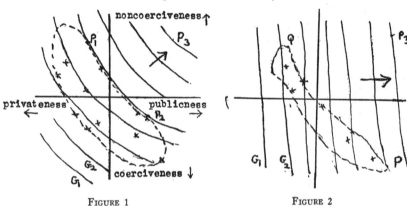

FIGURE 1   FIGURE 2

senting combinations of the subordinate "goods" which are regarded as equally "good." In the figure we suppose this function rises as we move upwards and to the right; i.e., noncoerciveness is regarded as "better" than coerciveness and publicness is regarded as better than privateness. The opportunities open lie in some kind of a limited field. In this case there is no need to limit the opportunities to a line. We suppose in Fig. 1 that the dotted line encloses all possible opportunities. We suppose that this area is long and narrow and slopes generally from the private-noncoercive region to public-coercive region, indicating in general that these qualities are roughly correlated. The "best" opportunity is, of course, that which lies on the "highest" indifference curve. If the opportunities are correlated in the same direction as the slope of the indifference curves, a state of ethical confusion or indifference may arise. Thus in Fig. 1 points P_1 and P_2 represent equally good situations, though one is high in the private-noncoercive field and the other is high in the public-coercive field. Suppose now that great weight is given to the ethical value of publicness but that little weight is given to the ethical value of noncoerciveness. The indifference curves will be steep, as in Fig. 2, indicating that goodness rises rapidly with increased publicness but rises very slowly with increased noncoerciveness. In this case a point such as P is likely to be regarded as the best of the opportunities, lying at the extreme of both publicness and coerciveness. This seems to be the communist case! If the indifference curves are flat, indicating a high sensitivity to noncoerciveness and a low sensitivity to publicness, a point such as Q at the opposite end of the range of opportunities may be chosen. In all cases, however, a broadening of the opportunity area is likely to lead to better situations. Thus if a point P_3 in the public-noncoercive quadrant becomes available, it is likely to be better than the previous opportunities.

This method of analysis of ethical judgments seems to be quite general. Any subordinate goods and bads can be measured along the axes. Most of the properties of the figures also survive the limitation that almost all goods and bads are ordinal magnitudes, or at least something less than cardinal magnitudes. These problems of measurement, however, are beyond the scope of this paper.

WAGES AS A SHARE IN NATIONAL INCOME

In: *The Impact of the Union,* D. McCord Wright, ed., New York: Harcourt, Brace, 1951, Chapter 6, 123-148.

Wages as a Share
in the National Income

THE problem of the distributional shares—that is, of the determinants of the proportions in which the national income is divided among the various "ranks of the people"—has interested economists at least from the days of the physiocrats. In classical economics the problem is conceived as a threefold division of the total product between wages, rent, and profit. In this paper we shall consider only the twofold division into wages (labor income) and "gross profits" or nonlabor income. Nonlabor income is the same as Marx's "surplus value."

In the classical system the problem of the distributional shares is recognized both as what we should now call a "macroeconomic" problem, involving the main aggregates of the system, and also as a dynamic problem, involving what happens in the progress of society and the course of economic growth or decline. Total labor income, or aggregate wages, is regarded as a constant at any given short period of time, determined by the wage fund, which in its turn is determined in some way by the decisions of capitalists as to the distribution of the use of their capital. Exactly how the wage fund is determined is never made quite clear, and this, of course, is the weak link in the whole chain of argument. Given the wage fund, however, nonlabor income is a residual—the difference between the aggregate total income and labor income.

Even with this crude apparatus the classical economists managed to develop at least the beginnings of a dynamic theory—i.e., a theory of economic development, and of what happens in the "progress of society." The subsistence theory postulated a perfectly elastic supply of labor at the subsistence level, wherever that might be. It assumed, that is to say, that there was some *average* wage above which the population would grow indefinitely, and below which the population would decline indefinitely. This average wage is the subsistence level, and it does not, of course, have to be determined by the level of physical subsistence. The average wage is equal to the wage fund, or total labor income, divided by the working population. If, therefore, the wage fund is constant, and the average wage is above the subsistence level, the population will grow, and therefore the average wage will decline until the subsistence level is reached and further growth of population ceases. In fact, however, the wage fund is not constant, but grows itself with the increase in capital. Hence we get the concept of the historical course of the average wage as the result of a race between population growth and capital accumulation, ending in the stationary state, where neither population nor capital grows. As population growth outstrips the growth of capital, the average wage falls; as capital outstrips population, the average wage rises; but eventually the race must be won by population—creation being no match for procreation—and the wage will settle down at the subsistence level.

It is instructive to examine a version of the classical system by means of graphical analysis. We suppose first of all that the aggregate income (Y) is a function of population (P) and capital (C). This function is shown by means of contour lines $(Y$-isomers) in Figure 1, where population is measured vertically, capital horizontally, and the solid lines marked 100, 200,

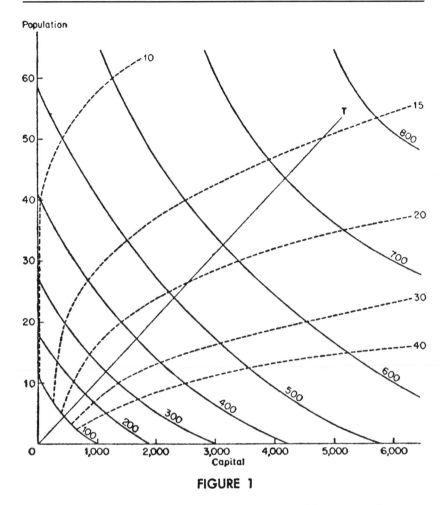

FIGURE 1

etc., are contours of equal aggregate income. These are drawn so as to exhibit a law of diminishing returns: An increase in both capital and population increases income at a decreasing rate, so that at high levels of population and capital a greater increase in population or capital is necessary to give a given increase in income than at low levels. This is reflected in the figure by the fact that the contours become further apart as we proceed upward or to the right. It is not necessary to assume any particular curvature in the contours, though a diminishing marginal rate of substitution between population and capital, as in the figure, is not unlikely.

By dividing the aggregate income at each point of the field by the population the per capita income can be calculated, and per capita income contours drawn (these are the dotted lines, marked 10, 15, etc.). It will be observed that the diminishing returns assumption—which is, of course, based on the assumption that there is some factor (land) which cannot be increased—results in a curvature in the per capita income contours, so that if per capita income is to be constant, capital must increase continually faster than population. If capital and population, historically, increase proportionally as along the line OT, per capita income will continually decline.

The classical system assumes that aggregate labor income is a function of capital, not population. In the extreme form of the wage fund doctrine it is assumed that aggregate labor income is some constant proportion of total capital. There is no need, however, to limit the model by this assumption, and in Figure 2 I have drawn, again on a population-capital field, aggregate labor income or wage bill contours, which are the solid lines marked 100, 200, etc. These are vertical, indicating that the wage bill is independent of population. I have assumed in the figure that the wage bill bears a diminishing proportion to total capital as total capital increases—a not unreasonable but by no means necessary assumption. From these wage bill contours average-wage contours can be constructed, the average wage at each point in the field being the wage bill divided by the population. It is assumed here that the population and the working population are identical—a rather general assumption in classical economics. The average-wage contours are the dotted lines marked 5, 10, etc.[2] Now suppose that the average wage

[2] The geometrical construction of the average-wage and per capita income contours is as follows: to construct the average-wage contour x in Figure 2 we take the points on the wage bill contours w_1, w_2, etc., at

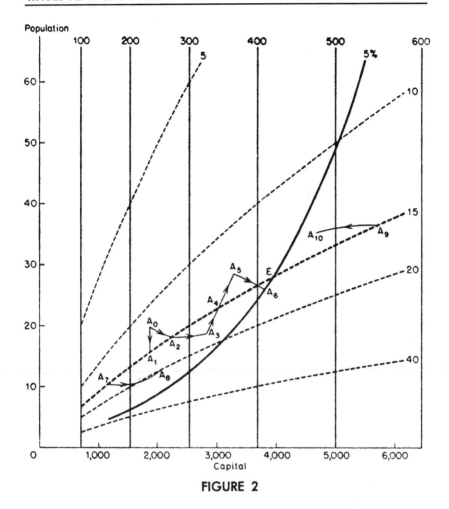

FIGURE 2

represented by one of these contours—say the wage of 15 units—
is the subsistence level. The corresponding average wage contour
is drawn heavily in Figure 2. At any point above and to the

which they are intersected by the lines $P = w_1/x$, $P = w_2/x$, and so on.
Thus the average-wage contour marked 10 in Figure 2 is constructed by
taking the point on the 100 wage bill contour where $P = 10$, the point
on the 200 wage bill contour where $P = 20$, on the 300 wage bill contour
where $P = 30$, and so on. The line joining these points is the average-
wage contour. A similar construction gives the per capita income contours in
Figure 1.

left of this line the average wage is less than the subsistence
level and the population will eventually decline; at any point
below and to the right of it the average wage is above the subsistence level and the population will eventually grow. The
actual course of population depends on the factors determining
the accumulation of capital and on the speed of response of the
population to a wage which diverges from the subsistence level.

The actual course of population and capital may be shown by
a line such as $A_0A_2A_3A_4$ . . . in Figure 2. A_0 represents some
initial position of population and capital. If there was no change
in capital the population would simply move to the subsistence
level contour at A_1. Actually however there may be growth
(or decline) in capital: if there is growth in capital, population
and capital together may follow a course such as $A_1A_2A_3$ . . .
etc. Population falls from A_0, as the wage is below the subsistence level contour. Capital continues to grow, however, and
if the population is not immediately responsive to the rise in
wages above the subsistence level we may move to A_3. The high
average wage, however, will stimulate a growth of population,
and we move back to the subsistence level contour A_4. The
growth in population may have some momentum, which will
carry us to A_5, below the subsistence level, this in turn producing a further decline to A_6. The more responsive the population is to the level of wages, the closer the actual population-
capital path will approximate to the subsistence level contour;
population will always just keep pace with the growth or decline
of capital. When population is increasing faster, per unit increase of capital, than the slope of the subsistence level contour
we see a decline in the average wage; when it is increasing more
slowly the average wage rises. This is the "race between capital
and population."

The foundation of Adam Smith's dictum that wages are likely
to be high in an advancing society and low in a declining
society can also be seen from this diagram. The basic assumption
involved is that the reaction of population to a divergence of the

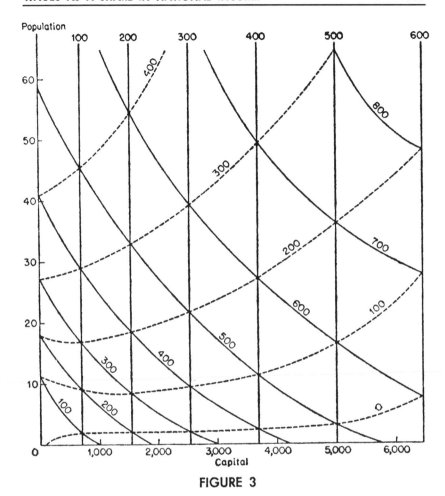

FIGURE 3

actual wage from the subsistence level is slow—slower, that is, than the rate of adjustment which would compensate for the change in capital. Thus in a society in which capital is increasing, even starting from the subsistence level, say at A_7, the population-capital course is likely to be like A_7A_8: the rise in population is not sufficient to bring the society back to the subsistence level contour. When capital is decreasing, however, as from A_9 to A_{10}, the population does not fall enough to keep pace, and the wage is continually below the subsistence level.

From the aggregate income and wage bill contours of Figures

1 and 2, contours showing the aggregate nonwage income can be derived as in Figure 3. Here the solid lines are identical with the aggregate income and wage bill contours of Figures 1 and 2. As the nonwage income is equal to the aggregate income minus the wage bill, the nonwage income contour, say, of 100 is drawn through the points of intersection of the 200, 300, 400 . . . aggregate income contours with the 100, 200, 300 . . . wage bill contours. The dotted lines are nonwage income contours. The "diminishing returns" assumption of the aggregate income function draws them upward to the right; the assumption of a diminishing ratio of wage bill to capital draws them downward to the right; in the figure the "diminishing income returns" assumption is clearly dominant.

The most interesting ratio in the case of nonlabor income is not the ratio to population [3] but the ratio to capital; this latter gives us a sort of gross "rate of return" on all capital. Thus in Figure 4 the dotted lines represent contours of equal "rate of return," constructed in a manner similar to the average wage contours of Figure 2. They slope sharply upward to the right, indicating that a rise in capital lowers, and a rise in population raises, the rate of return.

Suppose now that there is some rate of return at which capital will neither grow nor decline, and that above this rate capital will grow, while below this rate it will decline. We then have a long-run "subsistence" theory of the rate of return, or "profit." The "subsistence" rate of return need not be zero, as Ricardo seems at times to imply; indeed, in a society which is naturally averse to risk it is likely to be positive. In a highly risk-loving society it might even be negative. Suppose in Figure 4 that the subsistence rate is 5 per cent: the 5 per cent contour is then the subsistence rate contour. Putting this into Figure 2 as the heavy

---

[3] The per capita nonwage income is not a particularly significant figure, unless distribution of capital is practically equal. It is interesting to note in passing, however, that the per capita nonwage income function is quite likely to exhibit a maximum in the population-capital field.

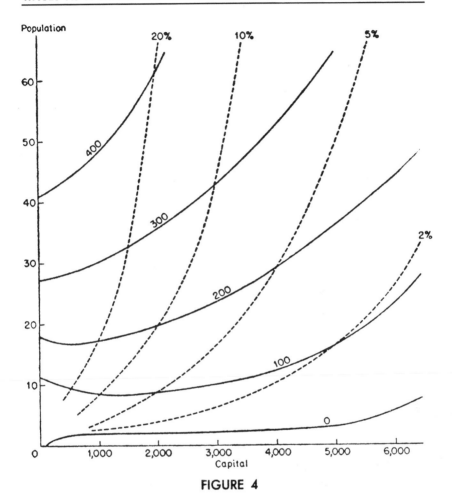

FIGURE 4

solid line, the "stationary state" is then found at E, where the subsistence wage contour and the subsistence rate contour intersect. This equilibrium is stable if the subsistence rate contour cuts the subsistence wage contour from below.

The model which I have outlined is substantially the same as that of classical economics. I have expounded it in some detail because I believe that it is much more relevant to present-day problems than is usually conceded. In modern economic thought the marginal productivity theory—or more generally, the refined marginal analysis—is supposed to have superseded the crude models of the classical school. In fact it has not done so. The marginal analysis has proved to be a very useful tool in dealing with problems of microeconomics. It is most instructive in dealing with the theory of the firm and with the demand, supply, and pricing of particular products and particular factors of production. It is not particularly helpful in dealing with the aggregates of the system, because its use is constantly likely to involve us in fallacies of composition. The functions which are deduced from the marginal analysis—e.g., demand functions for labor—are not aggregable, as they are derived on the assumption that other elements in the system remain stable. Consequently I can hardly help regarding the development of marginalism as a retrograde step as far as the theory of over-all distribution—i.e., of the macroeconomics of distribution—is concerned. The marginal analysis tells us a good deal about what determines the demand for plasterers in Podunk; it tells us very little about total wages. The famous "adding-up" problem relating to the homogeneity of the production function is quite unreal as applied to the whole economy, though it may have some significance in discussing the distribution of the revenues of a particular firm. Instead of superseding the classical analysis of distribution, marginalism has simply created a vacuum in this field. This vacuum has not been filled by the Keynesian analysis. In spite of one or two pregnant suggestions (e.g., the "widow's cruse" theory of profits in the *Treatise on Money* and the modified "wages fund" of the *General Theory*) Keynes never succeeded in developing a theory of distribution in macroeconomic terms, and this gap remains one of the prime weaknesses in his theoretical structure.

It is worth while, therefore, to re-examine the classical model to see how much of it actually remains valid in the light of present-day knowledge. We may examine first some misconceptions regarding the part played in the classical system by the wage fund doctrine. It must be confessed, of course, that the wage fund doctrine exhibits strong marks of that confusion between stocks and flows which is so characteristic of classical economics (and even more of Marxian economics!). In the form in which it is stated by Adam Smith and Ricardo it remains a somewhat inappropriate extension and generalization of a phenomenon which was clear enough in the agriculture of Adam Smith's Scotland, where wages were paid in oatmeal out of the barn, and the more oatmeal in the barn at the end of the harvest the higher wages would be in the forthcoming winter! [4] It is important to observe, however, that in the model outlined above no assumption is necessary that wages are paid "out of capital"; the only assumption necessary is that the total wage bill is an increasing *function* of total capital. This is a much less restricted assumption than is made in the usual exposition, and while it may not be particularly true, at least it is not ridiculous. The model could easily be extended, of course, by making the total wage bill a function both of population and capital, though we are in real danger here of postulating purely formal functions which have no basis in individual behavior. The really critical questions here are: (1) What are the *decisions* which actually determine the distributional pattern? (2) Can these decisions be expressed in terms of fairly simple aggregate parameters?

I cannot do much more here than sketch the outlines of the type of theory that will be necessary.[5] The basis of it may be

[4] In the course of the discussion Professor Knight raised the question as to why more oatmeal in the barn should mean higher wages. The answer is, of course, that the powers of consumption of oatmeal on the part of the capitalist are strictly limited, and once he has eaten his fill of porridge there is nothing he can do with his oatmeal but feed the "laboring poor and laboring cattle" with it. He will try to attract labor away from his competitors if he is particularly flush with oatmeal (perhaps to get gardeners!), and so will push up the oatmeal wage. The case is exactly analogous to the effects of increased money stocks of entrepreneurs on the money wage. Of course, if the laboring poor are so full of oatmeal that they cannot stand any more we will run into a "backward-sloping supply curve" for labor, but that is another story altogether.

[5] A more detailed exposition will be found in my book, *A Reconstruction of Economics* (Wiley, 1950), chapter 14.

called the balance-sheet view of the profit-making process. We suppose the accounts of the economy to be divided into two groups: households and businesses. Profits all accrue in business accounts, though they are of course distributed to household accounts as dividends, interest, and rent. Some practical difficulties of definition may arise here because of the confusion of household and business accounts in farming and other household-centered enterprises, but normally the distinction is clear enough in practice to make it valuable in theory. The accrual of profits is the same thing as the accrual of *net worths* in business accounts. If no profits were distributed the profit in a given period in any one account would be equal to the increase in net worth. If profits are distributed then the total gross profit accruing to the account is equal to the rise in the net worth plus 'the amount distributed in dividends, rent, and interest.

We thus see the profit-making process, in the case of an individual firm, as a process of manipulating assets by transformations through exchange and production in order to increase their total value in terms of the unit of account (usually money). This increase may be accomplished in two ways: (1) by increasing the physical quantities of assets in the account, or (2) by valuing existing physical quantities at higher "prices" or valuation coefficients. This means in effect that when one set of asset quantities is transformed into another set the value of the assets given up (cost) must be greater than the value of the assets which appear in the balance sheet as a result of the transformation. Profit, indeed, is the difference between the value of the assets produced by the transformation and the value of the assets given up—in more familiar terms, revenue minus cost. It is important to understand, however, that revenue and costs are not money flows: indeed, they need not be defined as flow at all, although a series of successive transformations can be so regarded. In the broadest sense cost consists of the assets which are consumed or destroyed or given up to another account;

revenue consists of assets created or received from another account.

For an individual business we can classify assets (positive and negative) into several groups. For purposes of a two-part model consisting only of households and business we need only seven classifications, including net worth, and can write the balance sheet as follows:

ASSETS		LIABILITIES	
Money	m_b	Debts to businesses	k'_{bb}
Value of goods (real capital)	q_b	Debts to households	k'_{bh}
Debts from businesses	k_{bb}	Net Worth	g_b
Debts from households	k_{hb}		

Treating contractual liabilities as negative assets, the balance sheet identity can be written in the form of a net worth identity thus:

$$g_b \equiv m_b + q_b + (k_{bb} - k'_{bb}) + (k_{hb} - k'_{bh}) \qquad (1)$$

This identity can be differentiated as follows:

$$dg_b \equiv dm_b + dq_b + d(k_{bb} - k'_{bb}) + d(k_{hb} - k'_{bh}) \qquad (2)$$

Here the prefix d before each symbol signifies the *change* (say increase) in the corresponding variable in a unit period of time. Each of the terms of this identity has economic significance: dg_b is the increase in net worth during the period, which may properly be called "business savings"; dm_b is the increase in the firm's money stock; $d(k_{bb} - k'_{bb})$ is the increase in the net debts owed to the firm by other firms; $d(k_{hb} - k'_{bh})$ is the increase in net debts owed to the firm by households. We are not considering here how these increases (or, if negative, decreases) arise from the particular transformations in which the firm engages; we are considering merely the end result.

Identity (2) can be summed (consolidated) for all businesses, and when this is done the term $d(k_{bb} - k'_{bb})$ reduces to zero,

as the debts of all firms to all firms must be equal to the debts of
all firms from all firms, being the same quantity. Every interfirm debt, in other words, appears in two balance sheets, once
as a liability and again as an asset. When all balance sheets of
firms are consolidated, then, these terms cancel out. If we represent by capital letters the sums of the corresponding quantities
for all firms, we have then

$$dG_b \equiv dM_b + dQ_b + dK_{hb} - dK'_{bh} \qquad (3)$$

This is a very important identity which may be called the *busi-
ness-savings identity*. From it can be derived immediately an
identity for gross profits (V), which must be equal to business
savings plus business distribution (D):

$$V \equiv dG_b + D \equiv dQ_b + (dM_b + D + dK_{hb} - dK'_{bh}) \equiv$$
$$dQ_b + T \quad (4)$$

The total product (Y) can be divided into two parts in two
ways: into the distributional shares, gross profits (V) and wages
(W); and into its absorptional composition, the increase in
business real capital ("investment"), dQ_b, and household purchases ("consumption"), C_h, for if we suppose that the product
originally is produced in business accounts, then that part which
is not taken off the hands of businesses by households must
still remain in the possession of businesses. We have therefore:

$$Y \equiv V + W \equiv dQ_b + C_h \qquad (5)$$

Comparing equations (4) and (5) we obtain an identity for
wages:

$$W \equiv C_h - (dM_b + D_b + dK_{hb} - dK_{bh}) \equiv C_h - T \quad (6)$$

This identity can also be derived directly from the summation
of household balance sheets. The item T

$$T \equiv dM_b + D + dK_{hb} - dK'_{bh} \qquad (7)$$

I call the "transfer factor": added to business accumulation it gives us total profits; subtracted from household purchases it gives us the total wage bill.

The significance of these identities is that each item in them, apart from W and V, represents in some degree a parameter of behavior, and is affected fairly directly by the decisions of broad classes of individuals. The item dM_b is essentially a balance-of-payments item as between businesses and households. In the simple identities above I assume no creation or destruction of money; however, they can be modified to include such changes. If, however, the money stock is constant, the positive (or negative) balance of payments of businesses must equal the negative (or positive) balance of payments of households; the money stock may be regarded as a shifting cargo, sometimes shifting out of household into business balances, sometimes out of business into household balances. Such a shift—other things being equal—clearly affects the distributional pattern. A shift into business balances shifts distribution into profits and away from wages, as the additional money in business balances increases the total net worths of businesses. A shift away from business into household balances diminishes profits and increases wages—assuming, of course, that national income remains constant. We may regard this internal balance of payments as determined primarily by the relative changes in liquidity preference (or velocities of circulation) of businesses and households. If both businesses and households change their velocities (Expenditure ÷ money stock) in the same degree (either absolutely or relatively), the total of payments will change but neither will succeed in forcing money stocks onto the other: if both businesses and households start spending more freely, in the same degree, both will find that their receipts expand in an equal degree; for the receipts of businesses are the expenditures of households and the receipts of households are the expenditures of business, interbusiness and interhousehold payments being neglected as they cancel out in the total. If, however, businesses increase their expenditures toward households more than households increase their expenditures toward businesses, then the money stock will shift out of business into household balances.

There may be, of course, important other results of a disequilibrium in the internal balance of payments. If the reactions to positive and negative balances are not symmetrical, as may well be the case, the appearance of positive and negative balances of payments in general—i.e., a shift in the ownership of the money stock—may produce marked effects on the *total* of payments. If we suppose, for instance, that a positive balance of payments (i.e., an increase in money stock) on the part of an individual produces a slower reaction than a negative balance of payments (a negative balance produces a rather immediate curtailment of expenditures, while a positive balance is allowed to accumulate for a while without producing a corresponding increase in expenditures), then a disturbance in the *balance* of payments is likely to produce a net decline in the total *volume* of payments, and this in turn may react upon prices, income, and output, depending on the varying flexibilities of prices and outputs.

In general it may be said that the longer the period we take, the smaller will be the balance of payments item dM_b in relation to the other items: i.e., in the long run the balance of payments of one sector of the economy cannot persist for very long, since otherwise all the money of the system would be concentrated into one part of it. We should normally expect positive and negative balances to succeed each other for any given part of the system as the money cargo surges first into one part and then into another part. Unfortunately we have very little data on these internal balances of payments, especially in regard to their movement through time. Over periods of a year or perhaps two years they may be quite a significant factor in the distributional proportions, though the fact that profits are so generally reckoned annually means that fluctuations of smaller period are not likely to be reflected in the accounts. With a total money stock of the order of magnitude of 100 billion units, however, a "surge" into or out of business balances of the size of, say, five billion in the course of a year is by no means out of the question, and some of the short-period fluctuations in the distributional pattern may well be due to this factor.

The "business distributions" factor D is fairly directly connected with business decisions as to "business savings." We run into a paradox here: If the other elements in the identity can be assumed constant, decisions of businesses to save (i.e., to add to their net worths) do not determine the total of business savings but the total of profits. In other words we have a "widow's cruse" effect: the more businesses distribute out of their profits, the more profits they will have to distribute! This proposition, of course, does not hold for individual businesses—it is the distributions of one business that help to create profits for all. Even for all businesses, of course, the "other things" may not be constant. Increased distributions may simply remain in the pockets of the households to which the distributions are made: in that case the increase in D will be offset by a decline in dM_b and there will be no shift in the distributional structure. Even in short periods, however, it is most unlikely that increased distributions would be completely offset in this way. There is also a possibility that increased distributions may be offset by a decline in consumer credit, which would render dK_{hb} negative, or by an increase in household holdings of business securities, which would create a positive dK'_{bh}. These changes, however, are not likely to be directly related to dividend policy. There may also be a relationship between business decisions to distribute profits and business decisions to accumulate (invest) which may be offsetting. With all these offsets, however, the longer the period of time that we take the smaller they are likely to be, relative to the total volume of business distributions. Subject to the above-mentioned qualifications, therefore, we can say that an increased "propensity to distribute" profits on the part of businesses is likely to lead to a shift in the distributional structure toward profits and away from wages.

The other items in the transfer factor, dK_{hb} and dK'_{bh}, may be dismissed briefly. The first represents mainly changes in consumer credit, and is clearly capable of spontaneous and decision-determined changes: an increased "propensity" to extend or to accept consumer credit is likely to have a direct effect in increasing profits at the expense of wages. Here also certain offsets are possible. An extension of consumer credit may cause a shift in the money stock away from households toward businesses, if households regard a "line of credit" as a substitute for holding money. This is a "negative offset," actually intensifying the shift toward profits. More consumer credit may also mean a depletion of the inventories of businesses, and hence a decline in dQ_b; changes in relative liquidity preference may do likewise. If, however, there is any elasticity in output, a decline in business inventories is likely to be made up from production, so that this offset is also smaller as the period taken is longer.

The second debt item, dK'_{bh}, represents mainly the increase in business securities held by households. This acts to shift the distributional structure *away* from profits toward wages—a somewhat paradoxical result, as it is usually in the hope of profits that securities are issued! Here again there may be the usual offsets: money may flow into business balances, thus raising profits; the sale of securities may permit businesses to expand their consumer credit; and so on. In this case, however, there is one offset which will not generally diminish in importance with longer periods; an expansion in business indebtedness to the public is very likely to be associated with an expansion in the real assets of business (i.e., an increase in dK'_{bh} is likely to be associated with an increase in dQ_b). If, indeed, business investment is financed entirely by the sale of securities to households these two items will be equal and will cancel, and the distribution pattern will be determined by the other items in our identities, or rather by the behavior patterns to which they correspond. Insofar, however, as business investment is financed out of profits (i.e., without the corresponding issuance of securities to households), this investment will itself create the profits out of which it is financed—another delightful "widow's cruse."

It is impossible to proceed much further in this argument without considering the impact of these various variables on total output and employment; and to discuss this in detail would carry us far beyond the scope of this paper. Two kinds of models can be constructed based on the above identities: (1) By postulating various functional relationships among the aggregates of the identities equilibrium models can be derived, on the lines of the Keynesian or the Walrasian systems, with equal numbers of equations and unknowns. The equilibrium models can then be used to discuss the effect of changes in the underlying determinants of the system by the method of comparative statics. (2) The other type of model is "period" analysis along the lines of the Swedish school, in which the identities are used to show how the decisions of one period determine the *data* of the next. I have developed some equilibrium-type models in my *Reconstruction of Economics* (Wiley, 1950). An interesting model is the one which expresses household absorption (C_h) as a function of total income (Y) and wages (W) (cf. the Keynesian consumption function), and in which business accumulations $(dQ_b,$ or $I)$ are written as a function of income and profits. As income is equal to wages plus profits, C_h and I can also be written as functions of wages and profits. We have, then, five equations to give us the five unknowns, C_h, I, W, V, and Y:

$$Y \equiv V + W \equiv C_h + I$$
$$T \equiv V - I \; (\equiv C - W)$$
$$C_h = F_c(V, W)$$
$$I = F_i(V, W)$$

In the above system T is supposed to be given by the complex of decisions determining its components. We can easily extend the system, however, to suppose that T also is a function of V and W, in which case we add another equation, $T = F_t(V, W)$, and another unknown, T, to the system.

This model is shown graphically in Figures 5, 6, and 7. In all three figures we measure V (gross profits) along the horizontal axis, and total wages (W) along the vertical axis. In Figure 5, the solid lines are lines of equal household absorption, or C_h-isomers: they are the contours of the "consumption function": $C_h = F_c(W, V)$. This consumption function is assumed to have two significant properties. A movement toward wages with constant income (i.e., an increase in the proportion of income going to wages), as represented, for instance, by a movement along the line $Y_v Y_w$ ($Y = 50$) from Y_v to Y_w, *raises* C_h, indicated by a movement to higher C_h-isomers. It is also assumed that at least after a certain point C_h does not increase proportionally with income, W/V being constant: thus, as we move out along a line OP, successive C_h-isomers become farther and farther apart. The C_h-isomers are likely to have some curvature also. The dotted lines marked CW_0, CW_{10}, etc., are $(C_h - W)$-isomers. Thus, the CW_0-isomer is constructed by joining the points where C_{30} cuts $W = 30$, C_{40} cuts $W = 40$, C_{50} cuts $W = 50$, and so on. Similarly in Figure 6 we have I-isomers marked I_0, I_{10}, I_{20}, etc.: contours of the function $I = F_i(W, V)$. These have somewhat similar properties to the C_h-isomers, except that they are assumed in the figure to be much more curved, so that as we move along a line of constant income $(Y_w Y_v)$ from Y_v (100 per cent profits) we find that investment rises to a maximum but then falls. This is a plausible but of course not essential assumption. We also assume that investment does not increase in proportion to the increase in income. The dotted lines VI_0, VI_{10}, etc., are $(V - I)$-isomers, constructed in similar manner to the CW-isomers of Figure 5.

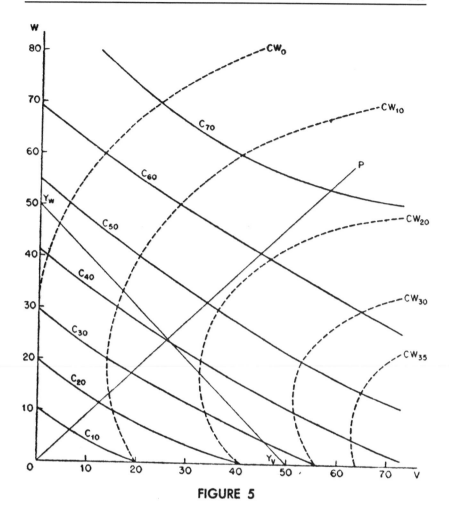

FIGURE 5

Thus VI_0 is drawn through points where I_0 cuts V_0, I_{10} cuts V_{10}, I_{20} cuts V_{20}, and so on.

In Figure 7 the dotted lines VI_0, VI_{10}, etc., and CW_0, CW_{10}, etc., are put together. The solid line $KLMN$ is drawn through the points of intersection of VI_0 with CW_0, VI_{10} with CW_{10} . . . VI_n with CW_n. This is the line corresponding to the identity $V - I = C - W$, or $V + W = C + I$.

If now the transfer factor is assumed given—say, $T = 20$—the point of equilibrium of the system is given at Q where the

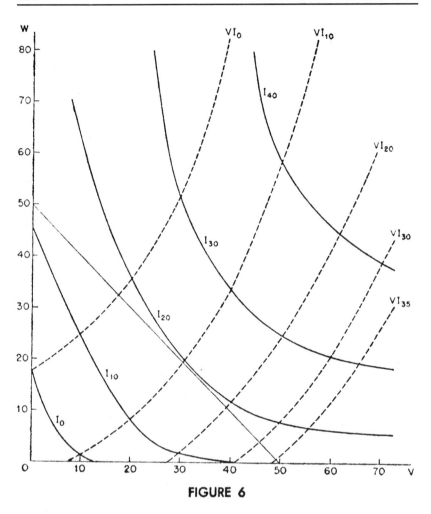

FIGURE 6

VI_{20}-isomer (or the CW_{20}-isomer) intersects with the line
$KLMN$. It will be observed that there are apparent double solutions: that for instance VI_{20} and CW_{20} intersect twice, once at Q
and again at R. Equilibrium, however, at points below M such as
N, R, etc., is unstable, and the only stable equilibriums are
above M.

Some interesting conclusions follow from this model. The
maximum total income which can be obtained on the line
$KLMN$ is at the point L, where the line is touched by a $45°$

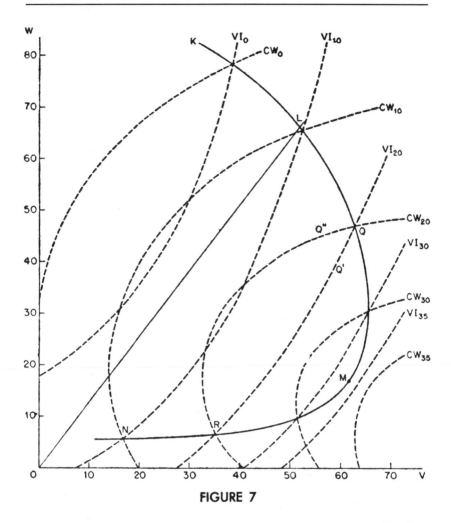

FIGURE 7

Y-isomer. We see also that a rise in T, moving the equilibrium point downward along the path KLQ, raises the proportion of profits and lowers the proportion of wages—proportionate distribution at a point, e.g., L, being given by the slope of the line OL. If T is below the value T_m which yields a maximum Y, then a rise in the profit proportion at the expense of wages through a rise in T will raise income: here "incentives" are more important than "markets." If T is above the value T_m than a rise in the wage and a decline in the profit proportion will raise in-

come: here "markets" are more important than "incentives."
It is not necessary, of course, for Y to exhibit a maximum
such as L within the possible range of values of the various
variables, but it is interesting to note that such a case is
by no means impossible. The national income (Y_m) at L
is not, of course, necessarily "ideal" income (i.e., the point
L does not necessarily represent full employment); ideal
income may be greater than Y_m, in which case no amount
of distributional manipulation will achieve it. These models,
like all Keynesian-type models, tend to break down as the
capacity of the system is reached, as no specific provision is
made in them for the mechanism of inflation; if the equilibrium
output as given by these models is "above capacity" then there
will be inflationary pressure of some sort which will shift the
functions themselves to adjust to the capacity income.

A fall in the consumption function (i.e., a decrease in the C_h
at each level of W and V) will push the C_h-isomers outward,
which will bend the CW-isomers outward and to the right also.
This will move the $KLMN$ curve of Figure 7 inward and to
the left, lowering the national income. The point of equilibrium
(with, say, $T = 20$) moves from Q to, say, Q'. In Figure 7
this represents a shift toward a higher proportion of profits, as
OQ' has a smaller slope than OQ: such a result is plausible,
but not absolutely necessary. Similarly, a fall in the investment
function may move the equilibrium from, say, Q along the
CW_{20}-curve to Q'', also with a fall in income and a rise in the
proportion going to wages.

To return now to the focus of interest of classical distribution theory: What is the implication of these macroeconomic
distributional models for the "progress of society"? If we examine the constituents of T (equation 7) we see that only the
business distributions item D has any future in the stationary
state. As we move toward the stationary state, investment (dQ_b
or I) must decline to zero—unless of course there is perpetual
inflation—the credit items likewise will decline toward zero, as

debt cannot expand forever; the balance of payments component of the increase in business money holdings obviously approaches zero in the long run, or at best fluctuates between positive and negative values. A perpetual increase in the money stock will, of course, be reflected in a positive dM_b, but this is a poor way out of the difficulty. It is evident, therefore, that in the stationary state business savings, along with all other savings, must disappear: there can be no building up of net worths if assets cannot increase. Profits then are reduced to business distributions; but this fact alone shows that *profits* do not disappear in the stationary state, and that therefore there is no *necessary* contradiction in capitalism. Profits are the price that we pay for a polylithic, nontotalitarian economy. If it were inevitable that this price would become insufficient, we should have to capitulate to Marx eventually as we approached the stationary state. The analysis of this paper shows, however, that such is not the case, and that the stationary state is not necessarily inconsistent with the institutions of capitalism.

A striking feature of the macroeconomic theory of distribution outlined above is that it shows quite clearly that the principal determinants of the distributional shares are human decisions rather than physical relationships. The success of the marginal productivity theory has given rise to a certain feeling that distributional shares are determined by the physical production function. Such a view is not of course implied in the marginal productivity theory when correctly stated, but the absence of any macroeconomic theory of distribution places a certain premium on the improper extension of the marginal theory to some over-all physical production function involving "Labor" and "Capital." The theory outlined above makes quite clear what the classical economists knew very well—that though production might be the result of the immutable laws of physics and chemistry, distribution was the result of human decision, and that consequently distribution could be changed within a wide range of values. The macroeconomic theory, however, also makes clear another point with which the classical economists were familiar—that distribution was not directly determined by what happened in the market for factors of production, e.g., in the labor market, but that it was determined directly by quite a different set of decisions. That is not to say, of course, that wage bargains cannot affect distribution very sharply. In regard to the over-all distribution between capital and labor, however, the wage bargain and the labor market only affect distribution indirectly, as they affect the direct determinants of investment, financial, loan, and monetary behavior. A rise in money wages will only raise real wages, and will only shift proportionate distribution toward labor, if it produces appropriate secondary effects on household absorption, business accumulation, dividend and financial policy, etc.

What we have done, therefore, is to effect a partial rehabilitation of the wage fund doctrine by defining more carefully the types of decisions regarding investment and finance which determine the total wage bill. The wage fund is perhaps more flexible than Ricardo thought (though certainly no more flexible than Mill thought). Nevertheless the general *conclusions* which follow from the wage fund doctrine, with the exception of the conclusion that the total wage bill is independent of income, are of the right order of magnitude—that distribution depends on decisions, and mainly on the decisions of capitalists about the use of their capital and their methods of finance; and that distribution, hence, is largely independent of what happens in the labor market. The history of trade unionism, and the evident impotence of trade unions in increasing the share of labor in the national income, are telling tributes to the accuracy of this insight.

IMPLICATIONS FOR GENERAL ECONOMICS OF MORE REALISTIC THEORIES OF THE FIRM

American Economic Review, 42, 2 (May 1952): 35-44.

IMPLICATIONS FOR GENERAL ECONOMICS OF MORE REALISTIC THEORIES OF THE FIRM

In the last few years a good deal of dissatisfaction has been expressed with the theory of the firm as it has come down to us from Cournot by way of Marshall, Chamberlin, and Joan Robinson. It is hardly necessary to say that the basic principle of this theory is the principle of profit maximization, and that the marginal analysis is merely an elaborate spelling out of this basic principle. There have been two main lines of criticism. The first is that the theory is unrealistic because it does not have enough variables in it, or because the variables of the theory do not in fact correspond to the significant variables of the firm. The second is more fundamental; it attacks the principle of maximization itself, on the grounds that it does not correspond to the actual principles which motivate and direct behavior.

The first criticism is one that is fairly easily remedied within the general framework of the marginal analysis by the simple process of adding new variables. Thus in the Chamberlin-Robinson versions of the theory, I myself have argued in several places, there is a serious deficiency in that the asset variables of the firm are not included except in a highly indirect way in the total cost. The Chamberlin-Robinson firm seems to have no balance sheet, no liquidity problems, no financial problems, no cash budget, and no investment program; it maximizes a curious income variable called net revenue, of which no accountant ever heard, and presumably lives happily ever after. It is not too difficult, however, to incorporate other variables into a more generalized marginal analysis, and I have made some steps in this direction in my *Reconstruction of Economics*.[1] The balance-sheet variables, in the accounting sense, are not the only ones which can be included in a generalized marginal analysis of this type. The psychological and sociological variables of the firm, insofar as they are subject to measurement, can also be included. Thus we can count "morale" as a psychological asset, and discuss morale-building expenditures as also subject to the marginal analysis, being carried on like any other to the point where marginal gain is just equal to marginal loss.

The second criticism of the marginal analysis is more fundamental. It is directed, not at the details, but at the basic assumption of profit

[1] K. E. Boulding, *A Reconstruction of Economics* (New York, 1950).

maximization itself. The criticism takes two forms: the first is that profit maximization is simply not what firms in fact do; the second is that even if firms wanted to maximize profits, there is no way of doing it. The criticisms of Hall and Hitch[2] and of R. A. Lester[3] are of the first kind; that of Stephen Enke[4] is of the second. Insofar as these criticisms have theoretical content, however, they come to much the same thing: that the maximization of profits is unrealistic because firms cannot possibly know when profits are at a maximum. Hence firms must adopt rule-of-thumb methods of behavior (like full-cost pricing) which do not necessarily maximize profits but which fit into their information systems. Profit maximization is ruled out because there is nothing in the information system of the firm which reveals the marginal inequalities which would be indicative of a failure to maximize profits. The information system reveals average costs; it reveals sales, production, inventory, debt, and other figures in the balance sheet and income statements. It does not, however, generally reveal marginal costs and still less does it reveal marginal revenues. If the firm cannot know when it is not maximizing profits, therefore, there is no reason to suppose that it maximizes them.

Much of this criticism seems to be destructive, in the sense that it seems to knock down an existing theory without setting up any other in its place. The criticism is grounded, however, in the beginnings of a general theory of organization and behavior which is emerging in many fields, notably in the work of Cannon the physiologist,[5] Barnard the theorist of organization,[6] and Wiener the founder and namer of cybernetics.[7] This general theory of organization begins with the concept of homeostasis; that is, of a mechanism for stabilizing a variable or a group of variables within certain limits of toleration. Every organism or organization is characterized by a group of such variables, and the organization consists mainly in more or less elaborate apparatus to maintain these variables between an upper and lower limit. Should any of the essential variables rise above the upper limit, machinery must be brought into play to reduce it; should it fall below the lower limit, machinery must be brought into play to raise it. An organization in this view consists of an aggregate of such governing mechanisms, sometimes called control or "feedback" mechanisms. The simplest

[2] R. L. Hall and C. J. Hitch, "Price Theory and Business Behavior," *Oxford Economic Papers*, May, 1939, pp. 12-49.
[3] R. A. Lester, "Shortcomings of the Marginal Analysis for Wage-Employment Problems," *American Economic Review*, March, 1946, pp. 63-82.
[4] Stephen Enke, "On Maximizing Profits," *American Economic Review*, September, 1951, pp. 566-578.
[5] Cannon, *The Wisdom of the Body*.
[6] Barnard, *The Functions of the Executive*.
[7] N. Wiener, *Cybernetics* (New York, 1948).

example is perhaps the thermostat, or a governor on an engine. The body contains dozens of such mechanisms, maintaining a great many physical, chemical, and even psychological variables within a limited range of toleration: temperature, blood pressure, water content, calcium content, and so on down a long list. Any organization likewise may be characterised by a long list of variables which have upper and lower limits demanding appropriate action.

A control mechanism always involves a number of parts. There must be first a receptor of information (*i*) which picks up information regarding the variable to be controlled and, in particular, picks up information regarding divergence between the actual value of the variable and the limits of toleration. In the simplest mechanism, all that is necessary is qualitative information about the sign of this divergence: the minimum information is that the variable is above the upper limit or below the lower limit of toleration. This information must be transmitted by a communications system (*ii*) to an executive, or decision-maker (*iii*). The function of the executive is to transform the information received into instructions; it (or he) can be thought of as a kind of production function, receiving information by one communications system and sending out instructions over another (*iv*). The instructions go to effectors (*v*) which carry out the instructions, and can produce an effect which is carried by another communications system (*vi*) to the controlled variable. Thus in the thermostatically controlled furnace, we have the thermostat (*i*) which registers divergence of the temperature from the tolerated limits (the upper and lower limits may in this case be contiguous). This information is transmitted by a wire (*ii*) to the furnace control (*iii*), which transforms the information into instructions sent by another wire (*iv*) to the furnace (*v*), which is capable of transmitting the effect (heat) by a system of pipes and radiators (*vi*) to the environment of the thermostat.

The theory of the control mechanism has been developed in some detail by Wiener, and we need only mention some conclusions here. One is that a control mechanism always involves a cyclical movement of the controlled variable, the amplitude of the cycle being a function of the sensitivity of the mechanism. If the mechanism has pronounced lags, the corrective effect may only be brought into play after an extensive divergence of the controlled variable from the norm, and the correction may go too far before the countercorrection comes into play. The famous contrast between the hand-fired furnace, where the house has two temperatures, too hot and too cold, and the automatic thermostat, where the cycle is practically imperceptible, illustrates the point.

The thermostat is a very simple control mechanism because the controlled variable (temperature) in the absence of control constantly tends to diminish, assuming that the tolerated temperature of the house is above that of the outside. Action, therefore, is only needed in one direction—that of supplying heat; the only action necessary when the temperature becomes too warm is to turn the furnace off. Where the movement of the controlled variable in the absence of control is random and may be in either direction, the problem of the "effector" becomes more difficult, and it is generally necessary to have two kinds of effectors: one to operate when the uncontrolled movement of the variable is downward (e.g., a furnace) and another to operate when the uncontrolled movement is upward (e.g., a refrigerator). This also requires greater complexity in the information system, which must be capable of detecting in what direction the uncontrolled movement of the variable would be going. Otherwise we will have the mechanism switching on the refrigeration unit in winter and the furnace in summer. In the case of physical variables, this task is not too difficult. In the case of social variables, however, the information system may have considerable difficulty in delivering information which will enable the executive to choose the appropriate effector. Thus suppose a firm is faced with inventories rising above what it considers to be the limit of toleration. A control mechanism of some sort will come into play. There is, however, a choice of mechanisms. The firm may reduce prices and institute a selling campaign in order to increase sales. Or it may cut back production and allow the existing rate of sales to lower the inventory. If the piling up of inventory is a result of a faulty price and sales policy relative to the general state of the market, the first technique may be effective. If the piling up of inventory is due to a general depression and decline in income, the second technique (from the point of view of the firm) may be more effective. Information about the mere quantity of inventory is not sufficient to distinguish between these two policies.

There is yet another complication of the control mechanism which is of great importance for social organizations. In organizations of any degree of complexity there is not a single variable to be controlled but a large number of variables, and the effectors which affect one may also affect others. If each variable to be controlled has an isolated effector which is capable of controlling it, the multiplicity of variables presents no problem. We do not in general find this to be the case, however. Action which is taken to influence one variable will almost always have some effect on the others. A great deal of human frustration arises from this confusion of effectors. It is a commonplace that when we solve one problem we generally create three others. If the effectors are sufficiently confused, the problem of control will become insoluble: in endeavoring to stabilize one variable we inevitably un-stabilize others; acute cycles may be set up and the organization may even disintegrate.

So far we have simply assumed the existence of certain controlled variables and of machinery to control them. Clearly, however, the theory cannot stop there. Two further questions must be raised. The first is what determines the limits of tolerance of the controlled variables and under what circumstances do these limits change. The second is under what circumstances is the organization itself changed, in one regard or another. In the simple theory of control, a divergence between the actual and the ideal value of the controlled variable sets in motion a control mechanism to bring the actual value nearer to the ideal. Suppose now that the mechanism is persistently unsuccessful and that the actual value of the variable seldom if ever falls within the ideal limits of toleration. Information of this type constitutes a different kind of challenge to the executive than simple information regarding divergence of actual from ideal values. The question facing the executive, then, is whether to adjust the ideal values in response to this situation or to reorganize the machinery itself. The answer to this question is likely to depend on the relation of the ideal values to the survival of the organization. In the case of the firm, for instance, a persistent failure to keep inventory within certain prescribed limits may result in a revision of the limits rather than a change in the organization, as action to keep inventory within specified limits is only incidental to the survival of the firm. If, however, the firm per-sistently makes losses (i.e., if there is a failure to keep profits above the lower limit of toleration), the executive will be seriously disturbed and will not revise the limits of toleration in the direction of being satisfied with taking losses, but will look around to see what steps, drastic if need be, must be taken in order to correct the situation.

A problem related to the above is that of growth and the life cycle. It is evident from the study of organizations of all kinds that they exhibit periods of growth, of relative stability, and of decay. This is perhaps the least understood field in the whole theory of organization. The existence of growth indicates that the controlled variables are certain rates of change through time. A firm, for instance, frequently regards some rate of growth as normal, and if its growth is not equal to this normal rate, serious concern will be aroused and steps will be taken. There are, however, important limits on growth. It is not merely that there may be certain rates of growth which are inherently unstable, as Harrod suggests for the economy as a whole and as the study of hormones indicates may be true for biological organisms. Growth at any rate, however, cannot take place without the organism eventually becoming "large" and diseconomies of scale may set in. The ideal rate of growth, therefore, may properly be regarded as a diminishing function of the size of the organization and will eventually diminish to zero. The problem of decay and death is even more mysterious, and the question as to whether death is inherent in the structure of organization itself or whether it is an accident is one that must remain unanswered, especially in regard to the social organization.

The kind of theory which I have outlined very briefly above is general and can be applied to the firm as well as to any other organization. Thus the first-approximation theory of the firm is a theory of "homeostasis of the balance sheet," treating the behavior of the firm as a reaction to changes in its balance-sheet structure, designed to restore the balance-sheet composition to its "ideal" value. On this theory, for instance, sales of product result in a distortion of the balance sheet, increasing cash (or accounts receivable) at the expense of inventory. In order to restore the previous values there must be production of product to replace the inventory lost by sale. This production will diminish cash and other items, which must also be replaced, and so on.

The next step is the theory of the selection of ideal balance sheets; i.e., what distribution of its assets and liabilities among the various items does the firm regard as best. It is at this level, if anywhere, that the theory of profit maximization becomes relevant. At this level, also, we cannot regard the firm as simply passive in regard to its income variables, and the problem of the selection of possible rates of turnover of balance-sheet items must also be considered. Profits are evidently a crucial variable in the case of the firm, as it represents probably the most important single variable which determines the firm's ultimate survival. We shall expect, therefore, that there will be some lower limit of profits below which a control mechanism will operate. There may also be an upper limit, above which the firm will take life easy and will not bother about profit-increasing activity. Somewhere around this range presumably profits are at a maximum. The theory of profit maximization assumes in effect that the upper and lower limits of toleration coincide at the point of maximum profits. This is an assumption which is not likely to be realized. However, it is a special case of the more general theory.

A word should be added on the subject of expectations and uncertainty, especially as this subject has received so much attention in recent years.[8] There have been a great many attempts to construct a theory of "rational" behavior in the presence of uncertainty—attempts which have not as yet produced agreement even on the problem of the

[8] Kenneth J. Arrow, "Alternative Approaches to the Theory of Choice in Risk-Taking," *Econometrica*, October, 1951, pp. 404-437.

measurement of uncertainty itself. The only conclusion which seems to emerge solidly from all the discussion is that uncertainty creates a preference for liquidity and flexibility in the asset structure. Liquidity is a measure of the degree of perfection of the market for an asset; i.e., the extent to which it can be exchanged for any other asset in indefinite quantities without loss due to worsening terms of trade. Flexibility is the extent to which an asset can be transformed into a variety of other assets in the course of the process of production. There may also be another property of the asset and income structure which increases in value with increased uncertainty; this might be called the property of security. It is measured by the "peakedness" of the profits function. If this function has a sharp peak, so that profits are high if exactly the right decisions are made but low or negative if slight deviations from the right decisions occur, the burden of uncertainty will be great. If on the other hand the profits function is a broad plateau, so that deviations from the "best" decisions do not involve disaster, uncertainty will not create acute discomfort. It is evident that there is a problem of the relief of uncertainty-discomfort in the process of decision making, through retreat towards more liquid, flexible, and secure positions as well as through the more conventional methods of insurance. I wonder, however, whether this process cannot be described in terms of the asset-preference structure for all purposes of the economist, and whether a detailed attempt to break up the problem into a "returns" aspect and an "uncertainty" measure is particularly useful.

It can hardly be denied, I think, that the type of theory which I have outlined so sketchily above is more "realistic" than the elementary marginal analysis, if only because it offers more hope of meaningful empirical studies of the firm. Economists have had enough of asking businessmen whether they equate marginal this to marginal that and· being met with utterly blank stares of incomprehension. It is quite evident that the marginal analysis, useful as it is as a tool of general static equilibrium economics, is not particularly useful as an instrument of analysis of actual business behavior. The economist, however, who asks businessmen what information comes to their desks, how they classify it, how they react to it, what kind of instructions follow from what kinds of information, what are the variables which they watch, what sort of weight do they give to various kinds of "trouble indicators," and so on, meets with an immediate response, and it seems not unreasonable to hope that armed with the kind of theory I have outlined above economists might even be of some use to businessmen, and their modest triumphs at the level of national accounting might be matched, in the next generation, in the realm of business practice. The question of this paper, however, is a different one. It is concerned with the impact of these newer theories of organization on the structure and conclusions of economics itself. Because the marginal analysis had been shown to be a rather highly special case, unlikely to be realized in practice, should we thereupon banish it from our textbooks, in spite of the admirable examination fodder which it makes, or at least relegate it to appendices which only specialists will ever read?

At the level of elementary teaching the proposal to ban the marginal analysis can perhaps be defended on the grounds that economics can get along so well without it. It is well to remember that for all practical purposes there was no theory of the firm in economics before Marshall and no theory of the individual consumer before Jevons and the Austrians. Even in Marshall the theory of the firm is practically confined to a sort of appendix on monopoly, and the theory of the firm does not become central in economics until the development of the economics of imperfect competition in the thirties. The whole of the classical economics, especially, was constructed with only the barest rudiments of a theory of the economic individual. The essential conceptual framework behind the classical economics is that of supply and demand analysis—the assumption of definite functional relationships between prices and quantities produced or consumed, and the further assumption that an improper relationship between production and consumption would have an impact on prices. The theory of maximizing behavior and the marginal analysis comes into economics at a second level of analysis—that of explaining the character of the supply and demand functions. As such it is not essential to economic analysis. It is a sort of porch to the main edifice, which may be remodeled without much affecting the central structure. No matter how much we revise the theory of the firm (or general economic organism), it would be surprising to find a conclusion that high prices generally discouraged production and encouraged consumption. We should even be surprised to find a theory that told us that under price discrimination the higher price would be charged in the more elastic market, or that a change in relative prices will cause substitution of the dearer for the cheaper factor or commodity. These conclusions which emerge from the marginal analysis will almost certainly survive a considerable failure on the part of the firm in maximizing its profits. We shall not be far wrong in concluding, therefore, that the impact of more realistic theories of the firm on static price analysis is likely to be small.

This conclusion is reinforced if we observe that many of the objections to profit maximization do not apply to the maximization of utility or preference. The substitution of a subjective for an objective maximand removes some of the difficulty in regard to the information needed for maximization. If utility is defined in terms of preference, presumably we always know at the moment whether one set of alternatives is preferred to another. Much of the marginal analysis can be rescued by substituting the maximization of utility for the maximization of profits, even in the theory of the firm. If the preference functions are reasonably stable, this theory has meaning and predictive power, for the preference functions can be investigated empirically. If the preference functions are not stable, of course, the theory amounts to little more than saying that people do what they do. Unfortunately there are many indications that the preference functions are not particularly stable, especially in regard to asset preferences. If this is the case, the only hope of rescuing the theory from sterility is the discovery of a genuine dynamics of preference; that is, stable difference equations relating present preferences to past variables. We are still a long way from this goal.

When we turn to economic dynamics in general, the impact of the theory of organization is likely to be larger, if only because the great weakness of the theory of maximizing behavior is that it has practically no dynamics in it. The general theory of organization as applied to the firm is likely, first, to draw attention to certain sensitive variables which the economist has previously neglected, such as the various asset ratios. Thus a shift in cash balances between firms and households may create considerable reactions in firm behavior, not because profit positions are affected so much as because asset ratios are disturbed. This is one of the points at which the theory of the bank, which has generally been discussed in terms of balance-sheet ratios such as the reserve ratio, could well be integrated with the general theory of the firm. In the second place, the possibility that the controlled variables exhibit a range of toleration introduces a "threshold" and time-lag phenomenon into the over-all movements of the economy. Profits, asset ratios, and other controlled variables will rise or fall for some distance without producing action until they pass the range of toleration. This fact is of great importance in the development of an economic dynamics, for it explains why the adjustments of the system are not instantaneous, and it determines the rate of adjustment. Generally speaking, the wider the range of tolerance, the slower will be the transmission of changes through the system. Even if the ranges of tolerance of the various controlled variables were stable, we would expect to find a certain asymmetry between "upward" and "downward" movements of the economy. Firms and households are more likely to be at one of the limits of toleration in one case and at the other in the other.

There is some possibility also that the general theory of organization may throw light on the theory of interactions among the few—one of the least satisfactory parts of almost any science, as the unsatisfactory state of the theory of oligopoly testifies in economics, and as the practical nonexistence of a theory of international relations testifies in political science. These interactions must clearly be confined to those variables which are in the information systems of the organisms concerned. Variables which are in the control of one organization may well be controlling variables for another organization. Consequently any change in the policy of one organization, insofar as it gets into the information structure of a second organization, may produce immediate reactions in the policy of the second, which in turn may react on the first, and so on in a kind of circular chain reaction. The nature of the information system may easily determine whether or not such a system is capable of equilibrium. There may be cases where ignorance is bliss! The phenomena of the price or advertising war and its counterpart in the arms race are good examples which need further study in the light of organizational theory.

One may conclude, then, that there is great need to integrate the general theory of organization into the body of economic analysis, and that such integration will immensely improve economics as a technique for analyzing the actual behavior of firms. Economists may even become useful to business! This extension of theory will not, however, overthrow the existing structure of analysis, which emerges clearly as an important special case. It is not likely to make any spectacular changes in a static theory; it may reasonably be expected to throw new light on economic dynamics.

WELFARE ECONOMICS

In: *A Survey of Contemporary Economics,* Vol. 2,
B. Haley, ed., Homewood, Ill.: R. D. Irwin, 1952, pp. 1-34.

WELFARE

ECONOMICS

It is almost as difficult to define the boundaries of welfare economics as it is to define economics itself. The subject must exist, for people write books and articles about it, but it is not easy to draw the line between what is and what is not included in it. At one extreme almost any discussion of economic policy which raises matters of principle or invokes standards of judgment might be included, and at the other the subject might be narrowed down to certain highly technical discussions of the conditions for a social optimum. Nor is it easy to delimit the topic historically. Some might argue that the work of A. C. Pigou, as represented by *Wealth and Welfare*[1] and in the various editions of his subsequent *Economics of Welfare*,[2] represents the emergence of the subject as a separate department of economic thought. Nevertheless, as Hla Myint[3] has pointed out so well, the English Classical economists had a great deal to say on subjects which could reasonably be brought within the compass of welfare economics, and Pigou's work itself is in large part a refinement and elaboration of some ideas of Marshall. It is also true that the development of welfare economics in the English language in the past fifteen or twenty years by Lerner, Hicks, Kaldor, Hotelling, Reder, Samuelson, and others[4] as something

---

[1] London, 1912.

[2] London, 1920; 4th ed., 1932.

[3] *Theories of Welfare Economics* (Cambridge, Mass., 1948).

[4] See especially: A. P. Lerner, "The Concept of Monopoly and the Measurement of Monopoly Power," *Rev. Econ. Stud.*, June 1934, I, 157–75; Abram Bergson (Burk), "A Reformulation of Certain Aspects of Welfare Economics," *Quart. Jour. Econ.*, Feb. 1938, LII, 310–34; Harold Hotelling, "The General Welfare in Relation to Problems of Taxation and of Railway and Utility Rates," *Econometrica*, July 1938, VI, 242–69; Nicholas Kaldor, "Welfare Propositions of Economics and Interpersonal Comparisons of Utility," *Econ. Jour.*, Sept. 1939, XLIX, 549–52; J. R. Hicks, "Foundations of Welfare Economics," *ibid.*, Dec. 1939, XLIX, 696–712; Tibor Scitovsky, "A Note on Welfare Propositions in

like a movement or a school of economic thought has not stemmed from Pigou, the perfection of whose thought makes it somewhat of a blind alley. It originated rather with Pareto, Barone, and Edgeworth, where it has not arisen spontaneously in response to the fine English tradition that it is much easier to think up something than to look it up. It is with this "new" welfare economics that the present article is mainly concerned. As it is getting a little too old to be called new, one may perhaps propose to call it the "Paretian" welfare economics after its forerunner (Vilfredo Pareto)[5] rather than its founders. The name of Pareto is particularly appropriate in this connection because he introduced the indifference curve (or preference function) analysis as a major instrument of economic analysis, and it is only a slight exaggeration to claim that modern welfare economics has developed largely as a result of the invention of this powerful analytical tool. It is a department of thought which owes its unity not so much to the natural boundaries of the subject matter which it is discussing as to the limitations of its tool chest, much as a carpenter is not so much interested in "furniture" as in things which can be manipulated with a saw and hammer. It is for this reason, perhaps, that the welfare economist is sometimes hard put to explain what his subject is *about*. There is a field of subject matter, presumably related to human welfare, and there is a field of technical and manipulative skill. Much of the apparently "precious" and over-refined character of welfare economics arises because the fields of subject matter and of skills do not altogether coincide. The more elegant any apparatus, the more specialized it is apt to be. Consequently it is not surprising to find welfare economists devoting their energies to tasks which may seem insignificant but which they can perform with their apparatus, rather than to the major problems of the subject matter which seem to defy analysis.

As it has developed, the Paretian welfare economics seems to have had three main objectives. One has been to clarify and quantify the vague concept of "riches" or, in the language of Adam Smith, "Opu-

Economics," *Rev. Econ. Stud.,* Nov. 1941, IX, 77–88; Oscar Lange, "The Foundations of Welfare Economics," *Econometrica.* July–Oct. 1942, X, 215–28; G. J. Stigler, "The New Welfare Economics," *Am. Econ. Rev.,* June 1943, XXXIII, 355–59; P. A. Samuelson, *Foundations of Economic Analysis* (Cambridge, Mass., 1947), Ch. 8. Probably the best three works of a systematic nature on the subject are: Hla Myint, *op. cit.;* Melvin Reder, *Studies in the Theory of Welfare Economics* (New York, 1947); and I. M. D. Little, *A Critique of Welfare Economics* (Oxford, 1950).

[5] *Cours d'économie politique* (Lausanne, 1897), Vol. I, pp. 20 ff.; Vol. II, pp. 90 ff.; *Manuel d'économie politique* (Paris, 1909; 2nd ed., 1927), pp. 354–64, 616 ff., 648 ff.

lence." A closely related objective has been to clarify what it is that economists have to say on matters of public policy. Economics has largely developed as a by-product of propaganda for policies of various kinds, and the economist has yet to be born who does not feel the urge to make his abstractions give birth to Proposals. Welfare economics then tries to set up standards of judgment by which events and policies can be judged as "economically" desirable, even though on other grounds (political, national, ethical) they might be judged to be undesirable. The search for such a standard of judgment leads to a further search for a definition of an economic "optimum," this being the position of all the economic variables at which riches are at a maximum, the test of economic desirability thus being an increase in riches. Of two events or policies then, the one which increases riches more would be judged economically the more desirable. Closely linked with these objectives is a third—to develop propositions which are "scientifically" free of ethical judgments, but which can nevertheless serve as a basis for conclusions with respect to policy alternatives by delimiting the area within which the final ethical judgment has to be made.

I. THE CONCEPT OF ECONOMIC WELFARE

The subject matter of welfare economics can be approached conveniently, therefore, by considering how the concept of "riches"—that is, economic welfare as distinct from other forms of welfare—arises out of the other interests of economists. Economics itself is an abstraction from the general melee of social phenomena based primarily on those magnitudes which are descriptive of the production, consumption, and exchange of commodities. Economics, then, is not primarily interested in men, but in commodities—in those things, material or immaterial, which are produced, distributed, exchanged, and consumed, rather than in the producers, distributers, exchangers, and consumers as people. Pure economic analysis discusses an abstract universe the constituents of which are (*i*) quantities of commodities (exchangeable assets) produced, consumed, and exchanged, and (*ii*) the derivative ratios of transformation of commodities or other exchangeables one into another through exchange or through production. Prices are rates of transformation through exchange; real costs or productivity ratios are rates of transformation through production. Thus economic analysis is a kind of astronomy of the economic universe, discussing the mutual determination of the position and magnitude of the various economic quantities much as the astronomer discusses the mutual determination of the position and magnitude of astronomical quantities. Indeed, the methods of the two sciences are strikingly similar; they both proceed by observation rather than by experiment, and both lean heavily on the concept of general equilibrium through the solution of simultaneous equations. The success of astronomy and the lack of success of economics in prediction arise mainly because of the greater stability and simplicity of the astronomer's universe—it is easier for him to discover stable difference (or differential) equations relating past to future values of the various variables.

Economists, however, in the language of David Ricardo[6] have always been interested not only in "value"—the positions of the economic magnitudes—but in "riches" or economic welfare. That is to say, they ask the question not only, "What determines the quantities of commodities produced, consumed, distributed and exchanged?" but also, "Am I—or are you—richer or poorer, better or worse off as a result of any given set of changes in the quantities of the economic universe?" This, oddly enough, is also the question which the astrologer asks of the stars. I am not suggesting of course that economists are to welfare economists what astronomers are to astrologers, at least in regard to the scientific respectability of performance! Nevertheless in regard to the *question asked* the relation of welfare economics to pure economics is almost exactly that of astrology to astronomy. The astrologer postulates a "welfare function" which relates the position of the heavenly bodies to human welfare, just as the welfare economist postulates a welfare function which relates the position of the economic "bodies" to human welfare. Whether we will regard either of these operations as nonsense depends on our confidence in the stability of the functions so postulated. For the astrologer some positions of the heavenly bodies are "better" than others; for the welfare economist some positions of the economic universe are "better" than others. If we are convinced that welfare economics is superior to astrology it is because we have better statistical and personal evidence that some "difference" is made to our states of being by shifts in the economic universe, whereas no apparent difference is made to these same states by shifts in the astronomical universe. Because astrology has in fact been bad science, deriving its hocus-pocus from traditional accretions rather than from careful observation, we do not have to conclude that its *problem* is ridiculous—

---

[6] *On the Principles of Political Economy and Taxation* (London, 1817), Ch. 20.

indeed, between sunspots and cosmic rays it is by no means clear that there could be no science of astrology, or that there could be no influences on human life of the astronomical universe.

However dubious may be the existence of an astrological welfare function we all have a strong feeling that there is something real about an economic welfare function. The proposition that Dives is richer than Lazarus but poorer than Croesus may not be true, and may be disputed, but we have a certain feeling that it is at least not entire nonsense. One of the persistent interests of welfare economics, then, is the quantification of this rather vague concept of "riches." What magnitude is it that is a larger number, or a higher order, in the case of Dives than in the case of Lazarus? This is the "welfare parameter"—some quantity, vector, or indicator which in some sense goes "up" as we move from poorer to richer positions of an economic universe, and which is at a maximum when the system is richest. The search for such a parameter is a legitimate quest, even though there is some danger in it. The danger is that the basic concept with which we are dealing is itself rather vague and ill defined, and that therefore attempts at exact quantification may result in a different concept from the one which really concerns us, and we may lose interest in the basic concept in our manipulations of the quantifiable substitute. Index numbers are a good example of such forced quantifications, and their use and misuse is a constant testimony to the value and the danger of such procedures.

Riches, then, are conceived first in terms of "dollars worth." A man with $10,000 is "richer" than a man with $5,000. We may note in passing an important ambiguity in the concept of riches. A sum of dollars may refer either to a capital stock or to an income flow. Generally speaking, it has been assumed in economics that the income flow was the more significant magnitude, and that when we said that A was richer than B we meant that in some sense he had a larger income. I have argued elsewhere that this has been a mistake, and that the capital stock is a better measure of welfare.[7] However, as this is a private feud between myself and the profession it does not deserve more than a brief reference here, especially as the principal problems of the measurement of riches apply equally whether we are considering a stock or a flow. We notice first of course that simple "dollars worth" figures are not satisfactory. We cannot say that $10,000 represents "more" than $5,000 in any more than a formal arithmetical sense. If for instance,

---

[7] K. E. Boulding, "Income or Welfare," *Rev. Econ. Stud.*, 1949–50, XVII, 77–86.

the index of the price level has risen four times we would be pretty confident that $10,000 represented in some sense "less" at the new price level than $5,000 did at the old. The question arises, however, less of what? We are here thinking not of a homogeneous sum of dollars but of a heterogeneous inventory of goods—so much cheese, so many eggs, so many Cadillacs, and so on, and the question arises, in what sense can we say that one such inventory is "less" than another. Whether the inventory is an inventory of stock or whether it is an inventory of flows does not affect the point in question; in both cases we have the problem of rating on a scale two lists of quantities of heterogeneous items.

The simplest way of reducing a heterogeneous aggregate to a single quantity or rating is by the process of valuation. This is no doubt why so many of the definitions of economic welfare center around measurability in terms of money.[8] The measuring rod of money, however, is more than we need to arrive at a meaningful aggregate of heterogeneous items. As long as there exists a system of valuation coefficients expressing the equivalence of a unit of any one item in terms of every other, the heterogeneous aggregate can be reduced to a single magnitude in terms of the unit of any one of the items. This is not the only way of doing it, but it is certainly the simplest. Thus suppose we have to aggregate 3 elephants, 15 feather beds, and 1,000 mousetraps. If we know, for instance, that 1 elephant is equivalent to 60 feather beds and to 8,000 mousetraps, we can express this aggregate as the equivalent of either $3 + \frac{1}{4} + \frac{1}{8}$ ($= 3\frac{3}{8}$) elephants, or as $180 + 15 + 7\frac{1}{2}$ ($= 202\frac{1}{2}$) feather beds, or as $24,000 + 2,000 + 1,000$ ($= 27,000$) mousetraps. Any of these figures is as good as any other, and as long as the valuation coefficients remain unchanged any change in the individual items of the aggregate will be reflected in equal proportional changes in any of the measures. If one elephant is always equivalent to 60 feather beds, then we can measure aggregates indifferently in one or the other unit, just as the constant equivalence of 12 inches to one foot means that we can measure length indifferently in either feet or inches.

Our notions of a system of valuation coefficients or equivalents are mainly derived from the existence of transformation coefficients, either in exchange or in production. If in the market one elephant can be exchanged for 60 feather beds this creates a sense of equivalence of these two quantities. The market equivalence is further based on equiva-

---

[8] Pigou, in *The Economics of Welfare*, defines economic welfare as: "That part of social welfare which can be brought directly or indirectly into relation with the measuring rod of money."

lence in production (i.e. alternative) cost: if giving up one elephant enables us to produce 60 feather beds, again a sense of equivalence of these two quantities is created. It must be emphasized, however, that valuation equivalents as psychological magnitudes may differ from price or cost equivalents—indeed exchange would not take place if this were not so. Furthermore, these psychological valuation coefficients may themselves be functions of the component quantities of the aggregate measured—the valuation function does not have to be linear, especially where there are *gestalt* configurations and complementary or competitive relationships among the various items.

The concept of a value-aggregate presents few difficulties as long as the set of valuation coefficients is stable. It is by no means unreasonable to say that within a given system of relative values a man with $10,000 is twice as rich as a man with $5,000. Interpersonal comparisons of utility, which will descend to plague us shortly, present no difficulties here, for we are not measuring utility or happiness or significance or any psychological magnitude, but simply a valued physical aggregate of valuable items—valuable not in their sense of significance for human life but simply in the sense that a unit of each can be assigned an equivalent number of units of any other. No troublesome psychological quantities plague us, for we are moving not in the world of men at all but in the economists' paradise, an abstract universe of commodities. The difficulties in measurement arise, however, as soon as the structure of relative values—that is, of the valuation coefficients —changes in the course of time or space. Then the unambiguous character of the valuation measure of riches disappears, for the measure according to one set of relative values does not even have to be the same sign as the measure according to another set. Suppose we compare, for instance, an aggregate of 3 elephants and 15 feather beds with an aggregate of 10 elephants and 5 feather beds. If 1 elephant equals 60 feather beds the first aggregate is $3\frac{1}{4}$ elephants and the second is $10\frac{1}{12}$ elephants: the second is the larger. Suppose, however that 1 elephant equals 1 feather bed. Then the first is 18 and the second is 15 elephants: the first is the larger.

For the aggregate of two commodities or items the problem can be clarified by a diagram such as Figure 1 (p. 8). Physical quantities of two items A and B are measured along the axes. The coordinates of P_0 and of P_1 represent two different collections or constellations of these items. The problem is whether P_0 represents a larger or a smaller total amount of "riches" than P_1. In comparing P_0 with P_2, which represents more of

both A and B than P_0, the answer seems fairly obvious, at least qualita-
tively, though the possibility of one or the other item being a "discommodity" makes even this conclusion doubtful: we might be "richer"
with *less* of one or more items than with more. P_1, however, represents
more of A but less of B than P_0, and the question as to which combination is the larger cannot be answered unless we have some means of
expressing the value of B in terms of A or of A in terms of B. The
simplest such means is the constant valuation coefficient, represented

FIGURE 1

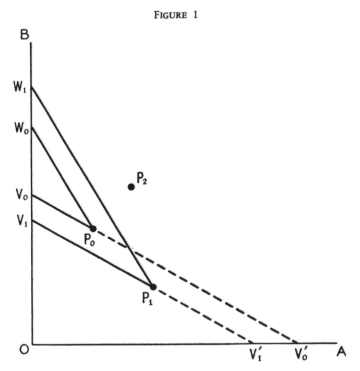

by the slope of a line in such a figure. Thus if the valuation coefficient
(the amount of B that is equivalent to one unit of A) is represented
by the slopes of the lines P_1V_1 and P_0V_0, OV_1 is the total value of the
P_1 combination, and OV_0 is the total value of the P_0 combination, both
measured in units of B. OV'_1 and OV'_0 are the corresponding values
expressed in terms of A. With this valuation coefficient, P_0 is clearly
"larger" than P_1. If, however, the coefficient B/A is higher, represented
say by the slopes of P_0W_0 and P_1W_1, the total value of the P_0 combination (OW_0) is now smaller than the value of the P_1 combination
(OW_1).

It is clear that if the fluctuations in relative values were as great as this we would lose all sense of their being a meaningful aggregate of the quantities involved. In fact we only have a sense that these aggregates—e.g. of national real capital or of national real income—are meaningful because the fluctuations in relative values are not so great as to make the limiting values meaningless. If according to one set of relative values (say "this year's" prices) the national income this year is 40% greater than last year's, while according to some other equally plausible and relevant set of values (say "last year's" prices) the difference is 50%, we would still feel that the comparison had some meaning—indeed, it would be good if the comparisons were stated in this way, saying "national income increased from 40 to 50 per cent" instead of trying to specify a more exact figure. If, however, one set of values gave an increase of 50% and another a decrease of 25%, the figures would have much less meaning. We cannot say, of course, exactly where are the boundaries of "significance" as they are not clear. It may even mean something to say: "National income increased from —25 to 50 per cent this year"!

Some readers may object that the problem I have discussed is simply one in index-number theory, which in a sense is true. I have discussed it in some detail, however, because it is the breakdown of the attempt at physical quantification of the idea of an aggregate of wealth or income which has led to the subtleties of welfare economics; did we have an unambiguous measure of physical wealth we could simply apply it in all instances where it was necessary to judge whether one situation was "economically" superior to another. The impossibility of such an unambiguous measure when relative values change is one of the drives underlying the development of utility theory: for if the objective measure fails, is there not hope in a subjective measure—that is, "utility"? Utility theory has not merely been an attempt to clarify the part played by the preference structure in the determination of relative values—there has also, from Bentham down, been the dream of a "felicific calculus" which would measure economic desirability in terms of a sum of satisfactions. It is not merely the breakdown of physical valuation which leads to a demand for utility theory. There is also a feeling that the economically superior must be judged not by any physical measure but by some measure of *significance*. Should we not say, for instance, that of two men with an identical physical inventory of assets or incomes, one is "really" richer than the other because he enjoys his riches more? And are not the valuation coefficients themselves, necessary to the calculation of any physical measure of riches, really derived from subjective valuations, and if so, in what way? The consumer's surplus analysis is an attempt to express "utility" in terms of money: its "rehabilitation" and refinement at the hands of Hicks and others[9] in the form of the various compensating payments is again an attempt to give a money value to a "utility" quantity.

It is not the business of this essay to go into the history of utility theory.[10] If, however, we are to have a psychological or subjective theory, utility or preference theory in some form is essential. As a measure of economic welfare, however, the utility concept runs into two grave difficulties. In the first place, no direct measure of utility has ever been devised, so that it can only be measured by its presumed effects on economic behavior—that is, on choices or potential choices. As choice merely implies greater or less, the thing chosen having greater utility than the thing not chosen, or two things having equal utility to which we are indifferent, a utility magnitude reflected in choices cannot be a cardinal, but can only be an ordinal magnitude.[11] That is to say, we cannot say that A has 5.867 times as much utility as B: we may say that it has more, or less, or equal utility. The fact that the measure of utility is choice leads also to a second difficulty; as nobody ever has the choice of being somebody else, the utilities of different individuals cannot be compared. This is the famous problem of "interpersonal comparisons."

---

[9] See especially, J. R. Hicks, "The Rehabilitation of Consumers' Surplus," *Rev. Econ. Stud.*, Feb. 1941, VIII, 108–16; *idem*, "The Four Consumer's Surpluses," *ibid.*, Winter 1943, XI, 31–41; *idem*, "The Generalised Theory of Consumer's Surplus," *ibid.*, 1945–46, XIII, 68–74. See also, A. M. Henderson, "Consumer's Surplus and the Compensating Variation." *ibid.*, Feb. 1941, VIII, 117–21.

[10] It may be observed that utility theory is not strictly necessary for the development of pure economics. Price theory can rest quite firmly on the assumption of demand-for-goods and supply-of-factors functions without going into the derivation of these functions from preference or utility functions. It is agreeable, of course, to find our hunches about the topography of demand and supply functions confirmed by our hunches about the topography of preference functions, but neither set of topographical hunches (e.g. the downward sloping demand curve on the one hand and the diminishing marginal rate of substitution on the other) actually demonstrates the assumed properties of the other. For an excellent history of utility theory the reader is referred to George Stigler, "The Development of Utility Theory," *Jour. Pol. Econ.*, Aug. and Oct. 1950, LVIII, 307–27, 373–96.

[11] Actually, utility is what Coombs calls an "ordered metric" magnitude: we can not only order the alternative choices in a rank of preference, but we can order the intervals between successive alternatives. Thus it makes some kind of sense to say not only, "I prefer A to B and prefer B to C" but, "My preference for A over B is greater than my preference for B over C." It seems to be curiously difficult to get a simple symbolic statement of this property. See C. L. Coombs, "Psychological Scaling without a Unit of Measurement," *Psych. Rev.*, May 1950, LVII, 145–58.

In spite of these two handicaps, however, utility theory, in its more elegant form of preference theory, has been exceedingly fruitful in the past generation. This fruitfulness is due mainly to the use of Pareto's ordinal preference function—especially in the graphic form of a system of indifference curves—as an instrument of analysis. The ordinal preference function is simply a "rubber" utility function capable of any amount of distortion in the direction of the utility axis under the limitation that the *order* of the utilities is not changed. Indifference curves (or surfaces) are contours of equal utility—i.e., they represent a set of combinations of the economic variables to which the subject is indifferent. Technically, the value of the ordinal preference function is generally supposed to be its liberation of utility theory from the assumption of cardinal utility. In fact, however, the rejection of cardinal utility has been a much less restrictive assumption than might at first appear: very few of the important properties of a cardinal utility function are not also present in its ordinal equivalent. One suspects that the fruitfulness of the indifference curve approach has been geometrical rather than analytical: it has permitted the geometric study of three-variable problems, including utility and two economic variables, and so has encouraged deeper study of the topography of the generalized functions.

II. THE SOCIAL OPTIMUM

In the case of the analysis of a single individual the restriction to an ordinal utility function is a very minor limitation, mainly because the main interest of the theory is in the position of maximum utility, and the maxima and minima of functions survive the kind of transformations which the ordinal property permits. This is even true in the case of multiple maxima: any point that is "above" another remains so through any amount of the kind of "stretching" that is permitted. The restriction imposed by the rejection of cardinal utility is somewhat more important in the case of the attempt to define a social optimum. If utility is cardinally measurable for the individual and if (what is not the same thing) the utilities of different individuals can be added, a total social utility function could be derived simply by adding the utilities of all individuals at each configuration of the economic universe. The maximum social utility in this function would then be the social optimum.

Even with the limitation of ordinal, nonaddable utilities, how-

ever, a more restricted concept of a social optimum is still possible, and
it is this concept which is at the center of the Paretian welfare economics of the past fifteen years. On this view, which goes back historically to Pareto,[12] but which was introduced into English-language
economics mainly by Lerner and Hicks,[13] a social optimum is defined
as a situation in which nobody can move to a position which he prefers
without moving somebody else to a position which is less preferred.
Stated negatively, the system is said to be *not* at a social optimum if it
is possible to effect a "reorganization" or rearrangement of commodities
through exchange or production which will make at least one person
better off, in the sense of moving him to a position which he prefers,
without making others worse off in the sense of moving them to positions which they do not prefer to the original. A situation in which A
is made better off at B's expense is regarded on this criterion as non-
assessable, as it would involve interpersonal comparisons.

Several points in regard to this concept of a social optimum need
to be noticed. One is that it does not define a "point" but a "range" of
values of the economic universe. If we suppose the economic welfare
function to be an n-dimensional mountain in which "height" represents
economic welfare, the social optimum in an absolute sense is the top of
the mountain. In order to find a single peak, however, it would be necessary to assume that the economic welfare of different individuals is
comparable. If this possibility is denied there is no way of finding a
single peak: the best that can be done is to build a fence across the peak
and say that it lies somewhere on the fence in the fog of uncertainty
that covers the mountain. That is to say, the Paretian social optimum
defines certain necessary conditions for the absolute social optimum,
but by an act of self-abnegation it prohibits itself from finding the sufficient conditions. The main trouble with this procedure—if we admit
the possibility of an absolute social optimum at all—is that points
which are not on our "fence"—which do not fulfil the conditions for
the Paretian optimum—may in fact be superior to points which are on
the fence. Thus suppose we have two possible societies, roughly comparable in per capita income and technology, in one of which income is
very highly concentrated in the hands of a small ruling class and in the
other of which it is widely distributed among an independent peasantry.
We might well rate the peasant society better off than the other, even
though it exhibited marked maldistribution of resources, imperfect

[12] *Op. cit.*, note 5.
[13] See articles cited in footnote 4.

markets, and other characteristics which placed it far from its own Paretian optimum, while at the same time the aristocratic society exhibited a perfect Paretian optimum within its own distribution of income. The Paretian welfare economist therefore seems to have worked himself into a position where either he has to deny that interpersonal comparisons of economic welfare have any meaning—in which case the "fence" can be supposed to run along a horizontal "ridge" and all points on it are equally good, or he has to admit that except for one unknowable point the society *might* be better off when his conditions are not satisfied than when they are. This dilemma seems to be forcing some welfare economists (notably I. M. D. Little) to work their way back to the rejected interpersonal comparisons—without ever quite getting around to saying how it is to be done.

Another important point to notice in connection with the Paretian optimum is that it raises the question of the *payment* of compensating payments. If interpersonal comparisons are rejected, then we cannot say that one position of the economic universe is better than another unless at least one person is better off and nobody is *actually* worse off. There has been some controversy on this subject: an attempt was made by Hicks and by Kaldor to state the theory in a form in which one position is regarded as superior to another if, after compensating payments are made, nobody is worse off and somebody is better off, even if the compensating payments are not in fact made. This view represented an attempt to define a "real income" concept which should be in some sense independent of its distribution. This attempt has now generally been abandoned, and in the hands of its later exponents such as Reder, Arrow, and Samuelson there has been a general return to the earlier position of Pareto and Barone.

It should be observed that the idea of a compensating payment is a generalization of Marshall's notion of consumer's surplus as a monetary measure of utility or disutility. If a certain economic reorganization necessitates Jones receiving a punch in the nose, or even more subtle disutilities, we supposedly ask Jones: "Will you let us punch you in the nose for $5?" If he says "No," we have to raise the offer: if he says "Yes," we can lower it. By a process of experiment we can presumably find that exact sum below which Jones is not willing to be punched and above which he is so willing. This is the compensating payment. Similarly, for some benefit we can find the greatest sum which Jones can be induced to pay. If the sum of these compensating payments, both positive and negative is positive, i.e., if the people who bene-

fit from the given change are willing to pay enough for the change to
bribe the people who are injured by it into permitting it voluntarily,
and still have something left over, then the change is judged to increase
economic welfare. We can only be sure that it increases economic welfare, however, if the bribes are actually paid.

From the Paretian definition of the social optimum a number of
marginal conditions can be derived which must be fulfilled at any position of the economic universe which conforms to the social optimum.

FIGURE 2

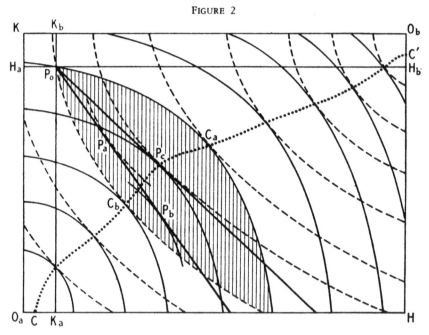

The derivation of these conditions in modern form is due mainly to
A. P. Lerner and J. R. Hicks,[14] and the most complete exposition is
to be found in Reder.[15] The principles can perhaps best be assessed in
the simplest (and probably the best founded) case of the redistribution of existing assets among owners through exchange. This is the
familiar case of Edgeworth's "contract curve." In Figure 2 the rectangle
O_aHO_bK is drawn so that O_aH is the total quantity of asset H and O_aK
is the total quantity of asset K in the possession of the two marketers,
A and B. Any point within the rectangle then represents a given distribution of these two assets between the two marketers. Thus at the

[14] See footnote 4.
[15] *Op. cit.*, Ch. 2

point P_o A has H_aP_o of H and K_aP_o of K: B has P_oH_b of H and P_oK_b of K. Indifference curve systems can be postulated in this field for both marketers. The curved broken lines are A's indifference curves: they can be visualized as the contours of a preference surface such that A prefers any point which is "higher" on it to any point that is "lower." Points on a single indifference curve or contour are equally desirable to him. The curves are so drawn that A prefers positions which give him more of both commodities to positions which give him less: the preference surface rises as we move "out" from A's origin O_a. Similarly the curved solid lines are B's indifference curves: in Figure 2 his preference surface rises as we move away from O_b.

FIGURE 3

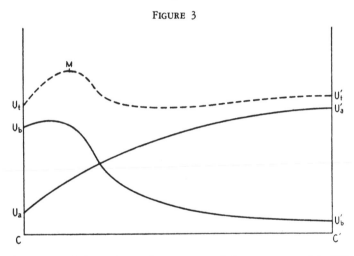

The locus of the points of tangency of the two sets of indifference curves (CC' in Figure 2) is the contract curve. From any point not on this curve, say P_o, we can move to the contract curve at C_a along a B-indifference curve P_oC_a, cutting successively higher A-indifference curves: that is, A is getting better off while B is getting no worse off. Similarly we can move along the A-indifference curve from P_o to C_b, with gain to B and no loss to A. A movement therefore from P_o to any point on the contract curve between C_a and C_b represents a gain to both parties. It is impossible to move from any point on the contract curve, however, without moving to a position in which at least one of the exchangers is worse off than before. Any point on the contract curve, then, represents a "social optimum" in the Paretian sense. The "marginal condition" in this case is the condition of tangency of the indifference curves, that is, that the marginal rates of substitution of the two exchangers should be equal. The marginal rate of substitution is the *slope* of an indifference curve: it is that amount of one commodity which can be substituted for one unit of another without feeling of loss or gain. When the indifference curves of the two exchangers are tangent, their slopes at that point are equal. The marginal condition in this case serves to *define* the contract curve. It is satisfied at any point on the contract curve and is not satisfied at any point away from it.

There still remains the significance of movement *along* the contract curve. As we move from C towards C', A is getting better off and B worse off. It is clear that we cannot say whether any point on the contract curve is "better" than any other, and so cannot define a maximum position on the contract curve, unless we introduce another function. This is the "Bergson Welfare Function,"[16] and it is illustrated in Figure 3 (p. 15). Here we suppose the contract curve to be stretched out along the line CC' and "social welfare" is measured in the vertical direction. A social welfare curve such as the dotted curve $U_t U'_t$ then shows the amount of social welfare at each point on the contract curve. The maximum position on this curve, M, is the "best" position then in the whole field. Now, however, we run immediately into a dilemma. If the social welfare function is constructed by somehow adding the welfare (utility) functions of each of the individuals, there is no particular problem apart from the assumption that the welfare of different individuals can be compared. If the indifference curves of Figure 2 are assumed to be contours of a cardinally measurable utility surface, then the social welfare function is obtained by simple addition of the two utility functions. Thus in Figure 3 if $U_a U'_a$ is the section of A's utility surface and $U_b U'_b$ is the section of B's utility surface, the social welfare function $U_t U'_t$ is obtained by adding the two curves vertically. This is clearly a highly special case of the social welfare function. In this special case we are sure that the maximum social welfare occurs somewhere on the contract curve. We can furthermore generalize the condition that limits this maximum to some point on the contract curve. It is not necessary to assume cardinal and additive utilities: as long as the social welfare is a monotonic function of individual (ordinal) utilities, the condition holds. In the most general case, however, if we visualize a generalized social welfare function as a "mountain" rising over the field of Figure 2, there is no reason to suppose that the summit of the mountain must lie somewhere over a point on the line CC'. Suppose, for instance, that

---

[16] Bergson, *op. cit.*

there is a strong social taboo against *A* having *H* and against *B* having *K*. Then the maximum social welfare, viewed in the light of the taboos and prejudices of the society, might well be at the point *K*, in spite of the fact that the individuals would prefer, as individuals, something different. The assumption that the optimum point must lie on the contract curve, therefore, itself involves an important value judgment: that people ought to get what they want.

It is evident that movement along the contract curve constitutes a redistribution of welfare in some sense, as one person is getting better off at the expense of the other. This has led to attempts to define the Paretian optimum as an "optimum of allocation" which can be defined without regard to distribution, and the fixing of a point on the contract curve as a problem in the "optimum of distribution."[17] Unfortunately the problem is not so simple, once the possibility of a generalized (Bergson) social welfare function is admitted.

These points may be clarified if the above analysis, which may seem at first sight to be very remote from real economic problems, is applied to a very practical economic question—the principles of collective bargaining. In bargaining about, say, the terms of a union contract there are a great many variables involved in the total settlement, each represented, we assume, by a clause in the contract. Let us suppose that each can be subjected to some kind of quantitative measure, and let us take a simple case in which there are only two such variables, say wages and length of vacation. Suppose the wage is measured along O_aH in Figure 2, and length of vacation along O_aK. Then, in general, the union will be better pleased as we move towards O_b, and the employer will be better pleased as we move towards O_a. Indifference curve systems can be postulated for each bargainer, and from their points of tangency a contract curve can be drawn. Then from any point not on the contract curve, agreement can be reached by *trading,* moving towards the contract curve: thus from P_o both union and employer might agree to give up some vacation in return for an addition to wages. Once the contract curve is reached, however, agreement by trading becomes impossible, and any move along the contract curve represents *conflict*—that is, a bettering of the position of one party at the expense of the other. This distinction between trading and conflict is essential in the bargaining process, and it is the main part of the skill of the

[17] Hicks, in his article, "Foundations of Welfare Economics," *loc. cit.,* pp. 696–712, suggests this point of view. A recent exponent is Maurice Allais, *Économie et intérêt* (Paris, 1947).

bargainer to know how to "trade"—that is, to start from a position where trading is possible and to trade in such a way, by a process akin to price discrimination, sliding down the opponent's indifference curves in a succession of small offers until he hits the contract curve at a point most favorable to himself. The theory can easily be generalized to the many-variable case: no matter how many variables there are in the bargain the contract curve with two bargainers remains a line in the n-space corresponding to the n variables, and conflict between two parties remains "one-dimensional" in the sense that it can be represented as movement along a line each point of which stands for a given collection of the bargained variables.

The introduction of more variables increases the possibility and the complexity of the "trading" process. This may well be why trade union contracts seem to get more and more complex, for the more clauses there are in the contract the more chance there is of trading clause against clause and the less likelihood there is of reaching an impasse on the contract curve. Reaching the contract curve does not necessarily involve a breakdown of bargaining: suppose for instance that the employer is willing to sign a contract on any terms more favorable than those represented by C_a, and the union will sign on any terms more favorable than those at C_b. Then a bargain can be struck anywhere within the range C_bC_a. If the union's sticking point were C_a and the employer's C_b, however, a bargain could not be struck, and negotiations would break down until some change had occurred in the underlying preferences. If one or both of the parties are unskilled traders, of course, there is no reason to suppose that the contract curve will be reached. In the above case where the range C_bC_a represents the possible range of bargains on the contract curve, the range of possible bargains in the whole field is in the shaded area bounded by the respective indifference curves through C_b and C_a. If one of the parties is an unskilled trader the other will be able to strike a bargain at a point off the contract curve which is better for him than the position to which he could be forced, by skilled trading, on the contract curve.

The real significance of the Paretian welfare economics, then, is that it sets forth explicitly the distinction between those changes in social variables which can take place through "trading"—i.e., through a mutual benefit of all parties—and those changes which involve "conflict," or the benefit of one party at the expense of another. In a civilization which is threatened with extinction because of an inability to solve the problem of conflict this distinction may be of considerable importance. Because conflict is costly, often very costly, and there is a reasonable presumption that it is almost certain to be more costly than trading, economists in general, and welfare economists in particular, have had a strong prejudice in favor of trading; and this is why the Paretian optimum is regarded as desirable. Considered merely as analysis, however, the contribution of the Paretian type of construction is the distinction between trading and conflict, and not the judgment between them.[18]

I have illustrated the marginal conditions in the case of exchange in some detail in order to bring out the essential nature of these conditions. Reder distinguishes seven such sets of conditions, all of which must be satisfied simultaneously if they are to define the optimum position of the system. They may perhaps be illustrated most simply by means of arithmetical examples; for graphical treatment Reder can be consulted,[19] and for analytical treatment Samuelson.[20] The arithmetical exposition of all seven conditions is shown in Table 1 (p. 20). The demonstration is conducted by showing that if the marginal conditions are *not* fulfilled a reorganization can take place which will leave one party better off without injuring the other.

The first condition is the one already discussed: that the marginal rates of substitution of two commodities should be the same for any pair of owners. Thus we suppose that for owner A, 1 of H can be substituted for 2 of K without loss or gain, and for owner B, 1 of H can be substituted for 3 of K without loss or gain: this violates the first marginal equality. Then we suppose that before the reorganization A has $20H$ and $10K$, and B has $5H$ and $20K$. The reorganization consists of exchange, A giving up 1 of H to B in return for 2 of K. This leaves A with $19H$ and $12K$, and B with $6H$ and $18K$. In A's case we know from his marginal rate of substitution that the reorganization leaves him neither worse nor better off. In B's case however we could have taken $3K$ away from him and we would have left him just as well off as before: for him, therefore, $6H$ and $17K$ would be just as good as $5H$ and $20K$. The reorganization therefore leaves B better off by $1K$, and leaves A no worse off. This could not be done if the marginal rates of substitution were equal.

---

[18] The reader should perhaps be warned that I have introduced the term "trading" and "conflict" into the discussion myself, because they seem to be best descriptive of the important distinction between reorganizations which involve no loss to anyone and those which involve loss to someone.

[19] *Op. cit.*, Ch. 2.

[20] *Op. cit.*, Ch. 8.

The second marginal condition relates to the allocation of products among various producers. The producers may be conceived of as firms, or as sectors of the economy, or as "countries," though the latter aggregates are open to some objections. This condition, therefore, determines the optimum degree of specialization of production. We suppose

TABLE 1

MARGINAL CONDITIONS: OPTIMUM POSITION OF THE SYSTEM

Condition Number	Parties	Marginal Rates of Transformation	Nature of Reorganization	Situation before Reorganization	Situation after Reorganization
1	Owner A Owner B	$1H = 2K$ $1H = 3K$	Exchange	$20H, 10K$ $5H, 20K$ $(5H, 20K$	$= 19H, 12K$ $6H, 18K$ $= 6H, 17K)$
2	Producer A Producer B	$1H$ for $2K$ $1H$ for $3K$	Reallocation of production	$15H, 25K$ $5H, 10K$	$16H, 23K$ $4H, 13K$
	(Totals)			$20H, 35K$	$20H, 36K$
3	Producer A Producer B	$1f$ makes $2K$ $1f$ makes $3K$	Reallocation of factors	$20f–40K$ $20f–60K$	$19f–38K$ $21f–63K$
	(Totals)			$40f–100K$	$40f–101K$
4	Producer A Producer B	$1f = 2g$ $1f = 3g$	Substitution of factors	$20f, 30g$ $10f, 20g$	$19f, 32g$ $11f, 17g$
	(Totals)			$30f, 50g$	$30f, 49g$
5	Consumer A Producer B	$1H = 2K$ $1H = 3K$	Substitution of products	$20H, 30K$ $20H, 30K$	$= 19H, 32K$ $19H, 33K$
6	Factors Preference Reward Paid	$1t = 2H$ $1t = 3H$	Substitution of leisure for product	$8t, 24H$ $8t, 24H$	$= 9t, 26H$ $9t, 27H$
7	Lender A Borrower B	$1H_1 = 2H_2$ $1H_1 = 3H_2$	Lending and borrowing without uncertainty	$20H_1, 10H_2$ $10H_1, 5H_2$ $(10H_1, 5H_2$	$= 19H_1, 12H_2$ $11H_1, 3H_2$ $= 11H_1, 2H_2)$

that producer A can produce $2K$ with the factors released by giving up the production of $1H$: this is his marginal rate of transformation of products under the condition that the quantity of factors used by him is constant. Similarly producer B could get $3K$ if he gave up $1H$. Before the reorganization, producer A is making $15H$ and $25K$, producer B is making $5H$ and $10K$; that is, $20H$ and $35K$ in all. We now suppose that A shifts from K to H and B from H to K, as in the table: we see that the production of K can be increased by 1 unit without lowering the production of H. An example could be constructed in which the production of both goods increased as a result of the reorganization. The second marginal condition may then be stated: if the marginal rates of transformation in production of any two products are not the same for all producers, the production of some product can be increased without diminishing the production of any other, by shifting production of each commodity towards its "low cost" producer.

The third marginal condition relates to the reallocation of a single factor between two producers. Thus we suppose that for producer A the addition of $1f$ of a factor adds $2K$ to the product, and that for B the addition of $1f$ adds $3K$ to the product. Then we see by the table that if $1f$ of the factor is shifted from A to B, the amount of commodity produced by the given amount of factor is increased: thus with $40f$ of the factor before the change only $100K$ is produced, and after the change $101K$ is produced. The third marginal condition can then be stated: if the marginal physical productivity of a given factor for a given product is not the same for two producers, the total product from a given amount of the factor can be increased by shifting the factor from the low to the high productivity producer.

The fourth marginal condition deals with the substitution of factors one for another. Here we suppose two factors, f and g. Producer A can keep his product constant if he replaces $1f$ by $2g$; producer B can do likewise if he replaces $1f$ by $3g$. In this case therefore producer A can produce the same product with $20f$ and $30g$ before, or with $19f$, and $32g$ after the change: producer B can do likewise with $10f$ and $20g$ before, and $11f$ and $17g$ after. A shift therefore of g towards producer A and of f towards producer B enables the same total product as before to be made with a smaller amount of factors. The condition may be stated: if the marginal rates of equal-product substitution of two factors are not the same for two producers, the same total product can be produced with a smaller expenditure of factors if each factor is shifted towards the producer for whom its marginal rate of substitution is least. Conditions two, three, and four can all be reduced to a single condition if factors are regarded as "negative products."

The fifth marginal condition relates to the substitution of products to conform to the structure of consumers' preferences. We suppose that consumer A can substitute $2K$ for $1H$ without feeling loss or gain. Producer B can substitute $3K$ for $1H$ without changing the amount of factors used. Then by shifting production from H to K the consumer can be made better off, without the producer being worse off; instead of the initial $20H$ and $30K$ he can have $19H$ and $33K$, whereas he would be just as well satisfied as before with $19H$ and $32K$: the change leaves him $1K$ to the good. This condition may be stated therefore: if the marginal rate of indifferent substitution of any consumer for two commodities is not equal to the marginal rate of transformation of these commodities in production, the consumer can be made better off by shifting production towards that commodity which has the greater marginal rate of equivalence in production.

The sixth condition relates to the substitution of "leisure" for product, and is concerned therefore with the *intensity of use* of factors. The concept of leisure does not only apply to labor, of course: it may refer to any factor which is withheld from use. Thus we suppose that the marginal rate of substitution of factor-use for product is $1t$ of factor use for $2H$ of product: that means that the owner of the factor would be indifferent whether the factor worked for $8t$ (say, hours) and received $24H$, or worked for $9t$ and received $26H$. The Marginal Reward is the increase in product acquired by the factor in return for a unit addition to the factor use; we suppose this is $3H$ per $1t$—i.e., working the factor another "hour" adds $3H$ to its total remuneration. In this case it will clearly pay to work another hour: $9t$ and $26H$ is just as good to the factor as $8t$ and $24H$: if it works another hour, however, it has $9t$ and $27H$—it is clearly $1H$ to the good. We can state the condition therefore: if the marginal reward of a factor exceeds the marginal rate of substitution of reward for use, the use of the factor will be increased.

The seventh condition relates to lending and borrowing in the absence of uncertainty. We suppose that H_1 and H_2 refer to qualities of asset H at times t_1 and t_2. We suppose that A is indifferent to having $1H_1$ or $2H_2$: B is indifferent to having $1H_1$ or $3H_2$. Individual A, that is to say, has a lower rate of time preference than B. Then it will pay B to borrow from A. Without borrowing we suppose A expects to have $20H_1$ and $10H_2$, B expects to have $10H_1$ and $5H_2$. Now if B borrows $1H$ from A at a rate of interest equal to A's rate of time preference A will have $19H_1$ and $12H_2$, and B will have $11H_1$ and $3H_2$, as A has transferred $1H$ to B at time t_1 and B has transferred $2H$ to A at time t_2. B however would just as soon have $11H_1$ and $2H_2$ as $10H_1$ and $5H_2$, as we know from his marginal rate of time substitution. He is therefore $1H$ to the good, and A is no worse off. The condition may be stated then: if the marginal rates of time substitution of two individuals for a given asset differ, it will pay the one with the smaller rate of time substitution to lend on the earlier date to the one with the larger.

These seven conditions correspond roughly to the list as given by

Reder. It is evident that there are others which have not been stated as yet explicitly in the literature. There may be other conditions relating to time preference, for instance: (8) that the own-rates of time preference for any one individual for two commodities must be the same; and (9) that the rate of time preference for an individual must be equal to the rate of time substitution in production (the marginal own-rate of return) for every commodity. There are also conditions relating to uncertainty and to liquidity (conditions 7, 8, and 9 assume certainty)— the marginal rates of substitution of all individuals for assets of different degrees of uncertainty and liquidity must be equal. There are also some conditions relating to equality of *rates* of uncertainty and liquidity preference, analogous to (8) and (9); the difficulties of quantifying these concepts makes these conditions rather vague. All these conditions may be summed up in two grand conditions: (*i*) wherever transformation of one variable into another is technically possible, the rate of indifferent substitution (that is, the amount of one variable which can be substituted for one unit of the other without feeling of gain or loss) must be equal to the rate of technical substitution—that is, the amount of the first variable which can be obtained technically by giving up one unit of the second; and (*ii*) all equivalent rates of technical and indifferent substitution must be equal.

The marginal equalities by themselves, of course, serve to define a minimum just as well as a maximum: that is why I have stated them in a negative rather than in a positive form, as this enables the statement of the second-order conditions to be worked into the condition itself. Stating them in this form, however, still does not guarantee that there is a real position of an optimum in which the conditions are satisfied. In the examples of Table 1, as long as the marginal inequalities persist it will always pay to make changes. If there is to be a real optimum we must invoke some "principle of diminishing returns" in each case. The generalized principle of diminishing returns may be stated thus: the movement of the system towards an optimum in the direction indicated by a divergence of marginal rates of transformation must lessen this divergence. If this law holds, the movement of the system from any position will lessen the divergence from the optimum until finally the system reaches the optimum point.

III. POLICY IMPLICATIONS OF WELFARE ECONOMICS

We may now pass on to some of the practical conclusions which have been drawn from welfare economics. The first is a strong predisposition in favor of "perfect markets"—that is, market situations in which the price of the commodity bought or sold does not vary with the *quantity* bought or sold by the individual buyer or seller. This predisposition arises from the fact that an individual operating in a perfect market maximizes his profits (or more generally his "advantage") by carrying every line of activity to the point where the price is equal to the marginal rate of transformation or substitution of money for the commodity in question. As in a perfect market the price is the same for all individuals this means that the operations of self-interest lead to an equilibrium of the universe of economic variables at a point where all the relevant marginal rates of transformation are equal to each other, because equal to the uniform price. We may illustrate from the equilibrium of exchange. Referring back to Figure 2 (p. 14), suppose that there is some price or ratio of exchange at which both parties can exchange any amounts. If we start with an initial position P_o such a price can be shown by any straight line (opportunity path) passing through P_o, such as P_oP_b or P_oP_c—the slope of the line being equal to the fixed ratio of exchange. Given this ratio of exchange, say P_oP_b, it is clear that (assuming profit or utility maximization) each party will proceed to the point at which the opportunity path touches one of his indifference curves—say P_a for A and P_b for B. We are assuming here a "market"—i.e., many other buyers and sellers—so that A and B do not have to deal only with each other. When there is a single price in the whole market at which the total amount offered for sale is equal to the total amount offered for purchase, the marginal rates of substitution for all marketers are equal and the marketers' positions lie on an n-dimensional contract function. It is not possible to illustrate this proposition graphically: however, the corresponding situation in the two-exchanger case would be the price (P_oP_c) at which both parties reach their optimum positions together on the contract curve at P_c.

We see, therefore, that welfare economics adds support to the classical case for perfect competition, as perfect competition is one form of social organization by which, theoretically, the social optimum can be achieved. This is not, of course, the main justification for a competitive economy in the minds of the classical economists, who thought much more in terms of the dynamics of social change than in terms of optimum positions of general equilibrium: the classical attack on protection is in terms of the ability of protected interests to prevent economic progress, rather than in terms of the wastes in the allocation of resources due to imperfect markets. Nevertheless, the welfare economists' case for perfect competition represents some clarification of the issues. Any argument for perfect competition immediately runs into the difficulty that perfect competition is impossible unless the size of the unit of economic decision is small relative to the market. Consequently, in cases where the efficiency of the economic unit (measured, say, by some reciprocal of average cost) increases with the size of the unit over a large range of output we run into a dilemma, that perfect competition can only be obtained at the cost of productive inefficiency. The only answer to this dilemma seems to be public operation or control of these large-scale enterprises in order to secure "marginal cost pricing"; for it is only when price is equal to marginal cost that the marginal conditions of the social optimum can be met.

This conclusion has been the subject of an extensive controversy in the journals, beginning with a famous article by Hotelling in 1938.[21] This controversy has been ably summed up by Nancy Ruggles in two articles.[22] The main issues from the point of view of welfare economics have been first, whether proportionality of price to marginal cost rather than equality would not equally well satisfy the conditions for an optimum: this was proposed by Frisch.[23] It has been shown, by Lerner, Bergson, and others, that equality is necessary if the third and fourth marginal conditions (those governing the allocation and substitution of factors) are not to be violated. A second issue of the controversy was whether complete compensation was necessary: this merely reflects the general controversy on the subject of whether the optimum conditions mean anything in the absence of full compensation. A third issue of the controversy concerned the means of raising money for the necessary subsidies: Hotelling advocated an income tax, but it can be shown that the income tax violates the sixth marginal condition, and distorts the economic equilibrium away from the optimal distribution of time between work and leisure. Perhaps the most important issue in the controversy concerns the administrative possibility of marginal cost pricing: this however lies outside the scope of welfare economics narrowly defined.

The marginal cost controversy pointed up another important con-

---

[21] *Op. cit.*

[22] Nancy Ruggles, "The Welfare Basis of the Marginal Cost Pricing Principle," *Rev. Econ. Stud.* (1949–50), XVII, 29–46; *idem,* "Recent Developments in the Theory of Marginal Cost Pricing," *ibid.,* pp. 107–26.

[23] Ragnar Frisch, "The Dupuit Taxation Theorem," *Econometrica,* Apr. 1939, VII, 145–50. See also on this point the earlier article by R. F. Kahn, "Some Notes on Ideal Output," *Econ. Jour.,* Mar. 1935, XLV, 1–35.

clusion of welfare economics: that all taxation as far as possible should be nonmarginal—that is, should be in the form of lump-sum taxes which are independent of the activity of the person or concern taxed. Thus there is a general predisposition against excise taxes on the ground that they distort the relative price and output structure away from the taxed commodities. There is a similar predisposition against income taxes on the ground that they distort the structure of activity as between "work" and "leisure." The general-welfare case against tariffs is part of the same argument, as they distort the geographic structure of economic activity. It can be shown that a tariff can benefit a single country, in the sense that it can create a situation whereby everyone within the country by a proper system of compensations, could be made better off as a result. This, however, is no more surprising than the proposition that a monopolist can benefit himself by restricting his output, even though the whole society suffers.

A rather surprising use of welfare economics has been in defense of socialism by some of the more sophisticated socialist economists. It is argued that as perfect competition is impossible in a market economy the marginal conditions for the social optimum cannot possibly be satisfied under capitalism and can only be satisfied in a socialist economy planned consciously to that end. This view—which is especially associated with the name of Oscar Lange[24]—should not be confused with the more Keynesian type of economic philosophy of Lerner,[25] in which the activity of the state is conceived as a governing mechanism, throwing a little counterweight in the directions where the system of private enterprise is failing to conform to the social optimum, rather than as the single-firm economy of the socialists. The assumption implicit in both these views, and especially in the socialist view, that there is nothing in the operations of a political and administrative system corresponding to imperfect competition in the market strikes me as naïve. Any realistic theory of the socialist or even of the governed economy must operate in terms of an equilibrium of political and administrative pressures, and I see no reason to suppose that these pressures will be any more "perfect" in a socialist than in the market economy. In any system action will affect the terms on which action is taken, whether the ac-

---

[24] "On the Economic Theory of Socialism," in *On the Economic Theory of Socialism*, B. E. Lippincott, ed. (Minneapolis, 1938). For a more detailed account of this aspect of the subject, see Abram Bergson, "Socialist Economics," *A Survey of Contemporary Economics*, Vol. I, H. S. Ellis, ed. (Philadelphia, 1948), Ch. 12.

[25] A. P. Lerner, *The Economics of Control* (New York, 1944).

tion be sales and the terms the price, or whether action be the placating of a superior and the terms the ratio of his pleasure to one's activity.

IV. AN ASSESSMENT OF WELFARE ECONOMICS

It is not perhaps the duty of the writer of one of these surveys to attempt an assessment of what he surveys. It is impossible, however, to be monarch of all one surveys without at the same time being a judge, and in a field as controversial as welfare economics the pretense of impartiality is more dangerous than the acknowledgment of bias. In the concluding pages, therefore, I propose to attempt some assessment of welfare economics, if only to warn the reader who judges differently to look for bias in my account.

In making this assessment some technical defects in the structure must first be examined. The first is of minor importance in principle, though it may be of considerable importance in practice. It is that the marginal conditions define a social optimum only marginally: i.e., the position which they define is superior to any other in the immediate vicinity, but it is not necessarily superior to any other over the whole possible range of the universe. This is the problem of the "maximum maximorum": there is nothing in the marginal conditions which can differentiate the top of a molehill from that of Mount Everest. This is a problem which has been of real concern to economists from Adam Smith on. Adam Smith's dynamics, based on the famous proposition that the division of labor depends on the extent of the market, is concerned with how one breaks out of a "low" equilibrium to a "higher" one. Marshall's case of the downward sloping supply curve intersecting the demand curve at three or more points is another example. The best treatment of this problem is that of Allyn Young:[26] since his day, until quite recently, there has been a curious lack of interest in the subject, in spite of its immense practical importance—e.g. in the development of underdeveloped areas. The preoccupation of welfare economics with the definition of a single optimum may well have done a disservice insofar as it has diverted attention from the critical problems of developmental dynamics. The problem may well be not how to get close to the top of a molehill, but how to climb *down* the molehill in order to start up the mountain. There is some recognition of this problem in Hicks' discussion of the "total conditions" in his 1939 article—a discussion

---

[26] "Increasing Returns and Economic Progress," *Econ. Jour.,* Dec. 1928. XXXVIII 527–42.

which has played some part in the marginal cost controversy. Hicks' total conditions, however, refer to the problem of whether capacity should be created; they are not adequate for dealing with the larger dynamic questions of economic development.

Somewhat related to this problem is that of the "boundary maximum." Where the actual range of variables of the economic system is sharply limited by institutional or other factors (e.g. minimum wage laws) boundary maxima are not at all improbable. That is, the boundary of the possible range of variables may represent a superior point to any other in the possible range, and yet the marginal conditions will not be satisfied at it. Thus suppose, in Figure 3 (p. 15), M represents the kind of maximum at which the marginal conditions are satisfied. It would be quite possible for U'_t to be a superior position, even though the marginal conditions would not be satisfied. One cannot assume offhand, therefore, in the presence of a bounded universe (and the economic universe is very sharply bounded by law and by custom) that the violation of the marginal conditions is necessarily significant.

A more serious technical defect is the assumption that the structure of individual preferences (as expressed, say, in indifference curves) is independent of any variable of the system except the quantities of commodity, and in particular is independent of prices and is also invariant with respect to the paths taken towards equilibrium. These assumptions are extremely shaky. If the preference structure is itself a function, say, of the prices or other transformation ratios of the economic variables, as well as of quantities of commodity, all the marginal equalities are invalidated. I have attempted to illustrate in *A Reconstruction of Economics*[27] some of the difficulties which arise in constructing a general theory of preference in which the preference functions (e.g. the indifference curves) are assumed to vary with the absolute level of price. It is not impossible to take these modifications formally into account. When the system is so modified, however, all the simplicity and elegance of welfare economics disappears, as well as most of its present conclusions. Virtually all the constructions of welfare economics, for instance (including our Figure 2), assume that the indifference curves remain stable as change proceeds, or as prices are changed. If every change in price necessitates drawing up a new set of indifference curves, the diagrams melt into chaos. It can be argued in defense of the simpler assumption that in fact preference functions will only vary with price if

---

[27] New York, 1950, Ch. 5.

there is a "money illusion" which should be neglected in welfare considerations, or if there is purely speculative behavior which cancels out in the long run. Thus a general rise in the absolute level of money prices may make many people "feel" worse off, even if their incomes rise accordingly, because they still think of the value of money in terms of their old money incomes. This is a "money illusion," but it hardly becomes a welfare economist to neglect it. If he builds solely on revealed (or revealable) preferences, he is no more entitled (as a welfare economist) to judge this an illusion than he is to judge a taste for whiskey immoral. A shift in the preference structure with a change in the absolute price is not "illusion" if the absolute level of price is regarded as an indicator of future levels. If price is thought to be "high" relative to some norm it may be perfectly rational to revise one's preferences towards money and away from commodity, in the expectation that prices will fall. This difficulty may be merely one aspect of a general weakness of present-day welfare economics—its failure to extend its principles to include the treatment of uncertainty.

An even more fundamental technical objection to modern welfare economics is the assumption that preference structures are invariant with respect to movement among the variables. This means assuming that there is no disutility of maximizing utility, and that "trading" in any of its forms is preferentially neutral. A great deal of human behavior and attitude, however, is explicable only on the assumption that both maximizing utility or profit (i.e. "economizing") and trading are acutely disagreeable, not to say unethical proceedings. There is a general assumption in welfare economics that "trading"—i.e. moving to positions of mutual advantage—is "good" and that "conflict" is bad, or at least neutral. One can see how a Marxist might jump on this as the intellectual product of a civilization of shopkeepers, and how the principles of dialectical materialism might lead to just the opposite conclusion—that trading was bad and conflict good. Indeed, much of the conflict between capitalism and communism lies precisely in a profound difference in preference in regard to trading—it is this which makes the disagreement so intractable. The same conflict may be observed between capitalist and militarist attitudes—indeed, militarism and communism can formally be regarded as sub-forms of the same preference system. In this system trading is regarded as "appeasement": the ideal of moving to positions where everybody is better off than before is positively rejected because a great positive value is attached to some people (enemies) being *worse* off than before. On this view the wicked should not be bought off: they should be knocked down. "Millions for defense but not a penny for tribute!"—the compensating payment again! The accusation that some welfare economists assume the permanent vesting of all vested interests is also part of the above criticism.

The act of economizing, and still more, the reduction of all values to monetary terms, likewise falls under criticism. This may be called the "romantic" preference field: it registers a high value for disinterested-ness, self-giving, not-counting-the-cost, daredeviltry, extravagance of life, and carelessness for consequences. It is a most important element in our civilization—witness our romantic attitude towards marriage and war. By this standard, welfare economics can be denounced as a set of variations on the shocking theme that every man has his price, and welfare economists can be stigmatized in the language of Oscar Wilde as people who know the price of everything and the value of nothing. Some things do not have a price at all, even in the form of compensating payments. It might be argued, for instance, that un-modified welfare economics would lead to the conclusion that slavery is desirable, as the establishment of any "inalienable rights" involves an interference with the ability to trade—i.e. to alienate.

The formal mathematical statement of the modifications which must be made in welfare economics to take account of these criticisms is quite beyond the scope of this paper—and of its author. It is possible, however, to see broadly some conclusions which might be expected. If the act of economizing itself is disagreeable (or agreeable!) the topography of the opportunity field itself modifies the topography of the preference field. There will be a preference for places where it does not much matter what we do, and where we do not have to hit the "right" conduct right on the head. That is to say there will be a prefer-ence for plateaus of opportunity, where we can wander around without disaster and even large errors are not fatal, to "peaks" where results are excellent *if* we make exactly the right choices but where even slightly wrong choices are disastrous. An extension of welfare economics into the fields of uncertainty and liquidity might clear up much of this problem.

The problem of the impact of the path followed on the structure of preferences is even more difficult. It may be that moving *anywhere* is painful, and produces a fall in the preference surface: this would result in a strong preference for the *status quo*, and the preference sur-face will bunch into peaks wherever we happen to be. Like a boy crawl-ing about under a sheet we carry our maximum with us; in which case why bother to go anywhere! The pregnant remark of Hicks that the greatest gain of the monopolist may be a quiet life is an insight which might profitably be worked into the formal structure of welfare economics. We may run into preferences against some paths—e.g. paths of price discrimination—which do not exist for others. What is worse, even the opportunity function may not be invariant to the path chosen: means determine ends, and ends means; history is irreversible, and often there are no roads back from errors committed. Thus instead of a relatively simple problem of climbing the preference mountain along the opportunity fence until we reach the highest point—which is the essential principle of maximizing behavior and of welfare economics—we find ourselves climbing a quaking jelly of a mountain that dips and sags as we walk across it, along a nightmarish fence which shifts and wavers as we walk beside it. It is little wonder that mankind has generally retreated from the quagmire of rationality to the solid highroads of taboo and principle, even though they may not go where we want them to!

This survey may well be concluded by asking to what extent has welfare economics attained the three objectives mentioned at the outset: to define "riches," to provide a guide for social policy, and to develop a "scientific" prolegomena to ethics. For the first some success can be claimed. The concept of a social optimum and the use of a preference function have clarified somewhat the meaning of "economically better," which perhaps has certain advantages over the older concept of utility. The question must be raised however whether in the process of refining the crude idea of riches some of the metal rather than the dross has been refined out, even in the notion of a preference function for an individual. When we come to the measurement of the riches of groups, the advance seems even more dubious. Samuelson[28] has shown that we cannot even be *sure* that group A is better off than group B even if A has collectively more of everything, and once more we seem to be thrown back on the rather crude comparisons of the Colin Clark type.

Turning now to the contribution of welfare economics to the discussion of economic policy, the record is not too encouraging. On the positive side there is a certain clarification of arguments which the earlier economists left fuzzy, for example, in the theory of tariffs or of taxation. As a realistic guide to social policy, however, the concept of a social optimum and of the marginal conditions has not been particularly

---

[28] P. A. Samuelson, "The Evaluation of Real National Income," *Oxford Econ. Papers*, Jan. 1950, II, 1–29.

fruitful—as the marginal cost controversy itself witnesses. One cannot
help feeling that the crude ifs and ands of plain price and monetary
theory are of much more importance to the policy maker than the elegant, but fragile, pots and pans of welfare economics. The policy maker
who learns that prices above some level lead to surpluses, and below
lead to shortages, or that exports, on the whole, are paid for by imports, or that a large increase in the quantity of money is likely to lead
to a rise in the price level, or that deflation is likely to lead to unemployment, knows something that is of use to him at least in avoiding gross
and clumsy mistakes. I doubt if a knowledge of the Seven Marginal
Conditions has ever proven of any value to the statesman, and an intoxication with the ideal of marginal cost pricing might mislead him
severely. One wonders even if the Paretian welfare economics has come
up with anything as practically useful as the famous Pigovian proposition that Smoke Is a Nuisance! And in fact all economic policy has to
be based on interpersonal comparisons, as compensation is hardly ever
administratively practicable. Even the conclusion of welfare economics
that poll taxes are economically more desirable than income or excise
taxes seems to be singularly useless as a canon of public finance—
simply because of its administrative difficulty. Perhaps the best that
càn be said for welfare economics as a discipline is that it is virtually
impossible to study it without learning a good deal of economics in the
process!

Then in regard to the third objective—the curiously platonic love
affair between welfare economics and ethics—one must admit that the
task of making value judgments explicit is a very important one. One
can dismiss fairly curtly the idea of a *wertfrei* system of evaluation: it
is obviously preposterous to suppose that one can set up criteria for
judgment which are somehow independent of ethical norms. Indeed, as
we have seen, the ethical judgments involved in the Hicks-Kaldor
variety of welfare economics—that people should get what they want
and that trading is ethically neutral—are not merely ethical judgments
but practically indefensible ones. In this respect the welfare economics
of the Bergson-Samuelson type which postulated a general "social
welfare function" is on much safer ground, even though its conclusions
grow more nebulous as they become more general.

What, indeed, welfare economics seems to be turning into is not
a prolegomena to ethics but a form of ethical theory itself. What we
are doing in economics, or in any other abstraction, is to carve for ourselves $n-k$ dimensional sections, along certain dimensions that interest
us, of some n-dimensional "feasibility function"—the feasibility func-

tion being that which shows all those combinations of social (or other) magnitudes which are in some sense "available." "Pure" economics is essentially a discussion of the topography of a section of the whole feasibility function in the dimensions of prices and quantities of exchangeables—a very small part of the total function, of course, but one which we can explore in some degree. Welfare economics tries to add another dimension, "economic welfare" (call it W), and to discuss the problem of where in the topography of the economic feasibility function this new variable is in some sense maximized. Ethics simply adds a further dimension (call it G for "good"), and discusses where in the feasibility function this variable is also in some sense maximized; for wherever it is not maximized there are possibilities of improvement.[29] If, however, the economic welfare function is an *empirical* function, in the sense that the value of W cannot be derived by *a priori* manipulation of the economic variables (prices and quantities), it cannot be any more (or less) scientific than the G-function, for both W and G share the empirical property that they can be observed in some sense by asking people questions (Is A *better* than B? Is A *richer* than B?). They run into the same empirical difficulty—that we get different answers from different people. It should be observed that the same difficulty is actually present in *all* empirical work, as anyone who has observed students at work in a laboratory will admit. The differences among the answers to the same question are larger from person to person when we ask, "Is A richer (or better) than B?" than it is when we ask, "Is A heavier that B?" But it seems to me that no difference in principle is involved. All empirical functions are fuzzy. If somebody wants to call the less fuzzy ones "scientific" and the more fuzzy ones "unscientific" he has the right of all Humpty Dumpties to make words mean what he likes, but he will run into grave danger of making an emotional rather than an intellectual distinction.

As far as I can see we run into no difficulties in inquiring into the G-function that we do not also run into in inquiring into the W-function: indeed, I suspect that there is a better chance of constructing empirical G-functions than W-functions. In this connection the recent work of Kenneth Arrow[30] and of Duncan Black[31] in exploring the construction of general welfare functions from individual welfare func-

---

[29] I have distinguished between the W-function and the G-function to allow for the possibility that duty might not be identical with interest.

[30] *Social Choice and Individual Values* (New York, 1951).

[31] "On the Rationale of Group Decision-making," *Jour. Pol. Econ.*, Feb. 1948, LVI, 23–34.

tions is of great importance, and is just as applicable to the investigation of the general ethical judgment as to the general economic welfare judgment. Their central proposition, very briefly, is that unique and transitive general welfare functions cannot be constructed from individual welfare functions unless certain rather narrow conditions are fulfilled, such that all individuals range their choices in a single rank-order. These discussions have thrown a great deal of light on the theory of consensus and of political decision. Thus we seem to be on the verge of an expansion of welfare economics into something like a social science of ethics and politics: what was intended to be a mere porch to ethics is either the whole house or nothing at all! In so laying down its life welfare economics may be able to contribute some of its insights and analytical methods to a much broader evaluative analysis of the whole social process.

THE FRUITS OF PROGRESS AND
THE DYNAMICS OF DISTRIBUTION

American Economic Review, 43, 2 (May 1953): 473-483.

THE FRUITS OF PROGRESS AND THE DYNAMICS
OF DISTRIBUTION

The classical economists devoted a good deal of attention to the problem of what happened to the various magnitudes of an economic system "in the progress of society," especially the structure of relative prices and the distributional shares. This is what Baumol has felicitously called the "magnificent dynamics." Since the days of Mill, however, economists have been preoccupied with developing equilibrium theory and comparative statics, and even the recent revival of interest in dynamics as a result of the use of difference equations (notably by Samuelson) has been confined to problems "in the small" rather than in the large. Moreover, the demise of the wage-fund theory left the classical dynamics in ruins, and no adequate macroeconomic theory of distribution has ever filled the gap.

The problem of filling this gap is of more than academic interest. One of the main appeals of Marxism is that it has a magnificent dynamics of its own. The weaknesses of the Marxist, as of the classical theory which it in many ways resembles, are apparent both in logic and in practice. Things have simply not turned out in the way that either the classical economists or Marx foretold. Wages do not move to a subsistence level, but the proportion of national income going to labor is almost stationary, or even shows slight increases, in the face of an enormous rise in national income. Profits do not exhibit any significant long-run downward trend, even in the face of enormous accumulations of capital. Rent does not swell to gobble up the fruits of progress, but becomes an increasingly insignificant part of national income. Nevertheless, all the facts in the world do not seem to be adequate to demolish an elegant and appealing theory. Only theory can kill a theory, and the intellectual appeal of Marxism depends in no small degree on the weakness of the alternative theories of long-run change.

One does not hope in half an hour to rebuild from scratch a major area of economic theory. Nevertheless, it may be possible to indicate at least the problems with which a magnificent dynamics must deal.

The main problem is the impact of progress on the structure of economic life. We must ask ourselves, therefore, what are the significant components of structure for this purpose. Suppose we take the short cut of defining technical progress as an increase in per capita real income of a society. There are great index-number difficulties in such a definition, but it is the only definition which seems to offer even a hope of quantitative analysis. Then the problem of long-run dynamics is concerned with the determinants of the changes in the distribution of total income among various significant categories as total income itself increases (or, of course, decreases).

The main focus of this paper is the problem of distribution according to functional shares. Nevertheless, it should be observed briefly that many other distributions of income are relevant to the general problem of the reciprocal relations of structure and growth. Interesting work has been done, for example by Colin Clark, on the effects of economic progress on the distribution of income by industry of origin. Here we have the famous proposition that in the course of economic progress primary industries (e.g., agriculture) undergo a relative decline and that in later stages even secondary industries (manufacturing) may decline relative to the tertiary service trades.

Another very interesting question is the structure of technical change itself and its impact both on general rates of growth and on the structural consequences of growth. The classification of technical improvements into labor-saving, land-saving, and capital-saving is of considerable importance here. From the point of view of growth of income per head, land-saving improvements, permitting a greater product per acre, may be a prerequisite of economic development. One might even make a special category of space-saving improvements, of which land-saving improvements are one part and transportation improvements another part. The main significance of these is, first, the impact of land-saving improvements on nutrition in crowded areas and, secondly, the external economies effect of space-saving improvements which permit greater specialization and more trade. An increase in output of food per acre, for instance, may be of more immediate importance to India than an increase in output per man: one will give immediately better nutrition; the other might merely create more rural underemployment. The capital-saving nature of an improvement is also of importance for the low-level areas, which need improvements which increase output per man and per acre without involving much accumulation of capital—hoes and land reorganization rather than dams and tractors.

With this brief glance at the wider aspects we can now return to the "classical distribution" problem, or distribution by functional shares. Cannan distinguished what he called "pseudo distribution," which is the problem of what determines wages per head, rent per acre, and interest per cent from the "true" distribution problem which is that of what determines the number of people in various size-of-income categories, or personal distribution. There is also another related problem, which is that of the determinants of the functional distributional shares; that is, the proportion of income going to labor, to land, and to capital or to any other interesting category of functional income. The link between all three aspects of distribution. is the distribution of wealth—that is, of various kinds of assets—among different holders or groups of holders. We suppose that income accrues to any individual as a result of the productive employment of assets which he owns. We include, of course, minds and bodies among assets; so that labor income is seen to be just as much derived from the employment of an asset as any other form of income. Then the income of any individual is the sum of the incomes which he receives from his various assets, and each of these is equal to the quantity of the asset owned, multiplied by the income per unit of asset. Given, therefore, the income per unit of asset and given the personal distribution of assets, it is a mere matter of arithmetic to calculate both the personal distribution of income by size groups and the proportion of income going to any particular asset factor. It would seem, therefore, as if the distribution problem were a mere matter of price theory, coupled perhaps with some notes on the dynamics of inheritance and the distribution of property. It is well known, for instance, that property tends to concentrate into the hands of elderly maiden ladies, that primogeniture and a caste system concentrate it, while equal division among children and class mobility tend to disperse it.

If the dynamics of property distribution can thus summarily be disposed of or perhaps handed over to the sociologists, it would look as if pseudo distribution in Cannan's sense is the heart of the problem. It is not, however, as it might appear, a simple problem in price theory. In effect that is the assumption of the marginal productivity theory as applied to this problem. The reward of each factor tends to be equal to its marginal productivity, which declines with increase in the quantity of the factor: the more we have of any factor, therefore, the less will be its remuneration per unit, following the declining line of the marginal productivity curve. This assumes, of course, that each factor is fully employed, or at least that the amount employed is limited only by voluntary withdrawals into "leisure" uses.

A fallacy of composition is involved here, however, analogous to that involved in the view that a reduction of wages is all that is necessary to secure full employment. We are facing a system of general price determination, and it cannot be assumed, as in partial analysis, that the demand functions for factors are invariant with respect to their prices. Even the general conclusions of the marginal productivity analysis need to be questioned: for instance, that if population is high relative to capital and land, wages will be low, or that if land is plentiful relative to population and capital, rents will be low.

What is needed to replace the classical theory is a macroeconomic theory of distribution. In this regard I find myself in a somewhat delicate position, having an axe to grind of my own. In my *Reconstruction of Economics* I put forward what purported to be a macroeconomic theory of distribution—or at least a stab in that direction. This theory has been received with catcalls and abuse from both sides of the Atlantic, as well as by some intelligent criticism. This is hardly the place either to state it or to defend or even to modify it. Nevertheless, as it occupies a predominant place in my own thinking and as I still believe it to be substantially correct in spite of many infelicities in its original expression and some rather legitimate misunderstandings on the part of the critics, I can hardly throw it altogether to one side. For the remainder of this paper, therefore, I propose to consider briefly what a macroeconomic model is and along what lines macroeconomic models of distribution might be constructed.

Any macroeconomic model consists, first, of two parts: one or more identities relating various aggregates of the system and sufficient behavior equations relating the aggregates of the identities among themselves to give an equal number of equations and unknowns and so make an equilibrium solution possible. The behavior equations may include variables not in the basic identities, as long as there are enough equations to determine all the unknowns. A behavior equation may be defined as a relationship among aggregates corresponding to some aspect of human behavior such that, if the relationship is not satisfied by the variables of the system, behavior will take place in the direction of changing some of the variables involved. The validity of any model—i.e., its usefulness in interpreting the phenomena of economic life—depends on two factors: The first is whether the aggregates which are the basic variables of the models are homogeneous enough so that changes in the composition and structure of the aggregate can be neglected. This condition can never be fulfilled perfectly, but if the aggregates are grossly heterogeneous, changes in their structure will affect the stability of the behavior equations. The second factor is whether the behavior equations do in fact correspond to stable patterns of human behavior. If the dynamics of the model are to be meaningful, the behavior equations must be capable of expression as stable difference equations, relating the values of one set of variables (the response variables) as determined by the values of another set (the stimulus variables) in a previous period or periods.

A model can fall short of these ideal requirements to a considerable degree and still be useful. A good example is the basic model of the Keynesian system (which I have sometimes called the sub-Keynesian system). This consists of an identity: Production or income $(Y) =$ Consumption (C) plus Accumulation (A), and two behavior equations, a consumption function $C = F_c (Y)$ and an investment or accumulation function $I = F_i (Y)$. The aggregates involved are extremely heterogeneous. Consumption, for instance, depends not only on the size of output (income) but also on its composition and distribution, in both space and time. The consumption function also is not very stable in time—a truth which was brought sadly home to the attention of economists by the debacle of the postwar unemployment predictions. Nevertheless, this model, crude and imperfect as it is, has proved to be the key which has unlocked the basic mysteries of the phenomenon of unemployment.

Consider, then, what we are looking for in a basic model of distribution theory. Let us take the simplest possible distribution of national income by functional shares: that into wages (W) and not-wages (V). Not-wages then includes profit, rent, and interest. By the principle that the whole national product is divided we have a basic identity.

$$Y = W + V \tag{1}$$

We can now postulate slightly more extended consumption and investment functions,

$$C = F_c(W, V) \tag{2}$$
$$I = F_i(W, V) \tag{3}$$

and we still have the basic composition-of-product, or "savings-investment" identity,

$$Y = C + I \tag{4}$$

This system is incomplete, however: it has four equations but five unknowns, so that it needs another equation to make it an equilibrium system. The question is, what equation should we postulate? The classical economists in effect postulated an equation $W = kS$, where S is the total stock of capital. This is the wage fund theory that the total wage bill is a certain proportion of the total stock of capital—a proportion determined by the tastes and habits of the capitalist. In a short period, S can be taken as given; so that the equation does not introduce an additional unknown. It does not, however, represent an acceptable behavior equation, as it is difficult to visualize any specific behavior which will result if it is not fulfilled.

The marginal productivity theory in effect postulates the equation $W = F_w(L)$ where L is the total labor force and is assumed given, for the theory that assumes that the average wage is equal to some "average" marginal productivity of labor, which in turn is supposed to be a function of the labor force. What this assumes in terms of behavior is that if there is unemployment, the average real wage will fall and that as it falls employment will rise; corresponding to full employment, there is a unique real wage per head and therefore a unique total wage bill. The difficulty with this behavior assumption is not only that it is unrealistic in modern society to assume that unemployment will produce much pressure even on money wages but that it is doubtful whether a decline in money wages will result in a decline in real wages, because a general decline in money wages will set off a fall in commodity prices and so may not lead to decline in real wages.

In my *Reconstruction of Economics,* I suggested another approach to the "missing equation," this time in terms of the aggregate balance sheet identity—one of the necessary relationships of the system which has been surprisingly neglected in economic model-building. Aggregate business savings are defined as the increase in net worths of all businesses. This must be equal to the increase in net business assets, which is composed of four other quantities: the increase in the value of real assets held by businesses ("Investment"), I: the increase in the money stock of businesses, dM_b, the increase in the debts of households to businesses (consumers credit, for the most part) dK_b, less the increase in debts of businesses to households (securities of businesses held by households) dK'_b. Total not-wages (V) now are equal to business savings plus business distributions in interest and dividends (D), so that we have

$$V = I + dM_b + dK_b - dK'_b + D \qquad (5)$$

Mr. Turvey, in his excellent review of the *Reconstruction* (*Economica,* May, 1951, page 203), pointed out, in effect, that I and dK'_b were not independent as, if investment is financed by the sale of securities to households I is exactly offset by the increase in securities in the hands of households, so that $I - dK'_b = 0$. This defect in the formulation, however, can easily be taken care of if we write $I - dK_b = I_n$, I_n then being internally financed investment; that is, investment financed out of profits. Identity (5) then becomes

$$V = I_n + D + dM_b + dK_b \qquad (6)$$

This same identity can easily be put into a "wages" form if we write

$$W = Y - V = C + I - I_n - (dM_b + D + dK_b)$$
$$= C + I_c - (dM_b + D + dK_b) \qquad (7)$$

where I_e is externally financed investment; i.e., investment financed by the issuance of securities to the public. Identities (6) and (7) are of course merely different forms of the same basic identity; they do not represent two independent equations.

We have now added a missing equation to our total system, but in so doing we have added five more unknowns — I_e, I_n, dM_b, D, and dK_b—and need five more equations! One of these is an identity,

$$I = I_e + I_n \qquad (8)$$

which leaves us with the necessity of finding four more behavior equations, governing the variables I_e (or I_n), dM_b, D, and dK_b. Each of these variables, however, corresponds to a specific area of decision. Their magnitude can be regarded as determined by the sum of other magnitudes, each of which is determined as a result of individual decision. Thus the total of both internally and externally financed investment is a result of decisions taken by individual businessmen. We can treat them simply as exogeneous variables in the model or they can be regarded as functions of some of the other variables of the system. The increase in the money stocks of businesses is a reflection of two factors: first, the relative liquidity preferences of businesses and households (a higher relative liquidity preference of businesses drawing money out of household into business balances), and second, the change in the total money stock. Again this can be assumed to be an exogenous variable without too much injustice to truth, especially as the longer the period we take the smaller this item will be relative to the others. Thus in a short period an increase in dividends may result in a shift of the money stock from business into household balances which will in part offset the increase in dividends, but over longer periods this effect will be unimportant. The consumers credit item may likewise be regarded as exogenous, or may be related in a consumers credit function to other variables such as W or Y.

It is not the purpose of this paper to examine in detail the properties of this model, especially as I have discussed the properties of a similar model in *The Impact of the Union* (Harcourt, Brace, 1951). What is relevant for the present purpose is the light which the model throws on the cumulative processes of society. There are three principal cumulative processes: the growth of population, of capital, and of knowledge. The growth of population increases consumption but it also increases investment; so that it is not easy to forecast the effect on the relative composition of national income into the two components. The growth of capital on the other hand may be expected to shift the composition of national income away from investment towards consumption, for as capital grows the opportunities for increasing capital usefully must eventually decline, while consumption, at least in the form of maintenance and depreciation, will increase. The growth of knowledge may postpone this process by opening up new fields for investment.

What, then, are likely to be the effects of these changes on distribution? In the long run, it is clear that we can neglect the items dM_b and dK_b. Businesses can neither accumulate money nor expand consumers credit for ever, unless there is a perpetual inflation. A general shift from investment into consumption as components of national income, reflected in a rise in the consumption function and a fall in the investment function, is likely to have a broad effect in increasing wages at the expense of not-wages. This effect may be offset in part if there is at the same time a shift in the structure of investment itself from externally financed to internally financed investment.

By far the most important conclusion which can be drawn from the model, however, is that the ultimate long-run tendency depends on the nature of the "dividends function." If firms on the whole distribute a constant proportion of their total earnings, these earnings will eventually shrink to zero, for in the final equilibrium, $I_n = dM_b = dK_b = 0$, so that $V = D$. The existence of contractual distributions in interest and rent will prevent the disappearance of not-wages altogether, but unless there is some level of profits at which total business distributions equal profits with positive dividends (i.e., a level at which there is no attempted net business saving), dividends will disappear.

Thus while it is perfectly possible to make assumptions about the behavior functions in the model which will give us a "day of judgment" on Keynesian or Marxist lines, in which accumulation is so great that all investment ceases, in which profits fall to zero and in which consumption is not adequate to absorb the full employment output, so that the system perishes in a slough of unemployment and profitlessness, such a conclusion is not necessary but depends on certain behavior functions which are themselves subject to public influence. It may be that even without public intervention the behavior functions will permit full employment and a sufficient distribution of national income to profits to permit the operation of a private enterprise system in, or as we approach, the stationary state. What emerges in any case from the analysis is a concept of long-run dynamics which is much less deterministic than that of the classical, the Marxist, or the marginal school. The historical movement of the relative shares is determined by how people behave or are induced to behave and is not predetermined by any iron physical laws.

The problem of the mutual relationship of the structure of technical change and the structure of distribution of income is another fascinating field of study to which very little attention has been given and in regard to which only a few brief suggestions can be offered here. The personal distribution of income will clearly affect the direction of technical change. Thus the technical skill which in ancient Egypt all went into the construction of mighty pyramids for the pharoah, in more equalitarian societies goes into the development of conveniences and luxuries for the masses. It is perhaps less obvious but equally true that the nature of techniques and the direction of technical change will affect the personal distribution of income. An improvement in food supplies can hardly help being fairly evenly distributed—the capacity even of the richest stomach being limited. Automobiles, likewise, if there are enough of them, can hardly help being fairly equally distributed. The improvements in tailoring brought good clothes to nearly everybody. On the other hand, improvements in the production of extreme luxuries cannot possibly be diffused among the people. There seems to be here a wide field both for theoretical and historical inquiry.

Another problem of great practical importance, but one in which our ignorance is virtually complete, is that of the effects of redistribution of income and wealth on the rate of economic development itself. The importance of this problem rests on a matter of simple arithmetic: that if redistribution towards any group causes a fall in the rate of growth of national income, no matter how slight, there will be some date beyond which the absolute income of the favored group will be less than what it would have been if the redistribution had not taken place. Thus in the Figure 1 we suppose that national income (in real terms) is OB at the base date and that this is divided into two parts, OA and AB. What the two parts are is immaterial. They can be wages and profits, or agriculture and industry, or rich and poor, or any dichotomy we please. National income grows, we suppose, at a constant rate following the line Bb on the log scale. The absolute value of the A-share follows the parallel line Aa, if the proportionate shares are constant. Now suppose that an initial increase in the A-share from OA to OA', the proportion to national income being again held constant, results in a decline in the rate of growth. National income follows the line Bb', and the absolute value of the A-share follows the line $A'a'$. It is clear that Aa and $A'a'$ must intersect. If E is the point of intersection, then at the corresponding date F the absolute income of the A-group will be just equal to what it would have been had there been no redistribution in its favor. Beyond F, of course, the absolute income of the A-group is less than it would have been had it not been "favored," and the disparity continually increases. If there is not time discounting, it is clear that it will never pay any group to accept a redistribution in its favor which lowers the rate of growth even by the smallest amount, even if our welfare function regards only the income of that group as contributing to welfare. If there is time discounting, the earlier gains weigh heavier than the later losses. Even so, there must be an absolute time horizon beyond which the present value of future gains or losses is zero before there can be a possibility of the gains from such redistribution outweighing the losses.[1]

In view of the extreme importance, therefore, even for the initially favored groups, of avoiding redistributions which lower the rate of growth of the total product, our massive ignorance concerning the effects of any kind of redistribution on the rate of growth is a matter for serious concern. It means that almost all major decisions of eco-

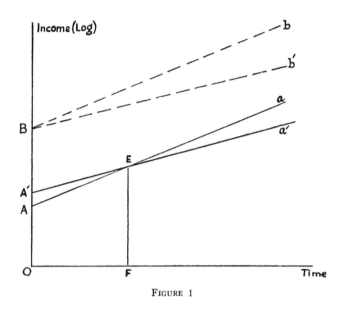

FIGURE 1

nomic policy have to be taken in ignorance of the most important effect which they have. It means that welfare economics has been forced to confine itself to what are almost trivial problems by comparison with the real issues in almost any policy decision. It means, also, that economic ethics has been seriously distorted by static and short-run criteria of value. "Justice" has been thought of too much in

---

[1] Let $A_1 = K_1 e^{\alpha t}$ be the growth equation before the redistribution, and $A_2 = K_2 e^{\beta t} be$ the growth equation after redistribution. Then when $A_1 = A_2$, $K_1 e^{\alpha t} = K_2 e^{\beta t}$, or $t = \dfrac{\log_e \frac{K}{H}}{\alpha - \beta}$. To get an idea of the orders of magnitude involved suppose $\dfrac{K}{H} = 1.1$, $\alpha - \beta = 0.01$. That is, a 10 per cent rise in the initial income of the A-group causes a drop of one percentage point in the rate of growth. Then $t = 9.5$ years—by no means a long time in the light of policy decisions!

terms of the division of a fixed pie rather than in terms of encouraging the baking of more pies. One of the simplest ways of dealing with an important area of ignorance is simply to ignore it. It is not therefore always a popular thing to do to call attention to such areas, especially when it is by no means clear what are the avenues of research by which the ignorance may be remedied. In the long run, however, it may be of more value to society to call attention to an unfelt need than to satisfy the felt wants.

What emerges from the over-all discussion, then, is that in the field of distribution, as in the field of production, man is not helpless in the grip of inflexible forces of historical development, but that his development depends on his behavior and his behavior is subject to rational analysis and to change in the light of that analysis. The great task of the social scientist is to find where are the aspects of behavior which make a real difference, even though the efforts may often be totally different from what is immediately apparent. The problem of ecological succession in social life can then be brought more under man's control, and social pressure of various kinds can be applied in the direction of molding the equilibrium closer to some heart's desire. But to what or whose heart's desire is a question for other occasion.

AN ECONOMIST'S VIEW OF
THE MANPOWER CONCEPT

In: *Proceedings of a Conference on the Utilization of Scientific and Professional Manpower,* New York: Columbia University Press, 1954, pp. 11-26.

An Economist's View of the Manpower Concept

When one has to raise a lonely voice in denunciation of a respected object one has the choice of two methods. One can keep the bad news till the last and then make an exit before the tomatoes begin to fly, or one can apply the shock technique and stun the audience into insensibility by letting the cat out of the bag at the beginning. It is the second of these alternatives which I propose to follow. Let me begin then by saying that I find the whole manpower concept repulsive, disgusting, dangerous, fascistic, communistic, incompatible with the ideals of liberal democracy, and unsuitable company for the minds of the young. This at least gives me something to defend.

The manpower concept is basically, I suspect, an engineering concept, and one of the main problems of society is to keep engineers in a decently subordinate position. It contemplates society as having a single well defined end which is to be pursued with *efficiency*. Society is conceived as a great machine, feeding Manpower in at one end and grinding out maximum quantities of the Single Well Defined End, which I propose to call the SWED, at the other. The manpower problem is, then, that of getting as much SWED per unit of Manpower as possible. The efficiency of the society is measured by the SWED/Manpower ratio, and, of course, we want to maximize this. I suspect, however, that the ardent proponents of Manpower want to do much more than maximize Efficiency. They actually want to maximize not merely Efficiency, but the Output of SWED. SWED is the thing, not men, and the more SWED the better. Rout people out of their beds, abolish arm chairs and hammocks, away with lolling on the beach or anywhere else, down with unused resources, with the vacant gaze and the cowlike meditation—to work, to arms, to something, increase Manpower, get out the SWED.

All this is fine and rousing. The only trouble with SWED is that it does not exist. There is no Single Well Defined End of Society, measured in bushels or gollops or even dollars. There are a great many different ends of a great many different people, some of which are competitive, some complementary, and some independent. Moreover, there is no such thing as manpower, save as a hot abstraction to be handled with long tongs. Not Manpower, but Men—with this cry I propose to arouse the populace to the threat which menaces them. I repeat, not manpower, but men: men in their infinite variety and sacredness, in their complex personalities and unfolding desires. Man as Manpower is all very well for a slave society, where man is a domestic animal, to be used for ends which are alien to him. But in a free society man is not manpower; he is not a donkey chained to a great churn for the production of SWED. He is a free being, the lord of society and not its slave, the creator of demand as well as of supply. In these days we are all in danger of being overcome by the great Feudal myth of Society, a frowning overlord to whom we are all too subservient, even if he has the impressive title of Lord National Interest or even Lord Social Interest.

I am sure that I cannot go on ranting in this vein for long without being called an anarchist, a rank, selfish individualist, or even perhaps an economist. I must confess that I like the anarchists and find them much more sympathetic than the socialists, but I must confess also that I have never quite been able to make the grade as an anarchist. There do seem to be, I regretfully conclude whenever I think about it, certain minimum functions of those attempted monopolies of coercion which arrogate to themselves the name of "governments." It will be useful, however, to start with a model of society which is as close to anarchy as we can get, to see what the "manpower" problem looks like under these conditions. Then we may be able to detect certain defects in the model which will lead to clarification of the nature of the minimum functions of government.

Let us suppose then a society in which the functions of government are confined to the definition and protection of private property. What does the "manpower" problem mean under these circumstances? It is a purely theoretical problem, of course, as nobody proposes to do anything about it. Nevertheless there is a theoretical problem, and it is an interesting one. It consists of two questions. The first is what determines the distribution of the population both geographically and between occupational groups—that is, what determines the number of doctors, dentists, shoemakers, and so on, in the various geographical divisions in which the society may be divided. The second is in a sense contained in the first, but is worth stating separately, and it is, what determines how great a proportion of its resources the society devotes to investment in human capital—i.e., to education and training.

The answer to these questions was really stated by Adam Smith, in two famous chapters of his *Wealth of Nations* which are almost the only part of that great work to remain almost completely unscathed and unmodified by the criticisms and discoveries of a hundred and seventy-seven years. If a people are free to move, either geographically or between occupations, then they will move if the gains from moving outweigh the cost. The gains from moving are the *total* differential advantages of the alternative places or occupations. In the case of movements which involve little or no investment and in which the returns are immediate, a simple balance of gain over loss is all that is required. The gains and losses here, it must be emphasized, are *total* gains and losses, not merely monetary or even those which may be measured in terms of money. Thus, a man might reasonably feel that he would not want to move to a situation or occupation with a larger *money* income than the one he now enjoys, because of the differences in the non-monetary advantages of the various occupations —prestige, pleasantness of work, burden of responsibility, nonmarketable goods such as climate and scenery, and so on.

We would then say that the *total* advantages of the two situations or occupations were equal. It is clear that if there were no difficulties or costs of movement of any kind between occupations or locations, that the population would tend to distribute itself in such a way as to make the total advantages of all occupations and situations equal. This is the principle which has been christened the "principle of equal advantage." It must be observed, of course, that when the total advantages of all occupations and locations are equal, the monetary advantages are likely to be very different. The total advantage of any situation is the sum of the monetary and the non-monetary advantages. If the total advantages of all situations are equal, then we would expect to find that the monetary advantages—wages or real incomes— would be high where the net non-monetary advantage is low, and low where the net non-monetary advantage is high. Thus, other things being equal (and I shall add later that they seldom are), we would expect pleasant, honorable, and decent occupations to be rather poorly paid, and unpleasant, dishonorable, and indecent occupations to be rather well paid. In the interests of charity, prudence, and friendship, I refrain from giving examples.

The principle of equal advantage must, of course, be modified when there are obstacles, natural or artificial, to the movement of people between occupations or locations. Differences in total advantage may be thought of as different levels of potential, like the level of water in different tanks. Potential differences tend to be eliminated by movement, but if the movement is impeded by resistances then the potential differences can persist for long periods or even indefinitely. The "costs" of movement should not perhaps be thought of as resistances, but as subtractions from the total advantages of the various occupations. Nevertheless, there are real resistances to movement which establish permanent differences even in the total advantages of different occupations and locations.

There are, for instance, certain occupations which require very scarce natural abilities. These abilities represent, as it were, a fence around the occupation preventing all but the most agile from getting into it. Under such circumstances the number inside the fence will be small enough to make the total advantages, on anybody's scale of preferences, high compared to the advantages of outside occupations. Yet, because of the natural scarcity of the peculiar abilities required, there is no net movement into the occupation sufficient to equalize the advantages. There may also be "artificial" barriers to entry into certain occupations or locations, in the form of high professional entrance requirements, high trade union initiation fees, "caste" relationships whereby only those connected by family with the existing tenants of the occupations are allowed to enter it, immigration restrictions into favored countries, and so on. Any of these restrictions on entry will prevent equilibrating movements in the form of *transfers* of individuals from locations or occupations of low total advantage to those of high total advantage.

Here, however, it may be well to notice a certain qualification introduced by the fact that people are born and die. We must not think of the distribution of the human population as consisting of apportioning a fixed population of unchanging individuals among various categories. The proportion and the absolute numbers of people in different occupations or locations change not merely because individuals *change* their situation, but because there are various rates of exit by death and entry by birth or by training. It is instructive in this connection to consider the theory of a pure caste society in which every occupation is a caste recruited only by birth and vacated only by death, and in which no individual can move from the occupation into which he is born. It might be thought that in such a society there is absolutely no principle regulating the proportion of people in different occupations. Such, however, is not the case. We can still appeal to the famous subsistence theory, and suppose that in each caste the population will increase by natural increase as long as the returns to the occupation permit it, but that in each caste also, as the numbers increase the returns will tend to diminish, and, when returns have diminished to the point where the population within the caste no longer grows, equilibrium has been reached. In such a society, then, the average income of each caste in equilibrium will be that at which it will just reproduce itself. If the only checks on the increase of population in any caste are starvation and misery, as in the classical Malthusian model, then the population will grow until it is sufficiently starved and miserable to prevent continuing growth. If, however, economic or other considerations can prevent the increase in population before the physical subsistence level is reached, then, of course, by voluntarily restricting its population a caste in such a society could maintain high levels of income indefinitely.

Most actual societies lie somewhere between the "pure caste" society and the absolutely "free" society. The "defense" of any group which maintains advantages higher than other groups then consists partly in the restriction of their natural increase, partly in the encouragement of emigration from the group (consider, for instance, the importance of younger sons in the establishment of colonial empires), and partly in the discouragement of immigration into the group. In addition, there may also be efforts directed toward increasing the demand for the product of the group, which would permit any given size of group to obtain higher advantages.

The principle of equal advantage, suitably modified by considerations of immobility, is sufficient to determine the distribution of real income among the different groups of society. It is not in itself sufficient to determine the number or the proportion of the population in each group. Such can very easily be determined, however, if we introduce a function for each group relating the total number of people in the group with the total real income of the group. This function, it should be observed, is then sufficient to determine both the average and the marginal real income of the group. If, for instance, we know that for a certain group 100 members would receive a total income of $500,000 and 101 members would receive a total income of $503,000, we can readily calculate the average income and also the marginal income for each size of group: a group of 100 would have an average income of $5,000, and the income of the 101st member would be $3,000. Suppose we call this function the "total real income function" for each group.

If the equilibrium of the distribution of the population is to be stable, the marginal income function must be a decreasing function—that is to say, the increase in the numbers in each group must result in a decline in the marginal income of the group. Otherwise, the movement of population between groups, whether by natural increase or decrease or by immigration and emigration, will have perverse effects on the potential differences which gave rise to it. Thus, suppose we have two groups, one of which enjoys a larger marginal total advantage than the other. We should expect a shift in the distribution of population so that the more advantaged group will grow relative to the less advantaged group. If this movement, however, results in the richer group getting still richer as it grows larger, and the poorer group getting still poorer as it grows smaller, obviously the movement is carrying us away from equilibrium, and the movement in response to the gap between the prosperity of the two groups is actually widening the gap rather than lowering it. Only if the transfer of relative numbers makes the rich poorer and the poor richer will it work toward a stable equilibrium. This does not mean, as we have seen, that in equilibrium all groups are in fact equally rich, only that the differences among them are not sufficient to overcome the resistances to change.

Let us inquire further, then, into the nature and determinants of the total income function for each group. Let us assume first, what is not actually quite true, that the marginal non-monetary advantages for each group are independent of the numbers in the group. Then the marginal total advantage depends only on the marginal real income. This in turn depends on two other factors: the productivity or efficiency of the group in producing its own product, and the "terms of trade" of the group—that is, the rate of exchange between its own product (which it sells) and other products which it buys. Thus, the total real income of the group is the *product* of its own output and the "price" or purchasing power of its output in terms of other things. If we take money as representing the "other things," it is clear that the income of a group is equal to the physical output of its product multiplied by the price of that product, and that the group's income can rise either because its physical output increases or because the price (i.e. the purchasing power per unit) of its product increases.

Why, then, should the marginal income of a group decline as its size increases? The answer must be found either in a decline in physical productivity, in the sense that successive additions to the population of the group result in successively smaller additions to physical product, or it must be found in a decline in the price or (marginal) purchasing power of the product as the amount which has to be sold increases. Both these things are likely to happen when the size of the group increases beyond a certain critical point. When the group is very small the movements may be reversed. That is to say, the growth of very small groups may actually result in an increase in their marginal physical productivity as an increase in numbers permits better organization, greater internal division of labor, and so on. It is even possible that at small volumes of sales, increased sales result in better terms of trade, again largely because of the greater specialization, or, perhaps, because of dynamic influences such as the growth of habits of consumption, and the reinforcement of demand by experience. Nevertheless, these upward movements cannot persist indefinitely. A point must come eventually when "diminishing returns" set in, both in the form of decreasing marginal physical productivity as the group grows large, and worsening terms of trade as its sales grow larger.

Suppose, then, for each group we know how much product will be produced at each level of population of the group. Suppose, also, that we know at what price each quantity of produce can be sold, so that we know also what will be the *value* in dollars or some other measure of each quantity of product. Then we know for each group what will be its total income at each level of population, and by comparing the total income at two adjacent levels of population we can find the *marginal* income at each level of population. Now, given the total population of the society, we can find how it must be distributed among the various groups so that the marginal incomes in each group are *equal*. This might be described as the first approximation to equilibrium. We can then approach a second approximation by showing how some groups maintain higher marginal incomes than others by being able to restrict their populations, either by natural or by artificial means.

A meaningful *equilibrium* distribution of the population among various groups is possible even if there is no single end of society, simply through the ecological interaction of the innumerable desires of innumerable people. What I have been describing is, of course, the famous "invisible hand" of Adam Smith—this extraordinary process in the operation of a market society whereby resources are in fact apportioned in what seems to be a fairly reasonable way, not by planning from above, not by the government telling anybody what he has to do or how he has to do it, but by the persistent pressure of the principle of equal advantage whereby if anybody knows of a better hole he goes to it if he can. This is the great principle which Adam Smith calls "natural liberty."

If now we are to justify governmental intervention in the allocation of human resources we must show in what regard either the equilibrium, or the process of moving toward the equilibrium of "natural liberty" is undesirable according to fairly well defined standards of judgment. That is, we must justify divergences from the state of splendid anarchy. Some divergences are, of course, fairly easy to justify in principle, though the question of *how much* divergence is desirable is always a matter of dispute. Not even the most anarchistic of liberal economists would deny the existence of certain "collective wants" which the mere apparatus of the market does not, and cannot, provide. There are certain "overheads" of society which are difficult to charge for on the basis of service rendered to individuals, mainly because of the cost of collection, as in the case of roads, or because of certain undesirable sociological relations which would be introduced by too strict adherence to the principles of the market, as in the case of police and justice, or because there are certain economies of monopoly, as in the case of the post office and certain public utilities. The case for the market, or at least for the abolition of state monopolies, is stronger in some of these instances than is generally imagined, but I am not disposed to argue these cases at the moment.

It should be observed, however, that the provision of these collective wants is generally accomplished through the system of public *finance*, not by any system of forced labor. That is to say, the state distorts the "natural" system of distribution of the labor force by providing a monetary demand for certain products and services. If inflation is to be avoided, of course, this monetary demand on the part of the state must be offset by a contraction of monetary demand on the part of private persons and institutions, a contraction which is generally accomplished through taxation. What we have here is the state nosing its way into the general system of equilibrium, attracting resources to itself, but not essentially destroying the operation of the principle of equal advantage. Men go into occupations which they would not otherwise have done because it has been made advantageous for them to do so through the financial power of the state, not because they have been forced unwillingly into these occupations by the threat of the police power.

We can see the distinction clearly if we contrast the feudal method of road building through the corvée—i.e., forced labor on the roads— with the modern method of road building through finance, i.e., through finding money to hire people to work on the roads. In both cases road building requires the withdrawal of resources from other uses. In the case of the corvée, this withdrawal is accomplished directly by the whip. In modern states the withdrawal is accomplished indirectly, either because the consumption of the mass of the people is restricted in some degree by taking money away from them through taxes or loans, or because it is restricted through inflation.

On the whole, the movement of the past few hundred years has been away from the "manpower" concept of directed or forced allocation of human resources toward the "financial" concept of the organization of human resources through the market. Slavery has been abolished. Serfdom has been largely abolished, corvées and press gangs have vanished. Only in one conspicuous area of life has this process been reversed. The last great stronghold of the manpower concept is, of course, in the armed forces. The growth of conscription represents a striking reversal of the movement toward a society of natural liberty, and it is a reversal which unfortunately seems to be gathering momentum. Conscription, like the corvée, is an attempt to satisfy a collective want by the exercise of the police power (the threat of legal penalties, prison, etc.) rather than by the financial power. The status of the conscript is technically similar to that of a temporary serf—he cannot leave his unchosen occupation before his time is up; he is outside the regular law and is rather at the mercy of his feudal superiors in the officer class. The conscript is "exploited" in the sense that because of the exercise of the police power it is possible to employ him at a much lower wage than would be necessary to attract him to his occupation in a free society. It is a device for forcing a major part of the economic burden of national defense on the unexempted young, and as such inevitably results in gross anomalies and inequalities. It is unquestionably the most disastrous social invention of the past two hundred years, and I find it difficult to forgive the French for inventing it. They have, however, had their reward. Where it has been long practiced, it results in an almost universal corruption of society, a decline in its morals and in its morale, a decay of that unfeigned and unforced love of country which is the only sure foundation even of military success, and the weakening of that exercise of free choice and the voluntary spirit which is the prerequisite of a healthy democracy.

Let me now try to apply some of these principles to the problem of the education and training of the professional classes. Suppose we return for a moment to the model of natural liberty, and see how a professional class arises and how its numbers are determined, in case we might be under the illusion that if government did not intervene there would be no doctors to cure us or parsons to bury us. Clearly, given a demand on the part of existing groups for professional services, then, if the numbers in the professions are "too small," there will be high remuneration for professional people and their numbers will grow until the net advantages of the professions are low enough to prevent any addition to their population. If there are so many professional people that their marginal remuneration is too small to make it worth their while entering the professions, recruitment will drop off, some will transfer themselves bodily to more advantageous occupations, and the numbers will decline. There seems to be nothing here which would lead to a breakdown of the principle of equal advantage.

There are, however, some complications. Entering the professions requires *investment* in education. The equilibrium value of professional incomes is that in which the excess over non-professional incomes is just sufficient to attract enough recruits in over the "wall" of the long and expensive education. We can calculate the rate of return on investment in education roughly—indeed, it has frequently been done. The greater the excess of professional incomes over non-professional, and the less the cost of education, the greater the rate of return. If the rate of return is "too great," many people will be induced to invest in professional education, and the numbers in the professions will increase and the differential advantage of the professions will fall. Here, again, it seems as if the introduction of the investment concept really makes no difference to the general principle: so far there seems to be no reason for regarding the professions as a "problem" requiring active intervention of government.

Now, however, I feel myself pursued by a host of indignant voices. What—am I arguing against education, that most sacred of all cows! Would I indeed leave education to private enterprise, to be enjoyed only by those whose parents can afford to pay! Do I believe in aristocracy, in a class society, in the perpetuation of privilege, in the shocking waste of talent and ability which goes on, even in our society, among the poor? If I can make my voice heard above the cries of indignation, I hasten to say Nay, indeed Nay! I would be indeed ungrateful if I spurned the very educational ladder up which I myself, by dint of being good at passing examinations, have scrambled. I have been making an extreme case, because it is comforting, to me at any rate, to realize that in spite of all the clamors that Something should be Done about Everything, if Nothing is Done about Anything at least the world will not come to an end, and, indeed, might have a better fighting chance of survival than it has now.

Let us then consider exactly *why* Something should be Done, which is the same question as why the equilibrium of natural liberty is not the *best* position possible. There are several good reasons why a position of natural liberty might not be optimal. In the first place, there may be a divergence between perceived private advantage and actual social advantage. In the market economy it is perceived private advantage which is the motive force, the potential difference which orders the distribution of resources. Perceived private advantage may differ from some reasonable if vague concept of social advantage for several reasons. There may be ignorance—i.e., a divergence between perceived and actual private advantage. There are situations in which ignorance is bliss, but this is probably not one of them. What we mean by ignorance in this situation is that there are people who do not now think it worth while to change their jobs or to undertake investment in education, but who, if they did these things, would finally be glad they had done them. If people are ignorant of their ignorance, there clearly cannot be any demand on their part for knowledge, and there is a clear case here for an omniscient government to undertake the provision of occupational and educational information, and a good case even for real governments doing so.

In the second place, there may be private monopoly, in which differential advantages are perceived but in which the organization of the professional group is designed to limit numbers and so perpetuate the differential advantages. Most of the professions are highly suspect in this regard, especially the medical profession, where monopolistic restriction of entry under the guise of high professional standards has been so great that it has resulted in the development of a number of sub-professions ranging from the osteopath to the Christian Science Practitioner who undercut the regular medicos in the sickness market. The most foolish and public spirited of all professions in this regard is, of course, my own. The teaching profession not merely fails to restrict its numbers, except perhaps through the relatively trivial device of the Ph.D., but actually encourages young people to enter it by the provision of scholarships and financial assistance of all kinds. Where these private professional monopolies exist, there is a clear case for undermining them by government action.

The third reason for a possible divergence between natural liberty and public interest is the existence of non-appropriable or unidentifiable benefits or misfortunes. This is the problem which is generally discussed in economics under the name of "external economies," positive or negative. What this means is that there are certain costs and returns which do not get into the private accounting system but which nevertheless must be included in any public appraisal of the contribution of any group or occupation. The man who beautifies his garden improves the value of his neighbors' property, but there is generally no way in which he can collect from the neighbors. The cost of collection from the enjoyers of some benefit or the perpetrators of some evil may be too great to make the attempt worth while, if the benefits and evils are very diffuse. This argument is particularly strong in the case of investment in education, where the benefits are great and yet are much too diffuse to be appropriated. This, perhaps, is the strongest reason for supposing that the mechanism of the market cannot be relied upon to yield an optimum position.

The fourth reason is that there may be inadequate arrangements in some fields, notably education, for the *finance* of investment. Investment in professional education is usually extremely profitable. One would think, therefore, that the impecunious but able student should be able to finance his education by means of loans, for, if rates of interest are moderate, the rate of return on his investment in education will be so large that he will still be much better off even after repaying the loan. Here, however, what might be called social risk and individual risk differ, and an investment which is clearly profitable for society is risky and difficult for the private supplier of funds, because of the difficulty of knowing just who, in advance, are the people who will justify the investment. I confess that I do not see any fundamental reason why specialized lending institutions in the finance of education should not have developed; the lack of such institutions, however, clearly indicates that there may be good reasons for their non-existence.

I seem to have argued myself out of my most extreme positions. There is, of course, a strong case for state support and intervention in professional training. But still a word of warning should be issued. The effect of the subsidization of *entry* into the professions, through the diminution of the private cost of education to the individual who gets its, inevitably results in a diminution of the different *returns* to education. This is not to be complained of; it is, indeed, one of the fundamental objects of such subsidization. We must distinguish the effect of this *cheapening* of professional services, which is a movement on the "supply side" from an increase in the quantity of professional services which comes from changes on the "demand side." The problem is complicated by a degree of interrelation between supply and demand, in that part of the demand for professional people arises from the necessity of passing on the skills to the next generation. Indeed, in the obscurer arts and sciences this constitutes almost the sole demand. These complications aside, however, the question of whether it is cheaper for society to subsidize demand or to subsidize supply is a very interesting and difficult one, and unfortunately is beyond the scope of this paper. There is a certain presumption, I think, in favor of subsidizing supply; the case, however, is not a clear one, especially if the subsidization of one part of the supply results in a decline in some other part of the supply. We might find, for instance, that extensive subsidization of professional training so lowered the returns to such training that no private capital went into it, and the state would find itself taking over the whole burden of the investment. On the other hand, if both supply and demand are rather elastic, a subsidization of demand (e.g., by providing public health service in the case of the doctors) might bring about a considerable expansion of the profession at rather small cost to the state.

The problem which the Ford Foundation faced in its attempt to expand the "behavioral sciences" is an interesting case in point: should the Foundation offer scholarships and bursaries to make it easy for young men to become "behavioral scientists," or should it subsidize the "demand" for behavioral scientists by "buying" research, etc.? This is not, of course, an either/or proposition—a little of both is usually indicated—but how much of one or the other gives the best results is a hard question to decide.

I suppose what I am ultimately protesting about in the manpower concept is its delusive simplicity. There has grown up in recent years a wave of protest against the use of financial standards and criteria and methods, some of which is perhaps justified. It is true, of course, that finance is a "veil" which hides the physical realities of the economic system, and that money is merely a symbol for men and things. It is tempting, therefore, to draw up "manpower budgets" in terms of "needs and requirements," to say that we "need" so many doctors or dentists or economists (?) per head of the population, and that if by these standards there is a deficiency of doctors in Dahomey or economists in Ethiopia, the answer is simply for somebody to send them there. This approach to the problem unfortunately neglects the no doubt deplorable multidimensionality of life and society and the immense variety of men, things, places, and cultures. For purposes of thought and decision it is true, we do have to force this multidimensionality into some kind of simple linear indices. We find it easy to perceive that one line is longer than another or that one number is larger than another. It is very hard to perceive immediately whether one great multidimensional splodge is larger or smaller, better or worse, than another great multidimensional splodge. Yet, reality is always a splodge; the lines and the numbers are always abstractions.

What I have been arguing is that the "manpower" abstraction is appallingly crude, and that the attempt to think of the problem of allocation as if it were simply a matter of counting noses not only misses most of the realities of the case, but leads inevitably to a *solution* in terms of a monolithic, military, communistic type of society in which allocation is made by threat of violence imposed by superior members of a hierarchy. The financial abstraction is still, of course, a crude abstraction from reality, and it is only a place to start from, not a place to rest in. But it does lead to the notion of a "multilithic" society, not dominated by any single will but guided by the interaction of the wills of all its members. Granted that the financial mechanism should not remain unmodified. But it should be modified, not destroyed.

AN APPLICATION OF POPULATION ANALYSIS TO THE AUTOMOBILE POPULATION OF THE UNITED STATES

Kyklos, 2 (1955): 109-124.

AN APPLICATION OF POPULATION
ANALYSIS TO THE AUTOMOBILE
POPULATION OF THE UNITED STATES

The principal purpose of this article is to estimate the influence of the distortion of the age distribution in the American automobile population on future replacements. The distortion in question was a result of the Second World War, when no private automobiles were produced for a period of over three years. The conclusion is reached that on fairly reasonable assumptions this distortion is likely to produce a deficiency in replacements which will rise to 600,000 per annum by about 1959, and then will rapidly disappear.

The method used is that of population analysis. This is one of the simplest, yet most fruitful applications of difference equation analysis, and can be applied to the projection ot the future course of any system which conforms to the basic concept of a population. There are four essential characteristics of such a system. (i) There must be a "population", consisting of an aggregate of objects, each of which conforms to a common definition. (ii) The aggregate must be augmented by "births" (the addition of objects to the aggregate which conform to the common definition) and diminished by "deaths" (the subtraction of such objects). (iii) It must be possible to divide the total aggregate into *age groups*, each consisting of objects in the same age range. (iv) Births and deaths in any one period ("year") must be functionally related in stable, well defined ways to the numbers in the different age groups in present or earlier years. If these birth and death functions are given, the course of the population, both in regard to its size, age composition, and annual births and deaths in each age group, can be projected through time, given one "present" size and composition.

Most of the applications of population analysis have been to human or other biological populations. There is no reason, however, why it cannot be applied to inanimate populations conforming to the above conditions. In particular it can be applied to populations of capital goods which conform to the essential conditions. The production of the goods constitutes its "birth", and its destruction, "death". The stability of the death or survival[1] functions, relating numbers destroyed or surviving each year to the numbers in the different age groups, is probably as great as for biological populations. The birth functions of goods differ markedly from those of biological populations, where it is usually reasonable to assume fairly stable relationships between the numbers in certain reproductive age groups and the number of births. Nevertheless it is possible to postulate birth functions for capital goods based on certain other considerations. We might assume, for instance, that the total population is to be stable, in which case the number of births in each year must be equal to the number of deaths, or we might assume that the population is to grow by a given amount, in which case the number of births must equal the number of deaths plus the increase in the population.

Table 1

Year	Births	Age Groups			
		0–1	1–2	2–3	3–4
0	B	a_0	b_0	c_0	d_0
1	B	Bs_1	$a_0\dfrac{s_2}{s_1}$	$b_0\dfrac{s_3}{s_2}$	$c_0\dfrac{s_4}{s_3}$
2	B	Bs_1	Bs_2	$a_0\dfrac{s_3}{s_1}$	$b_0\dfrac{s_4}{s_2}$
3	B	Bs_1	Bs_2	Bs_3	$a_0\dfrac{s_4}{s_1}$
4	B	Bs_1	Bs_2	Bs_3	Bs_4
5	B	Bs_1	Bs_2	Bs_3	Bs_4

1. A survival function is merely an alternative way of stating a death function, for if a proportion d of any group dies during a year, a proportion $(1-d)$ survives into the next year.

To make these processes clear, suppose we have a population of four age groups, 0–1, 1–2, 2–3 and 3–4 years. No member of the population survives the fourth year. Suppose then that we have a stable survival distribution such that out of each cohort of births B_0 in year 0, $B_0 s_1$ will survive to year 1, $B_0 s_2$ to year 2, and so on, the coefficients s_1, s_2—being constant. Suppose that we start with any age grouping, say a_0 between 0 and 1, b_0 between 1 and 2, c_0 between 2 and 3, and d_0 between 3 and 4. Suppose first that the number of births in each year is constant at B. Then the course of the population will be as in Table 1.

Thus, following the diagonal arrows, we see that the births B of year 0 become $B s_1$ individuals in the 0–1 age group of year 1, $B s_2$ individuals in the 1–2 age group of year 2, and so on. The proportion of the number in age group 0–1 which survives to the next year is $\frac{s_2}{s_1}$. The number a_0 in age group 0–1 of year 0 therefore becomes $a_0 \frac{s_2}{s_1}$ in age group 1–2 of year 1. The other values are derived similarly. By the year 4 an equilibrium population is reached, no matter what age grouping we start with. The number of deaths in each year can also be calculated. Thus in year 0 the number of "infant" deaths is $B - B s_1$, or $B(1 - s_1)$; that is, of the B births only $B s_1$ survive to be one year old. Similarly in the 0–1 age group the number of deaths is $a_0 (1 - \frac{s_2}{s_1})$, and the total number of deaths,

$$D_0 = B(1 - s_1) + a_0\left(1 - \frac{s_2}{s_1}\right) + b_0\left(1 - \frac{s_3}{s_2}\right) + c_0\left(1 - \frac{s_4}{s_3}\right) + d_0$$

Table 2

Year	Births	0–1	1–2	2–3	3–4	Population	Deaths
		Age Groups					
0	B_0	a_0	b_0	c_0	d_0	P_0	D_0
1	B_1	a_1	b_1	c_1	d_1	P_1	D_1
2	B_2	a_2	b_2	c_2	d_2	P_2	D_2

The number of deaths in each year can similarly be calculated. In the fourth and all subsequent years we have

$$D_4 = B(1-s_1) + B(s_1-s_2) + B(s_2-s_3) + B(s_3-s_4) + B(s_4) = B$$

That is, births equal deaths, which is the condition for an equilibrium population. The total population in each year, of course, is the sum of the numbers in each age group. The increase in population is the number of births minus the number of deaths.

The economic significance of this model is that it enables us to

Table 3

Number of Passenger Automobiles (ooo's) by

Age Groups (Years)

Year	0–1	1–2	2–3	3–4	4–5	5–6	6–7	7–8	8–9	9–10	10–11	11
1935	1386	1807	1420	1050	1867	2362	3613	2439	1526	1282	1565[a]	
1936	2181	2378	1825	1422	1051	1851	2288	3405	2160	1232	2105[a]	
1937	2383	3324	2351	1824	1409	1041	1816	2164	3048	1771	2365[a]	
1938	1231	3536	3262	2261	1759	1333	975	1682	1914	2481	2832[a]	
1939	1822	1739	3532	3261	2258	1759	1326	954	1610	1738	4232[a]	
1940	2321	2423	1746	3499	3234	2220	1697	1250	865	1438	4675[a]	
1941	3240	3112	2402	1733	3481	3175	2139	1591	1120	735	1211	12
1942												
1943												
1944			878	3941	3067	2336	1657	3252	2792	1639	1004	6
1945												
1946	448	0	0	0	997	4107	3182	2426	1736	3390	2893	16
1947	1367	2056	0	0	0	1065	4086	3113	2379	1679	3304	27
1948	1673	3100	2048	0	0	0	1012	4004	3093	2345	1662	31
1949	2638	2981	3066	2047	0	0	0	1006	4005	3089	2326	16
1950	2989	4935	3033	3052	2032	0	0	0	999	3955	3033	22
1951	2858	6114	4988	2964	2987	1975	0	0	0	966	3761	27
1952	1831	5387	6202	4969	2943	2953	1942	0	0	0	892	34

[a] Includes all subsequent age groups

predict what will happen to the total population (and age composition) of a category of capital goods if (1) production is constant from year to year and (2) the survival distributions are constant. The number of "births" in each year is the number of units produced. The number of "deaths" is the number of units destroyed (consumed). This is the "replacement quota"—that is the amount of production that would be necessary in that year to keep the total stock of the goods constant. The excess of births over deaths is the "growth quota".

Table 3

oups, U.S.A. 1935–1952 (R. L. Polk data)

Age Groups (Years)									Total Registration (Polk Data)	Privately Owned Cars Total Registration (U.S. Bureau of Public Roads)
2–13	13–14	14–15	15–16	16–17	17–18	18–19	19+	Not Given		
								432	20317	22495
								397	21898	24108
								346	23496	25391
								272	23266	25167
								278	24231	26140
								188	25316	27732
278	561	502[a]						215	27700	29254
										27869
										25913
369	642	624	576	403[a]					23782	25466
										25691
021	607	369	626	592	889[a]			185	25143	28100
592	967	568	346	596	1377[a]			236	27521	30719
657	1490	886	509	317	1732[a]			253	29968	33214
075	2495	1335	762	435	1738[a]			112	32731	36312
490	2709	2074	1053	567	1657[a]			100	35922	40185
996	1244	2126	1493	688	1451[a]			110	38516	42525
496	1687	973	1541	996	430	207	768[a]	99	39770	43646

More complex projections can be made if we suppose that the total population in each year is given. Table 2 shows the general case in our notation. Given a_0, b_0, c_0, d_0 and the survival coefficients we can calculate $b_1 = a_0\frac{s_2}{s_1}$, $c_1 = b_0\frac{s_3}{s_2}$, $d_1 = c_0\frac{s_4}{s_3}$. If now we are given P_1 we can calculate $a_1 = P_1 - (b_1 + c_1 + d_1)$. Then as $a_1 = B_0 s_1$, we can calculate $B_0 = \frac{a_1}{s_1}$. B_0 is the number of births we would need in year 0 in order to give us the required population P_1 in year 1. Similarly given P_2 we can calculate B_1, the number of births required in year 1 to give a population P_2 in year 2, and so on indefinitely.

This projection will predict the annual *production* of a good, on the assumption of a constant survival distribution and any given movement of the total stock (population).

Almost the only capital goods for which we have data on age and survival distributions, thanks to the accident of licensing, are the automobile and the truck. There is an opportunity here, therefore, to apply population analysis to these populations and to make projections of the types indicated above. Passenger automobiles, as the largest and most important group, have been selected for study.

The first step is to study the survival distributions. Table 3 shows the basic data, collected by R. L. Polk and Co. from registration figures and published in various annual editions of *Automobile Facts and Figures*. It will be observed that there is a discrepancy between the totals given by the Polk data and the totals given by the U.S. Bureau of Public Roads. This is almost entirely to be accounted for by the difference in date of the two counts: the Polk data are collected on July 1st, the U.S. Public Roads data on December 31st. The Polk data therefore underestimate the registrations of new cars, and the figures for the 0–1 age group therefore cannot be used.

In Table 4 then we show the *proportion* which has survived from the previous year in each age group. Thus in Table 3 the 1232 thousand aged 9–10 in the year 1936 are the survivors of 1526 thousand aged 8–9 in the year 1935: the ratio $\frac{1232}{1526} = .8073$ is put in the 9–10 age group of year 1936 in Table 4. Some interesting conclusions follow immediately even from the rather incomplete data of Table 4. It is clear that the automobile is getting more *durable*—the annual

Table 4

Proportion of Passenger Automobiles which have Survived from the Previous Year in each Age Group

Year	2-3	3-4	4-5	5-6	6-7	7-8	8-9	9-10	10-11	11-12	12-13	13-14	14-15	15-16	16-17	17-18
1936	1.010	1.001	1.001	.9914	.9687	.9424	.8856	.8073								
1937	.9886	.9995	.9909	.9905	.9811	.9458	.8952	.8199								
1938	.9813	.9617	.9644	.9461	.9364	.9262	.8845	.8140								
1939	.9987	.9997	.9987	1.000	.9947	.9785	.9572	.9080								
1940	1.0040	.9906	.9917	.9832	.9648	.9427	.9067	.8932								
1941	.9913	.9925	.9949	.9818	.9635	.9375	.8960	.8497	.8421							
1947				1.0682	.9949	.9783	.9806	.9672	.9746	.9644	.9504	.9471	.9357	.9377	.9520	
1948	.9961				.9502	.9799	.9936	.9857	.9899	.9643	.9523	.9359	.9162	.8961	.9162	
1949	.9890	.9995				.9941	1.0002	.9987	.9918	.9753	.9652	.9390	.8960	.8600	.8546	
1950	1.017	.9954	.9927				.9930	.9875	.9819	.9647	.9192	.8810	.8313	.7888	.7441	
1951	1.0107	.9773	.9787	.9719				.9670	.9509	.9212	.8895	.8349	.7848	.7199	.6534	
1952	1.0144	.9962	.9929	.9886	.9832				.9234	.9189	.8933	.8452	.7822	.7248	.6671	.6250

survival ratios increase, in the 6–10 age groups from 1936 to 1952. The very high survival ratios in the immediate post war years is noticeable: also a decline in survival ratios in the older age groups since the war. This is to be expected with the increasing abundance of cars.

It is clear also that by 1952 the survival ratios had stabilized themselves—at least there is not much change from 1951 to 1952. It is not unreasonable therefore to project the population on the assumption that the annual survival ratios of 1952 will persist. It will be observed that some of the annual survival ratios are greater than 1. This is of course impossible, and is simply a reflection of inaccuracy in the data. For the sake of simplicity then it was assumed that the survival ratios for the first two years were 1.0 and that all cars produced in each year survived into the next year. The survival distribution given by the data does not go beyond the 17–18 year age group. It was necessary to make a projection of the survival distribution beyond this age group, otherwise a serious error would be introduced into the population projections. If the survival distribution is not projected beyond this point the assumption is in effect made that none of the 17–18 year old cars survive the year. The number of cars in the 17–18 year group is still large enough so that this assumption would introduce serious error. The annual survival coefficients for 1952 were therefore plotted and the graph projected to the 22–23 year age group, numbers beyond this point being too small to make serious difference to the analysis. The annual and cumulative coefficients used in the projections are given in Table 5. The cumulative survival distribution was calculated from the annual survival ratios by successive multiplication. If v_1, v_2, v_3, etc., are the annual survival ratios for years 0–1, 1–2, 2–3, etc., the cumulative survival distribution will be $s_1 = v_1$, $s_2 = v_1 v_2$, $s_3 = v_1 v_2 v_3$, etc.

Three projections were then made on the basis of this survival distribution, assumed to be constant. The results are summarized in Table 6. Projection (1): Total annual production of cars was assumed to be constant at 5 million. For each year up to 1975 the total car population, the increase in population, and the "replacement quota" (total production less increase in population) was calculated, according to the procedures of Table 1. Projection (2): The automobile population was assumed to remain constant at the estimated 1952 level, 41,408,000, and the annual output required to maintain this constant population calculated. Projection (3): Automobile population was assumed to increase from the 1952 figure (41,408,000) by 2 million per annum, and the annual output required to maintain this rate of increase was calculated. The results are summarized also in Fig. 1. It will be observed that the replacement quota falls by 605,000 between 1953 and 1958, on the assumption of constant annual output of 5,000,000. This means, of course, that in order to maintain a constant annual output the annual increase of the total automobile population must *rise* by 605,000 between 1953 and 1958. Conversely, if the annual increase of the automobile population does *not* rise during this period, production must fall by about 600,000 per annum between 1953 and 1958, as shown in projections 2 and 3. This is the direct result of the distortion in the age distribution resulting from the absence of production in the war years 1942–45. We see that no matter what happens to the automobile population

Table 5

Survival Coefficients

Year	0–1	1–2	2–3	3–4	4–5	5–6
Annual Coefficient	1	1	1	.9962	.9929	.9986
Cumulative Coefficient	1	1	1	.9962	.9891	.9877

Year	6–7	7–8	8–9	9–10	10–11	11–12
Annual Coefficient	.9832	.9684[a]	.9534[a]	.9384[a]	.9234	.9189
Cumulative Coefficient	.9711	.9404	.8966	.8414	.7896	.7255

Year	12–13	13–14	14–15	15–16	16–17	17–18
Annual Coefficient	.8933	.8452	.7822	.7248	.6671	.6250
Cumulative Coefficient	.6481	.5478	.4285	.3106	.2072	.1295

Year	18–19	19–20	20–21	21–22	22–23	
Annual Coefficient	.5700[b]	.5150[b]	.4600[b]	.4100[b]	.3500[b]	
Cumulative Coefficient	.0738	.0380	.0175	.0071	.0025	

a Obtained by interpolation
b Obtained by extrapolation

the deficiency in replacement demand in these years is about the same order of magnitude. In the middle of the 1960's there is likely to be a peak in output due to the large replacements of the large post-war cohorts. This is shown especially clearly in projection 2: if the total auto population rises fast enough the effect will be masked, as in

Table 6

Projections of Automobile Population and Production,
U.S.A. 1952–1975 (000's)

Year	Projection 1 (Annual output = 5,000,000)			Projection 2 (Total population = 41,408,000) Annual Output	Projection 3 (Population rises by 2,000,000 per annum) Annual Output
	Total Population of Autos	Annual Increase in Population	Replacement Quota		
1952	41408			4200	4200
1953	43521	2113	2887	2887	4887
1954	45730	2209	2791	2791	4791
1955	48064	2334	2666	2666	4666
1956	50563	2499	2501	2493	4501
1957	53203	2640	2360	2336	4357
1958	55921	2718	2282	2256	4280
1959	58574	2653	2347	2280	4340
1960	61019	2445	2555	2424	4541
1961	63119	2100	2900	2668	4876
1962	64770	1651	3349	2990	5306
1963	65954	1184	3816	3328	5750
1964	66721	767	4233	3583	6138
1965	67179	458	4542	3704	6415
1966	67440	261	4739	3662	6575
1967	67580	140	4860	3496	6659
1968	67656	76	4934	3287	6694
1969	67961	35	4965	3081	6715
1970	67711	20	4980	2918	6734
1971	67724	13	4987	2804	6764
1972	67731	7	4993	2746	6826
1973	67734	3	4997	2747	6923
1974	67737	3	4997	2789	7060
1975	67739	2	4998	2864	7248

projection 3. It is interesting to note that with an annual output of 5 million (somewhat below the present capacity of the industry, which is certainly between 6 and 7 million) the equilibrium population of automobiles will be reached by about 1970, and will total about 68 million: that is, with this population and the current survival distribution the annual replacements would be 5 million. With a stable survival distribution the ratio of the equilibrium population to the annual production is constant and is equal to the average expectation of life in the equilibrium population. With the present survival distribution this amounts to 13.55 years. That is, for each million autos produced per annum the corresponding equilibrium population of autos is 13,550,000.

It must be emphasized again that these projections do not consti-

Figure 1

Projections of Automobile Output and Replacement
in the United States, 1953–1975

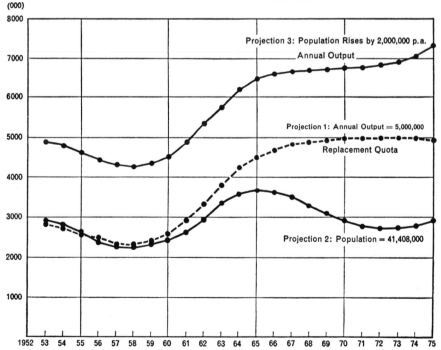

tute predictions, and it may be well to notice what further information would be necessary to make even fairly accurate predictions. We would first have to be sure of the stability of the survival distribution, or at least able to predict the changes in the survival distribution. This is probably the most stable element of the system, nevertheless it could be changed especially in the important middle section where the *total* of "deaths" is large. New models, for instance, may lead to different rates of obsolescence and a changed willingness to scrap old cars. The present distortion of the age distribution is so pronounced, however, that it would be necessary to assume large rates of scrapping in the *young* age groups to overcome its effect. This seems unlikely.

The most unstable element in the system is the growth (or decline) in the automobile population itself. Table 7 shows the total passenger car registrations in the U.S.A. since 1910, the annual increase in registrations, and the annual output. The difference between the output and the increase in population is a measure of replacements. It is not a very satisfactory measure of replacements as it includes cars going into or coming out of storage as well as cars scrapped, the population figure being for registrations, and not therefore including cars in existence but not registered. Thus the negative replacement figures for 1945 and 1946 must represent cars coming out of storage after the war, as the true replacement figure could never be negative. Even with these imperfect figures it is clear that declines in automobile output are strongly related to checks in the growth of the automobile population. Columns 6 and 7 of Table 7, show the increase in output and the increase in population increase (that is, the first differences of columns 4 and 3). In *every* year in which output decreased as compared with the previous year (1918, 21, 24, 27, 30, 31, 32, 38, 42, 43) the population increase declined also. The positive relationship is not so strong or so clear, but it is the decreases in output which create the problems. Further analysis of this problem would involve econometric models along the lines pioneered by C.F. Roos in his famous 1939 essay on the Dynamics of Automobile Demand, and recently developed by M.J. Farrell in his paper on the Demand for Motor Cars in the United States[2]. The problems created by *distortions*

2. *Journal of the Royal Statistical Institute*, Vol. 117, Series A, Pt. 2 (1954), p. 171–201.

Table 7

Automobiles in the United States, Output, Population,
and Replacements (000's)

Year	Total Population	Increase in Population	Annual Output	Replacement	Increase in Output	Increase in Population
1910	458		181		18	
1911	619	161	199	38	157	122
1912	902	283	356	73	105	5
1913	1190	288	461	173	87	186
1914	1664	474	548	74	348	194
1915	2332	668	896	228	630	368
1916	3368	1036	1526	490	220	323
1917	4727	1359	1746	387	− 803	− 531
1918	5555	828	943	115	709	296
1919	6679	1124	1652	528	254	329
1920	8132	1453	1906	453	− 438	− 373
1921	9212	1080	1468	388	806	412
1922	10704	1492	2274	782	1351	1057
1923	13253	2549	3625	1076	− 439	− 366
1924	15436	2183	3186	1003	549	− 179
1925	17440	2004	3735	1731	49	− 223
1926	19221	1781	3784	2003	− 847	− 860
1927	20142	921	2937	2016	838	245
1928	21308	1166	3775	2609	680	586
1929	23060	1752	4455	2703	−1668	−1839
1930	22973	− 87	2787	2874	− 839	− 556
1931	22330	− 643	1948	2591	− 844	− 855
1932	20832	−1498	1104	2602	457	1252
1933	20586	− 246	1561	1807	600	1402
1934	21742	1156	2161	1005	1113	− 403
1935	22495	753	3274	2521	405	860
1936	24108	1613	3679	2066	250	− 330
1937	25391	1283	3929	2646	−1909	−1507
1938	25167	− 224	2020	2244	869	1197
1939	26140	973	2889	1916	828	259
1940	27372	1232	3717	2485	63	920

Year	Total Population	Increase in Population	Annual Output	Replacement	Increase in Output	Increase in Population
1941	29524	2152	3780	1628	3557	−3807
1942	27869	−1655	223	1878	− 223	− 301
1943	25913	−1956	0	1956	1	1509
1944	25466	− 447	1	448	69	672
1945	25691	225	70	−155	2079	2184
1946	28100	2409	2149	−260	1409	210
1947	30719	2619	3558	939	351	− 124
1948	33214	2495	3909	1414	1210	603
1949	36312	3098	5119	2021	1547	775
1950	40185	3873	6666	2793	−1328	−1533
1951	42525	2340	5338	2998	−1017	−1219
1952	43640	1121	4321	3200		

in age distribution however have been somewhat neglected by these writers, and it is the limited purpose of this paper to estimate the order of magnitude of this distortion effect. The conclusion is that the size of the effect is large enough to make it an essential component of any predictions made during the next few years. Whether the decline and subsequent rise in output due to this distortion effect would itself have multiplier effects only a detailed econometric model could reveal; the possibility of these multipliers cannot however be left out of account. The general inference seems to be that the distortion effect creates a real hazard for the automobile industry, and indirectly for the whole American economy, at least until the end of the 1950's. If we add to the impact on the automobile industry similar effects in other durable goods industries, the magnitude of which cannot even be estimated for want of information in regard to age and survival distributions, the desirability of further information in this area is clearly indicated.

SUMMARY

Population analysis is the application of difference equation analysis to the projection of various variables associated with a population, such as its size, the numbers in different age groups, births and deaths. It is usually applied to biological populations, but it can equally well be applied to populations of inanimate objects such as capital goods.

The main object of the present article is to estimate the influence of the age distortion of the population of automobiles in the United States on future replacement demand. The distortion arose because no automobiles were produced for more than three years during the Second World War.

Data on age distributions of automobiles in the United States are available. The annual survival ratios were calculated for a series of years and for as many age groups as are available, the survival ratio being the ratio of the number in any age group to the number in the previous age group of the year before. The table of survival ratios shows some stability by 1952, so that with some interpolation and extrapolation a survival table was obtained for use in the projections. On the basis of this survival table three projections were made: (i) Assuming a constant annual output of 5,000,000 cars, the total automobile population, the growth in population and the replacement demand (annual "deaths") were calculated. (ii) Assuming a stable automobile population of 41,408,000 annual production was calculated. (iii) Annual production was also calculated on the assumption of an automobile population increasing by 2,000,000 each year.

The results of all three projections show a deficiency in replacement demand amounting to about 600,000 automobiles by the year 1958, after which replacement demand rises rapidly. The projections are carried to the year 1975.

ZUSAMMENFASSUNG

Anwendung der Bevölkerungsanalyse auf die Automobil-Population der USA. Bevölkerungsanalyse ist die Anwendung der Methode der Differenzengleichungen auf die Vorausberechnung verschiedener der Bevölkerung zugehöriger Variablen, wie zum Beispiel deren Grösse, die Besetzung der verschiedenen Altersgruppen, die Zahl der Geburten und Sterbefälle. Sie wird üblicherweise auf biologische Bevölkerungen angewandt, kann aber ebensogut bei Populationen lebloser Objekte, wie zum Beispiel Kapitalgüter, verwendet werden.

Das Hauptziel des Artikels besteht darin, den Einfluss der Verzerrung im Altersaufbau der Automobil-Population der USA auf die künftige Ersatznachfrage zu veranschlagen. Die Verzerrung entstand dadurch, dass im Zweiten Weltkrieg während mehr als drei Jahren keine Automobile für den zivilen Bedarf produziert wurden.

Die Zahlen über die Altersverteilung der Automobile in den USA sind verfügbar. Die jährlichen Überlebensraten wurden für eine Reihe von Jahren und für soviel Altersgruppen als möglich berechnet. (Die Überlebensrate ist das Verhältnis zwischen der Besetzung einer Altergruppe und der Besetzung der nächstjüngeren Gruppe im Jahr zuvor.) Die Tabelle der Überlebensraten lässt für das

Jahr 1952 eine gewisse Stabilität erkennen, so dass mit Hilfe einiger Interpolationen und Extrapolationen eine Überlebenstafel als Basis für die Vorausberechnungen erstellt werden konnte. Auf Grund dieser Überlebenstafel wurden drei Vorausberechnungen gemacht: 1. Unter der Annahme einer gleichbleibenden jährlichen Produktion von 5 Millionen Automobilen wurden die totale Automobil-Population, der «Bevölkerungs»-Zuwachs und die Ersatznachfrage (die jährlichen «Sterbefälle») berechnet. 2. Unter der Annahme einer stabilen Automobil Population von 41 408 000 Einheiten wurde die jährliche Produktion berechnet. 3. Die jeweilige Jahresproduktion wurde ferner unter der Annahme einer jährlich um 2 Millionen Einheiten wachsenden Automobil-Population berechnet.

Die Ergebnisse aller drei Vorausberechnungen zeigen einen steigenden Ausfall in der Ersatznachfrage, der im Jahre 1958 rund 600 000 Einheiten beträgt; nachher nimmt die Ersatznachfrage rasch zu. Die Vorausberechnungen erstrecken sich bis zum Jahre 1975.

RÉSUMÉ

Application de l'analyse de la population à l'ensemble des automobiles aux Etats-Unis. L'analyse de la population est l'application de la méthode des équations différentielles aux évaluations de diverses données variables de la population telles que sa grandeur, le nombre de personnes dans les différents groupes d'âge, les naissances et les décès. Elle est habituellement appliquée à la population vivante, mais elle peut également être appliquée aux objets inanimés d'une catégorie déterminée, comme par exemple les biens d'investissement.

Le but principal de cet article est d'estimer l'influence de la «distorsion» qui s'est produite quant à l'âge de l'ensemble des automobiles aux Etats-Unis sur la demande de remplacement dans l'avenir. Cette distorsion est née du fait qu'aucune automobile n'a été produite durant plus de trois ans, pendant la seconde guerre mondiale.

Il existe des données numériques sur la répartition par âge des automobiles. Les taux annuels de «survie» des automobiles ont été calculés pour une série d'années et pour différents groupes d'âge (le taux de survie étant le rapport du chiffre d'un groupe d'âge au chiffre du groupe d'âge précédent de l'année d'avant). La table des taux de survie montre une certaine stabilité pour 1952, en sorte qu'avec quelques interpolations et extrapolations une table de survie a été obtenue, permettant de faire des évaluations. Sur la base de cette table de survie, trois estimations ont été faites: 1° En admettant une production annuelle constante de 5 millions de voitures, l'ensemble des automobiles, l'accroissement de leur chiffre et la demande de voitures neuves pour remplacer les anciennes ont été calculés. 2° En admettant un nombre stable de 41 408 000 automobiles, la production annuelle a été calculée. 3° La production annuelle a été aussi calculée en supposant un accroissement de l'ensemble des automobiles de 2 millions d'unités par année.

Les résultats des trois évaluations montrent une insuffisance de la demande de voitures de remplacement se montant à environ 600 000 automobiles pour l'année 1958; par la suite, la demande de remplacement s'élève rapidement. Les estimations sont poussées jusqu'en 1975.

THE MALTHUSIAN MODEL AS A GENERAL SYSTEM

Social and Economic Studies, 4, 3 (Sept. 1955): 195-205.

THE MALTHUSIAN MODEL AS A GENERAL SYSTEM

The population equilibrium model of T. R. Malthus is not only of importance historically in both economics and biology but in its generalized form is applicable to almost any situation of population equilibrium or even dynamics. Moreover it is frequently misunderstood and it should be useful therefore to explain the model both in its simple and its generalized forms.

In its simple form the model assumes that there is some parameter S which is descriptive of the "average standard of life" of the individuals of a population, and that this parameter is a function of the size of the population, P,

$$S = F(P) \tag{1}$$

For the model to yield a stable equilibrium it must further be assumed that in the region of the equilibrium population this function is monotonically decreasing, so that a larger P is associated with a smaller S. In economic terms this property can be derived from the "law of diminishing returns" if it is supposed that the population represents one variable factor of population of S, the other factors (thought of, say, as "other resources") being held constant. The classical picture is that of a human population expanding in a limited land area with techniques of production constant.

It is then assumed that there is some value of S, S', which is the "subsistence level". This is *defined* as that value of S above which the population will grow indefinitely, below which the population will decline indefinitely, and at which the population will remain stable. From the age-specific birth and death rates of any population, if these are stable, a parameter r, the net reproductive ratio may be derived, which may be thought of roughly as the ratio of the size of each generation to the size of the preceding generation. According as $r \gtreqless 1$ the population will eventually expand indefinitely, be stable, or contract indefinitely. In the first case each generation is larger than the one which gave rise to it; in the second case each generation is the same size as the generation which preceded it, and in the third case each generation is smaller than the preceding one. The simple Malthusian theory then postulates in effect that the net reproductive ratio is a function (and for a stable equilibrium it has to be an increasing function) of S:

$$r = G(S) \tag{2}$$

that is, the "better off" the population is, the greater will be its net reproductive ratio. It follows that there may be some level of S at which $r = 1$. This is the subsistence level: above this, $r > 1$ and the population will grow: below this, $r < 1$ and the population will decline.

The equilibrium size of the population is that at which the standard of life as given by (1) is equal to the subsistence level. The model is illustrated in Figs. 1. In Fig. 1a the parameter S is measured vertically, r horizontally, and RQR_1 is the r-curve, representing equation (2). If then H is the point $r = 1$, HQ is the subsistence level, ON, in Fig. 1b. In Fig. 1b population is measured horizontally, standard of life vertically: TBM is the standard of life curve representing equation (1). The equilibrium population is OL, where LM is the subsistence level.[a]

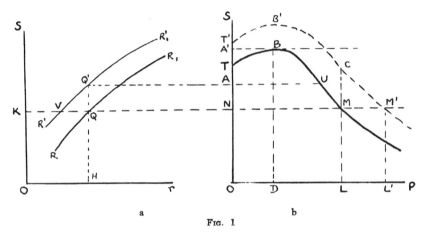

Fɪɢ. 1

Before going deeper into the implications of the model its "comparative statics" is worth examination. That is to say, we want to examine what happens to the position of equilibrium when certain changes are made in the functions which determine it. Consider first a change in the standard of life curve—say an "upward" shift from TBM to $T'B'M'$. What this means is that at each population the associated standard of life is higher than before: that is, there is an "improvement" in the resource position of the population. This can be due either to the discovery of new resources, such as an extension of the land area, or it can be due to improved techniques in the utilization of old resources—the nature of the improvement does not matter. If however the R-curve and therefore the subsistence level is unchanged the ultimate results are discouraging. The initial result of the improvement, with population still at OL, is that the standard of life rises to LC. At this point, however, it is above the subsistence level LM. Population therefore will expand, and will go on expanding until it reaches OL', where the standard of life is once again equal to the subsistence level $L'M'$ The ultimate result of the improvement, then, is not that the standard of life of the population rises, but that a *larger* population is living at the old standard of life.

[a]It should be observed that the validity of this model is not dependent on any particular form of function apart from the general characteristics described above. Thus the assumptions made by Malthus himself in early illustrations of the theory—that population expanded geometrically and food supply arithmetically—are quite irrelevant to the model.

We now see why economics was called the "Dismal Science"! If the only check to population is misery, the population will grow until it is miserable enough to check its growth. This is the Dismal Theorem. Furthermore, if the only check to population is misery, the result of any improvement is ultimately to enable a larger population than before to live in misery, so that resource-improvement actually increases the sum of misery. This is the Utterly Dismal Theorem.

Fortunately the Dismal Theorem can be restated in a cheerful form. The subsistence level of the model does not necessarily connote misery, and the Cheerful Theorem runs: if population can be checked by something else than misery, it does not have to grow until it is checked by misery. The subsistence level, as Malthus himself saw clearly, is not necessarily determined by some physiological limit of starvation, but is culturally determined. Indeed, there is no reason why S should even stand for food supply: any parameter which is related to population growth in the fashion specified will serve in the model. It is interesting to observe that in animal as well as human populations "cultural" rather than physiological factors tend to determine the subsistence level. Thus the population of robins is determined mainly by the shortage of available housing—the robin insists on a certain amount of living space, and fights off any robin that challenges his territory. The well-fed appearance of the bird is no doubt related to this "cultural" trait. In this case we could interpret the TBM curve of Fig. 1 as "living space per Robin" and the subsistence level ON as the "culturally determined" average living space. If the number of acres per robin is greater than ON the population, not being checked by food supply, will expand; if the number of acres per robin is less than ON some robins will not be able to find spaces and will perish in spite of the relative abundance of food.

Further consideration of the comparative statics of the model can also lead to more cheerful conclusions. Suppose for instance there is an "upward" or "leftward" shift in the r-curve in Fig. 1 from RQR_1 to $R'Q'B'_1$ That is to say, at each level of S there corresponds a smaller net reproductive ratio (for instance, KV instead of KQ at $S = OK$), or what is the same thing in view of the positive slope of the curve, at each r there is a higher value of S. The subsistence level therefore rises from HQ to HQ' and the equilibrium population falls from NM to AU. The equilibrium standard of life rises even if there is no improvement in the resource situation.

Two special cases deserve brief mention. Suppose first that the subsistence level is equal to the maximum standard of life possible with the given resource situation—say DB in Fig. 1b. The point B is then an odd one-sided equilibrium. It is stable when approached from higher populations, as if the population is above OD the standard of life is below S and the population will fall towards OD. It is unstable however when the population is below OD, as then the standard of life is still below the subsistence level and population will continue to decline until it becomes extinct. In practice this

means the position is unstable. If the subsistence level is above the maximum
possible standard of life the population will decline from any position to zero,
and there is no equilibrium. For a stable equilibrium therefore the standard
of life curve must have a negative slope at the subsistence level.

THE DYNAMIC MODEL

The next step is to consider the dynamics of the model under somewhat
more relaxed assumptions. Up to now we have supposed that the standard
of life-population function was invariant, or subject only to a single once-
over change. It may be, however, that the resources situation is itself affected
by the excess of the actual standard of life over the subsistence level, because
of the possibility of accumulation of capital. The problem is illustrated
graphically in Fig. 2. Suppose BM is the S curve, assumed here for simplicity
to be a straight line. NM is the equilibrium population, ON the subsistence
level as before. Now suppose a sudden rise in the S-curve to B_1M_1, creating
an ecess of standard of life above the subsistence level, MC_1. As a result

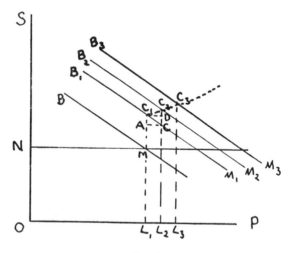

Fig. 2

of this gap the population rises in the next period to OL_2. If the S-curve does
not change the standard of life will fall to L_2C as a result of the rise in
population. Suppose now however that as a result of the initial rise in the
standard of life more is accumulated and hence the S-curve itself rises to
B_2M_2 as a result of this "induced" improvement in the resource position.
The standard of life is now L_2C_2. This results in a further expansion of
population to OL_3, but also results in a further rise in the S-curve to B_3M_3,
the new standard of life being L_3C_3. The dynamic course of both the population and the standard of life is thus shown by the dotted curve $C_1C_2C_3$

. . . and if the parameters of the system are constant can be projected indefinitely.

DYNAMIC MODEL I

The simplest dynamic model is shown in Fig. 3; this may be called the "Exponential" model. Three important cases of its dynamic path are shown. We suppose first that the population is in equilibrium at OL with a subsistence level LM, and that there is an initial improvement resulting in a

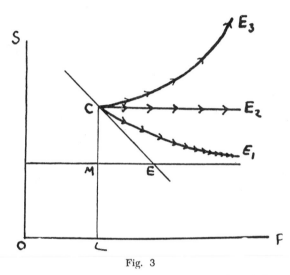

Fig. 3

shift of the standard of life to LC. If the result of this shift is a rapid increase in population but a slow rate of accumulation and improvement in the resource position the dynamic course will be like CE_1, with the improvement in resource position never able to compensate for the rise in population and a consequent continual decline in standard of life to the subsistence level again at E_1, where the population is somwhat larger than at E, where it would have been had there been no induced improvement. In the case shown by CE_2 the induced improvement is large enough so that it just compensates for the increase in population, and the standard of life remains unchanged. If the parameters are constant the same thing will happen in the next period, and in all succeeding periods, so that though population continually increases the standard of life does not fall. In the case shown by CE_3 the induced improvement more than compensates for the rise in population and both population and standard of life rises indefinitely as long as the parameters remain unchanged.

The essential features of this dynamic system may be further explored by going back to Fig. 2. Let $MC = C$, the initial disturbance. Let the resulting rise in population in the first period $L_1L_2 = \triangle P$. Let the rise in the S-curve (the "improvement factor"), $CC_2 = \triangle S$. Then there are three vital parameters of the system:

$$g = \frac{\triangle P}{C} \qquad m = \frac{\triangle S}{C} \quad \text{and } k = \frac{AC_1}{AC}$$

The ratio g may be called the population growth coefficient: it is the absolute amount by which the population grows in unit time per unit *excess* of standard of life over subsistence. The concept of the excess of standard of life above subsistence is so fundamental that we may give it a name: call it "surplus" ($=C$). The ratio m then is the "induced improvement coefficient" —the increase (in unit time) in the standard of life possible at *each* level of population induced by one unit of "surplus". The third parameter k is the slope of the S-curve: it is the amount by which the standard of life diminishes under *given* resource-use per unit increase of population. It may be called the "diminishing returns coefficient".

The growth in standard of life in period 1 then, is given by

$$\triangle C = DC_2 = CC_2 - CD = \triangle S - k\triangle P = mC - kgC = C(m-kg) \quad (3)$$

It is clear from (3) that as long as the improvement coefficient exceeds the product of the growth and scarcity coefficients the standard of life will increase ($\triangle C > O$); whenever the improvement coefficient is less than the product of the growth and scarcity coefficients the standard of life will fall. It is easy to show that the growth (or decline) will be exponential[a] if m, k, and g are constant, for then $\dfrac{\triangle C}{C}$, the rate of growth (or decline) of C is constant and equal to $m - kg$.

Dynamic Model II

The above dynamic model is not, of course, the only one, though it is probably the simplest. Liebenstein gives a somewhat different model, with significantly different properties [1].

Instead of assuming that the growth coefficient (g) of the above model is a constant, he assumed that the rate of growth of population, at least up to a certain point, is constant. He keeps the assumption that my "m", the improvement coefficient, is constant, and·that my "k", the scarcity coefficient, is constant.

In this model there are three types of movement, shown in Fig. 4. Again, if the improvement factor is weak and the population growth strong we may get a steady decline in standard of life after the initial shock, as in CF_1. If

---

[a]From (3) we have

$$C_1 = C_o + \triangle C_o = C_o(1+m-kg)$$
$$C_2 = C_1(1+m-kg) = C_o(1+m-kg)^2$$
$$C_t = C_o (1+m-kg)^t$$

Or, expressing the difference equation as a differential equation,

$$\frac{dC}{dt} = C(m-kg)$$

Whence $C = C_o e^{(m-kg)t}$

the improvement factor is somewhat stronger there may be an initial improvement in the standard of life, as in CF_2, but because of the "k" component in the improvement factor, at larger populations the population increase factor, which is assumed independent of the size of the population, dominates and the curves turn down and the system returns to subsistence level. If,

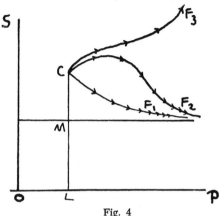

Fig. 4

however, the improvement factor is sufficiently strong relative to the initial increase the system may become explosive as in CF_3. It can be shown that with the other parameters given there is some critical size of the initial disturbance MC above which the system will be explosive and below which it will return to equilibrium at the subsistence level. That is to say, if this model is descriptive of reality, a society cannot escape from the Malthusian trap unless the initial disturbance is sufficiently large. The first model did not have this property: here the explosive or stable character of the system depended only on the three parameters, m, k and g, and not on the size of the initial disturbance.

DYNAMIC MODEL III

Another very interesting dynamic model can be developed in which the existence of a "surplus" produces a change in the subsistence level itself. In this case there may be a new equilibrium at a higher (or lower) subsistence level than before, depending on whether the existence of a surplus increases or diminishes the subsistence level. In this case also there is a possibility of an explosive outcome, though this is much less likely[a].

aContinuing the notation of footnote (a) on the previous page we may suppose that the ratio of the increase in the subsistence level, $\triangle B$ to the surplus C which which occasioned it is a constant, b $(= \frac{\triangle B}{C})$.

We then have

$$\frac{dC}{dt} = C(m-kg-b)$$

The solution will be explosive only if $(kg+b)<m$, which is even less likely than the explosive solution in the first instance $(kg<m)$.

The proliferation of these dynamic models can be continued almost indefinitely [2]. This very richness of the dynamic-model universe is an embarrassment. The real world is more complex than any of them, and on a-priori considerations one model is not much better than another. Nevertheless, it is important to explore some of the properties of the simpler dynamic models as a guide for parameters to look for in the real world. The task of empirical inquiry is the search for *stable* difference or differential equations. In searching for these a comparison between the *known general properties* of empirical systems and the known properties of dynamic systems may be of great help. Thus in the present instance we find that as between our dynamic systems (i) and (ii) there are fairly sharp differences in general properties. Thus in system (i) the course of the standard of life is either continuously upwards, or is continuously downwards towards the subsistence level after an initial disturbance. In system (ii) on the other hand we find that the standard of life may rise after a disturbance, but may reach a maximum and will then fall.

A Generalised Dynamic System

It is clear, however, on reflection, that none of the parameters of these systems are likely to be stable through time, though they may vary in fairly regular ways. Too great *specification* of the dynamic system will always be misleading, and it is important therefore to develop *generalised* dynamic systems, as illustrated in Fig. 5. Here again we start from a situation at M with an initial improvement which raises the standard of life from the old subsistence level LM to LC, creating a "surplus" MC. As a result of this, and the complex dynamic processes which follow, we suppose first that population expands, being in successive equal time periods, HP_1, HP_2 . . . HP_n. In the figure it is supposed that the population increase rises at first owing to the lag in the impact of the improvement, but that the increase

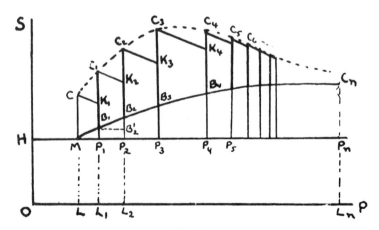

Fig. 5

eventually reaches a maximum (here between P_3 and P_4) and thence declines to very small levels, partly as a result of the diminishing surplus, partly under other impulses. We suppose also that in each period there is an "induced improvement", K_1C_1, K_2C_2 . . . etc. which raises the S-curve in successive periods as a result of the initial improvement. We have also drawn the improvement increasing to about period 3, then declining to zero by about period 7. The lines CK_1, C_1K_2, are sections of successive S-curves as the curve is raised by improvements. Thus had there been no improvements subsequent to the initial shock the standard of life in period 1 would be L_1K_1; the induced improvement, however, raises it to L_1C_1, and so on. Then I have further supposed that the subsistence level itself rises under the impact of the initial improvement, following the course in successive time periods LM, L_1B_1, L_2B_2, etc. I have assumed in the figure that the subsistence level rises at first, but at a declining rate, and eventually reaches a stable figure at L_nC_n. This means that the *surplus*, MC, B_1C_1, B_2C_2, etc. does not rise as fast as the standard of life, and eventually falls to zero after reaching a maximum. The position at L_n is the final equilibrium; population has ceased to grow, the surplus is zero, there are no further improvements, and the standard of life is stable at L_nC_n.

The difference between the generalized dynamic system and the special dynamic systems discussed above is that in the general system constancy of parameters is not assumed; there is no single stable difference or differential equation which characterizes the whole system; exact prediction is impossible and nevertheless the system is not formless: something can be said about its assumptions and the consequences of these assumptions. In a *special* dynamic system successive values of the variables are related in a stable manner. Thus if we were going to draw a similar graph for our first special system we would make $MP_1 = g.MC$, and then draw the vertical line from P_1: we would draw CK_1 with a slope k to meet this vertical line in K_1, and then would draw $K_1C_1 = m.MC$ to give us the point B_1. We would then repeat this procedure, making $P_1P_2 = g.B_1C_1$ drawing C_2K_2 with slope k to get K_2, drawing $K_2C_2 = m.B_1C_1$ and $B^1_2B_2 = b.B_1C_1$ to get B_2, By repeating the same procedure in successive periods the whole figure can be plotted and the dynamic course of all the variables derived. *Any* procedure which enables us to derive the variables of one period from those of the previous period (or of more than one previous period) can be applied in this way and used to plot out the time-course of the variables. The *procedure* is described by the basic difference or differential equation: the time-course is the *solution* of this equation (or equations).[a]

---

[a]It should be noticed that in order to "solve" a system of the first order in which the variables of one period depend only on those of the previous period one initial value must be given (*MC* in the figure). In a system of the second order two initial values must be given, and so on: thus if the improvement depended on the *increase* in the surplus we would have to be given the two values *CM* and B_1C_1 before the solution could be started. These initial values correspond to the constants of integration in differential equations.

Now perhaps it is the skeptic's turn to say "so what!" We have a system. what good is it? Does it give us "researchable hypotheses"? Does it contribute to the organization of knowledge of the real world, or is it merely an intellectual toy, or examination fodder?

The first claim which can be made is that the Malthusian system, especially as an *equilibrium* system, throws light on many historical situations. The light is clearest, of course, in situations where the notion of a subsistence level is least ambiguous—i.e. where there is some fairly clearly identifiable variable which has the necessary properties of being both population determined (having an S-function) and population determining (having a subsistence level). A population which is limited by "physical" subsistence, say per capita calorie intake, is a good example, and there are very many examples of such populations in human history: Ireland from 1700-1846, many South Sea islands, perhaps the far eastern countries today. There are certainly examples of Malthusian systems among biological populations, though here one is more likely to get into the still more general system of *interacting* populations such as that of Volterra. The generalization may be ventured, however, that "plump" creatures have their populations limited by other means than food supply such as living space (oysters, robins, domestic cats) whereas "skinny" creatures are limited mainly by food supply (coyotes, deer, alley cats).

A very interesting question is that of the application of the Malthusian model to the single living organism, conceived as a society of cells. All organisms originate as a result of an "initial disturbance" of a cell. All organisms exhibit "equifinality" in some degree. All organisms are population systems of different kinds of cells, most of which move towards an equilibrium at some "subsistence level". A cancer, on the other hand, looks like a "population explosion" of cells—something that can quite easily happen in a Malthusian system if the parameters are appropriate. It may not be all inappropriate for the cancer researchers to look for "subsistence" variables, and to look for growth, induced improvement, diminishing returns, and subsistence level parameters.

It must be emphasised, of course, that population systems, of which this extended Malthusian system is one, are only useful in situations where the population concept is a useful abstraction—that is, where "size" rather than any complex structure is the essential attribute of the system, "size" being a number of approximately homogeneous units. As we move towards higher levels of organization both in the biocene and in society the structural problems become more significant and simple population models are less adequate. Thus while it is tempting to regard knowledge, for instance, as a population of "wits" (units of knowledge analogous to the "bit" of information) and to regard the learning process as a population process in the birth and death of these units, care must be taken not to impose on a single model more than it can bear.

REFERENCES

1. LEIBENSTEIN, Harvey (1954) *A Theory of Economic-Demographic Development,* Chapter IV. Princeton.

2. HAAVELMO, T. (1954) *A Study in the Theory of Economic Evolution.* North-Holland Publishing Co., Amsterdam.

IN DEFENSE OF STATICS

Quarterly Journal of Economics, 69, 4 (Nov. 1955):
485-502.

IN DEFENSE OF STATICS

I

It has for decades been a complaint against economic theory that it is static. The complaint was not raised much against the classical economists, probably because for the most part their theory was not static, but involved what Baumol has so felicitously called the "magnificent dynamics." With the coming of the marginal school and even of Marshall, however, economists lost interest in the great sweep of the "progress of society" and devoted themselves to equilibrium models of greater and greater refinement. The underworld voices of Marx and Veblen were raised in protest, but the main course of academic economics proceeded in majestic indifference to the dissidents.

Now, however, all is changed. It has become almost a matter of personal insult to call a theory "static," and even the most academic of economists is resolved to be dynamic at almost any price. In all this there is some gain. The time may not be inappropriate, however, to examine this dynamic enthusiasm, perhaps to utter a few cautionary remarks, and to reappraise the contributions of statics, especially in the general area of the usefulness of economics in guiding the making of decisions, both public and private.

For the clarification of the issues involved we are all much indebted to Samuelson.[1] He has made two important contributions.

1. Paul A. Samuelson, *Foundations of Economic Analysis* (Harvard, 1947).

The first is the clear distinction between comparative statics and process analysis. The second is the demonstration that the stability of an equilibrium system can only be established if the equilibrium system itself can be expressed as a limiting position of a dynamic model. In comparative statics we postulate an equilibrium system consisting, for instance, of a set of simultaneous equations with some sort of a solution. The equations contain parameters, which are regarded as the determinants of the system, and variables, which are regarded as determined by the parameters. The "solution" is that set (or sets) of values of the variables which is consistent with a given set of relationships and parameters as expressed in the equations. In comparative statics we compare one "solution" derived from one set of parameters with another solution derived from a different set of parameters. The great bulk of the analysis found in textbooks of economic theory is comparative statics — demand and supply analysis, the marginal analysis, and the Keynesian national income analysis all fall into this category.

By contrast, "true" dynamics or process analysis consists of a set of difference equations or differential[2] equations, also having a set of parameters, assumed to be constant, a set of variables, one of which is a "sequence variable" (for example, time) and a "solution" which in this case consists of a function giving the value of each variable at each point of "time." It is worth noting, however, that the concept of a sequence variable is more general than that of "time" in a calendar sense, and that it is perfectly possible to write process systems of difference or differential equations in which the sequence variable is some sort of space, or is any other variable, such as population, which follows a regular sequential course.

The importance of process systems lies in their use in *prediction*. There are two forms of prediction, both of which, however, depend on the existence of stable difference or differential equations. The first may be called "conditional prediction." It consists of a proposition of the form "if A then B in time t." It depends on the establishment of a stable difference equation or relationship relating A and B in a time sequence. Most of the propositions of science are of this

2. A differential equation is simply the limiting case of a difference equation when the standard "time" or sequential interval of the difference equation approaches zero. It is largely a matter of mathematical or computational convenience whether process systems are expressed as difference or as differential equations — there is no difference of principle. Some solutions are easier in one form, some in another. Numerical computations (for example, by electronic calculators) are usually performed by expressing the system in the form of difference equations. For "well behaved" systems there is usually little difficulty in expressing the system in either form.

form. Physics for instance does not, and cannot predict that there will be an atomic explosion on a given calendar date: it can, and does predict that if certain things are done at dates t_1, t_2, etc., there will be an atomic explosion at date t_n, where the intervals between t_1, t_2 ... t_n are stable. The second form of prediction may be called "unconditional prediction." It is possible only where we have a closed system with perfectly stable parameters. So far only astronomy has had much success with unconditional prediction, and the success of the astronomers in predicting eclipses and less spectacular movements of the heavenly bodies has been the envy of their colleagues in other fields who have to struggle with less stable systems. It is not the virtue of the astronomers which leads to their success, however, but rather the virtue of the system with which they deal, which in simplicity and regularity exceeds any other scientific system. The geomorphologists and the geneticists deal with systems which have some characteristics of unconditional prediction, but with the advent of man unconditional prediction has become increasingly precarious even in these areas, and both land forms and mutations are in process of being profoundly modified by his activity. Indeed, it is an open question whether astronomy itself does not have to become a social science, for the continued rotation of the earth round the sun may come to depend on political rather than astronomical considerations.

For those who look to prediction as the supreme test of "success" in science, therefore, and especially for those who are enamored of unconditional prediction, the failures of the social sciences appear very glaring, and it is not surprising that they strain every nerve to make their systems "dynamic." There is a hunger for instance to make of economics an "astronomy of commodities" in which the various economic variables — prices, outputs, and so on — will dance in a lockstep as regular and precise as the music of the spheres, and in which the price of eggs is as predictable as the eclipses of the moon. I have no wish to deprecate any efforts to discover regular and predictable relationships in economic and social life. I shall argue, however, that the usefulness of such dynamic models as we have developed to date is extremely limited, and that while they throw some light on the nature of economic processes, they can be very misleading if taken too seriously. I shall also argue that the most secure propositions and the most reliable predictions, even though they are conditional predictions, arise out of comparative statics, and that when we are asked the awkward question "what good is economics to anyone," apart from its usefulness in providing a gainful occupation for economists, the defense rests mainly on the achievements of rather old-fashioned comparative statics.

The great weakness of process models is that they are too easy to make and too rigid once made. Once we start to set up difference or differential equation models, there seems to be no end to the variety of models which can be constructed. It is tempting to think that all we have to do is to study the properties of these models until we find one which reflects in fair measure the properties of the real world. The search, however, is that for a needle in a haystack. Models can be made of varying degrees, with various lags or leads, with the many variables related in all kinds of different ways, all of which seem plausible, none of which stand out as more plausible than the other. Do we, for instance, want a model that exhibits a cycle? Practically all process systems involving difference or differential equations of the second order, and even some of the first order, exhibit cycles. The cycles can be made damped, exploding, or recurring by small modifications of the parameters or the relationships. Do we want a model exhibiting growth? Again a great variety of possible relationships gives us the required property, and there seems to be no great reason to select one rather than another.

At the other end, even if we have accomplished the task of selecting a model, it is almost certain to let us down empirically. Relationships and parameters which we must assume, for purposes of the model, to be constant turn out to be highly variable in practice. The trouble with predicting the course of history is that it seems to be a process system of almost infinite degree — rates of change of rates of change of rates of change ad infinitum are all relevant and determinant. Predicting the course of human events by means of a process model is rather like instructing someone to drive to a certain destination by means of a simple rule, such as "always take the first on the right and the second on the left, and repeat indefinitely." Such a rule may get the traveler somewhere, but it is most unlikely to get him where he wants to go, or to describe where he has been!

II

I propose to illustrate these strictures with five examples of process models which have significance for economics. The first of these is the simple model of exponential growth — that is, growth at a constant rate.[3] This is much beloved of the planners, both national and corporation. It is the basis, for instance, of the General

3. The basic difference equation for such a model is $x_{t+1} - x_t = Kx_t$, that is, the change in the variable in the sequence interval unit is proportional to the value of the variable. The solution of this model is $x_t = x_0 (k + 1)^t$. The corresponding differential equation is $\dfrac{dx}{dt} = kx$, the solution of which is $x = x_0 e$.

Motors wage policy, and of most projections of national income. There is a magic 3 per cent, or perhaps 2 per cent, or something in between, at which everything in our society is supposed to grow — with occasional time out for wars and depressions. As a matter of fact, predictions based on this very simple model have been highly successful over moderately long periods. Many economic variables have a curious way of climbing back on the exponential bandwagon after a period of dissipation. Nevertheless it is a model that must be treated with extreme caution. One thing we are pretty sure of about growth is that with the possible exception of the whole expanding universe it cannot proceed at a constant rate forever. This is particularly true in a world where there are some principles of conservation, and in which therefore if one thing grows it is at the expense of something else. If the exponential model were sufficient, by this time there would only be One Thing in the universe, for anything which grew at a slightly faster rate than anything else would by now have gobbled up everything else. The whole biocene testifies to the impossibility of exponential growth, except for very short periods, and biologists have therefore devised more elaborate logistic models, in which absolute growth depends not merely on the size of the variable but also on the divergence of its present size from some equilibrium size. This model (in a great variety of special forms) gives us the familiar ogive or s-curve of growth. This, too, however, is likely to disappoint us, especially in the social realm. Growth processes in society get a new lease on life in the middle, or they collapse before they have worked themselves out. It seems sometimes as if parameters are most likely to change when we think them to be most stable, and that history is an elaborate practical joke with the predictors as butt.

III

The second dynamic system is that of population. The debacle of the population predictors is fresh in our memory. The system of prediction, however, is an elegant and quite sophisticated example of process analysis. The basic difference equations involved are survival or death functions, showing how many out of any given cohort of births survive into any given subsequent years. The simplest expression of such a relationship is a series of survival coefficients, s_1, s_2 . . . s_i . . . , the basic relationship being $a_t = s_i b_{t-i}$, where a_t is the total number in the population in year t of age i, and b_{t-i} is the total number of births in year $t - i$. In order to complete the model there must also be a birth function of some kind relating the number of births in each year to some other variables of the model. This can be a simple function of time, extrapolating the past movement of births, or it can be as complex as we wish to make it. From these relatively simple materials the whole course of a population, its age composition and its birth and death structure can be predicted. The failure of recent predictions illustrates the treacherous nature of these dynamic models, even in cases where we thought we had good grounds for secure predictions. The one thing we do know about the future is that everyone who is alive today will either be dead or a year older this time next year! This knowledge is not enough, however, and it has been abundantly evident that the dynamics of population is much more complex and less predictable than we thought.

IV

Coming now to the third illustration, more specific to economics, we have the accelerator-multiplier models developed with such elegance by Samuelson.[4] These are dynamic Keynesian models. The simple multiplier model is based on two relationships: the composition of income, or savings-investment identity, Y_t (total income) $= A_t$ (accumulation or investment) $+ C_t$ (Consumption), and the consumption function, which expressed as a linear difference equation becomes

$$C_t = c + kY_{t-1}, \tag{1}$$

k being the "marginal propensity to consume" of this year's consumption related to last year's income. Combining these equations we get

$$Y_t = A_t + c + kY_{t-1}. \tag{2}$$

It is easy to show that this system follows a path of simple exponential decline of D_t, the difference between Y_t and the equilibrium value of Y_e,[5] assuming that A_t is constant from year to year. There is no

4. Paul A. Samuelson, "Interactions between the Multiplier Analysis and the Principle of Acceleration" (reprinted from the *Review of Economic Statistics*, 1939, in *Readings in Business Cycle Theory*, pp. 261–69).
5. The equilibrium value Y_e is obtained by putting $Y_e = Y_t = Y_{t-1}$ in equation (2), the equilibrium value being simply that which the process will repeat indefinitely. We have therefore, if A_t is constant and equal to A,

$$Y_e = \frac{A + c}{1 - k} \tag{i}$$

(continued next page)

cyclical element in this model. A cyclical element is easily introduced, however, if we postulate an "accelerator" equation which relates A_t to the *change* in income,

$$A_t = a\ (Y_{t-1} - Y_{t-2}) \tag{3}$$

Equation (2) then becomes

$$Y_t = a(Y_{t-1} - Y_{t-2}) + c + kY_{t-1} = c + (a + k)\ Y_{t-1} - aY_{t-2} \tag{4}$$

This equation gives various types of solution, depending on the relative magnitudes of the parameters: it may give rise to damped, explosive, or stable oscillations: it may yield monotonic explosions away from or movements to equilibrium.

All this is very interesting, but does it really throw much light on the real forces of economic history? One may be permitted a few doubts. The doubts, of course, concern the stability of the parameters concerned. The famous failure of the postwar predictions of dire unemployment cannot fairly be imputed to intoxication with dynamic models, for this prediction was based essentially on the comparative statics, not the dynamics, of the Keynesian system. The breakdown of these predictions, however, arose from a deplorable (from the point of view of the predictors) or happy (from the point of view of society) upward instability in the consumption function — that is, essentially in the "c" parameter of our simple linear model. We all know now that the consumption function is far from being the law of the Medes and Persians which was sometimes hoped (or feared).

If even the stability of the consumption function is in doubt, there is double doubt about the stability of the accelerator function. There were shreds (pretty badly shredded by now, but still shreds) of evidence for the existence of a moderately stable consumption function. Nobody to my knowledge has ever put forward even a shred of evidence for a stable accelerator function. The accelerator is a pure construct of theoretical imagination, like Mrs. Harris. If we are honest we have to admit that we *have* no investment function, and that what is worse, we do not even know what we should put in it if we had one. Investment-planned or desired investment, that is, is the Holy Spirit of the Keynesian system. On it the whole fine edifice depends, but it insists on blowing where it listeth. In Keynes himself, of course, it depends on something which isn't in the system

$$D_t = Y_e - Y_t = \frac{A + c}{1 - k} - (A + c) - kY_{t-1} = k\left(\frac{A + c}{1 - k} - Y_{t-1}\right) = kD_{t-1} \tag{ii}$$

Equation (ii) as we have seen is simply the equation for exponential decline, as $k < 1$.

at all — a curious state of mind called the Marginal Efficiency of
Capital. But where this state of mind comes from, or goes to, is a
deep mystery which the system does not reveal. The accelerator is a
pebble cast hopefully into this chasmic gulf in the system. The most
one can say for it is that at least nobody ever attempted to predict
anything by it, and it remains a fine tour-de-force, retaining its hold
on the professional mind by its eminent suitability for regurgitation
in examinations.

V

The fourth dynamic system to be brought under review suffers
from defects like the third. This is the Harrod-Domar-Hicks dynamic,
or H-D-H for short. This has the peculiar attraction of being a very
gloomy dynamic, which in part accounts for its success, economics
having a strong masochistic urge to perpetuate its reputation as the
Dismal Science. It may conveniently be expounded graphically in a
version which is somewhat more general than that of its progenitors.

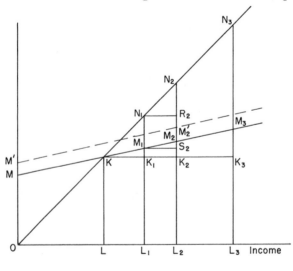

FIGURE I

Thus in Figure I we have the familiar diagram in which national
income is measured on the horizontal axis and its components on the
vertical axis. MM_1 is the consumption function, ON_1 the 45° line
representing the basic identity $Y = A + C$. With income equal to
OL_1 consumption will be L_1M_1 and "investment" (desired accumulation) M_1N_1. Suppose now that OL_1 represents full employment, or

capacity output. As a result of the investment represented by M_1N_1 the capacity of the system will rise, say to OL_2. If full employment is to be maintained in the next period, then, investment will have to be equal to M_2N_2. This investment again raises capacity to OL_3, and in the next period investment must be M_3N_3 if full employment is to be maintained. The maintenance of full employment therefore requires the continual growth of investment, and it is not hard to show that if the propensity to consume is constant and the "growth factor," the increase in capacity which is caused by unit investment, is also constant, this growth of investment must be at a constant rate — that is, the growth must be exponential.[6] This rate of growth is Harrod's "warranted rate." In the present case it is shown in note 6 that the excess of income over the "no accumulation income," OL, also grows at the warranted rate. This can be shown geometrically by the properties of similar triangles:

$$\frac{M_1N_1}{KN_1} = \frac{M_2N_2}{KN_2} \text{ and } \frac{KN_1}{KK_1} = \frac{KN_2}{KK_2}: \text{ whence} \frac{M_1N_1}{KK_1} = \frac{M_2N_2}{KK_2}.$$

Harrod's model is a special case of the above in which it is assumed that the consumption function goes through the origin. In this case the no-accumulation income is zero, and income itself also must grow at the warranted rate of growth in order to maintain full employment. There seems to be no need, however, for this very restrictive assumption.

6. Let A_0, A_1 be the amounts of investment at times t, $t + 1$. Then
$A_1 = M_2N_2 = S_2R_2 - S_2M_2 + R_2N_2 = M_1N_1 - kM_1S_2 + M_1S_2 = A_0 + (1-k)rA_0$
where k is the marginal propensity to consume and r is the ratio $\dfrac{L_1L_2}{M_1N_1}$ or
$\dfrac{\text{increase in capacity}}{\text{amount of investment}}$, the growth factor. That is,

$$A_1 = A_0(1 + r(1 - k)) \tag{i}$$

Investment therefore grows at a constant rate, $r(1 - k)$, if r and k are constant. Suppose now the equation of the consumption function is $C = c + mY$. Then

$$Y_0 = C_0 + A_0 = c + mY_0 + A_0, \text{ or } Y_0 = \frac{c}{1 - m} + \frac{A_0}{1 - m} \tag{ii}$$

Now let y be the income at which accumulation is zero (OL in the figure). Then

$$y = c + my, \text{ or } y = \frac{c}{1 - m} : \text{ hence from (ii)}$$

$$Y_0 - y = \frac{A_0}{1 - m}$$

A_0 however grows exponentially at the rate $r(1 - k)$. $Y_0 - y$ therefore must grow at the same rate.

The dismal character of the model arises out of the further hypothesis that the warranted rate of growth which is necessary to maintain full employment is greater than the "natural" rate of growth which the growth of population and technology permit. If this is so, the only way to have full employment is to grow faster than is possible in the long run: the only way to do this is to grow from a position of unemployment, in which case growth of income at a faster rate than the long-run "natural" rate of growth is possible — but only as long as unemployed resources remain to be absorbed. Once growth hits the ceiling of full employment it must come down to the natural rate. But it cannot stay at the natural rate: it has to be above the natural rate to maintain full employment. Hence income must come down in a depression until it is low enough to start the process all over again. This is the Hicks, or Hiccup, theory of the trade cycle.

It cannot be denied, I think, that this model sheds at least one or two rays of light on the real world — mainly, however, through its defects rather than through its virtues. Its great defect is precisely its rigid dynamism — the fact that it assumes a number of parameters constant which are almost certainly never constant for long. Its gloom is derived almost entirely from the assumption that the consumption function is stable — an assumption which we have already seen to be constantly violated by plain fact. It is perfectly possible to chase away the gloom, therefore, by assuming a sufficient upward movement of the consumption function in response to increasing accumulation of capital. Thus in Figure I suppose that in the second period the consumption function rose to the dotted line $M'M_2'$. The amount of investment required to maintain full employment is now $M_2'N_2$ which may be actually less than M_1N_1. We could perfectly well postulate a dynamic system, therefore, in which the consumption function rose steadily to the point at which there was no further accumulation and the system reached a stationary state with full employment and consumption equal to income! This assumption is at least as inherently plausible as the assumptions of the H-D-H system. OM we may suppose represents "fixed consumption," that is, that part of consumption which is a function of the capital stock, not a function of income. This fixed consumption clearly depends on the size of the capital stock, including the human population. The more people, livestock, houses, machines, etc., that exist in a society the more resources must be devoted to their mere maintenance, as anyone who has graduated from the ownership of a small house to a large house knows all too well. The maintenance is not automatic, of course, but it still represents consumption: if capital is not maintained this appears as disinvestment. It is not difficult to formulate conditions under which the investment required to maintain full employment will grow, be stable, or decline.[7]

This modification of the H-D-H system, though I flatter myself that it is an improvement, and at least has a slight potentiality of engendering a mathematically qualified cheerfulness, nevertheless still exhibits the fatal defects of any simple dynamic system, that it assumes constancy in parameters which are almost certainly never constant for long. Consequently its value in prediction would be small even if we could identify the values at the present time of the parameters concerned.

VI

The fifth and last example of a currently popular dynamic system or class of systems is the recent dynamization of Malthus into an embarrassing variety of systems of economic development. Drs. Leibenstein and Haavelmo[8] are the principal practitioners of this art,

7. Investment required to maintain full employment will grow, be stable or decline as

$$MM' \underset{>}{\overset{<}{=}} M_2 N_2 - M_1 N_1 \qquad \text{(i)}$$

Let us define d as the marginal durability of new accumulations, $= \dfrac{M_1 N_1}{MM'}$. The more durable the additions to the stock of capital, the less will be the increase in fixed consumption necessary to maintain them. Then:

$$MM' = \frac{M_1 N_1}{d} = \frac{L_1 L_2}{rd} \qquad \text{(ii)}$$

$$M_2 N_2 - M_1 N_1 = S_2 N_2 - S_2 M_2 - S_2 R_2 = R_2 N_2 - S_2 M_2 = L_1 L_2 (1 - k) \qquad \text{(iii)}$$

Inequality (i) therefore reduces to

$$\frac{1}{rd} \underset{>}{\overset{<}{=}} (1 - k)$$

That is, investment to maintain full employment must grow, be constant, or decline as

$$rd (1 - k) \underset{<}{\overset{>}{=}} 1.$$

The more durable the additions to capital, the more investment increases capacity, and the less the marginal propensity to consume, the more likely are we to run into the situation where the maintenance of full employment requires perpetual growth of investment.

8. Harvey Leibenstein, *A Theory of Economic-Demographic Development* (Princeton, 1954). T. Haavelmo, *A Study in the Theory of Economic Evolution* (Amsterdam, 1954).

the first using difference equations, the second differential equations. Again we may conveniently illustrate the general nature of the systems with a diagram, Figure II. Here we measure population on the horizontal, per capita income on the vertical axis. We postulate a "diminishing returns curve" R_0P_0 relating per capita income to population under a given resource situation. This is assumed to be linear for the sake of convenience. We suppose furthermore that there is

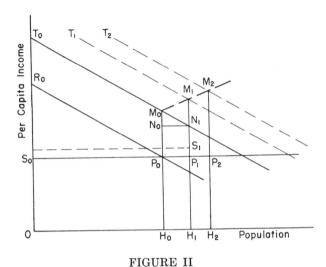

FIGURE II

some level of per capita income, OS_0, which is the "subsistence level," defined as that level of per capita income above which the population will grow, below which it will decline, and at which it will be stationary. The equilibrium level of population is S_0P_0, where the actual per capita income as given by the diminishing returns curve is at the subsistence level. Now suppose that there is an "improvement," reflected in a rise in the diminishing returns curve to T_0M_0. The first effect of this is to raise per capita income from H_0P_0 to H_0M_0. Now, however, there is a "surplus" — an excess of actual income above the subsistence level, P_0M_0. This "surplus" is the dynamic agent. It is likely to have two results: in the next period there will be an increase in population, to S_0P_1. There may also be an "induced improvement," raising the diminishing returns curve to T_1M_1. If there were no induced improvement the per capita income would fall in the first period as a result of the rise in population from H_0M_0 to H_1N_1. Because of the induced improvement, however, per capita income moves from H_0M_0 to H_1M_1 — which may be either a rise or a fall, depending on whether the rise due to the induced improvement exceeds or fails to exceed the fall due to the rise in population. The "surplus" above subsistence is now P_1M_1, and if the relationships are constant we can project the model into the second year with population S_0P_2, per capita income H_2M_2, and surplus P_2M_2. The dynamic course of the population and the per capita income is then represented by the heavy dotted line $M_0M_1M_2$ — and can be projected as far as we wish. Probably the simplest system is that in which the ratio of population growth to surplus, $\dfrac{P_0P_1}{P_0M_0}$ is a constant, g, the ratio of induced improvement to surplus, N_1M_1/P_0M_0 is a constant, n, and the slope of the diminishing returns curve is a constant, d. It can then be shown that the "surplus" will either expand exponentially without limit, or will decline exponentially to zero again, at a rate of growth (or decline) equal to $n - dg$.[9]

A great variety of other models can be constructed, depending on the kind of relationship assumed between the variables; and depending on the model chosen, various time paths for the variables — that is, various properties of the model — will emerge. We can have models in which the per capita income first rises and then falls to equilibrium, we can have models in which the nature of the path depends on the size of the initial disturbance, and so on. A very useful modification might be to suppose that a surplus gave rise to a change in the subsistence level itself. Suppose for instance in the figure that the surplus P_0M_0 created a rise in the subsistence level itself from H_0P_0 to H_1S_1. Then the surplus in the second period would be S_1M_1, not P_1M_1, and the dynamic would be modified accordingly. No matter how we modify the model, however, in its difference equation or differential equation form it again suffers from the fatal defect of constancy in parameters. It is extremely unlikely that any parameters of a simple model such as I have described above, or even of much more complex models, will maintain constancy for very long. We actually know very little about the many subtle forces which affect population. We know still less about the forces which

9. We have $g = P_0P_1/P_0M_0$, $n = N_1M_1/P_0M_0$, $d = M_0N_0/P_0P_1$. Then: $P_1M_1 = P_1N_1 + N_1M_1 = P_0M_0 - N_0M_0 + N_1M_1 = P_0M_0(1 - dg + n)$. That is:

$$\frac{P_1M_1}{P_0M_0} = (1 - dg + n).$$

The surplus, therefore, grows at a constant rate, $n - dg$. The bigger the induced improvement coefficient, n, and the smaller the population growth coefficient, g, and the diminishing returns coefficient, d, the more likely is the model to be explosive.

affect improvements. We do not even know very much about the forces of diminishing returns. It seems certain that only very loose relationships exist between any such vague quantity as a "surplus" and population, capital, and technological movements. It seems probable that whatever relationships occur exhibit "diminishing returns" or perhaps even "increasing returns" with time — forces spend themselves, or sometimes refuel themselves. An impetus to population may peter out: an impetus to technological change may reinforce itself. In any case the dynamics is far beyond the capacity of any simple system of difference or differential equations to portray.

VII

There are two possible avenues of escape from this fatal rigidity of the dynamic model. One is the use of stochastic variables, by which we add or subtract a number picked out of a hat to whatever answer our difference equations have given us in each period. This has some advantage in formalizing the ever present uncertainty, and in some cases even leads to fairly well determined equilibrium solutions, but it has the disadvantage from the standpoint of prediction that it yields usually a rapidly widening range of possible values rather than a specific prediction. Furthermore, in the absence of any real knowledge of probabilities it may be doubted whether the stochastic model does more than formalize ignorance in an elegant and perhaps even misleading manner.

The second possible avenue towards useful dynamic models is the development of short-range models with large numbers of variables in the manner of Lawrence Klein.[1] This is an avenue which is well worth exploring. It is a recognized principle of physical science that if a system does not predict it is because essential variables are missing from it. If we try to predict the volume of a gas from the pressure alone, variations in temperature will throw our prediction out severely. If temperature is included in the model very nice predictions can be obtained. If molecular size is included still better predictions follow, and so on. There seems to be no reason why the same principle should not apply in social systems, where the number of essential variables is much larger than in physical systems. All power, therefore, to those brave souls who penetrate the n-dimensional wilderness shouldering the heavy artillery of the electronic calculator,

1. Lawrence R. Klein, *Economic Fluctuations in the United States, 1921–1941* (Wiley, 1950).

especially if they are decently sceptical about their results, and are sensitive to the empirical frailty of empirical regularity. We primitive tribesmen who still cling to the bows and arrows of Demand and Supply will cheer you wistfully from the sidelines.

VIII

It is no deprecation of heavy artillery, however, to affirm that it is unfitted to the swatting of mosquitoes. I shall conclude, therefore, with a small paean of praise to comparative statics, as not only the mainstay of the textbook but the main justification for the usefulness of economics, on the grounds that there are a lot of mosquitoes which may be swatted with these primitive weapons. Suppose we ask ourselves the slightly embarrassing question *"To whom is a knowledge of academic economics useful?"* — apart, of course, from the academicians? I think we would have to confess that many business men get along admirably without more than a trace of economics. Even though we may, and do, comfort ourselves with the reflection that tennis players get along equally well without a knowledge of ballistics, it is slightly humbling to realize the magnificent irrelevance of most economic theory to the daily conduct of small affairs. As we move towards the large affairs, however, the maker of tennis balls may need to know something about ballistics, and the maker of large decisions — the central banker, the statesman, perhaps even the large corporation executive — may need to know something about economics. In making decisions about high economic policy we have a good deal of confidence that the special skills of the economist have relevance — not that they are sufficient, but that better decisions are likely to be made with them than without them. When we ask "what skills are relevant," however, I think we must admit that at least at present it is the skills of comparative statics and not our very rudimentary skills in dynamics which are crucial.

There are two broad areas in comparative statics which yield fruit for the policymaker. The first is the field of price theory, where anyone who ventures into the control or manipulation of prices certainly needs to know a little elementary demand-and-supply analysis. It is useful to know that in the case of any commodity there is usually some price above which we get into one kind of trouble which may be described roughly as "surplus" and below which we get into another kind of trouble described roughly as "shortage." Even this simple knowledge might have saved unwary statesmen from committing a vast number of economic boners over the long course of history. It is useful to know that price control almost always involves some form either of production control or consumption control. It is useful to know something about elasticities of supply and demand if one is going to tax commodities. It is useful to have some notions of general equilibrium, even if it is only to prevent total surprise when the solution of one problem creates three others. It is perhaps even useful to know that the power of monopoly depends on the absence of substitutes. All these little pieces of knowledge are simple in the extreme, and yet a surprising amount of trouble has been caused by ignorance of them.

As one moves towards problems which essentially involve dynamics, however, even in price theory, the beautiful simplicity of elementary knowledge is lost, and the economist takes on more and more the role of the magician. The sad state of antitrust policy is a case in point, where the contribution of the economist, especially in the area of monopolistic competition, has been a quite spectacular befuddlement, with the Department of Justice riding off on white horses in at least three different directions at once. The confusion here originates mainly in the fact that the problem of monopoly in the real world contains so many dynamic elements which cannot be treated under the simple rubrics of comparative statics. In terms of economic development monopoly seems to be less villainous than it is in the two-dimensional world of comparative statics, and we seem to have no adequate criteria to tell us where virtue ends and villainy begins. The same difficulty applies to the problem of economic development in general. The self-confidence with which the economist advises a price administrator collapses into frantic calls for an anthropologist in the house when the economist is roped into advising the government of an underdeveloped area on how to get rich quick.

The same picture is revealed in the other great area of economic competence, which is national income policy. This is probably the most impressive, even though it is the most recent area for the exercise of economic skills. The Keynesian contribution is, however, again essentially comparative statics — it is underemployment equilibrium which is the central concept of the system. Yet an appreciation of the simple Keynesian model, elementary as it is, makes the difference between being completely baffled by the problem of unemployment and depression and understanding its essential nature. On the policy side it means the difference between striking out wildly in all directions, and having at least a qualitative notion of the kinds of things that ought to be done. The statesman who knows that in a period of depression one should *not* at any rate increase taxes, make desperate efforts to balance the budget, and raise interest rates may not know much, but he perhaps knows most of what economics has to offer him, and that knowledge may make the difference between the survival or the nonsurvival of his society.

Again, however, when we come to the true dynamics of the problem the situation is confused and difficult. The problem of *when* to do things — how to interpret the economic signals — is a problem of true dynamics, and on this point the hand of the economist fumbles. We worry perhaps that ill-timed policies may aggravate fluctuations instead of alleviating them, but on the detailed matter of the when and the where it is still the intuition of the politician that governs and not the skill of the specialist.

IX

My conclusion, therefore, is that as economists we do not know very much, but we do know something that is not to be despised, and that what we do know is mostly comparative statics. This is not to deprecate the importance of economic dynamics: it is merely to register scepticism as to its existence. And our pretensions at dynamics in the shape of simple and rigid models of difference or differential equations must be seen for what they are — interesting exercises, and not much else. They have little value either for prediction or for policy. If dynamics is to be saved, it must be along two lines. On the theoretical side there is a real need for the development of a *qualitative dynamics* — process analysis which does not assume constancy in parameters, but which analyses the *general shape* of economic processes. Conceived in this sense there is something to be learned even from the accelerator models, from the post-Keynesian H-D-H dynamics, and from the dynamic Malthusian models of economic development. There is great need for the development of topological techniques in this field, analogous to the topological techniques which have been so useful in comparative statics, which enable us to describe the "shape" of processes without committing ourselves to detailed functions or constant parameters. It is to be feared that the enthusiasm for difference and differential equations on the part of our bright young dynamists has led them away from this more potentially fruitful area. On the quantitative side there is still hope for multi-variable econometric models. Even here, however, there is need for deeper theoretical work, especially at the level of integration of micro- and macroeconomic behavior. It is not enough merely to thresh around in the n-dimensional field, adding variables here and relationships there as fancy takes us. The growth of models should be in some sense "organic" and should be inspired by some principles of growth which are derived from fundamental theory. It is at this point that the long-awaited integration of psychology and economics may begin to take shape. We are looking for stable relationships among quantities differing in time position. What this involves on the theoretical side is learning theory, broadly conceived — the relationship between past experience and present behavior. What is learned here at the level of the individual cannot fail to affect our models of the aggregate, and may lead to that organic growth of testable model systems which is the dream of the scientist.

INDEX OF NAMES

SUBJECT INDEX